# Anastasia Again:

## THE HIDDEN SECRET OF THE ROMANOVS

## SECOND EDITION

J (JOHANNES) FROEBEL-PARKER

authorHOUSE®

AuthorHouse™
1663 Liberty Drive
Bloomington, IN 47403
www.authorhouse.com
Phone: 1 (800) 839-8640

Published by AuthorHouse  04/29/2020

ISBN: 978-1-7283-6005-8 (sc)
ISBN: 978-1-7283-6004-1 (e)

# NOTE TO READERS OF THE REVISED EDITION
# IN SOFTCOVER AND E-BOOK FORMATS

Since the original publication of this book at the centenary of the Romanov Tragedy, or perhaps more apt, Romanov Mystery, a myriad of developments in the quest for the true narrative of the fate of the youngest daughter of Tsar Nicholas II and Empress Alexandra Feodorovna has occurred. Waiting for the "right moment" to add to the original publication never leads to the "right moment" as the situation is so dynamic. As we begin the new decade, a version more accessible to the public seems in order.

Has the Patriarch of Moscow, Kirill, made any definitive statement concerning the so-called "Romanov Remains?" Only when the Church (Russian Orthodox) is satisfied with all evidence will they make a definitive statement. One can only assume that all evidence has not been fully reviewed at the time of this publication. What is NOT being said is a book in itself.

One sad note for me personally is the untimely death of Mr. Robert "Bob" Schmitt, whose cuttinge edge visual face recognition technology showed undeniable congruency between the faces of aka "Evgenia Smetisko" and Anastasia Romanov (both in 2D and 3D formats). Now online at YouTube, readers are encouraged to view his riveting video with explanation of the analysis at: https://www.youtube.com/watch?v=GnzegZlk38&t=425s

The Russian Investigative Committee, somewhat analogous to the FBI in the United States, also visited the Holy Trinity Russian Orthodox Monastery in Jordanville, New York in Herkimer County shortly after the hardcover edition of this book was published in 2018. An article by Lynda Edwards appeared in the Times Union (Albany, New York) on December 6, 2018 (ironically St. Nicholas Day) which mentions that Sledcom had visited the monastery. Sledcom never said that they had come to retrieve the DNA sample of aka "aka Evgenia" which was said to exist. Why would they? It is enough to know they were truly there for reasons known to them and probably only the highest official of the monastery: https://www.timesunion.com/news/article/Landmark-Tsar-Nicholas-II-exhibit-in-rural-NY-13352218.php

On June 18, 2018, on what would have been the 117th birthday of Anastasia Romanov, a cleric at the monastery agreed to perform a "panikhida" at the grave marked "Evgenia Smetisko" but sporting the date of birth of Grand Duchess Anastasia: June 18, 1901. A "panikhida" is a requiem for the dead in Orthodox tradition. The priest prayed for "Thy servant, Evgenia" yet the prayers were ascending heavenward on the birthday of Tsar Nicholas II's youngest daughter. The fact that the church acquiesced to pray for "Evgenia" on Anastasia's birthday is not to be easily dismissed, especially knowing that Sledcom was about to visit.

Again the Times Union of Albany chronicled the event with photos and information: https://www.timesunion.com/news/article/Photos-Memorial-service-for-upstate-s-Anastasia-13008245.php

Artist Barbara Green's iconic portrait of an adult Anastasia Romanov (see front cover) was based on a beloved portrait of Dowager Empress Maria (Dagmar) Feodorovna, nee' Princess Dagmar of Schleswig-Holstein-Sonderburg-Glücksburg, after studying Bob Schmitt's 2D/3D visual face recognition studies of "Evgenia" and Anastasia as well as countless photos of both at various ages. Although Bob, who had appeared on The History Channel using the technology, passed away 2019, his widow, Penny Schmitt, was to join the artist and this author for an interview on WGXC (90.7) FM in Hudson, New York with host, Garrett Roche of the Monday Morning Show. Barbara was ill that day but did submit a statement which will be included at the end of this Note to the Reader:

https://froebelgalleries.wordpress.com/2020/01/24/wgxc-radio-discussion-of-anastasia-romanov-and-visual-face-recognition/

Steve Gruber, host of Michigan's most popular radio talk show, was one of the first to interview this author about the research into Anastasia's exit from Bolshevik Russia and later life in the United States: https://tsarizm.com/news/2018/08/15/gruber-anastasia-again-parker/

A little known event in the life of Evgenia/Anastasia was her meeting with well known KGB defector known as Michael Goleniewski who maintained to his death that Anastasia Romanov had not died in 1918 and was living in the USA under the pseudonym of "Evgenia Smetisko." The author brought this to light in an article: https://froebelgalleries.wordpress.com/2019/05/11/soviet-intelligence-anastasia-romanov/

A dramatized reading of the Romanov-Goleniewski encounter was performed again in the Hudson, New York studios of WGXC Radio with host Garrett Roche as Goleniewski, Montessori educator Patrice Maynard as Evgenia/Anastasia, and Victoria Signorelli as the narrator: https://froebelgalleries.wordpress.com/2019/10/22/dramatized-1963-transcript-aka-evgenia-smetisko-anastasia-romanov-kgb-defector/

Barbara Green, nee' Korr/Kur who interestingly graduated from Erasmus Hall High School in Brooklyn, New York in the same class as singer/actress Barbra Streisand, gave a statement to be read on the WGXC interview about visual face recognition with Mrs. Bob (Penny) Schmitt. This Note to the Reader will close with her memorable thoughts about Anastasia, Bolshevism and her own family:

# STATEMENT BY BARBARA GREEN

Regrettably, I am sick in bed for this broadcast which I very much regret. When Mr. Froebel-Parker approached me to do a portrait of an adult Anastasia based on his book and the visual recognition analyses, 2D and 3D, by Mr Bob Schmitt, I was somewhat skeptical. Having done portraits for so many years and having studied many photos of Anastasia and aka Evgenia both in isolation and in the comparison analyses, I eventually felt there was, indeed, a factual basis for it being the youngest Romanov grand duchess. Based on these studies I created a likeness of the grand duchess at about the age of 40 as I imagined how she would have appeared in court costume had she remained in Russia with no Revolution. My own family escaped Bolshevism in 1918 fleeing through Harbin, China. They made it to Canada and entered in to the US from there. Their flight through Siberia, through China, to Japan to Canada to USA was a two year odyssey. Their ship was named ironically *The Empress of Russia* which they boarded in Japan. My father, having escaped Bolshevism, had a life long loathing of the system. I felt a great responsibility to be as truthful as to how I thought she would appear, based on Mr. Schmitt's work and historical photographs. I consider this portrait one of my best portraits and historically the most significant.

# INTRODUCTION

Year after year the search for the grave of the woman known simultaneously as "Evgenia Smetisko," "Eugenia Smith," and more daringly "H.I.H. Grand Duchess Anastasia Nicholaevna Romanova" continued. "She is in the new section!" One year it rained making the trek past rows and rows of Eastern Orthodox style crosses impractical. Cyrillic Script! Another challenge but not impossible. (http://learnrussian.rt.com/alphabet/the-history-of-the-cyrillic-alphabet/) Finally on Orthodox Pentecost 2008 while the faithful enjoyed the food booths, crafts and camaraderie of the Feast of Title near the Cathedral of Holy Trinity Seminary and Monastery in Jordanville, Herkimer County, New York (USA) the alphabet system introduced to Slavic lands by saints Cyril and Methodius finally made sense. There it was: *EVGENIA SMETISKO* (see photo in section dedicated to images).

What a feeling of elation to finally pay respects to the woman who is credited with donating wonderful Romanov albeit Romanov era objets d'art, religious artifacts, and memorabilia to the Foundation of Russian History Museum on the monastery grounds. Eve Kahn, reporter for the New York Times, duly noted "Evgenia's" contributions in *Treasures and Trivia of the Romanov Era* which was published April 3, 2014 (www.nytimes.com/2014/04/04/arts/design/treasures-and-trivia-of-the-romanov-era.html). Not only had "Evgenia" made sure that her precious donations would be displayed for the edification of others (something for which she had always striven according to her autobiography and officials at the monastery who arranged for her items to arrive there at her death), she had also planned her remarkable financial estate so that a *more than rather sizable* annuity in perpetuity would ensure the financial stability of the monastery museum in Jordanville, New York-USA.

Just as the historical Anastasia in Tsarist Russia, "Evgenia" was an avid and prolific artist, painting well into her nineties. After her death all the donated art was examined and the decision reached to sell those things which had no connection to the Romanov Era, namely her own work as an artist which had no worth to the museum as she was generally considered to be a "false claimant" to the identity of Anastasia Romanov. Eagerly, an offer was made for the work which was authorized with a blessing by the then sitting Metropolitan Laurus. (*Genealogically noteworthy as he was born in what is today Ladomirova, Slovakia, where paternal relatives of this author had resided*) These delightful paintings, embroideries, *Hinterglasmalerei*, and needlepoint creations were the basis of the 2014 publication (Authorhouse) *The Art of the Authoress of Anastasia: The Autobiography of H.I.H. The Grand Duchess Anastasia Nicholaevna of Russia* by J (Johannes) Froebel-Parker.

Finding the grave was a way to say *thank you* to "Evgenia," yet another surprise awaited us as the initial joy of deciphering the name from Cyrillic script was acknowledged. In all immigration documents, ship manifests, and other publicly accessible sources about her, "Evgenia's" date of birth had been given as January 25, 1899. Surely that had been on her own death certificate and expected to be on her grave cross. Yet another date of birth was plainly visible on the cross marking her sanctified eternal resting place- June 18, 1901. On that day the Anastasia of history, daughter of Tsar Nicholas II and his German wife, Alexandra (Alix) von Hessen und bei Rhein, had come to the world at Peterhof Palace in St. Petersburg, Russia. "Mrs. Smetisko" was *Evgenia* in the name spelled in Cyrillic script, yet she was *Anastasia* in the date of birth on her official grave marker. A rare event for an alleged impostress! Conundrum!

Christian teaching instructs us: (Mark 4:22) "For there is nothing hid, which shall not be manifested; neither was any thing kept secret, but that it should come abroad." An "error" of such magnitude, especially given contentious proclamations to the contrary of historians, forensic scientists with their diverse conclusions accompanied often by caustic declarations by *opionistas* around the world would make this date problematic. By itself it could have become the catalyst for a debate to rival that of yore concerning how many angels could dance on the tip of a pin.

When the question was raised about the discrepancy, the answer was swift albeit terse from those in a position to know, "Someone must have made a mistake." As there are "no coincidences" that answer was not satisfying. To this day questions linger to the true identity of the lady known as "Evgenia," but conceivably there are LESS at the time of this writing. Perhaps a definitive answer is prefigured by this expanded version of "Evgenia's" 1963 book thanks to easier access to documents and the use of biometric analysis.

Verified via the website *Nonprofit Facts of the State of Rhode Island*, "Evgenia's" association, the St. Nicholas House Foundation had wealth only dreamed of by struggling nonprofits. Where could such monies have originated (one of the questions remaining) which would have allowed her to so abundantly endow the upstate New York museum in *perpetuity*?

Ostensibly, she was not a "woman with a mental disturbance," a term heard more than once uttered by those who rejected her claim. Indeed, few Eastern European immigrants coming as to the United States as an unaccompanied female in the early decades of the twentieth century would have been so instrumental in their death to make the dream, her specific dream of a museum dedicated to Russian history and culture, a reality. Easily, she was neither "mad" nor "disturbed," rather she exuded determination, fearlessness, and savvy- all with a penchant for art and history.

Historians will note, while other readers will smile, that "Evgenia" not only had conflicting dates of birth but also varying statements of nationality. In one ship manifest she is listed as *German* and on another *Ukrainian*. Via her mother whose German family she was said to most resemble, Anastasia would have indeed had derivative qualities to claim German citizenship (*see image in illustration section of the biometric overlay between Empress Alexandra and the lady known as "Evgenia"*). When she was born Ukraine was part of the Russian Empire, so that too makes sense. That they both appear on identity documentation begs to be noted. The image of a woman involved in international intrigue begins to emerge from a perusal of her paper trail from Europe to the USA. Had Hollywood known of her chameleon-like identity in the 1960's she would have easily been a main character in a James Bond movie. A note of thanks is due to Ancestry.com for enabling the discovery of such primary sources which formerly would have been proverbial "needles in a haystack."

The casual reader of "Evgenia's" 1963 publication might read the names of various friends and supporters without pausing to consider that these social relationships could reveal clues to her special set of circumstances. An initial investigation reveals that many were part of the politically connected, Chicago circles of literati, doyennes, and successful people in business. Again, this was a unique social circle for a a recently arrived Eastern European immigrant dismissed as "misguided" or worse, "deceitful."

"Evgenia" credits much assistance with her initial manuscript to two sisters from the Kohlsaat family.

The Kohlsaat grandfather, Reimer, had been an immigrant to the United States from Schleswig-Holstein, a region claimed at various times by Denmark and Germany. The Romanov family belongs to the noble House of Schleswig-Holstein-Gottorp-Romanov, sometimes referred to as Holstein-Gottorp-Romanov. However, Reimer's son, Judge Christian Cecil Kohlsaat, attained great professional heights as the son of this immigrant father. Surely Christian as well as perhaps the daughters, Helen and Edith, would have spoken German while Anastasia Romanov had been tutored in it. Christian Cecil was nominated in 1899 by President William McKinley to a seat on the United States District Court for the Northern District of Illinois which had been recently vacated by Peter S. Grosscup. Six years later President Theodore Roosevelt nominated him to a seat on the United States Court of Appeals for the Seventh Circuit on which he served until the year of his death, 1918, which was the same year of the alleged Romanov assassinations by Cheka operatives under the direction of Lenin and Bolshevik revolutionaries.

The Kohlsaat sisters whom "Evgenia" credits with their immense assistance in the preparation of her autobiography manuscript had ties via their father to the highest level of the United States federal government. Their paternal grandfather was the conduit to cultural ties with Schleswig-Holstein. Helen Kohlsaat (later Wells) was a 1904 graduate of Vassar College. Edith Kohlsaat traveled 1918 to Great Britain for "relief work." Evgenia" called her a "good friend." Had Edith gone to Great Britain on behalf of the US government to prepare the way for Evgenia/Anastasia to eventually emigrate? How "Evgenia" made the acquaintance of the Kohlsaat family is unclear at this point, but we do know that the woman with two dates of birth (even three as 1909 is given on one travel document) and various purported nationalities came as an unaccompanied woman though listed as "married" on her paperwork.

Life Magazine of October 18, 1963 boasted a front cover titled "The Case of a New Anastasia" in which the purported husband, Marijan Smetisko, neither a German nor a Ukrainian but rather a Croatian, denied he had ever been married to "Evgenia," moreover had never even met her and certainly had no idea who she even was. Nonetheless, he appears on her immigration records and never seems to have come to the United States. His existence, however, had been useful in creating a new identity for her travel documents. Was he the Croatian with whom "Evgenia" states she crossed the border out of Russia? She would have had time to make mental notes of his identity which she could then later easily manipulate to create a new identity.

In the acknowledgments of "Evgenia's" 1963 autobiography aka "Grand Duchess Anastasia Nicholaevna Romanov," John Adams Chapman of Chicago is mentioned. In fact, Chapman's father, John Edwin Chapman, is listed in *Chicago: Its History and its Builders*, Volume 5 by Josiah Seymour Currey. The Chapmans were of old New England stock which had produced a long line of successful businessmen.

Marjorie Wilder Emery was a member of the governing board of the Illinois Industrial School for Girls and the mother of Mrs. Norman Hanson whom "Evgenia" also thanks.

Mr. and Mrs. Louis E. Laflin, Jr: Laflin was a well-known playwright. He is mentioned in a Chicago Tribune article (by Ruth De Young) dated May 17, 1933 for his play concerning the life of Civil War hero Colonel Ellsworth titled "Ellsworth of the Zouavers."

Francis Beidler II and wife, Eleonor Chapman Beidler (sister of John Adams Chapman): From a Chicago Tribune obituary (dated June 27, 2004) we learn: "Eleanor Chapman Beidler, 94, resident of Lake Forest for 62 years, died June 23, 2004, at Lake Forest Hospital. She served as president of the Lake Forest League of Women Voters and was active in the McCormick YWCA of Chicago, the Lake Forest-Lake Bluff YWCA and the Coterie. She belonged to the Colonial Dames and was a lifelong member of the First Presbyterian Church of Lake Forest. Wife of the late Francis Beidler II (1984).

Mr. Beidler's father is well known for the Francis Beidler Forest: (http://sc.audubon.org/Centers_FBF.html) Francis Beidler Forest is a 15,000 acre wildlife sanctuary and natural area jointly owned by the National Audubon Society with The Nature Conservancy and managed by the National Audubon Society.

Another noteworthy person intimately involved with "Evgenia's" transformation in the public mind of that time to "Anastasia" was the renowned Grover Cleveland "Cleve" Backster, Jr. (February 27, 1924 – June 24, 2013). He was an interrogation specialist for the Central Intelligence Agency (CIA). He is credited with establishing the CIA's polygraph lie detection unit which still uses his techniques.

We learn by "Evgenia's" own account that she had been subjected to 30 hours of interrogation during which at some point Backster suggested that she was "withholding information" when stating that she was a "friend of Anastasia." Backster asked her to answer from the viewpoint of her really being the Grand Duchess. When she did, she passed her polygraph test and his muster. After this "switch" he declared that the woman who was not the wife of Mr. Smetisko, had purported to be a German and a Ukrainian, and who possessed two dates of birth, was telling the truth when it came to her imperial identity. To his analysis she was, indeed, the youngest daughter of Tsar Nicholas and Tsaritsa Alexandra. Hence, she had not died on July 17, 1918 in Ektarienburg during the alleged massacre in the Ipatiev House, infamously dubbed "The House of Special Purpose."

The circumstantial evidence that "Evgenia" was really "Anastasia" living under a useful and protective pseudonym has been impressive. The involvement of an expert from the CIA also indicates that the real identity of this well-connected woman could have been of national albeit international importance.

The Anastasia of historical accounts was also a talented artist and creative individual. (*A more in depth study of her work with color images is provided by the author in the above mentioned The Art of the Authoress of Anastasia published 2014 by Authorhouse*). By coincidence or design "Evgenia" and Anastasia were accomplished artists. If definitively proved by DNA analysis from the body of "Evgenia" that she was (and is) Anastasia, the prolific paintings of memories from her childhood in Russia may have had a double benefit of helping her to work through Post Traumatic Stress Syndrome which would have been a normal outcome after witnessing such a violent attack on her family.

Short of DNA there is another technology which can be employed for deeper insight into one's identity-biometric analysis. In 2013 while casually watching The History Channel a segment devoted to the fate of outlaw Jesse James was televised. The clever Jesse seems to have faked his own death, placing the body of a local man from a poor family in his grave. Meanwhile, James family members claimed that he had not died at all but had lived under a pseudonym well into his nineties. Mr. Robert (Bob) Schmitt, an expert and pioneer in biometric analysis, compared the photos of the young Jesse and the bearded nonagenarian whose family claimed that he had been Jesse all along. Using 2D technology, the features of both matched and merged. A later DNA analysis of the remains on the man who had lain in the James grave indicated he was not related to that family at all. The biometric analysis had driven the agenda leading to a DNA confirmation that Jesse had never been in the grave.

After contacting Mr. Schmitt (visualfacerecognition.com) about the puzzling story swirling around "Evgenia" he kindly agreed to analyze her photo at the approximate age of 62 to a verified photo of Anastasia as a young teenager. When he sent the result one could only gasp and sit down in wonder: "It is a 99.9% match." Subsequent conversations spoke of a new generation of 3D technology soon available. The day came in late spring 2017. Mr. Schmitt, "Bob," would be happy to look again at the relationship of the face of the older "Evgenia" and the younger "Anastasia." Not only that, he would look at the symmetry between "Evgenia" and Anastasia's mother, Empress Alexandra. We met at the historic El Patron Mexican Grill and Cantina at 198 Central Avenue, Albany, New York, built in the early 20<sup>th</sup> century and used as a backdrop in Albany native William Kennedy's motion picture IRONWEED with Meryl Streep and Jack Nicholson, based on his novel of the same title. Perhaps another historical event would occur within its walls.

First things first. We enjoyed sizzling fajitas with refried beans and generous portions of guacamole before discussing this chapter of Russian history and the artwork of Bob's late brother-in-law, Abdias do Nascimento, from Brazil. From the time of the original Dutch settlers Albany (earlier Beverwijk) had been known as a place of cultural fusion. A brief introduction to the mechanics and science of visual face recognition technology served as our dessert. First the case of Abraham Lincoln and an early alleged image of him. Next a verifiable young Thomas Edison and a more mature version. It was convincing to see the images separately and and then gradually joining in one even though age had changed appearances to the naked eye. After our meeting I viewed Bob's analysis of the earliest known image of composer, Richard Wagner, viewable at https://youtu.be/TMznhdlpj9w.

"Evgenia?" With calm the images of the Empress and that of the woman entombed with the last name "Smetisko" but inhumed with the date of birth of Russia's youngest Grand Duchess were examined. The 3D process places 22 points of reference onto each of the faces of the two images to be examined. A grid mask is created to connect these dots and then both masks are examined. Even to the uninitiated layperson "Evgenia" and the mother of Anastasia were highly congruent. When "Evgenia" and Anastasia were examined, restaurant owner Delma D. Hernandez and I were dumbstruck with the similarity. After so many years of studying the claimant's case and being aware of the earlier 2D analysis it was not really a surprise. Nonetheless, to see the two images seemingly float in space to create one face and to then regard two congruent faces side by side was breathtaking. Was this to be the evidence needed for some authority to request albeit demand an exhumation to check her DNA?

This publication will look at new biometric evidence in addition to bringing to public attention other contextual evidence that "Smetisko's" claim, substantiated first by 30 hours of interrogation by famed interview Backster, is more credible than ever.

Her own words will be reviewed in two forms: rewritten, but true to content, first person narration from her 1963 autobiography with indented first person verbatim quotations and original text.

Robert Speller and Sons Publishers are to be commended for having then lent credence to Evgenia albeit Anastasia's claim. They seemed to have been more prescient than many could have ever expected.

There are more aspects of this journey which should be shared only in private with those who have a sense of spirituality and respect for God. There are many dimensions to reality. As the Nicene Creed of the Christian faith clearly states: *We believe in the visible and the invisible.* In some ways, "Evgenia" albeit Anastasia has always had a journey partially seen and equally unseen but always WHOLE.

NOTA BENE:

Photos, the index, and other parts of the 1963 autobiography, originally published by Robert Speller and Sons Publishers, are not in this rewritten version. The original photographs, although interesting, offer little to inform the readers of today to help understand the realities of biometric visual face recognition. The goal of this section of Froebel-Parker's work is to glean insight from the words of the original authoress herself. Anastasia's first person quotations and selected text in original phraseology are indented in this edition.

# FROEBEL-PARKER'S ACKNOWLEDGEMENTS

Janis Froebel Parker

Robert "Bob" Schmitt

Penny Schmitt, nee' Larkin

Dr. Larisa Semenova-Head

Barbara Green, nee' Korr/Kur and Frances Eugene Green

The Late Consuelo Serrano L.

Delma Duarte Hernandez

Frank and Linda Kallenda Bruno

+ Pater Franz Maria Schwarz, Priorat Skt. Wigberti (Werningshausen, Thueringen)

Susan Gosselin

Roderick Hinkel, Schlossherr zu Boerln bei Leipzig

Robert Chiquin Martin

Garrett Roche

Patrice Maynard

Victoria Signorelli

Linda von Schatzabel, nee' Signorelli

Paul Grondahl

Catherine Ritchey and Delma Duarte H.

Let us review to whom the original authoress with love and esteem dedicated her account:

*To My Family:*

*To My Father, His Imperial Majesty, the Emperor Nicholas II, To My Mother, Her Imperial Majesty, the Empress Alexandra*

*Feodorovna,*

*To My Brother, His Imperial Highness, the Tsesarevich Alexei Nicholaevich,*

*To My Sisters, Their Imperial Highnesses, the Grand Duchesses Olga, Tatiana, and Marie;*

*To those dear and understanding friends who perished with My Family in Ekaterinburg;*

*Dr. Eugene Botkin, Mlle. Anna Demidova, Ivan Kharitonov, and Trup;*

*To those faithful friends and companions who, because of their loyalty to us, perished before or after the tragedy which befell My Family:*

*Countess Anastasia Hendrikova, Mlle. Ekaterina Schneider, Prince Vasily Dolgorukov, Count Ilia Tatishchev, Nagorny, Chemodurov, and Ivan Sidniev;*

*To My Brother's youthful companion and helper, whose fate I never learned:*

*Leonid Sidniev;*

*To My Uncle, His Imperial Highness, the Grand Duke Michael Alexandrovich, and his secretary and friend, Nicholas Johnson, both of whom disappeared, apparently murdered by the Bolsheviks;*

*To My Aunt, Her Imperial Highness, the Grand Duchess Elizabeth Feodorovna, and her faithful nun, Varvara, who were brutally murdered by the Bolsheviks;*

*To other members of the Imperial Family who were murdered by ·*

*the Bolsheviks;*

*To all members of the Imperial Family who died during the First World War and the Civil War in Russia,·*

*To all members of the Imperial Family, living and dead, who survived the Bolshevik revolution,·*

*To those dear and helpful friends:*

*Count Apraxin and Captain Nilov,·*

*To the two officers who came to pay their respects and salute My Father for the last time at the station at Tsarskoe Selo just before our departure for Siberia:*

*Kushelev and Artasalev (?);*

*To friends who voluntarily accompanied My Family into exile,· To my rescuer, Alexander;*

*To Nikolai,· to the Serbian, the Croatian, and the former Austrian soldier; and to all others who befriended and aided me during the long journey from the vicinity of Ekaterinburg to a refuge in Bukovina;*

*To those millions of heroes of the Russian Empire, sung and un sung, who gave their lives in defense of their country against the Central Powers and against the Bolsheviks,·*

*To all members of the Imperial Armed Forces who served their Emperor and their country faithfully and loyally at all times,·*

*To the millions who died in Russia from execution, starvation and other causes deriving from Bolshevik cruelty, tyranny and misrule,·*

*To the members of the Imperial Armed Forces who are now living outside their homeland and
    especially those among them who are maimed and destitute;*
*To all who have helped me in any way since I left Russia,·*
*To all these-departed and living, known and unknown, relatives
and friends-I am eternally grateful.*

*Anastasia*

# HER ACKNOWLEDGEMENTS

Mrs. Helen Kohlsaat Wells, Mr. John Adams Chapman, Mrs. Marjorie Wilder Emery, Miss Edith Kohlsaat, Mr. and Mrs. Norman Hanson, Mrs. John Adams Chapman, Mr. and Mrs. Louis Ellsworth Laflin, Jr., Mr. and Mrs. Francis Beidler II.

The original autobiography was divided into thirty-four chapters kept here for the ease of the reader:

# THE PREFACE OF THE AUTHORESS

Some weeks after my arrival in Bukovina-after I had had time to endure the emotional and nervous shock and body wounds that I had suffered at the time of the tragedy on the night of July 16-17, 1918. I was determined to put in writing the story of my home life with my beloved family, regarding our arrest, regarding our exile in Tobolsk and Ekaterinburg, regarding the assassination of the family in Ekaterinburg, and regarding my rescue and subsequent escape across the frontier.

I created myriad notes, totaling over 300 pages. I spent hours and hours penning my memories, days and nights of self-examining experiences, of grief and horror. I wrote taking refuge in a peasant house in a lonely village dotted with thatched-roof homes. I wrote at the hours of darkness with only the dim light of a beeswax candle, in pain over my story. Occasionally the sole relief I had from my misery was the howling or barking of a local dog. I remembered my beloved Father's words, "Dearest ones, are you awake?" Tear after tear dropped as I labored.

I recalled additionally my father's express wish that an historical account of Russia ought to be composed by an individual from our family. Father had at the top of the priority list that such a history may be composed by my two most established sisters and, keeping that in mind, he gave them much important data. As it has turned out, it is the most youthful sister, the one least capable to do as such, upon whom is bestowed the assignment of composing such a book, on the off chance that it is to be composed. That is something to yet be determined. In 1918, after my escape, I believed that the book I had chosen to compose about my family and myself might incorporate authentic information and translation which would bear some significance with the world and would be of advantage to the Russians and our common Motherland. I especially needed to let the world know the realities about the capture, outcast and murder of my parents, sisters and brother, and about the idea of the Bolshevik government in my nation.

These early notes sadly vanished in 1919 when I was en route from Rumania to Serbia-second country to us Russians-while in the region of Tumu Severin. I had acknowledged another traveler I thought was an Italian-his kind offer of a cut of bread and a bit of ham. Three or after four hours I turned out to be sick and needed to leave the compartment. When I returned some time later, the heartless explorer, who had no pity for a young lady voyaging alone, had vanished alongside my bag and a blanket. The bag contained not just my valuable notes, so laboriously penned, yet additionally some personal effects, a few letters, and a summary of around one hundred names of the men who were responsible for a large portion of the malice inflicted on Russia and on my family. These names I had recorded from memory, in light of information recited to me by my rescuer, Alexander. The vast majority of these names were at that point already well-known to me.

In Yugoslavia I continued work on my book. I proceeded with the undertaking later in Rumania and again in Yugoslavia. I composed many pages of notes, utilizing a pencil stub and pieces of paper. Various passages of these notes stayed neat and were used consequently in the arrangement of the main draft of the present book.

Afterward, in the mid-thirties, a few years after my landing in the United States, I started to amend my materials which were in a somewhat scattered state, however for the most part still in quite comprehensible condition, helped by my great companions, the late *Mrs. Helen Kohlsaat Wells*, and her sister, *Miss Edith Kohlsaat*. Amid this period of the undertaking I was resolved to finish the book as quickly as time permitted and to make arrangement for its production upon my death.

For around twenty years, I was not able work on the composition, because of the need of making my own living (*recorded on immigration papers as milliner*). During this period I gave no consideration whatever to the manuscript content which I had entrusted for supervision to my attorney, a companion who knew about my bonafide character and who wished to help me eventually to contract a publisher.

Five or six years before this present time I chose to continue to labor at the book. An entire modification and revamping of my materials were again required. Afresh I had the advantage of Helen Wells' help and advice.

I had additionally the considerable and esteemed support of my great companions - the late John Adams Chapman and Mrs. Marjorie Wilder Emery.

In the early months of 1963 I expressed to a companion in New York, who was ignorant of my true indentity, that I had previously possessed a manuscript full of content on the Russian Revolution. He proposed I connect with a dear associate, Dr. Jon P. Speller of Robert Speller and Sons, Publishers, Inc. This I did. The main individual from the firm with whom I talked was Mr. Robert E. B. Speller, Jr., who shocked me with the profundity of his insight into my family. I craftily suggested to him that the Grand Duchess Anastasia herself had left the composition with me, a dear family friend, right before her passing in [sic] 1919. I had desired gullibly to accomplish an early production of the manuscript in its entirety all the while keeping my true identity a secret. Dr. Jon Speller at that point joined the discussion. He inquired as to whether I would take a polygraph examination to substantiate my assertions. Upon my consenting to do as such, they finally agreed to peruse the composition. The Spellman father, Mr. Robert E. B. Speller, Sr., president of the firm, subsequent to examining the original copy conceded, based on a plethora of considerations, that the composition could only have composed by a member of the Imperial Family. They questioned me at length, and finally I confided to Dr.

Jon Speller and then to Mr. Robert Speller, Jr. that their suspicions were correct, that I was Anastasia, but that, if possible, I would like to retain my anonymity.

Consequently the polygraph examination, given by the prominent polygraph master Mr. Cleve Backster (*Grover Cleveland "Cleve" Backster, Jr.*), was commenced by testing me on my declaration that I was a companion of Anastasia. Mr. Backster immediately perceived that I was withholding relevant information, even to the degree that I could be Anastasia; at long last I conceded my genuine and veritable character to him. In a series of interrogation meetings stretching over thirty hours taking all things together, Mr. Backster emerged noticeably persuaded that I was verifiably Anastasia. I inked an agreement with Robert Speller and Sons and started modifying my book with Mr. Earl L. Packer, senior editorial manager of the firm, and Mr. Robert Speller, Jr.

My purposes behind bringing forth the book before the world right now will, I trust, be promptly perceived. They are not muddled. To start with, I wished to act as a bulwark for the protection my murdered mother and father, against whom numerous unwarranted allegations and criticisms have been and are still being made. Second, I felt that conflicting narratives of history which have been given wide audience should be rectified. Thirdly, I wished to reveal the deceptive claims and cases of different people to purportedly be me, namely Grand Duchess Anastasia. Fourth, I wish to found an association or foundation which will set up a museum or historical center, associated with little house of prayer or church or perhaps with a chapel in it out of respect for my family who so passionately cherished Russia with all loyalty and furthermore to guarantee, in so far as I may have the capacity to do as such, reserves for its upkeep, endowing it with finances for its maintenance (*editor's note: this she has done with the museum located in Jordanville, NY, at Holy Trinity Monastery and Seminary*). Fifth, I wish to financially support former Russians soldiers and officers with any profits generated by the publication of my books; 6th, I am planning to financially help other philanthropic and charitable organizations and causes which I have already chosen.

Sometime earlier I had come to doubt that, if publication of the book were postponed until after my death, as I had earlier resolved, my projects would ever materialize. Also, I thought unlikely the possibility that anyone but myself could or would make knowledgeable and effective defense against whatever criticism might·be made of the book and myself upon its publication.

I have had the blessing of being able to lead a a moderately calm life in the United States, where I have had the relative opportunity to avoid the undue attention and scrutiny to which I would have been subjected had I revealed myself to the world any time before this. Be that as it may, my motivations, as listed above, would not have been able to be implemented by obfuscating my true identity any longer. So I have decided to focus on the benefits of my endeavor instead of any unwarranted incursion into my life and peaceful existence in order to further carry out my desire to be an authoress and publish my work in the future. A.N.R. 1963

✳

# PART I

## *The Youthful Years*

# I     EARLIEST MEMORIES

𝕴T WAS June 5th, 1901, by the Russian calendar (*Julian calendar dubbed Old Style or OS*) June 18th by the new (*Gregorian dubbed New Style or NS*). Intrigue and excitement were rife at Peterhof (*dubbed Russian Versailles*)

The delivery of the Tsarina's baby was immediately anticipated. The fourth of her issue, without a doubt this time it would be a male. Russia bowed to the little Grand Duchess Olga, at that point to the child Tatiana. Yet, Marie, the third girl in progression, had been altogether too much. In any case, all would be made aright if this fourth imperial infant were the feverishly anticipated Tsarevich. Finally, the boom of coordinated rifles being fired was heard: the child had arrived; a three hundred firearm salute would report an Imperial Grand Duke and beneficiary to Russia's most highly honored and prayed for position. One hundred and one weapons would report a Grand Duchess. The firearms saluted yet again. The general population delayed to tally three, four, five; endlessly the rhythmical blasts continued. The people stood short of breath. Twenty-three, endlessly, one hundred, one hundred and one; the weapons ceased. No, it simply cannot be. It was unrealistic. "C'est domage!" The fourth offspring of the Tsar and Tsarina of Russia was yet once again another little girl. Dejected due to disappointment, the common man tarried on in his daily routine, yet the officials associated with Imperial Court murmured "humbug" and inwardly loathed the Tsaritsa who could not satisfy the expectations placed on her and demanded of her in her capacity as Empress. The Tsar and the Tsaritsa acknowledged the unavoidable and stated, "The Lord hath spoken."

> All the while I, the unconscious cause of this frustration, had lain peacefully in the same little crib which had cradled the three sisters before me. It was not long, however, before the unwelcomed wee one won the hearts of its parents and I was christened Anastasia (*from the Greek anastasis meaning resurrection*), but to the world outside I was *number four*, almost forgotten beyond the family circle.

As a tyke, my boyish girl soul prevailed and I was permitted to enjoy this characteristic up to the point when I progressed toward becoming somewhat of an oddity at court greatly steeped in custom. Nothing satisfied me more than a group of people, particularly when they gestured and whispered "adorable."

My next, more established sister, Marie and I were indivisible. At an early age my most noteworthy enjoyment was to stir her interest. Regularly when we were in the midst of some pretending and playing at make-believe, I would all of a sudden dash away. Marie was as easily reengaged in her own activity as I was snappy, so I would slip far away into one of my hiding places. At that point started the chase I delighted in. The searchers went around, as I tuned in from my vantage point, murmuring with fulfillment when I heard the call, "Anastasia, where are you? Be a decent young lady and do tell us, dear!" These diversions started good naturedly, yet regularly when the chase became less insistent, I lost interest and felt obliged to divulge my whereabouts.

Mysterious spots for hide and seek turned into a fixation for me, particularly little ones so cozy I needed to press into them. There I regularly stayed absolutely delighted over the bewilderment and possible fury of those whose searched for me. Once, when I was very youthful, I slipped out of the nursery onto the gallery. It was late toward the evening and the long shadows captivated me; and I must have lingered there unobtrusively for an inordinately long period of time. All of a sudden I heard agitated voices and I chose to keep impeccably calm. At nightfall, in the diffuse light, I straightened myself against the wall bathed in the shadows. The sentries were spreading out over the recreation center; the fear for my well-being was growing. I was excited when I knew they were hunting me down, yet I was somewhat afraid due to the disappearing light. I ran rapidly down the stairs and to the ground floor. Mother was conversing with one of the officers when her eyes all of a sudden fell on me.

"Anastasia," she cried, "where have you been?"

"Up there on the balcony," I replied with all the happiness in my voice that I could marshal. Nearly before I could get the words out Father was close to me. He took me by the hand. Taking one gander at his face cautioned me that something was off-base. Without a word he motioned to the bothered servant. Her face was flushed. She walked me to my room, and I never dared to cast even one look of triumph as she changed me into my nightgown. She did not utter the slightest peep until the moment I was ready to slip into nocturnal slumber. At that point she sternly stated, "You were an exceptionally underhanded young lady to stress your Mother so. She was extremely flustered."

Mother dependably came to kiss me goodnight each and every night. I did not crawl under the duvet in order to not miss her approaching footsteps which I could hear clicking on the floor outside my door. At last I heard her drawing nearer with my sisters; their voices sounded glad. She halted at the entryway for a slight instant, and Marie came into the room alone. At the point when the governess turned out the lights, I understood that Mother was not going to kiss me that night. The next morning a penitent little girl asked herself: "Will Mother come to me now?" And: "Will she be cross with me?" I was full of contrition, but how could I express it if Mother were not in a receptive mood? My eyes fastened on the door, hoping to see Mother's face. Suddenly she appeared. I ran to her and wrapped myself around her neck. I promised never to worry her again.

Mother's custom each day was to come to the nursery the first thing every morning before breakfast to say a prayer with us children and to read one chapter to us from the Bible. (*A very Lutheran custom surely informed by her Protestant upbringing in the Landgraviate of Hesse-Darmstadt*)

She was generally attired in an lovely robe of white, infrequently in other delicate hues, her hair plaited and attached with silk strips to coordinate the trimming of her outfit, a propensity procured from her grandmama, Queen Victoria of England. These were valuable minutes to us youngsters. She was a fairytale sovereign: stately and wonderful.

On July 30ᵗʰ, 1904, by Russian reckoning, August twelfth by the new, my younger brother was delivered on a Friday at midday. Three hundred firearms reported the appearance of the heir apparent to the Russian Crown from the Peter and Paul Fortress in St. Petersburg.

Around the same time, it was being reported that the Russian armada at Port Arthur had been sunk on August tenth by the Japanese naval force. My Mother frequently said it was simultaneously a day of daylight and a day of dark haze. It would have been customary to celebrate with a substantial meal to praise the introduction of a beneficiary to the position of authority yet Father would not entertain the notion. Rather, supplications were offered in the places of worship for the lost ones adrift and for the infant Tsarevich (*child of a Tsar*). Throughout the day chimes rang out from all the places of worship of Russia. After thirteen years Mother talked about this day as being as desolate as the day we touched base in Ekaterinburg. It was on Alexei's thirteenth birthday celebration and about that hour in 1917, that the family was ordered that they should leave their dearest home in Tsarskoe Selo.

I do not remember Alexei's christening (*Orthodox custom is to baptize, chrismate with holy oil, and immediately commune all new Christians even infants*) since I was but a toddler, but I have heard accounts of it and have often inspected his christening mantle and the cross which he wore on a golden chain around his neck. These were shown in a glass vitrine alongside the baptismal gowns of his sisters. Olga's was a detailed replica of that of Marie Antoinette's little princess of a daughter. It had been sewn in Lyons, France. Olga and Tatiana held a side of the long mantle which was pinned to the *coussin* due to its weight. Alexei's esteemed godparents were his grandmama, the Dowager Empress Marie Feodorovna (*born a Lutheran Danish Princess \*26 November 1847 +13 October 1928 christened Marie Sophie Frederikke Dagmar*); his sister, Olga Nicholaevna; his aunts, Mother's sisters, the Princesses Irene of Prussia and Victoria of Battenberg (eventually Marchioness of Milford Haven). The godfathers were his great uncles, the Grand Duke Alexei Alexandrovich and King Edward VII of Great Britain; his cousin, Kaiser Wilhelm II of Germany; his greatgrandfather, King Christian IX of Denmark; his uncle, the Grand Duke Ernest Louis of Hesse (*Ernst Ludwig von Hessen*), the Empress' only brother, and his Aunt Irene's husband, Prince Henry of Prussia. To commemorate his birth the cornerstone for the Feodorovsky Sobor (Church) was ceremoniously placed in Tsarskoe Selo.

Since this nice looking little brother had arrived, the hitherto burden of my young life, that of being a young lady, appeared to be to some degree mitigated. Alexei was a lovely young boy with a light appearance and wavy reddish-brown hair which my Mother brushed affectionately into a twist in the center, huge blue eyes, long eyelashes and a most appealing grin. He was the most interesting thing in my young world, so whenever there was a chance, I kept running into his nursery bestowing different toys on him. Mother had many pet names for him, among them: "My valuable Agoo" and "Kroshka" which is a Russian nickname which means a crumb of bread. Olga and Tatiana were allowed to hold the infant; Marie and I could just hold his feet.

One of my most clear memories from childhood, when I was almost four years of age, occurred on a Sunday when we sisters, as was our custom, were wearing white, prepared to go to Divine Liturgy. We heard strident voices and saw Mother running upstairs.

> This frightened us and we all ran after her to the nursery. There I saw a spot of blood on little Alexei's shirt. While the nurse was bathing him he sneezed, thereby causing a discharge of blood from his navel.

Despite the fact that I was extremely youthful, I could perceive without any effort from from the strain on the faces around me that something was not right. At that time I could not totally comprehend that which I could intuitively sense. A couple of years after the fact, when I was around seven, we three youngest siblings playing in the garden when our little brother fell over his truck. Before long a huge black and blue swelling appeared around his lower leg. At the point when Mother came she blacked out at the sight, knowing it was the feared hemophilia that might rob the life of her child. Accordingly, Father and Mother were ostensibly disheartened. Father sought the world's finest expert on the disease leaving no stone unturned, to no practical avail.

We were persistently reminded that we should be watchful of Alexei. He was so prone to being hurt. The toys which I loved to bring him as gift were quickly dispatched before he could ever put his hands on them. When he fell on his head his face swelled so appallingly that his eyes were practically shut and his entire face became a purplish yellow, a loathsome sight. At one minute he would be superbly well; after a hour, he would lie in bed genuinely sick. We were told not divulge what we knew about him to absolutely anyone. Naively and quite innocently we did entrust our insight with some of the staff who convinced us deceptively that they already knew about Alexei's mysterious malady.

Mother was continually next to him, failing to trust anyone else to minister to him. Each time, when he recuperated, Mother was totally depleted of energy, to such an extent that she was not able rise from her bed or leave her chambers, not even for a moment.

At the point when Alexei was well and had become his ordinary rotund self, it was difficult to recall that we must be watchful when we played with him. I frequently felt pugnacious when he prodded me saying, "Leave, you are playing like a young lady; you do not have a clue about this game." I kept up my self-control truly well and once in a while struck back by declining to play with him, however he severely whined because of such treatment. All of a sudden he would be well again at which time it was hard to control him from getting excessively frisky or undertaking games that might end in great misfortune.

Alexei had a few bodyguards known as Cossacks who were dependable and obliged to do their duties both day and night. Each morning they looked through the castle grounds before any individual from the family could stroll about in them. Alexei likewise had two exceptional chaperones. One was Derevenko, nicknamed Dina, an enormous solidly built mariner, an individual from the sailing crew of Father's yacht, the "Standard." He was no member of Dr. Derevenko's family, Alexei's doctor. Dina administered hot packs and light back rubs to Alexei, when they were required. Dina likewise gave froth medications, and always bore him in his arms when he was not capable of walking. Tragically Dina betrayed his young master during the chaos and upheaval of the Revolution and was later captured by the Soviets when they discovered some of Alexei's assets in his gear.

The other bodyguard was Nagorny. He was the last to give Alexei the care needed on a daily basis. Nagorny assumed responsibility of him amid the upheaval of the Revolution, and was murdered in Ekaterinburg in light of the fact that he possessed property which was Alexei's. These two, Dina and Nagorny, were continually next to Alexei to see that he did not do harm to himself. They helped my brother to experience an almost ordinary childhood by utilizing the activities recommended by Dr. Derevenko and the recommendations of M. Pierre Gilliard, our French mentor. They deftly carried out their responsibilities in such a way that my darling little brother never speculated that he was being protected. For he was never told of the genuine nature of his disease but rather was to acknowledge it for himself when he reached adolescence.

At his birth Alexei received many titles: "Hetman of all the Cossacks," "Knight of St. Andrew," "Knight of the Seraphim of Sweden," "Head of the Battalion of the Horse Infantry," "Head of the Siberian Infantry," "Head of the Cadet Corps" and others. Alexei loved everything military.

I think he had a uniform for practically every military unit in Russia. He was so pleased to wear every one, and conducted himself with genuine military bearing. From adolescence he had worn a white mariner suit with stripes around his neckline. When we traveled in the Baltic, he wore a white mariner top with the name "Standard" in white on a blue band. While cruising on the Black Sea he had a dark band with yellow lettering.

One day in a snow storm I pulled Alexei on his sled. At that point he demanded to change roles and pull me. Before long his hands wound up noticeably swollen, however, luckily this did not instigate one of his genuine assaults. He was not allowed to partake in sports with abandon like other boys, however he was permitted to ride a tricycle and later a bicycle too, at which times he was painstakingly trailed by Dina. At long last he was permitted to drive a little motorized auto with his cousins or circle of young friends.

Alexei had playmates other than myself. I recall a particular young boy who was driven up up the drive joined by a bodyguard and well supplied with many toys. He had in addition to other things a container of powdered chalk. Considering my brother's pal a kind of interloper and, unfit to conceal my envy, I grabbed the case from his hand and scattered the substance everywhere throughout the floor. Everything happened so rapidly that nobody could stop me. Before long I was escorted to Mother. When she received me I was all grins yet somewhat distressed no doubt. She sat quietly and held my little hands, examining them and thinking about how they could do something such as this. I looked at her face, putting on my most winsome smirk. Mother guaranteed me that "Grins won't help." Just at that point Father came in and sent me to my bedroom for whatever remained of the day.

Later he came to see me and stated, "You should not battle with your younger playmates. Always be on your guard to be a young gentlelady." "I would prefer not to be a woman," I said rebelliously. Father replied, "At that point you cannot live in this place." "Where will I live at that point?" "In one of the sentry's houses," said Father. My dear father regularly apologized for Alexei and myself.

Delicate as Father might have been, I considered those comments important, because I knew he generally stood by what he said. So I dedicated myself to "being a woman." It soon paid off. At some point later when I was wandering through the estate gardens I perchanced upon two laborers who were battling in the gorge. It looked genuine and urgent. With all the ladyship I could marshal I bade them stop. To my surprise they did. The differentiation between little me and those two, so colossal and threatening, persuaded me that there must be something in this elegant business all things considered.

By nature I delighted in the unpleasant and all that was rumble-tumble, while being a woman implied being noble, sewing, rehearsing on the piano, as a rule following in the strides of Olga and Tatiana. I would much rather have played the same games that Alexei delighted in. Marie disliked these past times by any stretch of the imagination. She favored dolls, which I thought were not half as much fun as shooting off cap guns. I frequently held the firearm while Alexei slid down the toboggan slide on the lap of his bodyguards Derevenko or Nagorny.

The esplanade encompassing our home at Tsarskoe Selo (*Tsarskoye Selo, "Tsar's town," 15 miles south of St. Petersburg*) fulfilled my anxious wish to investigate my general surroundings, albeit even this could not fulfill my interest about that piece of the world which lay past the fence. One evening I found an owl opposite the fence in the garden. I had seen something flying which tumbled to the ground. When I raced to it I found an owl which did not move. I needed to lift it up, yet was informed that it was misfortune to do as such. Notwithstanding the undesirability of my action, I got the winged creature and stroked and encouraged it. In a brief time it turned into a genuine pet so it could even perceive my footsteps. It generally remained close-by, jumping about within a little area, however it didn't appear to be harmed. At whatever point it heard me, it would fly up and sit on the rail of the veranda. While the owl was roosted there, it appeared to gaze at me and I could not resist strolling about interested by its winding neck and gazing eyes which obviously followed my every gesture.

More often than not I was wont to meander through our fairyland surroundings with my sisters and our little brother, the heir to the throne and future Tsar. Its excellence was overwhelming with fine vistas encompassing greenhouses, gorges, lakes and even islands. We frequently played with our toy vessels on the lake or paddled Alexei in a pontoon. Now and again we sat on shore watching the diverse reflections on the surface of the lake. These included reflections of the Feodorovsky Sobor (*Nicholas and Alexandra's parish church*) with its brilliant dome, or again a look at the lush tree tops, or the quickly changing cloud shapes. On the lake the swans floated forward and backward in effortless magnificence, however, when they drew close to our shores, with one stroke they removed all the pictures before our eyes.

These swans were my extraordinary pets. I more often than not came laden with bits of bread to toss to them. One day in an evil mindset, I made them think I had come to feed them. When they swam toward me eagerly, I fled. All of a sudden I was tossed to the ground, and the biggest of the swans with his wings spread wide hovered over me. He started to beat me with his wings. My shouts brought assistance from one of the bodyguards, who drove off the swan. When I quit wailing I had not lost my adoration for the swans, but rather I had learned I should not prod or provoke them.

Father discovered time to visit us at play each day, regularly just for a couple of minutes, yet he delighted us with these visits. At times he watched us as we went down the slide which had been erected in a spacious room on the ground floor. He produced a tootle of glee as each of his offspring scooted down the slide while the rest of us shouted in absolute joy.

A few times, as an awesome treat, we children were allowed to bathe in Father's enormous tub, lined with elegant tiles and sunken in the floor. It was so deep and spacious that he could permit himself a few swim strokes. After our ablutions we frolicked over the tremendous chaise longue in Father's changing area, watching the tongues of fire flickering in the fireplace.

Mother called Father's office "No Man's Land." We youngsters were not permitted to enter it, which of course made me fairly inquisitive about it. I regularly kept running a few doors down, trusting that I would figure out how to get into his space yet there was dependably somebody who might send me back. In the event that I could have discovered what Father did there, I would have been fulfilled. One day I figured out how to sneak past the narrow hallway of his changing room and opened the entryway which opened up into the office. I was short of breath with anticipation, yet stayed silent. I was going to open the entryway for a little look, to check whether Father were there, when I heard the sound of footsteps. I chose to withdraw discreetly as though I had arrived by mistake. Be that as it may, as I retreated I moved too quickly. I moved down a few steps directly into the center of Father's indented tub. Luckily, I was not harmed, but my feelings and emotions were. I removed myself and went back down the corridor amidst much giggling. I never knew the identity of whomever it was who sensed I was there.

My interest was as yet not fulfilled, and I was resolved to continue attempting. I utilized a wide range of reasons for setting off to his office with pressing messages or little gifts. Yet, Mother talked with severity: "Father can't be irritated in his work." Notwithstanding Mother's words, the opportunity did present itself. One day I stood trembling at the entryway. There was Father at his work area looking engrossed in something at hand. I stood on my tippy-toes to take in all that I could see, so far forward that I lost my equilibrium and fell head over teacups into the room. I was frightfully terrified, yet Father raced to me and with a grin lifted me up saying: "What are you doing here, child?" Then he sat me down at his work area and held me on his knees. I was confused to think I was in the prohibited place. I looked at heaps of papers and then immediately at Father's face. With an embrace and a kiss he led me back into the corridor. "Now keep running along, my little Curiosity." I skipped away elated and I could barely contain myself to tell Marie that I had really been in "No Man's Land."

I was frequently instrumental in getting my sister and little Alexei in naughty situations. When we headed to Pavlovsk (an Imperial bequest close St. Petersburg), a short distance from Tsarskoe Selo, I looked for the minute when the nanny was in discussion with my cousin's bodyguard. I snapped my fingers-a flag to dash to the stream for the mud battle. Within seconds our little faces and white outfits were mud caked to the point of being unrecognizable. These mud battles made the nurse furious. Once when she reprimanded me, she said it was a pity I had not been born a little boy instead of a girl. This caused me such distress that I went to Mother with the inquiry, "Do you adore me, Mother?" "You know I do, little *Shvibzchik*," was her answer, utilizing her pet name for me. "Be that as it may, on the off chance that I had come to the world a boy, would you cherish me more?" I made my inquiry with tears in my eyes. Mother comprehended immediately; she shook her head and whispered "No" and I was put at ease.

At various times after tea, I slipped into the servants' quarters to partake of tea once more, since I thought they would surely have additional fascinating things to eat. I was very wrapped up in my little world without understanding that there was some other. But then being a member of the imperial family, despite everything, I still had to continue to ponder whether I ought to have been born another person. I thought about whether my grandmama, the Dowager Empress Marie, had ever excused me for not being a little boy. That may clarify her basic state of mind toward me. I thought I detected an unsympathetic bearing in her and I frequently struck back by being bad tempered which substantiated her assessment of me. Things being what they are this same grandmother may have understood me more thoroughly, more profoundly that anyone else. At the point when all had thrown all expectations regarding me to the wind, she would state, "Don't fret she'll tame down before long." This may have been an encouraging idea to my family, however not to me. I would not like to resemble my grandmama, not in the least. She was short, dark-eyed, with a deeply pitched voice but always elegantly coiffed and comely. I needed to resemble Tatiana, tall, lovely and elegant. Frequently after I was tucked in bed, I whispered a petition for intercession that God might change me overnight·into a young lady like Tatiana. Grandmama was Alexei's top choice. He adored her more than we sisters. She was Father's mama and there was a solid bond between them.

I remember the satisfaction I felt when some Danish relatives were visiting us and my Grandmother said to one, "Anastasia is certainly small," and the relative replied, "You are not very tall yourself." This kind person must have sensed that I was touchy about my height and she attempted to defend me before Grandmother. (*editor's note: An immigration record available at ancestry.com state's "Evgenia's" height at just over 5' 01"*)

At the point when Father's toils and labor were complete at the end of the day, he would enter Mother's chamber and warble tunefully. This was the signal for a family get-together or for an activity outside. Now and again Father took me on a walk alone. He listened intently to my little worries and complaints, while putting on a show pretending to be worried about my negligible issues. I swelled with pride at the idea that he considered my little world was as vital as his. He was an admirer of nature, and this information made our strolls much additionally fascinating. Father had the notoriety of being a talented and avid tennis player. He played with the best experts in the Crimea and won more often than not. Olga and Tatiana regularly played with him and I anticipated the day when I would have the capacity to engage him in a genuine match. However, that day never came. Prior to the war I was far too young, and amid the war there was no chance. I did fetch balls infrequently when father was playing or practicing.

*(Editor's note: Olga and Tatiana were affectionately called Big Pair while the younger Maria and Anastasia were Little Pair. They often wrote poetry, knit, embroidered, painted, and crocheted together. In order to honor their Romanov sisterhood they created an acronym based on the chronological order of their birth using the first letter of their first names: OTMA. Embroideries from that time created by them are usually inscribed with this acronym in beads. Later paintings by the lady known simultaneously as "Evgenia Smetisko" and Anastasia Romanov are generally signed OTMA.)*

# II    SCHOOL DAYS

**W**ITH EXCITEMENT I anticipated my first day of school. I was on edge to establish a decent connection with my educators. Wearing a blue or white pinafore and with ribbon bows on my hair, holding my Mother's hand, I had the sensation that I was quite mature as I joined Marie in the school room on the second floor of the imperial residence. I was pleased to hear Mother say that I was a good girl, tranquil, and intelligent as I sat at a medium sized table across from my teacher, taking notes as he asked questions. Be that as it may, to Mother's chagrin my laudable behavior did not last much longer. As the days passed, I started to feel corralled, and I yearned for the outside. School turned into a proverbial cross to bear, and my instructors found me problematic. My mind wandered to the outside of the classroom entrance. Only the fear of punishment caused me to go to classes, yet once I was seated I immediately longed for and mentally arranged my after school activities.

My mind envisioned Vanka, the little donkey, when she came as a present to Alexei. She was splendid and to a great degree persistent. She was named for a character in a hilarious Russian melody of the time. Vanka was clever. At the point when Alexei hurt himself, she laid her head on his shoulder as though she were crying. She could shake hands, dance as though she heard music, and feigned being a coquette. She seemed to comprehend each word we stated, regularly shook her ears in bliss. Be that as it may, when things were not to her liking, she gazed directly at us. Her ears stood up and curled almost into a cone. She could have been an animal performer at a circus, however she would just perform when she felt like it. Derevenko, the mariner, could make her walk while I rode her, yet she needed a piece of sugar in regular installments as she slowly trotted along.

"Anastasia, please do pay attention," and suddenly I left my pleasant thoughts of Vanka and focused once again on my studies at hand. I liked numbers juggling and drawing. I would frequently doodle until my pencil was taken away and the lessons continued. In the spring it was more of a task to be mindful of my lessons. The warm, sweet air and the tweeting birdies outside would just not allow me to sit still.

Frequently after school, Mother would take me to my favorite barnyard and livestock pens where I felt absolute liberation. Here were numerous cute animals to cuddle: sweet little pink piglets, toy-like sheep, calves and colts, the cutest I had ever seen. There were other children, as well, members of the farmhands' families, however Olga had a method for bestowing her devoted attention to them. Each place we went the youngsters were joined at our hip.

They all spoke with animation and enthusiastically about all that was new at the farm. We professed to be astounded, which encouraged them to recount every story over once more.

There was one time when a farm manager gave me a little chick, hatched late in the season. We placed it in a tiny basket with some straw in it. I shrouded it with my embroidered hankie and ventured out in front of Mother to uncover it in the carriage where I cuddled it eagerly. I was worried about the possibility that that this teeny tiny chick would pass away before we had gotten home. Not long after Mother heard the chick cry, she said, "You have taken an infant from the mother hen. You should keep it healthy and glad." This chick taught me my first lesson in obligation. You never could have observed so much pampering showered on such a little thing. I encouraged it most gently and gave it my dainty doll's pillow. Regardless of my dedication and benevolence the chick's chirping became weaker and weaker until one morning I discovered it lying on its back. It was the cause of absolute distress to me.

I chose to give my chick a burial service. I dressed it majestically with cloak and outfit and, as an extraordinary concession, I enabled Marie and Alexei to help lay the little chick body on a sleeping cushion of flower petals in a pretty box. A bunch of white blossoms was set on its bosom. At that point we welcomed everybody to the memorial service. Plus, I wanted all those in attendance to admire how perfectly I had arranged my pet. Alexei was the clergyman, Marie and I intoned the traditional funeral chants. Derevenko, the mariner, arranged the grave. The casket was opened for all to see. Finally the case was shut and put over a stretcher, which was raised up on the pallbearers' shoulders. I, the main griever, led the funeral parade with a dark band on my arm. We covered the crate with an abundance of flower petals and blooms and then adorned the burial site with the loveliest of stones.

For seven days I grieved at the grave each day, ruminating about how the chick was faring on its journey to the highest heavens in Paradise. At long last, I uncovered the burial case. I opened the cover expecting that the little blessed one had taken off, however rather I hurried to Mother to disclose to her that worms were eating my pet. Mother clarified that the casket contained only the lifeless body of the chick, the spirit had already taken off while Nature was now reclaiming the body.

I was socially inclined and engaged anyone at the royal residence in conversation. I talked with all about diverse subjects. "On the off chance that Olga and Tatiana ever wed, will they abandon us? Olga pressed an orange peel yesterday and it squirted directly into my eye. Do you realize that Mashka (Marie) put on her clothing incorrectly inside out and refused to put it on with the right side out, it was a true misfortune. Did you hear that "babykins" (Alexei) painted a saggy mustache all over with a colored pencil? Olga says, he resembles the Cossack in Riepin's famous painting. Have you seen that artistic portrait? Why do you figure Marie did not bathe in cold water today? Olga says that mother kangaroos shroud their infants in a sack on their bodies and the babies jut their heads out to see where they are going. Why doesn't daddy get infant cribs for the *kangarooshkas*?" These thoughts or others like them were communicated to all in five to ten minutes of these social visits. In some cases I requested they recount to me stories like the Golden Apple and the Princess. I applauded and expressed my gratitude to them for the most enjoyable story. On the off chance that anybody was not well, I was prepared to play nursemaid. My one cure for those who were under the weather was invariably a wet towel on the brow.

Some of my most pleasant early memories about Mother were the times when she told us stories. There was one favorite she was asked to repeat over and over. One day she changed the words slightly and I burst into tears, saying: "But, Mommy, I like the old story better."

Some years later, Mother read to me an American book called *Ramona (Helen Hunt Jackson's book published in 1894. It was later made into a silent film with Mary Pickford and Henry B. Walthall.)* As much as I could understand, it was a fascinating story about an indigenous American girl, a little Indian girl.

The tale greatly impressed me and left me with the feeling of a most tender friendship for the Indian young lady. Quite a while later, when I heard that a respected man, a true gentleman from the United States was going to pay Mother a visit, I asked to be permitted to meet him. I recollect that I wore my best new dress, of white silk, a present to me from Queen Alexandra of England. This dress had smocking at the midsection. I had been informed that it had been purchased at a well-known shop: Liberty's of London. I kept this dress until, during the war, at which time I offered it away in a charity drive.

At the time of the said American's visit, the nanny had arranged to bring me to the ground floor when Mother rang. Be that as it may, when I heard that it was time to descend, I instead ran ahead, and flew down the winding stairway as quick as my feet could convey me, whereupon I burst enthusiastically into the room. A tall dapper man rose and kissed my hand as we were presented. Bothered and quite beside myself I looked sideways to him as I blurted out in astonishment: "Mother, he cannot be American!

He doesn't have feathers in his hair or blanket about his shoulders." The poor man, whoever he was, attempted his best to clarify, yet to me, despite everything he was not a true American.

Mashka (Marie) had the most magnificent way about her, however I frequently got her into hot water. We used to practice piano in a room over Mother's bedchamber where she could hear us. Once when our teacher, Mr. Konrad, happened to venture out for a moment, we started to roughhouse. Before long the phone rang and we knew it was Mother on the line to remind us to pay attention to our lessons and not to play around.

Mother understood that we missed having playmates of our age, and she compensated for it by creating a more tightly woven family circle of our own. Once in a while we saw the Tolstoy lasses or the children of General Hesse, once Father's confidant. We took a few lessons, practiced dance steps and played with them: two young men and a young lady about the age of my sister Olga. In any case, no undue closeness whatever was permitted. We immensely enjoyed Aunt Xenia's children, our cousins, when they were at home.

At the point when Alexei was close to seven years of age, he had a governess named Maria Vishniakova. She exasperated Olga and made her cry. Vishniakova disclosed to Mother that the *muzhik* (*Russian for someone from the countryside*) Rasputin purportedly had been upstairs in our private apartments and had acted shamefully. As indicated by the tradition of the Russian court, no men were permitted in young ladies' rooms aside from the two Negro concierges, Apty and Jim. Father turned out to be so angry with the report that he actually personally confronted Vishniakova. She was sly, and indicated one date and then yet another. Father disclosed to her that Rasputin who had been implicated in the report had not even been close to St. Petersburg during those dates; she conceded her entire story was a fictitious creation and that it was a malicious relative of the Imperial family who had enticed her to make the accusations she had. No sooner had she confessed then she burst out crying; obviously she was dismissed from her duties. It was then that the assault on Rasputin started.

Another episode which caused a lot of perplexity a few years before the war began included our tutor, Mlle. Tutcheva, a local citizen of Moscow. She was fluent in various tongues, however no English. Aunt Ella (*the Grand Duchess Elizabeth Feodorovna, later sanctified a holy saint and martyr, Saint Elizaveta Feodorovna*), Mother's sister, had suggested that she be considered for this position. Tutcheva was a refined lady and originated from a fine family, yet she also was overly candid and overbearing. She detested the English so that she issued an edict that she would not tolerate English to be uttered in her presence; she regularly excoriated the English, particularly when we she reviewed the photos of our various visits abroad. She even grumbled to us about our own Mother, that she was English and not a Russian, and continually traded sharp words with Mlle. Butsova, one of Mother's most favored female royal attendants, speaking also to her in a harsh way, yet Mlle. Butsova did not hold back when answering her either. This disquieted us children making us unnerved. Mlle. Tutcheva was likewise in a ceaseless clash with others in the royal residence. To our disdain she likewise talked unkindly of Princess Maria Bariatinsky. Later she maliciously proffered to Aunt Ella that Rasputin had gone to our bed chambers in spite of the fact that at no time had any of us sisters seen the man in the upstairs above the ground floor. (*Editor's note: The rumor mill must have been in full swing with this disinformation albeit misinformation sweeping through courtly circles, probably believed by many up to and beyond the Revolution.*)

Mother's sister, our Aunt Ella made an exceptional trek to Tsarskoe Selo from Moscow to inform her of this calumny. This occurrence likewise went to Father's notice and he went to our rooms to enquire about it. We as a whole said we had not seen him in our personal quarters ever. The police records demonstrated that Rasputin was away on those days. Tutcheva at long last conceded that the story was false and that she had never in her life seen Rasputin. She was expelled.

Father adored everything about Russia: her subjects, her customs, her music and her national dishes, especially was he enamored of black peasant bread. It was prepared in the military kitchens and was generally delicious. He likewise appreciated a glass of *slivovitsa*, a plum liqueur. Amid the war he favored beverages with no alcohol content and followed his own proclamation during national prohibition, making no exemption for himself. Be that as it may, some wine and different alcoholic beverages were still served to high outside military officers in Mogilev. Father detested and regularly dismissed taking medicines prescribed to him even given the fact they were deemed essential for his gastrointestinal maladies. He accepted, as did his Romanov precursors, that Nature was and remains the best pharmacist.

Father had the most ideal academic instruction and preparation. One of his most loved educators was the well-known Konstantin Donostsev. This man was an exceptional scholar and attorney. He introduced Father to both law and religion, so that Father's confidence stayed solid to the very end. Another most favored instructor was General Danilov explained military strategies. He was painstakingly chosen for this most critical course of study for a tsar. Father had a Swiss teacher who instructed him in the French language and literature, and an English instructor named Charles Heath who helped Father improve his command of the English language and literature.

Father had the most extraordinary memory. He was able to recite many Russian, French and English poems, including passages from Shakespeare.

He could read and write with alacrity, his sentences being short and compact and constantly written in ink. He appreciated the works of art. His personal library included additionally titles by Gogol, Gorbunov's stories of Russia, and Feodor Dostoevsky, a significant number of whose signed books were on the racks of our library; along with literary works crafted by Longfellow (*relative of this editor via William Brewster of the Mayflower 1620*), Dickens, Wordsworth and many others.

He was familiar with international law and often commented that many diplomats made mountains out of molehills, dealing in such a complicated manner with matters whose solutions were really quite simple.

On the "Standard," the Imperial yacht, he had in his cabin the complete works of Shakespeare and other English contemporary authors, with a collection of books selected for us by our teachers which we were to read during out cruises.

The discipline expected by Father's father, the Tsar Alexander III, was the reason for such order. Had Father not felt bound by his oath of office, I can say with surety that he would have rescinded some of the restrictions he had inherited from his own father. His love for his people and his Christian nature were often displayed when he mitigated the punishment of soldiers by their officers. He believed in a close family relationship and once, after receiving a request, he allowed the Jewish mother of an ill prisoner to visit her son in the prison hospital as often as she wanted in recognition of the love of a mother for her child.

Father was always a loyal friend to those who were close to him. Generally he did not like gossip and avoided what might be called idle chatter.

At times requests from subjects were never delivered to him so that he never learned of them to begin with. In other cases, actions were taken in his name without his having ever sanctioned them. Often he would never hear about these actions which were taken in his name but without his express authorization. (*Editor's note: This is somewhat reminiscent of the execution of Mary Queen of Scots by her cousin, HM Elizabeth I Tudor of England. Court operatives executed Mary without the express declaration of Elizabeth to do so. When Her Majesty finally learned of it she was understandably furious. Although she had signed an order, it came with the express caveat that it was not to be carried out without her direct verbal mandate.*)

In spite of previous attempts on his life, he had resumed the ancient custom of the "Blessing of the Waters" on the river Neva in St. Petersburg.

When a little girl, I heard a story of how there had been an explosion on the river during one of these ceremonies in which several were injured included Father's personal physician. The Winter Palace had suffered damages to some extent. With this in mind Father ordered this ancient tradition to end. However, an illness took hold of the city in epidemic proportions and the people attributed it to the discontinuance of the ceremony. So the order was lifted and the Epiphany (*also known in Orthodoxy as Theophany and associated with Christ's baptism hence the emphasis on water*) celebration began anew. I was able to attend this centuries old celebration once.

Ecclesiastical and governmental luminaries all assembled at the Winter Palace. The procession grouped there and marched to the river, followed by other church dignitaries. Father positioned himself in front of a crimson and gold canopy. An opening had already been chiseled into the ice. At the end of the liturgy the Father received the cross from the priest which he placed and withdrew from the water, raised high and used to make the sign of the holy cross in the air above the people. This was repeated thrice. The air was so frigid that the drops of water froze as they fell on the ice. All of the participants returned to the Palace and were seated to enjoy a sumptuous luncheon together. The image they created, seated all in their sparkling court regalia, was magical indeed.

The ladies seated at the reception were indescribably lovely in their long court dresses of various pastel colors and jeweled filets (*kokoshniki*) from which fell soft and gentle veils. The diamonds, rubies, emeralds, sapphires and alexandrite gems shone sparkly and bright in the light. Alexandrite is a rare gemstone found in the Urals in 1833, named after the future Alexander II, my great-grandfather.

Many officers wore their regiments' uniforms: the Horse Guards were in white and gold; the Cossacks in deep blue or crimson; and the Hussars in white and gold with scarlet dolmans (*editors' note: a long, loose garment with narrow sleeves and open in the front, of Turkish origin*) over their shoulders.

This Theophany ceremony was conducted the last time in January 1916. It did not evoke the same spirit as previously. This time there were many high ranking dignitaries in attendance, among them the foreign High Command, such as our friend, Sir John Hanbury-Williams, and, naturally, Sir George Buchanan, the British Ambassador.

My first years of life were spent in the Winter Palace with all its rococo inspired fancifulness. (*Editor's note: to great extent Elizabethan Baroque*) Tsarskoe Selo became our new home, however, during the war with Japan. It was there that my earliest memories formed.

The Alexander Palace at Tsarskoe Selo was our permanent home. Many members of the Imperial family had their residences in this suburb and nearby; it was only fourteen miles south of St. Petersburg.

Our Palace was located in the epicenter of a spacious estate of about six hundred acres, in which one could find stables, greenhouses and diverse churches, including the *Feodorovsky Sobor* and Our *Lady of Znamenie* which was my Mother's most cherished houses of worship. There were also islands nearby. On the "Children's Island", Alexei had a small house; time had not touched the four rooms which were as if in a time warp from the time of Alexander II. The book cases boasted books by the poet Zhukovsky and also by Byron, Schiller and other poets which he had translated into Russian. Zhukovsky was the tutor to Alexander II and spent much time with him before his ascending to the throne.

Many tiny docks were located on the water where boats could be moored. An Elephant house and other specialty buildings were on the estate. A White Tower, a building dedicated to photography and an armory were also there. Military regiments had their barracks nearby as well.

Cabinent members were ushered in to see Father before the war. Invariably they brought all kinds of military reports for him to review. Father, however, did go to St. Petersburg too at time to meet with his ministers and other officials. The General Chamber of the Winter Palace was also used once a week in an effort to save time and expense. Father spent only minutes per meeting as there were hundreds on one day. There was no time even to sit, so they were held standing. After his morning constitutional Father would have one half hour, 10am-10:30am to be exact, for reports from high officials.

> Several hundred attendants took care of the grounds and buildings; many of them lived outside. The personnel included the Grand Marshals of the Court, Masters of the Hunt, Masters of Ceremonies, Equerries, Chamberlains, coachmen, valets, butlers, chauffeurs, gardeners, cooks, maids, etc.

An intricately wrought iron gate surrounded the Palace of Catherine the Great at Tsarkoe Selo, and a high fence surrounded the entire palace grounds. Priceless rooms of amber, malachite, mosaics, and gilt graced this museum-like palace. Of these chambers two are marked indelibly on my mind: an antechamber in which Catherine displayed her renowned collections of snuffboxes, and a drawing room with a ceiling created with ivory silk satin, in the center of which one viewed a tremendous double eagle which had been hand embroidered. In a third room, the walls were of satin, with exquisitely embroidered golden wheat and pastel blue cornflowers. There was another room with a double eagle inlaid in its mosaic wooden floor.

The choir of the private chapel was located in a large balcony. The private chapel had a large balcony for the choir. Catherine's Palace was grandiose and highly decorated while we always felt that the Alexander Palace had a cozier atmosphere, more family-oriented.

During my childhood tours were permitted of the Alexander Palace when we were not there. However, we soon learned that the tour guides were allowing their relatives to enter our private quarters in our absence. Mother was incensed and felt abused by this fact, so that these tours were soon discontinued. Thereafter the park became restricted so that anyone coming to visit had to apply for and receive a special permit from the House Manager to even enter the grounds of Tsarskoe Selo. Even those who were workers at the estate had to have a permit.

# III    CRUISES

ur summer holidays were usually on the yacht, but we were inland at Tsarkoe Selo. Hence, our journey started at Peterhof located on the Gulf of Finland. We always looked forward to these excursions with great anticipation.

The great palace of Peterhof was too formal with its many groups of fountains and Peter the Great grandeur. We preferred to stay in the little Alexandria Cottage, while we waited for Father to get away.

In the exciting process of packing our luggage I often slipped in myriad slips of paper on which I had written my personal secrets. I also included personal treasures such as a favorite slipper which the dog loved to chew.

To the east of Peterhof lay the Alexandria Cottage which was two buildings actually, connected by an enclosed walkway. In the greenhouses with their glass walls and ceilings, we enjoyed our "wintergarden" which displayed palms, flowers, and tropical plants. We would take luncheon there, and, when it rained, we girls would play with our dolls on garden chairs and in a doll house which was also there.

My second great grandfather, Nicholas I, had originally bought this estate and he was the first to occupy it. There was a saying that Peterhof started with Nicholas and would end with Nicholas. The natural beauty of the park with its landscaped gardens, meandering walkways, gorges and awe-inspiring white birch trees and green spruce have been preserved since the time of Tsar Nicholas I. (*Editor's note: a look into the Ahnentafel of Nicholas I from the website Fabpedigree: http://fabpedigree.com/s096/f662161.htm*)

The view from the entrance of Peterhof grounds was enough to take away one's breath. The roadway was graced with beautiful trees on both sides which formed an arch over the road. Statues in bronzes depicting historical events and then fountains were interspersed among the trees. Magnificent flower-filled urns also added to the grandeur. We could view everything that was happening on the Island of Kronstadt from a tower in a pavilion nearby. Divine Liturgy was held in the Alexander Nevsky Church dedicated to our national hero from the thirteenth century who protected the sovereignty of the Russian Motherland. From Peterhof we took a tender (*a kind of railroad car which immediately follows the locomotive*) to Kronstadt, the naval base on the island bearing the same name. The dock at Peterhof was not sufficient enough for the yacht "Standard" (*Standart*) so it had to moor elsewhere nearby. A sailor was assigned to watch over each of us children. My poor sailor had his hands full since disappearing was almost an obsession with me. (*The editor has boldened this sentence as it relates to her subsequent "escape" and hidden identity.*) I once climbed over the rail and would have slipped into the water had my sailor-watchman not caught me in the knick of time for which I am still grateful.

The cabins which we occupied where quietly elegant and upholstered in light chintzes while each had a washstand, cold and hot water, dresser and desk. Olga and Tatiana occupied one cabin; Marie and I, another. In the dining salon located on the upper deck we would take our meals. We would not miss church on the yacht as we had our own chapel in which we would attend Divine Liturgy. Mother stood behind a screen just as she had at home, while the chaplain recited the prayers and conducted the service. The "Standard" (*The authoress known simultaneously as Evgenia Smetisko, Eugenia Smith and Anastasia Romanov painted a number of pictures in advanced age of the yacht on voyages*) boasted a striking paint scheme of black with gold decorations at the bow and the stern. Two-decks and two smoke stacks were part of its construction.

Every day at dusk a gun salute was fired which often scared me. My ears hurt from the loud blasts compelling me to run down the hallway to the other side of the vessel with hands over my ears. In the morning at 9:00 am the flag was raised with dignity and then lowered at dusk.

My father enjoyed the company of the captain of the "Standard:" Charles Dehn whilst my brother was Captain Dehn's constant shadow. Alexei never questioned anything "Pekin Dehn" said (*Karl Alexander von Dehn, 1877-1932*). Dehn's wife, Lili, was Mother's intimate and cherished friend, as well as of us children. Mother was their son's godmother. The boy, Titi (*Alexander Leonid von Dehn, *1908- +1974 in Caracas, Libertador, Capital District, Venezuela*), at times came to visit us. He was linguistically gifted and could speak a number of languages already by the time he was seven years old. His manners were impeccable and he enjoyed sitting next to Mother at tea time asking her politely, "Madam, sugar? And, how many?"

Another of Father's close friends was an officer of the yacht, Drenteln, an aides-de-camp and thoroughly devoted to my father; Drenteln always accompanied us on our trips. When they were both young, both Father and he had been attached to the Preobrazhensky Regiment. Their evening conversations sometimes stretched well into the wee hours of the morning.

Father was an avid sportsman with interests, and talent, in tennis, boxing, swimming, diving; we admired how he could stay under water for as long as he could. With expert skill he could ride horses, but although he was a good shot he was nor particularly keen on hunting. Navigation was of immense interest to him, being as he was so devoted to the navy, and he spent many hours studying it. Our yacht had been built at Odense in Denmark at the time of the marriage of Mother and Father. I remember visiting the shipyard where it had been built on one holiday cruise. Honeymoon memories flooded Mother's mind when we were onboard and she commented more than once, that the happiest memories she had were of times spent on the yacht.

For us a cruise meant spending a part of each day on shore, tramping in the Finnish forests. On the yacht our attendants turned a rope for us girls to jump. Then there was the tug of war with an admiral or a captain and other officers joining in. Sometimes we roller-skated on the deck.

Mother and Alexei would sit and watch, as neither could participate in our merriment, but when we laughed we all laughed together with mutual glee.

Dowager Empress Marie, Father's mother and our Grandmama, sailed nearby many times at the same times as we. Her yacht was called the "Polar Star," and we would then receive word that she would be arriving for a visit on onboard. Admiral Prince Viazemsky was also present. The fun times and merry-making had to come to an abrupt halt, while we all shifted into a more serious mode of behavior. We did this because Grandmama wanted to see how much we had progressed in our music lessons, especially as she was m musically gifted herself. Her entire family in Denmark played instruments and constituted their own chamber orchestra. Even her father (Apapa), our great grandfather who later became King Christian IX of Denmark, and her mother (Amama), our great grandmother, subsequently Queen Louise, were also talented musicians.

Grandmother *Minnie,* as she was dubbed, was the cause of much tension when she arrived. I did not like being warned to be on "good behavior" which brought out a rebellious side to my character. Because we were somewhat "ansy" as people say, that is unable to sit quietly through formal dinner, we would have our supper earlier when our grandmother was in attendance. It was rather impossible to live up to the high expectations that one had for behavior in Minnie's presence, no matter how earnest our endeavors were, or at least my endeavor was. The moment she left, the atmosphere was lifted, and we all began to enjoy ourselves again.

We liked nothing better than to hunt for mushrooms when were anchored near land. Although Mother and Alexei seldom joined us, on the occasions when he did, he enjoyed immensely looking behind trees, this way and that, smelling the distinct woodsy fragrance of these succulent fungi. The ground was spongy with pine needles and moss which lent a springy feeling to our leaps and bounds across the forest floor. Twigs would crack under our feet which was an unforgettable sound of our mushroom hunts.

To keep up with Father who walked so quickly was a chore. However, he once jumped over some mossy rocks in a stream to which we had come, and he urged me to jump too promising to grab my hand and help me over. Unfortunately, I did not jump quite well enough and slipped ungraciously into the middle of the creek. Upon lifting myself up I noticed that I was covered head to foot in muddy clay, almost the color of mustard. My frock, my face, my canvas docker shoes were all covered with the wretched stuff. Upon returning to the "Standard" I took a well-deserved nap exhausted from the walk in wet and dirty clothes.

The Fredensborg Palace in Copenhagen was a destination for us every other year before World War I began. We children loved visiting Hvidore's white villa with the wide vistas of the sea it offered, all from a location nestled amid flower laden bushes and trees on terraces narrowing from the bottom to the top as one reached the villa.

How we enjoyed the relaxing and tranquil sight of sailing vessels and little boats in the bay. Danish farms with typical roofs of thatch surrounded by stretching fields of golden wheat, red poppies, dotted with willowy poplar trees added to the site's majesty. My tiny grandmother, her sister Queen Alexandra of England, and Thyra, Duchess of Cumberland, owned this magnificent place. Here happy family reunions full of cheer were held in the warm summer months.

The arrival of Queen Alexandra and Uncle Bertie (*King Edward VII of Great Britain*) on their yacht "Victoria and Albert" was the occasion for much joy and excitement when they met us at Reval (*Editor's note: now Tallinn, Estonia*). I King Edward came clad in typical Scottish kilts. Grandmama Marie and Aunt Olga sailed to meet us on the "Polar Star". Uncle George, who later became King of Great Britain, arrived along with his wife, May (Queen Mary) and children. The eldest son David, later Edward, Prince of Wales, was in attendance. Many other children were there too from related families. The family reunion was enjoyable and memorable full of a wide range of scheduled activities. The day was replete with swimming, fishing, rowing and frolicking in the shallow waters of the bay. Swings had been installed especially for us children. All the ports in the Baltic were known to well instructed Alexei as young as we were at the time. Count Alexander Benckendorff, Russian Ambassador to London, was of the opinion that my little brother was uniquely bright and perceptive or gifted. Before we knew it we had reached Norway with its fabulous fjords. As we approached Oslo (Christiania) many other sailing vessels surrounded our yacht to the point that we actually had to retreat. The press had leaked the news of our arrival.

Royal Copenhagen porcelain creations depicting summer and winter scenes were souvenirs which we took home from this holiday. Many included lovely animals and other animals in the colors so typical of Danish art, soft blues, whites and a hint of brown so delftly painted by skilled traditional Danish artisans.

Another relative, Kaiser Wilhelm II, was once cruising on near us on his own yacht so that Father had a salute be fired to him as a royal greeting. The kaiser's yacht reciprocated, and soon the leader of Germany had climbed onboard to greet his cousins. He embraced Father with a kiss and the words "My most valued friend." The Russian national anthem was offered as a musical tribute by the German band accompanying the Kaiser. Not to be outdone, the Russian band played the German anthem as well. "My litte Jokester" the Kaiser called me, especially as he had taken a liking to me. (*Editor's note: most probably than not he would have used the German expression "Mein kleiner Spassvogel!"*)This German relative who was to later cause us so much grief and agony and also danced in a manner which my mother found repulsive. She exclaimed many times how she thought it was not suitable or becoming of any national leader of his rank.

Father's mother, Grandmama Marie, joined us in Reval. Queen Olga, her sister-in-law, came along. King George I, my grandmother's brother, was husband to Olga. Later he was murdered. This deed made a fearful impression on us. I remember when Granny cried, "Why do they want to kill an innocent man?" The bald spot on King George's head was quite prominent. Once he heard the Kaiser jokingly inform him that he had his own 'private moon" which was typical of the Danish royal family in any case. The Kaiser was known to refer to his Danish kin as the "deaf, bald-headed Danes." We once traveled to Stockholm, Sweden to visit King Gustavus V and Queen Victoria of Sweden who had earlier visited us on their yacht.

Not infrequently our cruises were marked by undesirable events. Once in Finnish waters, a British freighter did not maintain correct distance from our yacht. They ignored frequent admonitions to keep their distance, so that when a precautionary warning shot was fired it inadvertently wounded one of the British crew.

Mother's brother-in-law was Prince Henry of Prussia whom we once visited at his gorgeous estate overlooking the sea at Jagernsfeld. He wanted us to see the Prussian fleet at Kiel, but the weather did not cooperate that day, so after the brief visit we continued on to England.

In the British port at Cowes on the Isle of Wight the "Standard" was greeted by the traditional twenty-one gun salute. The Russian warships returned the courtesy and our vessel sailed down the center of countless vessels on either side. The "Victoria and Albert" were now alongside our boat. Salutes, applause and cheers filled the air. King Edward VII presented himself the next morning on the boat's bridge attired in the Russian uniform which an admiral of the Imperial Fleet would normally wear. Father stood next to him in the uniform of a British admiral. The anthems of both nations were played underneath the flags of both snapping in the breeze. Many pleasantries were exchanged and amid the salutations and reveries, numerable photos were taken which we added to our growing photo albums of which we were so proud.

A seemingly endless table was the setting for our ensuing luncheon. King Edward was seated in the center whilst Mother, resplendent in white looking as lovely as ever sat next to him. Father sat next to Queen Alexandra who was opposite the king. Not to be outdone, Alexei persisted in his attempt to garner the king's attention until at some point the monarch relented with the words: "All right, Alexei, what do you want?" Dejectedly Alexei retorted, "It's too late now, Uncle Bertie; you ate a caterpillar with your salad." Pink roses graced the table as decoration arrangements while the porcelain was trimmed in gold.

The Crown Prince of Sweden, the Prince of Wales (later George V), Princess Beatrice, and Princess Irene, wife of Prince Henry of Prussia were amongst the other guests at table. The "Standard" played host with Mother in charge of arrangements for a dinner for the ladies in honor of Queen Alexandra. Many elegant and beautiful ladies, several hundred of them were among the list of guests at various dinners held onboard our yacht. They consisted of friends, relatives, English, Swedish, German and Russian. King Edward, calling Mother "my dear niece," expressed his gratitude for her hospitality.

The lawn of the Royal Yacht Club served as the setting many times for tea. Mother knew all the hundreds of guests who were for the most part all related with some friends also present.

On one occasion Princess Henry, Mother's sister, and Princess Beatrice played with us on the lawn of Osborne House. Present were Marie, Alexei, his playmate, and myself. Alexei proudly showed off his white sailor suit. However, both boys were rather naughty. Before afternoon tea, Alexei had managed to climb all over the new automobile belonging to a relative causing his white suit to become wrinkled and smudged with dirt from head to foot. Happy to stay and play in and on the car he informed us, "You girls can go to the tea; I am happy at what I am doing." We girls were shocked at our brother's disrespectful behavior. Finally, Derevenko, the sailor and watchman for Alexei, removed him from the car. We pretended he did not belong to our family while we were taking tea, gesturing towards him as though he were an unwanted and unknown guest. This brought him, however, almost to the point of real tears to which he blurted out, "What is the matter with you girls? I do not like your attitude. If I were not ashamed, I would cry."

Olga and Tatiana once walked around the town of Cowes in their grey suites without an chaperones or guards. In front of a shop window they paused and then entered to buy postcards for our photo albums. A carriage with Count Benckendorff and a friend stopped on the opposite side of the street. With the idea that they would surprise Count Beckendorff, they ran across the street to the carriage unescorted, at which time a large crowd began to gather as the people had heard that our family was visiting in town.

With a constable blocking the entrance to give my sisters a change to escape, they ran through the shop to the other side. At this time two carriages appeared with one for the girls and the other for the policeman. The crowd grew and the constable decided they should all take refuge in a neighborhood church. As unique as this adventure had been, it was to be the first and the last of its kind, but it did generate myriad questions from us all as we delighted in the excitement of this news We reviewed the story many times when we looked together at the photos of it in our photo albums. Nonetheless, there was an air of triumph to it all in the fact that girls of our position could go out unescorted in public.

Before he became King Edward VIII, Prince David had come came by torpedo boat to Osborne House from Dartmouth as he was a student at the Royal Naval College. He gave Father a tour of the college before we left. Alexei, Father opined, might do well at Dartmouth and the subject was discussed with David. Our visit had now come to an end. We were bidden goodbye by our royal family, namely King Prince Edward, Queen

Alexandra, Prince George, then Prince of Wales, and Princess Mary and all the children. The visit was, to say the least, highly memorable.

Per the norm our entourage included Princess Obolensky, Mlle. Butsova, a cherished lady-in-waiting, of whom we all were so fond; also Mlle. Tutcheva, the governess with whom I did not at all get along due to her envy of Mlle. Butsova. However, I was also very cross with her for speaking so nastily about our English relatives. Count Fredericks, Father's chamberlain, Ambassador Izvolsky, Prince Beloselsky-Belozersky, Dr. Botkin, Dr. Derevenko, Captain Drenteln were also present along with various crew members from our escort ships.

Now to France we sailed, indeed to Cherbourg, where President Fallieres was to arrive on his yacht, the "Marseilles". Dense fog and storms plagued our journey and reduced our sailing velocity, so that we did not arrive in a timely manner at our destination. The French fleet was reviewed by French President and Father. As an extra treat we children were allowed to take photographs of submarines which had honored placed in our photo albums. Although these photos were confiscated during our arrest in the year 1917, they previously had given us great pleasure whenever we would remember this enjoyable trip we had taken as family.

A dinner on the deck of a battleship was arranged by the French presideng in honor of my family. The table had been arranged in the shape of a horseshoe in the middle of which the Russian Coat of Arms had been crafted with flower arrangements using roses of various colors. French and Russian musical pieces entertained us as we ate played by the band. A display of floats on the water were later illuminated depicting scenes from famous operas including Wagner's *Lohengrin*. Someone must have informed them that Mother loved this opera by Richard Wagner. The dramatic spectacle of it all made a lasting impression on us all. Floats were created to resemble dolphins, sea creatures, serpents, the swan from the opera, a huge egg in which a man played a mandolin and on top of which an image of rooster appeared seeming to pull a gondola. The figures of swans seemed to pull another boat in which a band played while fireworks continued to brighten the night sky for hours. A film, a moving picture, of the entire event had been made and sent to us as a gift. When Alexei was ill he enjoyed operating the projector himself and watching it over and over.

The yacht's chapel was the setting for a Divine Liturgy to offer thank to the Almighty for such a successful trip and for the new friends we had made along the way. The French president appeared later with gifts, and knowing that Alexei loved all things military he offered him gifts of miniature rifles, guns and drums. Alexei also received a military tent ready to use with a miniature cot, table and folding chairs. Alexei was elated. Countless hours of entertainment and diversion were the result of this thoughtful present. During our arrest in Tsarsoe Selo officers of the provisional government confiscated this toy gun from Alexei while he was playing with it in the garden. Olga's gift was a handsome writing desk set of dark blue enamel inscribed beautifully with her initials. A travel clock was destined for Tatiana which accompanied her to Tobolsk. Marie's present was a two story doll house completely furnished, including a bath tub and electric lighting. A beautiful doll with a complete trousseau, was given to me. She even came with veil for a bride. Just as at Cowes earlier, a twenty-one gun salute marked the end of our sojourn in France.

All during the cruise I had admired the graceful manners and lady-like ways of Olga and Tatiana. They seemed to have been born to be princesses with their tall, graceful stature, while I seemed to have not grown at all during these years. Alexei was even an inch or more taller than me. Marie was tall also. I would be short like my Grandmother people opined. When I sat down I was talle enough, but my arms and legs were not long enough to suit me. I should hop on one foot, then on the other, three times a day the captain of our yacht told me, assuring me that that would produce the desired results. I doubled and tripled his recipe, but to no avail. Later on a subsequent cruise I confided to him that his remedy had not produced any positive results. He nearly keeled over in utter laughter which I never forgave him for, as I suddenly felt utterly ridiculous and gullible at that.

Mother's doctors were not satisfied with the lack of improvement in Mother's health in spite of the various cruises we had embarked on in 1909. Neuralgia was one of her maladies. We progressed to Uncle Ernest's castle at Friedberg, because Karslruhe had been suggested as a place of treatment. We met Princess Louis of Battenberg and her two sons there as well. Darmstadt was Mother's old home, so we went to Wolfsgarten near Darmstadt where as a young lady she had resided with her brother Ernest who became the reigning Grand Duke on the death of his father. Ernest (*Editor's note: Onkel Ernst*) was like an ersatz parent to Mother who was quite fond of him, hence we were also disposed to draw near to him. Our maternal uncle we thought was handsome, kind, musically and artistically inclined. Mother shared these talents with him. Eleonor (*Onor*) was his second wife and also a delightful person. Mother and she had known one another since childhood so that their friendship grew only stronger with time. Our trip was meaningful therefore for the entire family.

So little of our stay remains in my memory. A constant flow of Mother's relatives and uncountable numbers of royal children came and went. One bedroom had to suffice for us four sisters, while Father could receive visitors in only one small room. Mother's sister Irene (*Amity*) and her husband Prince Henry, the Kaiser's brother, were in attendance. Her tender affection won our hearts, especially when she called us "the dear children." Mother was closer to her than to any of her other sisters. A new cousin, aunt, uncle or a friend was always being presented to and we were called in continuously to make their acquaintance. I do remember that one of our kin had a rather unpretty nose, yet I did not associate her face to a name I could remember. The Kaiser and Kaiserin (*German for Emperor and Empress*) had invited Father to Potsdam as their guest.

The Kaiser's physical impediment gave me cause for concern. He rode his horse in his Hussar's uniform I can remember clearly. His reins were stuck into his belt; with fingers resting partly on his hip he cleverly manipulated the reins. We seemed to think that he leaned his weight heavily to one side. The reality of his left arm was explained to us by our aunt. She explained: "All rejoiced when Prince Wilhelm was born because he was the boy they had been hoping for. However, he did not immediately show signs of life. All measures possible were taken to get him to breathe. He was slapped, tossed, swung by his teeny feet for over an hour. At least a weak cry was heard from him. No one beyond the doctors and those present knew about this rough post natal treatment. When his mother finally was informed she became despondent. The blame for his injuries and suffering were clearly placed by her on the doctors and nurses in attendance. Because his left arm had been pulled out of its socket it became atrophied forever."

In the spring of 1910 most of our relatives were in deep mourning for King Edward VII of England (Uncle Bertie), who had gone to be with God that spring. In the Oranienburg Forest near Berlin Kaiser Wilhelm had been hunting with Father. Wilhelm beheld the ladies in their deep mourning garb and in the presence of the widow, Queen Alexandra, and of the new King George V and Queen Mary, and was reported to have quipped:

"Everyone is dressed in black because the old rooster has died." Queen Alexandra was partially deaf and could not hear his rude comment; but there were various others who actually did, including the beautiful Princess Alice and her husband, Prince Andrew of Greece, who accompanied Cousin George from England.Those heard reacted with visible disapproval, while others stated, "Wilhelm must be mad."

That the Kaiser was tactless was common knowledge amongst the family. As heir apparent he never hesitated to remark how he detested having to wait so long to inherit the throne. Even before his grandfather and own father died, he had written the Proclamation, preparing himself for the moment when he would ascend to the throne. The young Emperor, Wilhelm II, on the very day he ascended the throne, ordered everyone in the palace to be placed under surveillance, including his own mother, the Empress Victoria which caused Aunt Irene and Mother to weep openly; this came as a surprise as he had given his own father his sacred oath that he would protect the reputation of the royal house. Courtiers were called parasites and were objects of his disdain. Later they would be the ones to wrest power from him during the war and hold him practically under house arrest. His only joy he said was at the Yacht Club, while at the same time he hated his mother's ladies-in-waiting.Uncle Bertie had called him "the boss." He skillfully steered the sailboat with one arm, but so very skillfully that one could hardly believe it.

Augusta Victoria was always a beautiful *kaiserin* with a clear, almost transparent complexion, was wonderfully friendly but rather quiet and retiring. She wore a black ribbon around her throat which intrigued me. The kaiser and kaiserin showed us photos of the palace at Potsdam. One room stood out from the others which we found to be lovely but this one I personally thought was in bad taste. This room had ornate pillars full of all sorts of precious and semiprecious gemstones and odd-shaped shells. Father had donated a large uncut diamond bejeweled behemoth, which also included geological specimens, and petrified snakes entwined around the pillars, turtles and crocodiles in creeping or crawling positions.

Father went one day with the kaiser to the royal mausoleum to lay a wreath at the tomb of the Emperor Frederick III, the kaiser's father. The entire event was photographed and Mother later exclaimed during the war "Papa would rather lay a wreath on Wilhelm's tomb." Pictures of the Kaiser were cut out of all our photographs. Alexei ripped to shreds any photos he had of the Kaiser taken in Germany. He added a particularly hurtful invective that the Kaiser did not even deserve to be his godfather, and indignantly stomped on all the old photographs with his feet. I followed suit. I purposely broke several gifts from the Kaiser always pretending that it was an accident after our arrest and imprisonment in Tsarskoe Selo.

Father gave the kaiserin a magnificent gift of a pendant of pearls and sapphires before we departed for home. We had previously proudly displayed the lovely piece of jewelry to our friends for their approval. The Empress was dear to us and we often pitied her because she had to put up with such an ornery husband. A sewing basket complete with all necessary equipment was given to us girls by the kaiserin. In 1914 we gave them away as we no longer wanted to see these gifts with their origin in Germany. We were escorted to the rail station by some of the Kaiser's sons, shining in their immaculate uniforms and helmets encrusted with the German eagles. We noticed that they frequently clicked their heels as they saluted us, making our departure a gala affair. The kaiserin was *verboten* to accompany us to the station. Mother had taken this as a personal insult, but a later letter from Aunt Onor (Eleanor) explained that the empress had been slapped by the kaiser early that very morning and had suffered slap marks of his five fingers on her face, hence was embarrassed to appear in public.

Father was dressed in his civilian overcoat and Alexei wore his beloved dark-blue sailor suit, while we girls wore our traveling suits given that the cold weather had already set in. Alexei confessed to us on the train: "I was scared of those cousins." Father, as a gesture of courtesy due to our visit, appointed Kaiserin Augusta Victoria honorary colonel-in-chief of the Grodno Hussars. Needless to say, Grandmama Marie was not pleased at all with this "honor" being bestowed on the kaiserin. She cried with frustration and informed us that she hoped that Wilhelm's wife would never ever put on the uniform; I would wager that the kaiserin never did in any case. Aunt Ella (Elizaveta Feodorovna) sent word to father while were on en route that two Russian millionaires whom he knew had committed suicide. Such news saddened us beyond measure. Mother received a Christmas gift from Kaiser Wilhelm after we arrived home - two enormous red enameled vases. Surely there were made by the porcelain manufacturer with the royal patent. We placed these on console tables in our living quarters.

Soon we were back to our normal routines, although finding suitable playmates for Alexei was still a preoccupation. The two sons of Derevenko, the sailor who guarded by brother, were younger than Alexei yet they became my and his playmates. Mother, however, bore the brunt of sometimes severe criticism for allowing this arrangement.

# IV    THE CRIMEA

Attending classes was never easy for me to get used to, especially when we were on our way to spend time in The Crimea. We loved this place as our hearts were quite in tune with the sea. Father's favorite estate was as it had been for the preceding two generations of Romanov tsars. Yalta on the Crimean peninsula was its geographic location, but its sunshine and warmth were in pleasant contrast to the gloomy, cold days spent in our more northerly home at Tsarskoe Selo.

Dr. Botkin, Mother's physician, asked for permission to bring his children on board our yacht. He was convalescing and she assured him that they could come as often as they liked while he recovered. One's Christian duty is to not forsake the ill and suffering so I visited him daily like a little old lady and sat there with my hands folded on my lap trying to make him feel better. Our fondness for him was shared by all. Story telling was one of his many talents which kept us hanging on every word. I would then recount, with my dramatic flourishes thrown in for good measure, everything he had told me to Marie and Alexei. I used to wait for him at home in the room next to Mother's sleeping chamber as I knew he would walk by after her physical. He would politely listen to my childish gibberish and imagined difficulties. I stopped him and opened my heart to him with my childish problems. He would invariably ask me many questions and I, in turn, would learn details about his family. As I always had scraps of paper with me, I would jot down as notes the important elements of what he would tell me.

Tatiana and Gleb, his two children were coming to visit their father the fact of which filled us with great excitement. We felt we already knew them, because he had already told us so much about them. Gleb was at first timid while his sister, Tatiana was more outgoing. After we got to know one another, however, we had a marvelous time with many peals of laughter. We younger children were more involved with Gleb and Tatiana than were our older sisters, Olga and Tatiana, dubbed "Big Pair." Dr. Botkin was resting on a chaise longue while I was attempting to hide on Tatiana behind the drapery, but Dr. Botkin could see me and kept telling me so. Little did I know that my shoes were poking out from beneath the curtains betraying my hiding space. I did not answer him. I was one trick ahead of everyone. Tatiana finally came to the curtains to open them expecting to find me. However, all she found were my empty shoes. Indeed, I had quietly taken them off and left them there only to run to a new hiding place which she did not expect.

As a good father, Dr. Botkin enjoyed the happiness we had in our childish games. In my eagerness for his children to have a good time, I asked him confidentially what I could do to make his family happy. He replied, "Just being with you is the greatest pleasure you can give." As his children called him "Papula" I also began to call him this in Ekaterinburg. In times of sadness there I used to say, "Cheer up, Papula; all will be right."

It was rare in Tsarskoe Selo, that we girls would ever have any chance to play with children our own age with the exception of some cousins when they would come to visit.

Hill of the Cross (*Krestovaya Gora*) was one of the most unforgettable sites at Livadia. We gazed upon it with eager eyes each time that we entered the Bay of Yalta. At the top of this towering mountain there stood a monumental cross which I found mesmerizing. Was not the peak one of the umbrellas which held up the world? I could not believe it was really round, and fantasized that such peaks were the pinions which kept the Earth in place.

I truly wanted to explore this site and I devised a plan to include Marie in my venture. One day when the nanny was preoccupied with some task or other, Marie and I ran through the bushes and were on way up to the peak. Thinking that the bushes behind which we hid would protect us from those who would pursue us, we continued onward finally realizing that our destination was actually much farther away than we had originally imagined.

We trod on bravely. We gradually slowed down, our little legs not able to go quickly any more. Our destination was still quite a ways away. Dejected we returned home, exhausted. Guards suddenly rushed toward us to our astonishment and gladness.=. "Here they are," a voice sang out, and we two adventurers were hastily brought back to the palace.

One particular memory of mine involves Alexei. To everyone's astonishment he was suddenly not with us. All thoughts turned morbidly to tragic scenarios including drowning, kidnapping, or any other some such tragedy. All household personnel were dispatched in all directions.

Instinctually, Father made a beeline straight to the seashore. Quite contentedly, little Alexei was playing alone with all the sea shells of diverse shapes and colors he had collected, oblivious to the uproar his absence has caused for others.

Fruit orchards were a special characteristic and blessing at Livadia. The orchards became refuge for us where we could spend our leisure time. Each season the gardeners would display the corresponding fruit including apples, peaches, apricots and cherries. At Massandra there were vineyards of which we were also proud. Every sort of grape imaginable from white, purple, to red grew in abundance: each one a perfect specimen and larger than normal. In the wine cellar we found large bunches of artistically displayed waiting for us on platters in the reception area. Someone had taken care to display the grapes with corresponding leaves which heightened the esthetic sensation of the clusters. After tea, cakes and grapes were shared among us.

The elevator took us down further where there were other store rooms. The Russian double eagle was embossed on the labels of many of these bottles, lying on their side in the seemingly endless racks. Deep red, white, blue were the colors of the bottles which contained wine from previous generations as well as our own. The age and quality of the wines stored there were commented on by Father who perused the contents on platforms and in large barrels holding several hundred gallons of wine to age. Coronation wine was made and bottled here.

At the time of the Revolution much of the wine was still stored here. Some of these bottles in storage were for exclusive consumption at Tsarskoe Selo. Father was not what would call today a "big drinker." In fact, he disliked champagne but would indulge now and then in a glass of sherry.

The water of the Black Sea was the center of many of our free time activities. Ironically, none of us (except Father) were good swimmers. Quite on the contrary, we were afraid of the deep water, especially since that life threatening incident in which I was swept under by a huge wave and was saved from death by drowning by Father. A platform, albeit break water, was erected soon after as a precaution for us children.

We stopped for a few days in Kiev to visit Crown Prince Boris in 1911. (*Boris III, *1894- +1943, son of Ferdinand I who had similar ancestral background as Empress Alexandra, born Maximilian Karl Leopold Maria of Saxe-Coburg and Gotha*) Boris was heir to the Bulgarian throne and with Father and the court ladies in waiting we all went to the opera. Confusion broke out and agitated voices began to be heard. In the front row, someone had shot Prime Minister Stolypin who sat in a white coat. Passing through his cross and piercing his chest he expired. A man who had gotten a pass from someone from the Okhrana, made to believe that he was anxious to enjoy performance, had committed the dastardly deed. All returned home earlier than expected. Pale as a corpse Father returned to the train with Olga and Tatiana who were trembling. Mother was in a state of absolute shock having already learned of the tragedy. The rumor mill had it that a certain Minister, Count Witte, had wanted to regain his former position, lost to Stolypin, and had hence exchanged sharp words with him shortly before the killing. Father did not seek revenge and deferred to court action to settle the matter. This decision provoked sharp criticism.

The experience of the Stolypin family during the Japanese War was confided to us by Madame Narishkina. The Stolypin home in St. Petersburg was bombed and nearly twenty-four people were injured; one was to become a paraplegic. All over the garden were strewn arms, fingers, and limbs.

One of Mother's closest friends was Mme. Anna Vyrubova (nee Taneeva) who not infrequently verbally clashed with members of the staff. Anna Vyrubova made a declaration of war on Mlle. Butsova. Mother said: "To Livadia she shall never return," but she broke her promise repeatedly. The maiden name of Anna's mother was Tolstoy and her husband was a relative of General Voyeykov, the commandant of the palaces in Tsarskoe Selo. Many disliked him also for some reason.

Anna was invited by Mother to come to the Crimea despite prevailing sentiments. Indeed, Anna had been our friend for a long while and we thought of her as "one of the family." She had a house in Tsarskoe Selo conveniently located a short distance from the palace gate. As children we loved to go to Anna's where we often raided her well stocked cookie jar. The atmosphere at Anna's was casual and child-friendly. She was full of friendliness and understanding, so that we became ever fonder of her. Father and Mother sometimes came together to Anna's which was a unique experience for my parents. Precisely at her house Mother and sometimes Father saw the *Starets* (*Russian for a revered elder of the Orthodox faith admired for wisdom and spiritual guidance*) Rasputin. All messages to Mother from the starets came through Anna.

It was hard to avoid the malicious tongues which related stories about Anna's purported relationship with Rasputin. Detailed investigative reports, however, proved that Rasputin had never been at Anna's when Anna was alone.

Mother had even encouraged Anna to marry an officer who had been shellshocked during the Russo-Japanese war. Divorce ended the marriage. After Rasputin's murder, Anna moved to our house because Mother feared she might also be a murder victim with time. Anna's father, Alexander Sergeevich Taneev, was held in high esteem by Father, and he held a position at court. He was a talented musician from whom Anna also inherited this gift for music.

Music was the cement which bonded the friendship between Mother and Anna. As a young princess in Germany Mother had taken voice lessons, learning arias from many operas. Music might have become her profession had she been born to some other family other than the one through which she came to the world. Miss Baumgarten or Miss Clements usually accompanied Mother during her voice lessons. Mother could play many challenging compositions on the piano; the more difficult they were the more she enjoyed them. She possessed great patience and would never stop until she had mastered the piece. Her rings were placed on a tray when she played as she felt they interfered with the clearness and softness of the melody.

Our house was graced with frequent visits from Anna while Father would occasionally drop in to listen and enjoy the simple musical interludes Mother and Anna had together. Sometimes in the evening we children would slip into the salon to hear Anna and Mother singing classical pieces. At these Mother was radiantly beautiful and she carried the melody with much expression and feeling; we were often deeply touched. There was an expression of sadness in those melodies and the plaintive ones were those she sang the best. Father enjoyed Mother's informal concerts but never encouraged the presence of strangers during these intimate musical evenings. He also was musical and while young often played the piano with Madame Narishkina.

Baroness Iza Buxhoeveden (*Baroness Sophie "Isa/Iza" Buxhoeveden was of Danish ancestry; her father Buxhoeveden's father, Karlos Buxhoeveden, was the Russian minister in Copenhagen, Denmark during World War I*) was another musically gifted friend and also the lady-in-waiting.

Mother's happiness was greatly enhanced by the interaction with these people. In 1912 Mother withdrew from many of her earlier activities which she had always enjoyed so much because of Alexei's illness. She stopped singing all together when the war broke out, although she did chant in church, especially when we were in captivity.

*Father encouraged all sorts of artistic endeavors.* (The editor italicizes *this as it gives us insight into aka "Evgenia/ Anastasia's" later artwork into her 80's and 90's*) The tsar wished for culture in all of its forms to be available to subjects from all walks of society regardless of their economic station. In 1901, the year I was born, he sponsored *Narodny Dom*, a cultural center in St. Petersburg, not far from the Cathedral of Sts. Peter and Paul. Large concert halls, a theatre and a cinema were integral parts to this center. Imperial Theater artists and performers were now able to be heard and seen in this cultural center, at the cost of only a few kopecks (*1/100 of a Russian ruble*).

Livadia was more beautiful than ever at the discovery of a new palace there which had replaced an old wooden one which had stood for generations. The new royal residence had begun to be built in 1910 and completed in 1911. It was large with forty or fifty rooms. It rose naturally from its surroundings as if it had grown out of the fertile soil itself. The former palace had been demolished due to a fungus which had begun to grow there, smelly even, which was deemed to be hazardous for our health. All that was left of it was our memories. Such a contrast to the new building full of light and airiness constructed with steel and white Crimean Inkerman stone. Dazzling is the word I would use to describe it as it seemed to rival the sea itself and was the cheeriest place of all the residences at our disposal.

Mother found it quite appealing, especially in the color scheme which placed worth on harmony. Mother's feeling of contentment made a home of it immediately. Mother was ubiquitous, participating in every detail and activity: she directed the hanging of the art collection and placement of blessed icons, or the arrangement of vases (designed by her) of marvelous bouquets of flowers on tables and surfaces she selected. Mother's favorite flower was lobelia, and Father made sure the gardeners had planned the landscape to be filled with these and other of her favorite flowers. Her predilection for lobelia with its purplish-blue hue gave her the motivation to ask that that the same shade of velvet be set into the stair rail, next to the Byzantine-style chapel leading to the second floor.

Father's big improvements included removing the old porcelain stoves and heating the palace was heated by hot water. Direct bells were installed in every room and were connected to the rooms of officers on duty at all times who had the authorization to enter any room if requested or necessary.

Telephone booths, at Father's request, were installed all over the estate so that he could be found at any time for more instantaneous communication. Trained guard dogs protected the palace grounds. White marble was used for the colonnades and for the balconies while some of the lower rooms were in lemonwood, mahogany and redwood. Krasnov was Mother's architect and with his help she selected all the needed articles. A painting of wisteria vines she had created herself hung in one of her rooms in the Alexander Palace in Tsarskoe Selo (*Editor's note: proof of her artistic talents and also a hint as the artistic talent of "Evgenia Smetisko" who painted well into her nineties.*). In our chapel there she had a glass screen of that same color, behind which she prayed undisturbed.

Father was equally enthralled with our new home, but his natural focus was more oriented to the outside environment: to trees, bushes, shrubs and their horticultural characteristics. The temperate climate of the Crimea created a perfect environment for agricultural experiments. Father invested a great deal of time to incorporating speciments from the famous Nikitsky Botanical

Garden nearby. Father enjoyed his free moments by he enjoyed working in the gardens under the bright sun. Every spring we awaited the flowering of various varieties of hyacinths in bloom, white, purple and pink. Flowering trees and shrubs of many sorts embellished the beauty and elegance. Mother's beloved combinations included that of wisteria and smoke tree. The year before the commencement of the war a storm destroyed many of these rare trees which were soon replaced.

A lovely, life-sized, reclining statue of female figure in pure white marble was positioned in front of the palace, facing the sea, but Alexei and I discovered a hole on the side of the figure. It was miniscule but still large enough to squeeze a kopeck into, which we did because we could. With all the inquisitiveness of childhood we ran out the next morning to see if it were still there.

The happy times we all shared there and the beauty of the place will never be forgotten.

To me the Crimean peninsula was a concentration of nature's best: snow-capped mountains with little Tartar villages nestling on their slopes, high plains under cultivation, and valleys full of wild flowers and berries. The estate itself was especially beautiful, with its wide lanes, lovely gardens, and many orchards bearing every kind of fruit. But, perhaps, most beautiful of all, and certainly the accent for all the other natural beauties surrounding Livadia, was the sea itself.

Happy memories still come to mind when I reminisce about the Crimea. Pictures of vividly colored flowers, soft green-blue waters and deeper skies swim before my eyes, meshed together in the vitalizing sunshine of the Russian Riviera. The life we led here was more family oriented with more time for Mother and Father to spend with us. Our visits were usually planned for the spring and fall, while the seemingly endless winter became for all of us one long period of anticipation. Right before World War I, when I was almost thirteen, we had our last visit.

A special Imperial train took us to Crimea. First we headed to Sevastopol, where Father inspected the naval installations. The admiralty, naval barracks, hospital, and other buildings were part of this inspection.

The Officers Club was where Father usually took lunch with the officers. As we continued our journey we stopped at Tsarskaya Pristan (dock) to finally land at Yalta where we were greeted by the people formed lines on both sides of path as our carriages passed through. The arrival of the Tsar's Family was considered a national holiday.

Our grandmama from Denmark, Marie, had not visited the Crimea since the death of her husband, Alexander III, in 1894. The new palace in all its majesty amidst the carefully planted trees was not enough to convince her to come. Ironically, however, she was forced to flee to the Crimea during the Revolution.

Father once got up one morning before dawn when we were in pre-war Crimea and dressed himself in a soldier's uniform. Cleverly he eluded the guards and walked toward the rising sun and the nearby village. He personally witnessed people working in gardens and fields. Happy and content they seemed to be as he passed by him. Perhaps Father was motivated by the example of his great uncle, Alexander I, who had dressed as a beggar walking for weeks through the villages until he reached a Siberian monastery. History books officially report that Alexander I died of sickness in Taganrog. On the other hand many others believe he was seen escaping into the woods on the day he was supposed to have died. Truly his wife had planned only the most simple of funerals for him attended by a handful of worshippers. Alexander I's corpse was brought to St. Petersburg where it was entombed in a mausoleum in the Cathedral of Saints Peter and Paul-where all the Russian emperors were inhumed. Legend insists that the buried body was not the Emperor's rather that of a soldier who had died in Taganrog at the same time that Alexander I had escaped. To this day many believe he lived out his days as a monk in a monastery. Later when the monk's body was exhumed the birthmarks on the body were the same as those of the Emperor. The Cathedral in St. Petersburg was later flooded and, when the coffin that purportedly holding the body of the Emperor for eternity was made open, it was found to be empty. Supposedly the coffin had earlier been pried open and the body taken.

However, in this case our father did, indeed, return after walking all day and talking to the peasants All the authorities, such as the police and his staff officers, were terribly worried over his disappearance. Father, on the other hand, was happy. Father reported that it had been one of his most pleasant walks for he had seen how his people lived. General Dumbadze, responsible for Father's safety1 remained disturbed about this incident for a long time.

Father once again tried, this time unsuccessfully, to leave the palace in Tsarskoe Selo, dressed as a soldier. He was saluted by one of the guards as he passed. Father asked him: "Do you know me?" The guard quickly replied: "I do, Your Majesty, by your kind eyes."

Mother and Princess Bariatinsky were in preparation for their charity bazaar for which they were well known. This bazaar was held every year with funds earmarked to the support the Children's Tuberculosis Sanatorium. Located on the Imperial estate of Massandra, it was housed in an absolutely gorgeous building overlooking the sea surrounded by spacious grounds with rose bordered avenues and rare species of carefully labelled shrubs and trees.

The Imperial vineyards were connected. Several hundred children were cared for here and educated. When their tuberculosis was cured many entered schools of higher learning. These children, both rich and poor, came from all over the Empire. Donations, concerts, plays, bazaars, selling flowers and photographs all added up to constitute the great sums of money needed to finance this institution. Mother, her friends and my sisters and I eagerly pitched in to make articles for this bazaar. We three younger siblings were thoroughly engaged to help find buyers for the flowers and concert tickets. The public was always known for its generosity .

Alexei was empathic with the plight of these young patients and felt much sympathy for them. Aunt Ella once appeared on our private train on the way to the Crime. Our widowed aunt also brought items to sell at the bazaar.

Easter eggs were sold on the train with much success and, by the time we reached the Crimea, the donations had come rolling in in great sums. While some one of our group carried the basket, Alexei would walk up and down the aisles of the train with this heart wrenching accounts of suffering among the young patients so that he literally had donors compelled to donate. A stickler for details, Alexei kept meticulous records as to who had donated and given gifts. His donation basket held, after many times being emptied, several hundred thousand rubles. Prince Dolgorukov submitted a check for 50,000 rubles. Alexei always looked forward to the next year's event and never forgot the many acts of generosity. When he was subsequently praised for this, he answered cheerfully: "I never had more fun in my life!"

Princesses Nina and Xenia Georgievna, our own cousins, helped us in this charity project when they were at their estate in Kharaks. In Ai-Todor, adjoining Livadia, other relatives always helped us as did those of the Youssoupoff family. Countess Vorontsova-Dashkova (*daughter of Count Hilarion Vorontsov Illarionovich - Dashkov and his first wife. The countess was known for her elegance and beauty*), that beautiful woman, was a great supporter of this charity.

Box after box was carried off the "Standard" in 1914 with items to be sold at the annual bazaar. The Governor of Yalta was in charge of this particular event. Most wanted to purchase items that Mother had made or even just touched. Madame Zizi (Elizabeth) Narishkina was of great help to Mother. She handed to guests whatever Mother asked her to. This could be a child's bonnet, a cushion, or a scarf. They always insisted on kissing Mother's hand afterwards. We four sisters I sold at different stalls. Great quantities of beautiful handmade boxes of all kinds of shapes and sizes, in lapis azuli, malachite, leather, or in the famous transparent enamel were sold as were hundreds and hundreds of the lacquer boxes of papier mache. An evening concert was performed by Madame Plevitskaya, dubbed "the nightingale of Russia." She sweepingly bowed gracefully before her appreciative audience, her fingertips even touching the floor. Her main fame was for her singing of national songs. Friends and cousins attended plays which were produced and performed in our honor. As to be expected, Alexei was a bit naughty during one performance. During the intermission he jumped up and down like a young horse not yet broken and trained. Of course, his playmate egged him on in this exhibition of bad manners. First a chair then a table became his podium. He pretended to give a speech. He modulated his voice, utilizing a weird accent in pronouncing certain letters. Marie and I wanted to crawl under the table we were so mortified at his behavior. Mother said that from now on he would not be allowed in public without his older sisters there with him to chaperone.

Besides from the bazaar many made extra donations of great sums. This sanatorium was in part converted to an officers' hospital during World War I so that they could recover quickly and return to combat.

Father had a specific purpose in mind when he took long walks. He wanted to see how it felt for soldiers to do mandatory distances per day in their service and training. Frequently he did more than was expected, exceeding the limit by several miles. He carried only water and bread.

(Editor's note: In Anastasia's narrative the image of a Tsar more benevolent than oft depicted in contemporary reports emerges. Later one will read of her assertion that he did not know of a well-known pogrom, becoming angry when he learned of it and demanding accountability. He has his son with him during military strategy sessions and afterwards takes time in private to entertain and answer any questions that Alexei has for him. He does not even seem to fit into a Victorian framework of what a father was imagined to be and somewhat resembles the hands-on approach of his wife's grandfather, Albert, husband of HM Victoria. Anastasia writes of him as humble, religious, principled, compassionate, philanthropic: even endowing a museum in Ekaterinburg where the later execution would take place. In this aspect, Anastasia known simultaneously as "Evgenia Smetisko" and "Eugenia Smith," followed in his footsteps for she had always dreamt, she informs the reader, of founding and endowing a museum dedicated to Russian history and culture. In great measure she was successful, as the Foundation of Russian History Museum located at Holy Trinity Monastery in Jordanville, New York gives evidence. Indeed, this multi-named lady has endowed said museum with a generous annuity in perpetuity, while also enriching it with donations of religious items, art, and other museum objects. Throughout her story, the woman who claims to have been the Tsar's daughter, great respect for both parents is evident, with great love for both and a special awe for Nicholas II.)

## V       SPALA: 1912

We were once again at Peterhof in the summer of 1912. Yet another cruise was embarked upon for official reasons. The German Kaiser arrived to inspect the Viborg infantry as was their honorary colonel-in-chief. He was so overt in his laughter that Mother dubbed him "The Comedian" (*Editor's note: probably the German der Komödiant*) He sailed with us in Finnish waters.

One of his men made a quip about "my men, while the Kaiser turned as on a dime twirling his moustache and responding nervously, "Once again, they are my men." He was cheery one moment and gloomy the next, so that my sisters assessed him with the words, "There is something wrong with him." (*Editor's note: today he might be diagnosed as bi-polar*) At my then tender age, I focused only the humorous side of his nature. I was amused with his amusing anecdotes and clever caricatures, drawn by himself, mostly humorous depictions of his own relatives. He reserved some measure of envy of Mother, because he could not understand how she managed to become fully russified, when his own English mother had never become totally germanified. He professed to admire our yacht, the "Standard," and said cheekily to Father, "Nicky, I would like to have the 'Standard' myself, but with a German crew." Father blushed deep crimson. He understood full well the meaning behind Wilhelm's comment. The utterance of the German emperor was meant to telegraph triumphalism this time naval, that is a feeling of absolute superiority of one culture over another. After a pause, Father retorted: "We are very fond of the 'Standard'; it is quite comfortable and the family enjoys it a great deal." (*Editor's note: Nicholas II here practices extreme diplomatic skills by addressing the obvious topic-the yacht-while avoiding any other ulterior motives embedded in the rest of the German kaiser's comment to him.*)

With frequency the Kaiser hit Father up for donations to his various charities which was difficult, albeit night on impossible for Father to deny. This infuriated my mother. During this particular cruise Mother was more perplexed than ever by her German relative. "I remember when he was a young man he used to provoke Granny with his sharp words. But Granny did not spare him, either."

When it was time for Kaiser Wilhelm to depart he startled all in attendance by kissing Father's hand in front of the Russian Foreign Minister Izvolsky. The latter muttered audibly to many, "A kiss on the hand and a stab in the back." The minister, in retrospect, seems to have been prescient in his understanding of what would happen in World War I. Elated were we all that the Kaiser had now sailed off on the "Hohenzollern." Our Danish grandmother was also not kindly disposed toward Wilhelm as the Germans had annexed the ancient duchy of Schleswig-Holstein (*the land of origin of the Kohlsaat family which was so helpful to Anastasia, aka "Evgenia's" work with this manuscript*) whereby Danes were expelled from their ancestral lands. Grandmama did not enjoy when Kaiser Wilhelm came to Denmark as she could still feel the salt in this cultural wound. To top if off, Wilhelm hated every living Slav, and often I have ruminated on the fact how he must have felt in his heart when he accepted expensive gifts from us and sat at table with us all. Father, after all, who was not only a Slav but the defender of Slavic culture. Napoleon was defeated at the Berezina River in 1812 and our family celebrated at the Monastery of Borodino.(*Editor's note: our Froebel ancestor, Johann Gotthelf "August" Froebel, eldest brother of Kindergarten founder, Friedrich Wilhelm August Froebel, had been a sharpshooter with Thuringian albeit Prussian troops fighting Napoleon. He seems to have disappeared from the family record and was thought to have fallen in the Russian Empire. However, with new DNA analyses we have found relatives in the noble Korotkevich Family from Belarus with their rank originating in the Grand Duchy of Lithuania. They report to us a German Lutheran military ancestor in the same generation as ours who disappeared fighting Napoleon.*) Alexei received memorabilia from the War of 1812 while the people cheered and applauded our arrival.

Although Father was not a big fan of hunting he occasionally went in the fall to hunt on his estates at Belovezh in the government of Grodno. We landed in Reva where Alexei laid a stone at the harbor to Peter the Great. While Mother and we girls visited the Nicholas Institute for Girls, Father went to review the Sixth Army Corps. We resided in our new large red brick hunting villa in Belovezh. It boasted several watch towers and a fine balcony whence we viewed the game brought in after the day's hunt. On one side of the villa we had our living quarters and on the other there was a collection of fantastic stuffed animals from generations before. A forest of pine and white birch trees surrounded by picturesque hills and ravines formed the scenic site where the hunting lodge was located. Belovezh and Spala formed the area where the best hunting was to be found.

The hunting lodge at Spala was not quite as cozy and consisted of a two-story, gloomy, wooden villa near a river and a park. The forest was so thick in trees on one side that little sunshine penetrated, making it necessary to keep the lights burning in the corridors and hallways. English chintz was used throughout the entire house.

White birch and fragrant pines framed the sandy and winding paths throughout the forest on which we four sisters rode our horses. Yellow milk mushrooms covered the forest floor creating an almost fairy-take like impression. The locals found them so tasty that they had the custom of eating them totally raw. We never missed an opportunity to play in the park or fish in the nearby streams while occasionally Father and his guests enjoyed a game of tennis.

Generation upon generation these forests had been filled with game, intentionally stocked, for the visits of royal hunters. Deer, wild boar, lynx, and wild fowl roamed these almost primeval woods. Absolutely the most rare and sought was the *auroch* an unusual variety of bison found only here and in the Caucasus mountains. As the sun set the hunting party brought back its catch which it laid carefully on the lawn, sometimes decorated with pine and other greens, for the admiration and inspection of all. Mother was not keen on this carnal display and might appear briefly on the balcony but usually made an excuse to stay indoors for she did not like to witness such killing. Her generous and sympathetic heart saw human suffering in the fate of the animals.

Throughout the house there were displayed many mounted heads from the hunting events of years gone by. Mother ordered some of them to be removed, especially from the dining rooms. Other heavily and ornamentally framed landscapes and horse portraiture did brighten the room, but Mother removed others which glorified the hunt. She found the paintings of dogs with fowl in their mouths or deer with arrows in them beyond the pale.

Alexei had an unfortunate incident on the yacht in which he bumped himself on the knee which broke a blood vessel and created a black and blue swelling up into his groin area. His suffering was so acute that he did not want the doctor to even examine him. With time the swelling was reduced and he felt somewhat better until, while riding in the carriage, his lump began to swell again and which time he became feverish and delirious.

Princess Irene who was Mother's siter, wife of Prince Henry of Prussia, and their son, Prince Sigismund, happened to be with us at this time. Irene was a great shoulder for Mother to lean on as she had also lost a son to Alexei's same blood disease. (*Editor's note: the term hemophilia, in this text usually with the British spelling variant, was understood then differently from today. Whether Alexei would today be diagnosed with standard hemophilia or a malady diagnosed uniquely today is not yet known. Another claimant, as yet unverified, to be Alexei, namely Vasily Filatov, lived into his late eighties and also had a blood disease which would have been generally labelled hemophilia in the time of Alexei. Research continues concerning his claim.*) Mother's sister had immediately understood the nature of Alexei's illness from the very beginning as she was so acquainted with the topic, even while those outside the family did not truly understand the severity of its true nature. Irene proved to be a great asset to Mother as she knew exactly what to do to take care of her nephew having cared for her own son with the same condition. Months ago we had planned our trip to Spala and Aunt Irene had planned to come. Had we cancelled our trip it would have aroused suspicion about Alexei's condition, which we wanted to avoid.

The villa was full of house guests from many parts of Russia and foreign countries. Out of Warsaw came some family friends joining us for dinner and entertainment. We danced and entertainers did their best to make the events enjoyable for our guests. Such joy was problematic for Mother to feign as she was worried about the fate of Alexei who could be snatched from her in death. Often she would run upstairs to check in on our brother with Father continuing as host and Princess, Aunt to us, Irene replacing Mother as hostess meanwhile.

Our guests were treated to a play in French given by us four sisters. Our Swiss tutor, M. Pierre Gilliard, gave me a part that contributed largely to the success of our little performance for which I was more than delighted. However, live entertainment often provides opportunities for unforeseen moments, and this happened when I could not hear the prompter feed. I began to ad lib my lines to the great amusement of those assembled. At the same moment an elastic band holding up my ruffled petticoat snapped and my undergarment fell unceremoniously to the floor. The audience became well-nigh hysterical and laughed far more than if I had remembered my lines.

I had always been vexed by the clandestine nature of whatever was ailing Alexei. I could understand as a child that bleeding was part of his malaise and that it somehow implied that he had something like a wound that would not get a scab on it and stop bleeding. Neither Marie nor I understood much more than any of the general public.

Quietly I would slip into Alexei's room where I would espy Mother resting for a moment on her chaise longue. There was a porcelain basin filled with pieces of gauze which she had applied to Alexei's swelling. When he became worse the entire family would join her tending to him. Although I would have preferred to be outside far away from the agony of my brother's moaning and groaning I was nonetheless compelled by something more profound to stay at his side. All of us in the family were there hoping beyond hope for a respite to our and Alexei's suffering. As they prayed they had to be unaware of my own inner struggle. I thought the better of it and slowly inched my way in to the front of the group near my brother.

Mother tenderly enclosed Alexei's hand in hers as though she were trying to transmit thus her strength to him in this manner. I noted that was not lying in a pool of blood as I had always expected but looked quite normal, with the exception that he was pale and moaning, so I knew he could not be well. His face seemed changed and his eyes seemed sunken almost like an elderly person on his deathbed. "You will be well soon," Mother assured him kneeling by his bed. Alexei knew that as long as Mother continued in her encouragement, he could hope for better health. Although her heart was breaking inside, she maintained her outward countenance of composure. Left only to the care of nurses, Mother knew the boy would stop fighting. It was simply Mother's fortitude which kept Alexei from sinking into total despair.

Some evenings Aunt Irene and Dr. Botkin would spell Mother for a while in order for her to rest. More doctors, namely Dr. Fedorov, Dr. Dreifuss and Dr. Ostrogorsky, were all summoned to repeat all the treatments which had helped in previous attacks. Dr. Fedorov had the esteemed reputation of being a renowned specialist in haemophilia, and was the care manager for Alexei. The good doctor had been successful in assisting Alexei to get over previous bouts after which Dr. Derevenko, who was Dr. Fedorov's assistant, took over as Alexei's personal physician. No matter the efforts the new doctor made, Alexei did not seem to improve. Mother's faith, however, was unshakeable even if the doctors themselves were dismayed at their lack of success. Mother intuitively understood every agony of the boy and seemed to be able to relieve his suffering. There was a unique understanding, a profound bond, between Mother and son, between the two, although Father was suffering from hopelessness.

Should anything ever happen to Alexei, Father feared that he would suffer a double loss and that my mother's heart would fail. He was not prepared for double torture. Where we sisters and Father may have given up hope, Mother never would, never could. Simply put, she would not give up. We found ourselves in a constant preparation to face the worse that could occur. Mother, though pale with worry, never gave up the calm and presented it to Alexei as a gift as his eyes searched hers. At the very end she sent a telegram to Siberia to the home of Rasputin, imploring him to pray for Alexei's recovery. Mother sent for Father Vassiliev to administer the holy sacrament to our brother the next morning. Alexei and Mother stared lovingly into each other's eyes; the love and tenderness hers emitted were received thankfully by his. She was his rock.

Father issued a press release about the current situation believing that the Russian people had the right to know what was happening to the heir to the throne, although he had long suffered at keeping it a secret. Simultaneously, Father told his ambassadors and emissaries to search far and wide for a blood specialist, that is a hematologist, who could treat Alexei. Not one was found or came forth.

With sweat on their foreheads the doctors did all they could. Again and again Alexei would groan and Mother quietly asked, "Has no word come from the Starets?" Although we were all, with the exception of Mother, ready to accept the inevitable, even wished for it at some level to release our beloved brother from such torment, Alexei did not expire.

Father received a telegram from a guard who came swiftly to him. It was read aloud to all of us in his clear voice. "The little one will not die, do not let him be bothered too much." (This was the sense of the telegram; the words are my own.) The air as filled with hope anew. Alexei had to have been aware of it too as he suddenly relaxed and fell into deep slumber. It continued for so long that Mother kept listening to his heart to make sure that he was still with us. At his awakening we all noticed that the bleeding had stopped. We were not sure if it was the medicine, the prayers or intercessions of the starets, that is Rasputin, which were the cause of this amelioration, but we were absolutely convinced that Alexei had miraculously been spared death. We had seen a miracle before our very eyes. From that moment on, the boy's ravaged body began· to mend.

Rasputin's reputation as a holy man and servant- vessel of God's will for healing were clear to us. Although I had only seen him three to four times after this event, but still he made an indelible impression upon me. Verily, he was not at all like other people. His eyes pierced into the deepest sanctums of my soul. This fact disquieted me, indeed even frightened me. "Is this the little one?" he asked the first time we saw one another. I felt trepidation that he might touch me, but he never did. His garb was a long cassock with a cross hanging down on his chest. He appeared almost monk-like. We heard that he did not have money for a train and so walked without shoes long distances, though he wore boots in our presence. He was like a wild plant, a soul of the earth, nourished only the accident of Nature.

Grigory Rasputin had never taken vows to enter holy orders at all, and was loosely associated the Church. He was known as a *Starets*, a pilgrim and lay preacher among peasants. Was he like Elijah from the Bible thought to have returned to life from heaven? I wondered. He was well aware of natural medicine and efficacious folk remedies. Although modern medicine often looked with disdain at these cures, Rasputin held them in esteem. Just as God had made provision for food and drink for his Creation, so did Rasputin believe that he had created fruits, berries, herbs to cure illness. His remedies were simple as Nature itself; it was difficult for many to believe they could be of value. It was said that he put dried berries into his tea. High Bush cranberries and raspberry juice was employed for bronchitis. None of his natural remedies were used, however, for Alexei, and our parents preferred to believe that only God was the final arbiter of health and alleviation of affliction.

Religious services were held twice daily in our camp chapel which was inside a large garden tent until we left in the fall. In the meantime, Alexei had received many gifts from all over Russian including gem encrusted icons of St. Alexius and the Theotokos with Infant Jesus set in gold. (*Editor's note: Oklad or riza- a metal covering, either silver, gold or gilded metal, which protects parts of the icon and heightens its esthetic value*)

Prayers and blessings for Alexei's improved health were implicit in these lovely gifts.

Despite the many kindnesses and courtesies we showered on Alexei after his almost mortal experience in Poland he was still a normal, unspoiled little boy who had been born to a royal family. His charisma was magnetic and truly irresistible, yet trying to be the best parents they could be, Mother and Father were still firm with him. Mother's most important gem in this life was her little boy, and we all were well aware of it. Whatever the condition that befell him would befall us all; our fate was sealed in his. Each morning we began by asking about his health, "How his Alexei?" Assessing Mother's mood we knew the answer without her input; if she were happy, he was fine. If she were dismayed, something was wrong.

All kinds of defamatory rumors about Alexei's health reached our ears. How people can be so cruel is even today beyond my comprehension.

Alexei took things to heart very easily and sometimes ran to Olga for a sympathetic ear when Mother reprimanded him for this thing or another. His adoration for Olga was beyond measure saying he would marry her one day. He was quite solicitous of her attention especially when others unknown to him were in her presence, when he actually displayed jealousy. Alexei could deflect any attempt to scold him by using the strategy of distraction. Fully aware of his little diversionary tactics, we had a hard time to say anything harsh to him when he was making us laugh at the same time.

Somewhat before Christmas later in the year, snow blanketing the ground, we took Alexei, now better, to Tsarskoe Selo where he could further recuperate. His left leg was now somewhat shorter as the attack had somehow damaged a nerve. A pad created especially for his foot was inserted into his shoe to compensate for this fact. After that his limp was only very slight, almost imperceptible.

Mother was no longer her old self due to all the effort she had expended in taking care of our little brother. Although she was elated that Alexei had been spared the fate many had feared, she was also on the point of mental and physical exhaustion. Hence she lay on her back for weeks on end. She could not even attend church services intended to give thanks to God for Alexei's improvement which was very disappointing to her. When she finally said she felt better enough to get up, Dr. Botkin examined her again and found her heart to be yet more weakened than before.

In the period in which Mother rested and tried to regain her strength, she turned to intense religious study. She was now fully dedicated to the Almighty out of undying gratitude for having saved the life of her son and future Tsar. She lived fully consumed in a world of religiousity. As a bibliophile Mother possessed a rare collection of Bibles which were brought to her from St. Petersburg and Moscow. She wrote out comparative analyses of these editions much like a theologian or academician. Father, who also found religious studies interesting, would engage her in conversation about them, although he did not have the amount of time he would have liked to be able to delve further into them.

The royal library, that is Father's own collection, had some rare scrolls and texts. They originated in Egypt, Persia, Palestine, Sinai, and elsewhere. The Codex Sinaiticus, dating from the fourth century AD, was in this collection. It had been first discovered by the German scholar Tischendorff in a monastery on the Sinai peninsula. Alexander II, my great grandfather, had later acquired the manuscript and published it in 1862.

Early Russian texts were also to be found in this collection. As they were precious they could only be seen behind glass and were locked away in the case. Father understood the history and origin of each book. Our children's library was quite separate. We had access to Russian fables and stories. There translations from the Danish were also on hand. Some originals were even signed by Hans Christian Andersen himself.

Mother was reared and educated in England and Germany and distinguished herself in her studies. She, herself, was a philosopher and often discussed philosophy with her friends. She saw things the others could not see and sometimes con nected religion with the writings of the great philosophers. However, she was not a fanatic as many described her, but she could see and understand things the others did not. She was well informed on various subjects. She understood and reasoned the value and depth of her religion. Her and Father's knowledge of history surpassed that of many historians and their vocabulary was powerfully rich.

When Mother was strong enough, we children joined her at luncheon or tea. In the winter she selected a sunny room where a folding table was used for the occasion. One of Mother's rooms was decorated in her favorite color, mauve, and was cosy with matching brocades, curtains and upholstery. One wall was covered with a collection of icons which were gifts from different people. These were continually lighted by two lamps, one blue and one pink. Some of these icons were the most beautiful that Byzantine art could produce, others were very simple, but all were symbols to Mother and a means of remembering the donors. Mother loved every one of them, and was most appreciative when people presented her one of these religious treasures. Some of them she carried with her from Tsarskoe Selo to Alexandria and Livadia palaces and later to Tobolsk and Ekaterinburg. She wanted to have the most meaningful in her room. Others hung in one of the small rooms of the chapel together with some of her Bibles and a panagia. She also had some icons of great historic importance. Icons of these types were made only by the Greeks, Russians, Serbians, Bulgarians, and Rumanians. No statues were permitted in our churches, since we discarded the pagan idols at the time of the adoption of the Greek orthodox religion. A lot of the best treasures in the country were looted during the revolution. Other gifts were hung in the long hall which ran the whole length of the palace including all kinds of plates and other objects of historical value which we had received during many trips in Russia and abroad.

Mother presented a shocking image after her recuperation. It was almost impossible for her to walk the entire length of the hallway and made her way to the elevator which would take her to Alexei's room only with the aid of a wheelchair. Alexei was permitted to go to the music rooms, sit on the sofa there and play with his electric trains. He busied himself building villages, fountains, churches out of blocks. (Editor's note: these were quite probably the blocks of wood developed by the German educator from Thuringia, Friedrich Wilhelm August Froebel and still available today. Other blocks based on Froebel's concepts were produced then and now in Thuringia, Germany, under the brand name Ankerstein. Alexandra would have been well aware of these Froebel items, given her own familial connections to Thuringia. However, an earlier Romanov, Maria Pavlovna then Grand Duchess of Saxe-Weimar-Eisenach, had also been an ardent supporter of Friedrich Froebel, embroidering a rug for him to auction off to raise funds for his educational programs. It is very plausible that she introduced these blocks to Russia as she would have been acquainted with them and their developer, Herr Froebel.)

We sisters read to him and entertained him with other games and activities as best we could. Alexei used a blue nightshirt after his evening bath and appeared wearing it before retiring for the night. Mother listened to him nightly as he said his prayers (Editor's note: also a very German Lutheran custom which she must have brought with her from Hessen und bei Rhein.) Mother put on a good act in a sense as she did not want anyone to know how utterly exhausted she really was from taking care of her little boy. She was aware that press releases about Alexei's not being well had been sent out and reported on in the press. Nonetheless, the deeper nature of his illness had not been revealed, as to do that would be to implicate hopelessness to the people. As soon as the health and well-being of Mother and Alexei were sufficiently better we did go to the Crimea which was always a welcome place for us to be, hopefully beneficial for both.

Alexei's periods of malaise were difficult for all of us, no less because our education was thereby interrupted. We could not focus on anything really beyond his condition and health. Adversity brought us closer together as a family and this fact evoked a change in my own life.

I gained a sense of selflessness and I was no longer enticed by childish, self-centered notion. It was night on impossible to be light-hearted and free as my entire being was intertwined with the well-being of my family.

To my chagrin I realized I was taming down, through sorrow, not discipline. My childhood pastime of painting took a more serious turn. (*The editor boldens the previous statement as it gives insight in to her later painting activity.*) My attempts at authorship continued as I tried my hand at writing fictional stories about animals, which pleased Mother. She forwarded one to Aunt Irene saying, "See what our little Nastia has done." If I were to sing as well as Olga and Mother I would have to be more diligent in my practice, and I was willing to try harder and harder. Olga had much compassion for her littlest sisters, so much that I often kissed her hand in gratitude.

It was always a challenge to focus my attention on any one thing for more than a week or two. Although I would, at times, revert to my childish ways, I did so with less zeal and conviction. Nonetheless, my ill gained reputation of being a problem child did not dissipate. People often asked, "Where does the little one, small in size, store so much, much energy? She has an endless supply of jokes and pranks." I had my admirers who found whimsy in my actions, but still others were not amused at all.

My younger sister, Marie, and I had many little devices and small toys at our disposal to help us in our practical jokes. Our "Circus Kingdom" consisted of a mechanical mouse, a yellow iridescent snake with a moving head and a red, sharp tongue, a snapping turtle which might become entangled in a victim's dress. Marie and I would feign equal fright when one of our "victims" would scream and jump on a sofa for what they thought they were seeing.

The servants were often informed to be on the lookout for any practical jokes that I might instigate. Usually I was the ring leader and also the one which carried the most disgrace when we were found out.

"You must have been born in a dry summer, your jokes have outgrown you." Alexei once informed me while sprinkling me at the same time with water. Perhaps my most effective tool for playing pranks was a large doll with brown glowing eyes that shone in the dark. She could move her head and eyes when I wound her up seeming almost human in her gestures. Marie watched one day as we awaited the approach of our next victim. When we heard the oncoming footsteps I would up the doll and faced it toward the door on the floor. We then jumped into our beds and pretended to be deep in sleep. As she approached she saw the eyes glowing and blinking so that she ran screaming out of terror down the hall waking all who were sleeping on that floor. A warning sign was put on the door, "Enter only by permission of Olga and Tatiana." In this way, Marie, Alexei and I would not go in when we wanted.

But in light of our family situation I was less and less prone to be a practical jokester.

(Editor's note: Prankster, artist, dramaturge, actress- all self-attributed characteristics of Anastasia throughout her narrative. These seemed to set her apart from her older sisters. Almost presciently she will later intimate that even in the cellar of the Ipatiev House, dubbed The House of Special Purpose, moments before volleys of shots were fired at the Imperial Family, she was standing somewhat apart from the others which leads one to assume that this had something to do with her special grace to have survived.)

# VI     JUBILEE: 1913

THE SPRING OF 1913 (*the woman known simultaneously as "Evgenia Smetisko" and Anastasia Romanov painted a picture depicting the Romanov family during a Divine Liturgy to mark the 300ᵗʰ anniversary. Another objet d'art in the illustrations included in this author's earlier work, The Art of the Authoress of Anastasia, is the bead replica of necklaces worn by Anastasia and her sisters during that anniversary liturgy, purportedly presented to their tutor, Mr. Gibbes and acquired by Froebel-Parker when he purchased pieces of art from the monastery deemed unwanted for the museum there*) commemorated the three hundredth anniversary of the Romanov dynasty. A great jubilee marked the commencement of celebrations in St. Petersburg. We took up our residence in the Winter Palace in Tsarskoe Selo a few days before. Our first stop was the Cathedral of Our Lady of Kazan and on our way there people lined the streets as our carriages made their way to this important church. Inside the church candles burned brightly, jeweled icons glistened in the light and the golden vestments of the clergy brightened our world, yet outside the day was dark and gloomy.

It was an ancient custom for the tsar to be the first to enter, followed by the tsarevitch, Alexei. This frail little brother of mine, heir to the throne of Russia, seemed frail and weak. Grand Dukes and dignitaries bowed to this nine year old boy carried in the arms of a Cossack. How sad we are all were. How fervently we had hoped that Alexei would be able to walk on his own accord but he was not sufficiently well to do that. In the middle of the magnificent church we gathered under a canopy. It was necessary for Alexei to sit in a chair most of the time. Alexei was the cause of much worry for Mother. We were all to watch out for him also. Dr. Derevenko was not far away in case he was needed. Mother and we girls were all dressed alike in white. Mother sported the blue ribbon of St. Andrew, the order studded with diamonds and rubies. We four sisters wore the red ribbon of the Order of St. Catherine with its sparkling star. (*Editor's note: there is a red Order of St Catherine ribbon in the collection of the museum in Jordanville, New York*) Diamonds, rubies and emeralds adorned our grandmother, Marie, who bedazzled all who gazed upon her. The St. Petersburg elite were gathered here, a a sight to behold and the high clergy were clad in golden robes and elaborate headdresses. Military high dignitaries were resplendent in uniforms embroidered with gold.

During the service a dove flew into the Cathedral and criss crossed above our canopy. (*This dove is an element in the painting signed OTMA by aka "Evgenia Smetisko and simultaneously Anastasia Romanov found in the group of illustrations The Art of the Authoress of Anastasia*) Some friends confided to us after that they had held their breath hoping that the dove would not start a fire by hitting a candle. However, after its symbolic appearance if flew out an open door. The Christian faith puts much importance on the symbol of a dove, a sign of the Holy Ghost. It was logical that we all wondered if this event were a portent of special significance. (It is worthy of comment that also during the coronation, Father said, "A pigeon flew during the ceremonies." Later, in Ekaterinburg on the same date as the tragedy, while we took our last constitutional in the yard, a pigeon flew thrice over us and then kept hitting itself against the window.) (*Editor's note: this incident noted by the authoress "E.S." or "A.R." is personally known as it was commonly uttered in the home of Froebel grandparents and is an ancient saying in German culture. Given their German heritage, the family may have been aware of it. Perhaps it exists also in Russian culture.*) In afternoon having returned from the ceremony we changed into our national costumes just as had our guests. Mother wore her high traditional *kokoshnik*, behind which fell a long delicate veil. Her white robe was exquisitely embroidered in silver. For the evening soiree she wore a tiara which had belonged to Catherine II and a magnificent diamond necklace. The value of it was placed then at several million rubles. Its weight made it almost impractical so that she used it in all ·only a few times. Olga and Tatiana chose soft pink of fine tulle while Marie and I being younger, sported white silk and lace.

The Winter Palace was the site of a formal ball a few nights later. The important affair was almost like being debutantes for Marie and me and we were terribly excited.I Mother preferred that we leave early and return to our rooms while Grandmama Marie sided with us and bade Mother to allow us to stay just a bit longer promising she would look after us personally. Mother suddenly shed tears with the preoccupation: "These women of St. Petersburg might talk about the girls, and Anastasia's jokes might be misinterpreted."

I was very unhappy that evening for fear that every move I might make or every word I might speak would be used against me. All the innocent joy was taken from me that gala night for fear of those women's sharp tongues.

(*Editor's note: The authoress writes of the women's sharp tongues which robbed her of the joy she would have experienced, she believes, had her sisters and she stayed longer.*

*This theme appears in Froebel-Parker's Grandma Rebecka and the Witches' Tree, published 2014 by Authorhouse.com, In that publication, the author explores the life and suffering of his maternal 11th great grandmother, Rebecka (Towne) Nurse, first of others to be hanged as a "witch" 1692 in Salem, Massachusetts Colony. In investigating the ancestry of this ancestress, the family "de Ferrers" from Tutbury Castle appeared as her ancestors.*

*The "de Ferrers" as well as Anastasia's great grandmother, Victoria, could claim many of the same Plantagenet ancestors. Rebecka would have agreed with Anastasia in that the sharp tongues of Salem's young ladies and her neighbors had led to her subsequent condemnation and execution. Sharp tongues led to much calumny for the Romanov family, perhaps most infamously regarding the Starets, Rasputin.*

*The hatred of the Bolsheviks and similar groups for the Romanov Family, the Orthodox Christian Church and opponents of Marxism-Leninism with its inherent atheism, are themes actual at the time of this publication. The term "witchhunt" so applicable in 1692 New England could easily be applied to the Bolshevik Revolution and current political situations of many stripes.)*

To Moscow now by train leaving from St. Petersburg where the Jubilee continued. Mother wore the exquisite crown jewels. When first married an unfortunate incident had occurred which left its mark on Mother who had only recently married. Grandmama Marie although no longer on the throne truly felt that she still was entitled to wear the crown jewels instead of the new young Empress. Below the Winter Palace were safety vaults where Mother kept her own collection of personal jewelry. She notified the court chamberlain, Count Benckendorff, anytime she wanted to use them. The count, then, sent sent several responsible persons with papers of authorization to retrieve the desired pieces which were then taken upstairs under heavy guard to Mother. We were never to spend another night at the Winter Palace, our childhood home, after these anniversary festivities. My sisters often stopped in the rooms for a glass of tea after meetings for our various charity organizations during the war. Sadly I ponder what became of the treasures which had been stored for generations in those vaults. They belonged not only to the Imperial family but to the Russian people as well. Worth billions of rubles, they were safe until the leaders of the revolution, Lenin, Trotsky (Bronstein), Apfelbaum, Rosenfeld and others got their paws on them. Another rumor claimed that much of it was divided among relatives of the Bolshevik leaders who came to our country expressly for that purpose to kill and loot. Our Russian national treasures, so long guarded by the Imperial family, have been sold off now to people in many foreign lands.

From Moscow we continued Vladimir, then to Nizhni Novgorod and to Yaroslavl. Yaroslav was an ancient historic city with a view of the wide river. Words cannot begin to describe the most marvelous reception we received. Throngs of children, cadets, the nobility and the townspeople lined the streets right down to the dock. What a delightful and luxurious sight from the river-this beautiful city on a little hill!

In every city guests had been especially selected to honor my Father and my Mother. At Father's dinner his guests were mostly men while Mother received ladies in separate drawing rooms. The *chanteuse extraordinaire*, Plevitskaya, sang again and bowed gracefully before the glowing audience. We made many new friends during these spectacular performances.

Poor Tatiana, was exhausted and muttered, "People and more people-I am tired of them!" Mother was able to hear her say it and let her know that it was unkind and impolite to express such sentiment.

We sailed on the Volga on our way to Kostroma. People waded out to their waists to greet us while many others waved from the shores. "God Save the Tsar" was sung to us from the shore when we made an unforeseen stop in the river while some mechanical problem was dealt with. There was a delay and we in the Imperial Family arrived later than scheduled in Kostroma. The Romanov dynasty had its official beginning here in this terraced city. Now the three hundredth anniversary of the Romanov family was to be marked in a special ceremony.

We finally reached the monument of Susanin. On this column there loomed a bronze bust of the first Romanov Tsar, Michael Feodorovich. The peasant, Susanin, supported the erection of this column, hence the name. Susanin was the Russian patriot who deliberately misdirected the Polish army which had invaded Russia and requested that Susanin lead the way to the Tsar who was in hiding. The Polish army fell for the ploy, was destroyed and sent out of Russia because of Susanin's ruse. The famous opera, "A Life for the Tsar" by Glinka, is based on this heroic incident. Father loved this opera. Feodor Romanov was the origin of the frequent patronymic taken by brides of many Grand Dukes upon marriage.

The Ipatiev Monastery was the next stop after the column. This was where the first Romanov was sheltered in 1613. The Cathedral of the Holy Trinity is found at this monastery in which one can see the within the iconostasis and the throne of Tsar Michael Feodorovich. A tatar prince built the Cathedral and was the first to be baptized there.

Michael's living quarters, to us they seemed like dark rooms, were on our schedule to be visited. The chairs were adorned with the beautifully embroidered double eagles on their backs. We took tea from the original cups at the same table once used by Tsar Alexei. A portrait of Michael and Alexei Romanov hung in a different room. They both somewhat resembled my Father. Both my father and Alexei were born on the day dedicated to St. Job. Both Father and Alexei could claim sad experiences, yet those of my father outshadowed Alexei's.

A luxurious wreath wrought of silver in the shape of the cap of Monomakh was placed on the grave of Michael. (*The Cap of Monomakh, Hinterglasmalerei, in private collection, appears in the illustrations of The Art of the Authoress of Anastasia*)

What a strange and mysterious coincidence that in Ekaterinburg in 1918 in the Ipatiev House, Nicholas II the last Tsar of Russia, meant his mournful demise. On the other hand the Romanov dynasty was born in the Ipatiev Monastery in Kostroma in 1613 and ended in death the Ipatiev House in Ekaterinburg, a full three hundred and five years later. A legend from history recounts that at the election of Michael Feodorovich Romanov, a lame beggar woman who claimed to be a wandering saint had foretold that the Romanov dynasty would be born with Michael and would die with another Michael. Oddly this was exactly the case. Father's brother, Michael, briefly took the throne when Father abdicated but soon gave it up, lending credence to the utterance of the prophetess.

Before we arrived in Kostroma another odd symbolic even occurred. An ancient tree which the first Michael had planted, of enormous circumference, had been cut down. It had been preserved as a relic of historical significance.

Prince Dolgorukov was with us on this trip who was a direct descendant of the family which founded the city of Kostroma and also built the first church in the Kremlin in Moscow. Prince Dolgorukov was a loyal who followed us all the way through our series of incarcerations until Ekaterinburg where he met the same frightful end as the rest of our family.

1913 was the bicentennial of the transfer of the seat of government to St. Petersburg from its former seat in Moscow.

Our photo albums brimmed with photos of these historic events in which we had just participated. On our way back to St. Petersburg we made a stop at the Nicholas Palace in Moscow. Mother wore the traditional Slavonic robe and the Imperial crown jewels at the functions here. After the end of the Jubilee celebrations she never wore them again. Many commemorations and anniversaries happened in 1913. It was the centennial for several regiments. There was a reconsecration of The Naval Cathedral at Kronstadt in recognition of its centennial. Our attendance was mandatory at all of these functions.

Our daily routines finally began again at Tsarskoe Selo. Baroness Iza Buxhoeveden was named a lady in waiting, replacing the young Princess Elizabeth (Lili) Obolensky suffering now from impaired health. Lili had been with us in England and on various other trips. Buxhoeveden had already taken on certain palace responsibilities before becomeing a lady-in-waiting. A requirement for such ladies-in-waiting were they had to be unmarried and to be born in titled families.

Mother was not a great fan of all the old court etiquette with its staid traditions and harsh restrictions. It did not matter to her in the least what rank these ladies had or did not have. She selected them on their individual merits based on ability, education and culture. Baroness Buxhoeveden had her origins in an old Baltic family which had produced several ambassadors. Her father had been an ambassador to Denmark.

A lady in waiting was an honorary position to which many a young lady aspired. Their various diamond studded brooches designated their rank within Mother's staff. This bejeweled badge had Mother's initial and a crown on its top. According to their length of service some were set in silver and others in gold. It was not permitted for them to discuss political affairs at any time and they were sworn to strict discretion and confidentiality. They were also allowed to fraternize with officers or others on duty in the palace.

They were expected to accept telephone calls for Mother and for us girls, jot down important details and note incoming and outgoing telegrams. These were to be file by date with an accompanying memorandum of all telegrams and letters. At any event in which we girls were to leave the palace, the ladies-in-waiting were to be with us and watch over us. They lived well with maids, a footman and a carriage provided for their comfort. If, on occasion, other ladies were needed, they were called in to help. When later under arrest in Tsarskoe Selo, our letters and telegrams were read and scoured for information. Iza went with us and suffered with us all the way to Tobolsk, Siberia, but was not permitted entry into the governor's house.

✳

# PART II

## *The First World War*

_____

# VII     EVE OF THE WAR: 1914

We went to Livadia early in the spring of 1914. Full days of school work were continued here. Our tutor, M. Pierre Gilliard as well as our Russian tutor, M. Peter Vasilievich Petrov, were with us as per custom. At time they joined us for lunch and then hiked with us in the sunshine or some other recreational undertaking. These walking journies led us through the park or along the shore to Yalta or to the Church of Alexander Nevsky on a nearby hill. The central point of the day, however, was dinner with friends and relatives. Among our favorite dinner guests were Prince Igor Constantinovich and the Grand Duke Dimitri Pavlovich. Aunt Ella, Mother's older sister, the widow of the Grand Duke Serge, brother of Alexander III, was another adored guest. Mother and she shared similar religious views, having inherited this mysticism from their mother, Princess Alice, Grand Duchess of Hesse, Queen Victoria's daughter.

I was told that Grandmother Alice had been a student of religious history and movements, having been inspired by her tutor, a theologian who was a close friend of the von Hessen family. His influence on Mother was markedly direct. Thoughts and the terrible fear of sin were imbedded into her by this ardent theologian. We children witnessed her long struggle to leave this deeply ingrained mysticism and return to reality. Father's mother, Marie Feodorovna's extreme criticism of her coupled with the unsympathetic attitude of the Russian court led her to seek comfort in this mysticism so that once again her whole soul anew overflowed with it. The misfortune of her son's illness forced her to turn even more ardently to it. Her upbringing informed her to try to ignore the criticism that surrounded her and yet her sensitive heart suffered. Being unable to utter the words of response that she would have otherwise wanted to express, her heart seemed to harden. She was seen by courtiers as a heartless, cold and eccentric woman. Queen Victoria had raised this granddaughter of hers to be very English, reserved, determined. Although eternally English in upbringing, her faith informed by Orthodoxy grew more fervent so that she became in manners and thought more Russian and a better Russian than many who were born Russians.

From the Baltic Sea via the North Sea our yacht had been brought to the Crimea and we now boarded our the "Standard" for several short cruises on the Black Sea. We approached Constantsa on the Rumanian coast to reciprocate a visit of King Carol and Queen Elizabeth (Carmen Sylva) of Rumania. The future King Carol II, their great nephew, accompanied them. At her late age Carmen Sylva was still beautiful as was Princess Marie (Missy), wife of Prince Ferdinand who later became the reigning monarchs of Rumania. Princess Marie and my sister Olga developed a close friendship during this visit. Thankfully the strained relationship between Mother and Missy's sister Victoria, divorced from Mother's brother Ernest, greatly improved; now all was forgotten. In a pavilion which seemed to rise right out of the sea we enjoyed luncheon together. We could see many yachts and smaller boats cruising back and forth for a closer look at the "Standard" from this vantage point.

Tea was served on board the "Standard" for the members of the two families in the afternoon. A great many dignitaries joined us on board ship after tea. A grand banquet was held in the adorably adorned pavilion overlooking the sea in the afternoon. On the water one enjoyed the reflection of the light as various craft sailed by while the sound of music wafted over the sea. Many garlands and flags fluttered in the gentle breeze heightening the gala aspect of this grand event. It had been rumored that this fete had really been organized in the expectation that Olga might marry into the Rumanian Royal Family. Olga and Prince Carol sat side by side at the table and ostensibly enjoyed themselves. The red, white and blue tricolors decorated the table at which there was an exchange of small gifts. Olga was gifted a Rumanian national costume with absolutely beautifully embroidery. Fabric of a dark color woven in a pattern of gold and silver thread was used in the fabrication of the lovely skirt, while the blouse sported dainty embroidery in white. Princess Marie was not shy in recognizing her own beauty especially her blue eyes. The eldest daughter of Prince Alfred, Duke of Edinburgh, and the Grand Duchess Marie Alexandrovna of Russia she had been named Marie Alexandra Victoria, in honor of both of her grandmothers the Russian Empress Marie Alexandrovna and Queen Victoria of Great Britain. As previously noted, her younger sister Victoria Melita (Ducky) was the divorced wife of Mother's brother Ernest of Hesse (*Editor's note: von Hessen-Darmstadt*) now married to the Grand Duke Cyril Vladimirovich. Alexandra (Sandra), married Prince Ernest of Hohenlohe-Langenburg (**see editor's note at end of chapter*) Beatrice (Baby B.), the third sister, was wife of the Infante Alfonso of Spain, first cousin of Alfonso XIII.

I was experiencing a new intense interest that was unique and unknown to me. After sailing away that night, we were told that it had been decided Olga was too young to marry. Olga did not want to leave Russia and expressed the notion that she would rather remain single than leave her Motherland. We girls were elated that we would not be losing our sister, we even teased her good naturedly about "losing a husband." Alexei, thankfully, never knew about this aspect of his beloved sister, Olga, as he would have been sick with worry that she might leave Russia. In retrospect, it would have been better had Olga married at that time as she might be alive today.

Prince Carol came to Russia several times during the war to astay with us for a few days. Prime Minister Bratianu came with him one day. There was no way, however, that Olga was to be left alone with Carol for even a slight moment without a chaperone. Ladies-in-waiting were omnipresent and the rest of us scurried in and out constantly. Neither could she have a chance to steal a kiss or innocently hold his hand.

In Tobolsk Mother finally realized her mistake in not allowing her older daughters more independence.

Olga was named in recognition of Aunt Olga. A tall, slender, blonde she was blessed with a lovely fresh complexion. Her eyes were dazzling blue, her nose slightly upturned. She had humorously dubbed it "little stub". Her smile revealed beautiful white teeth. In retrospect I increasingly appreciate of her fine character. She read voraciously including some stories she sent to Aunt Missy, Queen Marie of Rumania, who reciprocated by presenting to Olga stories she had written. Olga destroyed her own poetry. Her religious faith was deep so that she often sat with patients at the hospital praying that God might spare the young soldiers' lives. Her command of the piano keyboard was masterful, and she was able to flawlessly perform most difficult compositions of Tchaikovsky, Wagner, Mozart, and Beethoven. Duets were performed by Mother and Olga on the piano. From her Danish and Romanov family lines she inherited her penchant for writing and composing as those pedigrees had boasted a long line of artists, poets, sculptors and musicians. She sang as a mezzo soprano while memorizing musical compositions very easily. Her musical instructor, as well as ours, was Mr. Konrad. Father's preferred piece of music was Tchaikovsky's "Chanson Sans Paroles". His face lighted up with pleasure when she played for him. Her love for Father was a tender one. During troubling times Father discussed his problems with Olga with no other family member permitted to be present. Her love for children was unbounded which was evident in her support of some who were confined to life in a hospital bed.She set aside funds for their education from her own allowance.

My memories float back to our Rumanian cruise where we arrived at Odessa in the middle of the night. There the Imperial train was ready to take us to Kishinev for the public viewing of the monument to Alexander I. Alexei's lack of proper behavior is one reason I remember it so well. Surely his fatigue brought on by the heat on the train was one of the causes. We were the guests in Kishniev of the Governor, an old friend, whose beard was the absolute longest I have ever seen, reaching almost to his waist.

Champagne was served at the tea which followed. Before anyone could stop him Alexei had latched onto a glass of the bubbly libation, downing it before anyone could stop him. The effect was almost immediate and he became overtly cheery so that all the ladies, old and young gathered round. It was the first time that I realized his amazing sense of humor. Naïve as he was he did not realize how the champagne had affected him. The family was mortified at this display. Back on the train after sobering up, Father gave him a dispatching to his bed.

It dawned upon us that Alexei's illness and the Jubilee had brought an abrupt end to our formal studies. Alexei and I had begun by studying French together, but his fluency far outpaced mine. In contrast to me, French came naturally to him but not to me. I found no inspiration in any of my studies. I became melancholic when in a classroom long, but ran out of the room like a bullet when classes were over. Thus I felt my tutors were displeased with me.

Hardly were we returned home when we were all shocked at the news of the assassination of the Archduke Francis Ferdinand of Austria and his wife in Sarajevo, on June 28th, 1914. Father spent very little time with us subsequent to this sad event. Father was always in conference with his ministers, diplomats and the Grand Dukes. M. Poincare, the French president, spent four or five days with us at Alexandria Cottage in Peterhof. He was as pleasantly agreeable as President Fallieres his predecessor. Father felt an affinity for him from the very first meeting admiring his diplomacy and amicability. The Imperial family received him at various state dinners in his honor. Ironically, everyone had a countenance of impending doom so that I perceived that matters must be serious. How could the assassination of an Austrian be so detrimental to Russia? The only explanation given to us younger children was that Russia had signed a treaty which might implicate the nation in the case that the matter could not be immediately resolved. At the departure of the French president, Austria declared its intentions against Russia and Serbia.

Two things in this chaos were clear to me: Father's pallidness and Mother's heartfelt albeit emotional supplications imploring that Russia be kept out of war. Mother repeatedly echoed, "The country is not recovered from one war before it is in another." Of course she was reliving the horrors of the war with Japan still fresh in her mind. In Mother's face we could see the foreshadowing of unavoidable doom.

There was an annual review every summer of regimental maneuvers at Krasnoe Selo (near Tsarskoe Selo). They were held that year in honor of King Frederick Augustus III of Saxony (*Editor's note: his full name was Friedrich August Johann Ludwig Karl Gustav Gregor Philipp, *1865- +1932)*

Horses were a favorite pastime for us sisters. Each of us had a favorite horse of our own. Tatiana was quite informed about these animals, since she had learned the art of riding with an accomplished riding master as the rest of us. Olga and Tatiana were more graceful riders than either Marie or I.

The horses belonging to Cossacks were especially mesmerizing to me, since they appeared to have extra-sensory perception in able to understand the very thoughts of their masters. Tatiana explained to me how the Cossack and his horse grow up together. The young Cossack is given a horse, a progeny of a Cossack horse, whose training fits the requirements of the Cossack regiment. The boy and horse become inseparable so that each must learn from the other and each understand the other's personalities. The body of the unit is the horse, while the boy, later a Cossack, is the head.

As they gradually merge into a cohesive unit the boy is then allowed to become a Cossack. I often wished I were a boy so that I could be a Cossack and sit atop a noble steed resplendent in my polished and tailored uniform.

The crowds cheered as we speeded by. We watched the magnificent maneuvers from the Imperial pavilion. A large unit trotted in perfect formation when suddenly all the riders jumped off their horses in unison only to jump back on their saddles without a single horse breaking its gait or changing its speed. Another performance involved a horseman's throwing his black cape around his own shoulders then over his horse skillfully so that the cape covered both horse and rider. Soon followed many stunts and jumps over wide trenches filled with water into which not one ride fell. In the midst of such magnificence and at luncheon no less, served under tents following the exercise, a message came stating that Austria-Hungary had declared war on Serbia (August 1st, 1914). Immediately we left and returned home.

In the years leading up to 1914 I distinctly remember the review of the troops each May. All St. Petersburg high society felt compelled to pay hundreds of rubles for a box seat at these maneuvers. The sale of tickets created proceeds which were destined for certain charities. Upon our approach a signal was given and cheers erupted along the quays.

Two pairs of pure white horses drew our carriages. Father's was always left of Mother's and Grandmother's equipage with their accompanying liveried footmen. Our children's carriage followed swiftly between the rows of troops until our destination at the Imperial box under a green tent. The troops were reviewed by our father. Father's own Preobrazhensky regiment followed by the Hussars, the Pavlovsky regiment, the Lancers, the cuirassiers et al.

Father did not think that the Emperor Francis Joseph

(Editor's note: *1830- +1916, His full title was
His Imperial and Royal Apostolic Majesty,
By the Grace of God Emperor of Austria,
King of Hungary and Bohemia, Dalmatia, Croatia, Slavonia, Galicia, Lodomeria
and Illyria;
King of Jerusalem, etc.;
Archduke of Austria;
Grand Duke of Tuscany and Cracow;
Duke of Lorraine, Salzburg, Styria, Carinthia, Carniola and Bukovina;
Grand Prince of Transylvania, Margrave of Moravia;
Duke of Upper and Lower Silesia, of Modena, Parma, Piacenza and Guastalla, of
Auschwitz and Zator, of Teschen, Friaul, Ragusa and Zara;
Princely Count of Habsburg and Tyrol, of Kyburg, Gorizia and Gradisca;
Prince of Trent and Brixen;
Margrave of Upper and Lower Lusatia and in Istria;
Count of Hohenems, Feldkirch, Bregenz, Sonnenberg etc.;
Lord of Trieste, of Cattaro and on the Windic March;
Grand Voivode of the Voivodeship of Serbia.

The editor wishes to make a genealogical note that David Vondracek of the University of Prague is currently studying the biological relationship between the Austrian emperor and the first president of Czechoslovakia, Tomas Garrigue Masaryk, friend of the editor's great grandfather, Jan Grega, with whom his grandmother once waltzed at a charity function in New York City. Some of the editor's biometric data on all three has been sent to Professor Vondracek.) would wage war against Serbia due to the murder of the Archduke and his wife. Father was of this pious opinion due to a comment Father himself had heard the emperor make, in which he criticized the Austrian archduke with the disparaging aside that he was unfit to wear the crown of the Austro-Hungarian Empire.

As the war progressed we were astounded to hear that some high level Austrian officers who had been captured confessed that the old Austrian emperor had personally orchestrated the Sarajevo attack and that the archduke had been sent there on purpose. Such nefarious news was told to General Tatishchev, the Court Chamberlain. Further it was explained that the archduke had been hated and murdered by oppressed Bosnians of the Dual Monarchy in an overt attempt to incite an armed conflict in order to destroy Serbia completely and then bring it under Austria's control as had happened with Bosnia-Herzegovina. Relatively small Serbia would then not be able to protect itself against Austria AND Germany. They knew that this little country would not be able to resist the two powers, Austria-Hungary and Germany. Serbia would not go down lightly, and they were willing to die for their freedom and the right to live on their own land.

It would be more reasonable and less deadly, Father thought, to try the Austro-Hungarian-Serbia dispute in front of the International Arbitration Court at the Hague. To this end he sent a telegram to Kaiser Wilhelm Afterward he notified King Carol of Rumania that he should follow suit and telegraph the Kaiser that Russian did not wish war. Sadly, all was for naught. The assassination of this goodfor-nothing Archduke as a deliberate excuse, even though the murder was committed by their own citizens who resented the Dual Monarchy. It was common knowledge that Russian mobilization which was under way was directed against Austria, not Germany.

(* Editor's note: Prince Ernst II von Hohenlohe-Langenburg, *1863- +1950; members of the family von Hohenlohe-Langenburg assisted Friedrich Froebel, educator from Thuringia who founded Kindergarten. Bernhard II Erich Freund von Sachsen-Meiningen, who helped raise money for Froebel's project, also allowed Froebel to educate the first women who would become certified Kindergarten teachers at his hunting villa, Marienthal in Bad Liebenstein in the Thuringian Meiningen Duchy. The duke's mother was Luise Eleonor von Hohenlohe-Langenburg. Later Friedrich's nephew, Carl Ferdinand "Julius" Froebel, began as editor the newspaper Sueddeutsche Presse in Munich, in part due to his friendship with Chlodwig, Prince of Hohenlohe-Schillingsfürst, Chancellor of Germany from 1894-1900, whose mother was Princess Konstanze of Hohenlohe-Langenburg)

# VIII    NO CHOICE BUT WAR

apid were the events which now unfolded in succession. Serbia had war declared on her by Austria and Germany. Father was increasingly shut away from us, trying with all his might to divert conflict with Russia. Russia was, nonetheless, an ally of Serbia. There was no alternative. Troops from Germany and Austria were already mobilizing and maneuvering near our border so that war with us seemed totally inevitable. Mother wept inconsolably. "Why," she wondered," should millions of Russians lose their lives because one man is killed? Wilhelm has done this; I never trusted him. I never forgave him for the humiliation and indignities toward our Granny (Queen Victoria)." Quickly my memories raced to the visit in Germany when the Kaiser was my still my friend. Two short years ago we had exchanged jokes. Now he was the enemy of all Russia, Mother's enemy, and also mine. Mother's own cousin, Wilhelm!

In an instant the Austrian troops threatened the old Russian fortification of Bendery. I had a feeling of foreboding. Dreams were indicative of the future to me, and I attempted to interpret a dream I had had just before this news arrived. In the dream the forest on the Russian western border was on fire. Audible was the crackling of the timber and the fire raging high into the sky was visible. I suddenly remembered this dream when I crossed these same forests during my escape. During my flight on foot out of Russia the trees were not on fire but rather lay with their huge roots ripped out of the ground-witnesses of the horrific misery and anguish that had transpired there.

That evening at Tsarskoe Selo, knowing now that the Germans were advancing, we knelt in prayer to the Most High God, imploring Him to avert disaster and maintain peace. Father appeared late for dinner and we instantly realized how much he was suffering. His face was palid, his face emanated dispair. He declared clearly: "Russia has no choice but war, when the armies of Germany and Austria are already on Russian soil." Mother collapsed and wept, as did we all. That evening we could not finish our meal. We arose and left the table. Shortly thereafter, Foreign Minister Sazonov and the British Ambassador, Sir George Buchanan, conferred with Father into the early hours of the morning. Father was at his desk at five in the morning, well before breakfast. Alexei did not learn of the war until the next morning as he was sick.

All of us except Alexei made our way to the Winter Palace, where Father's subjects gathered in the square and surrounded us as they cheered. In accordance with established Russian tradition the people kissed Father's shoulders and the hem of Mother's skirt. Such public loyalty made Mother teary-eyed. At the huge Nicholas Concert Hall Father attended a meeting with the ministers and generals. Then the *Te Deum* was sung (*Editor's note: A Christian hymn of praise to God from the Latin Te deum laudamos, which is Thee O Lord, we Praise*). Father now appeared on the balcony of the Winter Palace to read the Manifesto declaring war with all of us children and other relatives behind him. Suddenly the voices hushed and the entire assembly was still. Not a breath could be heard from those congregated. The Thousands of people gathered in the square knelt. With one unified voice they sang together "God Save the Tsar." Father took a solemn oath that he would not sign any peace treaty as long as any enemy to the man remained on Russian soil. He swore a promise to his people that he would defend all Slavs, even if called upon to offer his own martyrdom. It was extremely demanding of my Father to announce to the people that war was no longer a fear rather a reality.

After a few days we left for Moscow. The same enthusiasm met us there. The bells in the church towers peeled without end as we passed the station to the Kremlin. Wherever one looked people were gathered, on trees, rooftops, balconies, wherever they could see the royal cortege. Frequently we heard the Russian national anthem as we passed along. Poor Alexei was not well so that he had to be carried to the Cathedral of the Assumption to hear the Te Deum. For three days there were public demonstrations of heartfelt patriotism. "Ura" (hurrah) resounded everywhere. We left Moscow and went to pray at the famous Troitsko-Sergievskaya Lavra in Sergievo.

The monastery was the richest and most important one in Russia and the crowds seemed limitless along the route. The monastery estate encompassed an expansive territory surrounded by a high thick wall dotted with many towers. A dozen churches were located within its environs containing countless historic and ancient treasures. The monastery was renowned for its heroic defense by the monks against the Poles in 1608 which has been depicted in countless history books. The tombs of Tsar Boris Godunov's tomb and those of his family were there. Father received an icon at the monastery that he was to carry with him through the battles. Until the very last this icon was revered at the field chapel of the General Headquarters. (*Editor's note: in the illustrations contained in The Art of the Authoress of Anastasia is a painting, signed OTMA, from the "Smetisko Collection" which depicts the Tsar holding an icon in front of his troops.*)

Now that war was no longer a possibility rather a tangible reality the people were resolved to have an early and decisive victory. Father was greeted enthusiastically on his travels. There were times when we would hear his addresses to the people, because we traveled with him on those occasions. Unity was thick in the air, and a strong bond of unity between us and the family seemed more intimate than ever. Students wrote Father letters begging to be allowed to leave school to fight for their country. "A beautiful patriotism," Father said. "But how little they understand what war is."

There was a great surge of patriotism during these early days of the war. Some of our own relatives returned to Russia to do their part for the war. Some relatives were so distant that we had no idea who they were. They all pitched in to do anything they could for the cause.

Grandmama Marie did all she could to help in the hospital. She later went to Kiev with our Aunt Olga, her daughter and Father's sister, who toiled in her own hospital as a Sister of Mercy. She received the most critical of cases as she worked so close to the front.

The pace of life in the palace became more hectic. Mother's sole preoccupation was the hospitals and their mission to tend to the wounded. She wondered aloud if they were adequate for the most certain heightened demand which was surely in the future. Mother was fully aware of the exigencies which awaited these medical units. Mother had actually studied medicine early in her adulthood precisely because she knew that the "bleeding disease" might appear in her descendants. Should any of her children inherit it, she wanted to be prepared to take care of them. Her previous preparation served her well in the care she was able to give Alexei and also to others during the way. Mother also had a medical library on the second floor in Tsarskoe Selo where in addition to textbooks, one could find all kinds of anatomical diagrams. Mother was an excellent organizer of hospitals and charitable institutions even before the war. She was particularly interested in orphanages. Mother had studied philosophy in one of the German universities in addition to her interest in the medical field. In fact I recall the very drawer in the desk in a room on the balcony where she kept her documents and other papers of this nature. I have the extreme assurance that Mother was determined to meet with courage any problems she had to face. An introduction to nursing course was now planned for Mother, Olga and Tatiana, so that they might serve the wounded more efficiently.

Soldiering was no longer a past time for Alexei, for he now had to be obligatorily in serious military training. There was always a chair for Alexei in Father's study, where he sat on certain days listening to the diverse reports presented by the Ministers. There was no permission for Alexei to comment on any matter in these conferences, although when in private with Father he could ask questions that puzzled him.

Why can Alexei participate with Father and not I? Mother said, "During a war there are first duties. Yours is to continue your education in order to be useful later on." How disappointing. Yet the war-electrified patriotism compelled me to dig in at my school work and to pursue my formal education. Stirring sounds of bands and marching feet often disturbed my good intentions. I learned the meaning of discipline and self-sacrifice from the men under arms.

I did not want to waste a moment due to the awakening of the growing awareness of my environment. I joined a group of young women who hemmed children's dresses for various charities in addition to my studies. Marie supervised work the in the palace workroom sewing garments for which we often called officers of Father's own regiment on duty in the palace to turn the wheels of the sewing machines and sort the garments.

We had learned sewing at an early age because Mother had always stressed its importance in any woman's life. (*Editor's note: until recently, and perhaps still in areas, an integral part of girls' German public education and generally inter-generationally encouraged at home*) Mother was expert at sewing and during the early years of her marriage created some of the layettes for us infants. Many of her embroideries sold at benefits and some hand-made blouses in silk or linen, beautifully tucked and embroidered, went as gifts to our relatives in England and in Germany. (*Editor's note: the reader is urged to view images of fine needlework, albeit embroidery signed OTMA in* The Art of the Authoress of Anastasia)

Grandmother was also a skilled seamstress and delft with a needle and thread. If any of her exquisite handkerchiefs were in need of mending she could repair it in such a way that no one could ever detect that it had been touched. She could knit well, too. During the war she knit fine wool gloves which she sent to the front and also to Father. Socks, gloves, and caps were the focus of Marie and my handiwork. We listened to war news while doing our evening knitting. We learned responsibility in the hard school of our own mutual problems and war. As the honorary chief of a regiment, the 148th Caspian Infantry, I received monthly reports of my regiment which included news of the losses in dead and wounded. I became frightened reading these reports, so I ran to Olga for advice for what could be done to ease the situation. She said; "Hundreds of wounded are coming every day and it is horrible the way they suffer." German losses were even greater we were told.

I wanted to follow in Mother's footsteps with her interest in medicine and become a doctor when I was bigger. Marie and I were now allowed to visit our own hospital more often.

They were carrying a wounded man with bloody bandages as we entered the building. He went directly to the operating room but he was to be removed a moment later. He had already died when he was brought to the operating room. Suddenly I became nauseous and faint. Impossible that I could ever be a doctor. I shall never be able to forget the sight of that poor boy. The phantom smell of blood remained in my nostrils. The color red haunted me wherever I turned so that even medicines of that color revolted me.

Olga and Tatiana worked daily beside Mother at the hospital. Arising at seven, they attended lectures only to resume their hospital work. While they knit in the evening they also read. Their endurance of all that was happening was a mystery to me. Olga was just like me in that neither of us could bear to witness suffering and this gave me great satisfaction. Just as Mother, Tatiana had an ability to see the relief that loving care granted beyond the suffering. Due to the scarcity of doctors, Mother assisted in many operations. She prayed each day the Znamensky Sobor, the little church she had restored, imploring the Almighty that her hands might be enabled to help each wounded soldier. Her obligation she felt to each one was to nurse them back to health herself. She prayed for the war to end each time she saw a new wounded soldier. Her entire day was spent at the hospital and when she returned each day she lay for a bit on her sofa to gain a modicum of rest.

Father ordered strict austerity given the war effort. To benefit the soldiers each kopeck must be accounted for. The palace staff was reduced by Mother. Our meals became plainer. The Court, Father ordered, was to follow all these restrictions also. As children we had not been raised to expect such exaggeratedly luxurious extravagances. Idleness and wastefulness were frowned upon. These ideals were now more imperative. (*Editor's note: these sound like values common in German Lutheranism in which denomination the Empress had been raised from childhood until her conversion to Orthodoxy)* Whatever we received with did so with appreciation.

Few dresses were in our closets. My older sisters often gave me their hand me downs. As I was smaller, the fit was not always perfect and tucks and hems were needed to fit me. The times when we did receive new frocks we were almost afraid to sit down in them so that they would not wrinkle or be soiled. We each had household chores and mandatory duties to perform.

Olga and Tatiana never stopped working at the hospital while continuing their studies. They were also charged with making out the daily schedule for Marie and me. Additionally they checked supplies for the hospitals, charitable organization meetings, and supervised money raising efforts through concerts and plays. The leading artists of the day donated their services while enormous sums of money were collected to improve and expand hospitals and other charitable efforts. hospitals and other charities. Our friend the singer Madame Plevitskaya proved most beneficial by generously donating her time and her talent to the war effort. Mother always waiting with expectation to see how much money had been made with these ventures.

Gramophone records selected by Marie and me were to be sent to the convalescent wards, also books which we thought the soldiers might like to read. Fruit, candies, cakes, games, stationery, soap and pencils were all ordered by us. Hospitals received box after box. Dominoes was a favorite pastime with us and the men. We sometimes watched those well enough to play croquet or we helped them to write letters to their families.

We realized our playrooms were now deserted. We had stored Alexei's electric automobile under a slide. He had chores and duties to do besides his homework and studies. When he did take the electric automobile out for a spin with his playmates he did so pretending they were out doing a special project for the war effort.

Any *joie de vivre* from before was now extinguished due to the war. Social gatherings were now almost exclusively charity benefits; it was out of vogue to not be helping in some way. There was a great sense of camaraderie in making these a success.

We sold photos of our family, that is the Imperial Family, to help raise funds. The press helped to set aside days for various members of the family who were publicized throughout the empire so that it became a competition to see which family member would sell the most photos and thereby raise the most money. Tatiana proved to be one of the most desired photos in the scheme.

Homes of noble relatives and friends were often turned into field hospitals for which the host family often paid the expenses themselves. The devoted their time and themselves to the wounded. Up to seventy patients were housed in their residences. An historical commemorative calendar was designed by Tatiana, and orders rolled in by the thousands. Father's own sister, Olga, our Aunt Olga, made drawings and paintings which brought large sums to charities. Large sums of cash were also donated. One well known banker, Yaroshinsky, donated over a quarter of a million rubles. He was assistant manager of Mother's own hospital train. I mention him later in the sections of this book dedicated to Tobolsk and Ekaterinburg.

There were occasional officers' balls in 1915 before Father took over the Supreme Command of the Russian Armies in the Field. Father and Mother put in brief appearances at these balls never knowing if it might be their last. Although Olga and Tatiana attended these functions, Marie and I were still too young. The always came to show off their gowns and jewelry to Marie and me so that we could participate vicariously. It made them happy to be able to change out of their nursing smocks and appear gowned in public if even for a little while.

They radiated loveliness in their complexions and sparkling eyes, so that I am sure more than one prince saw in them his future wife. Mother did not want her daughters to be coquette in public and expected them to act naturally. The romantic nature of it all was exciting to me so that I could not wait for time enough to pass so that I could also participate in such social events. Because Marie and I could not attend, we expected to be filled in on each detail over and over after our older sisters, dubbed Big Pair, arrived home. Father's sister, Olga, also realized that the ladies at the home front appreciated some diversion while the men were at the battle front so she also threw a few parties in Petrograd, the new moniker for what had been St. Petersburg. At these Sunday gatherings we would meet other young people. There were other occasions when we were invited to see dramas staged at Countess Sheremetieva's. The Countess was a close friend of our Aunt Olga. We had delightful times at these parties.

Aunt Olga and we were extremely close, more like sisters than nieces and aunt, because she was only thirteen years older than my sister Olga. The art of living was something she fully understood, so full of life and joy was she. She seemed to take the fun and joy with here when she left. Olga was an avid sportswoman and besides tennis she enjoyed skating and skiing; she played a good game of billiards, often with her mother our grandmother; also croquet and many other games. She was known for her painting skills and her art of a religious nature was appreciated in my churches. Olga was a woman of faith and loved our Orthodox religion. Religion was a topic that Aunt Olga and Mother often discussed. Aunt Olga sang beautifully and played several instruments. She was known as an excellent linguist and spoke Russian, English, French although she also had some command of both Danish and German.

The peasants were objects of her love and appreciation. Olga was a woman of little formality often bypassing the rules of etiquette de rigueur for the royal families. She considered them relics of times gone by. Dressing like a peasant brought her enjoyment. Her liberal views made her a target of cheap gossip. Prince Peter of Oldenburg, her husband, was chronically ill. Uncle Peter was fabulously wealthy but Olga was unable to bear him a child. Grandmama Marie was directly responsible for this marriage. An annulment was achieved after many years of marriage, albeit against my Father's wishes, upon which she married Colonel Nicholai Koulikovsky, a tall handsome officer, who was her former husband's aide-de-camp and the head of her hospital in Kiev. Gossiping women criticized her for her new betrothal, but Aunt Olga felt it was a matter of her own personal happiness and not that of ladies who were useless in their own right except for interfering in the lives of others.

Although Prince Peter was pleasant enough companionship alone was not enough to make their marriage completely successful. Due to the ensuing family tension this domestic issue caused, Aunt Olga was exiled, but even in Tobolsk Father continued to correspond with her.

In what was now called Petrograd Grandmama Marie, when she was there on short visits, met with her friends to roll gauze bandaging. After their meetings in the Winter Palace Olga and Tatiana often drove to the Anichkov Palace to take tea with Granny. We heard all her news from them. Mother sent us children to see her when she was not well. Some delicacy or other was always taken along as a token gift. I felt uncomfortable and selfconscious in Grandmother's presence for reasons I cannot explain. However, I did admire her as she carried herself in such a stately manner in her gorgeous frocks, mostly black.

Mother took us to Moscow to see our Aunt Ella (Elizabeth), whose husband, the Grand Duke Serge, had been assassinated by a bomb. The only image I have of Aunt Ella is of her dressed in a nun's habit with its draping simple lines which totally covered her head and hair, but her facial features were beautiful and symmetrical. There were noble men who would have done anything to wed her in a second marriage even asking Mother for assistance but it as to no avail, as Mother knew it would be impossible.

She was a wonderful source of information about history. When she first came to Russia as the bride of Serge Alexandrovich, she had studied the Orthodox religion with the court priest for the long period of several before she felt sufficiently capable of becoming a member of the Church. As a surprise on the night before Uncle Serge's name day, she informed him, "I have a gift for your name day." "A piece of jewelry?" "No, my dear, something more precious to you." Next morning she informed him "My gift to you today is my embracing the Orthodox religion." Uncle Serge replied: "This is the happiest day of my life since our marriage."

Aunt Ella was with us 1914 in the Crimea when she related to us sisters that during the Japanese war Uncle Serge had offered to take command of the army with the extreme confidence that he would win and prevent a civil war. Count Witte, the Prime Minister, on the other hand, opposed it. The ensuing controversy caused the two men to become enemies. The peace treaty, now signed, encouraged by the President of the United States, Theodore Roosevelt, caused Uncle Serge and Count Witte to fight and never come to terms. (*Editor's note: Theodore Roosevelt had also elevated Judge Kohlsaat, father of "Evgenia/Anastasia's" friends, Edith and Helen, whom she credits as being of immense help with her manuscript and "good friends," to a newly created joint seat on United States Court of Appeals for the Seventh Circuit and the United States Circuit Courts for the Seventh Circuit. The editor finds it interesting that Anastasia's uncle was involved in Theodore Roosevelt's plan and that later the daughters of a judge Roosevelt knew well befriended "Evgenia/Anastasia" almost immediately after her arrival as a married, yet husbandless immigrant from eastern Europe in the USA.)*

It was not soon after that as Uncle Serge was leaving the Kremlin in a sleigh a bomb was thrown into it killing him instantly. Aunt Ella knew the explosion was intended for her husband when she heard it. With her lady-in-waiting she ran out to find only bits and pieces remaining of his body which the two gathered with their bare hands for burial. Pieces of his shredded uniform were also gathered and kept almost as holy relics in a cross shaped container in her nun's cell. Aunt Ella joined the convent of Martha and Mary soon after this terrible murder. She wore a habit of her order (*Editor's note: which she helped to design*) in soft pale gray, which was dramatically and beautifully draped around her head. Count Witte, she maintained to the end, was behind the man who killed her husband. Nonetheless, she forgave them. To the prisoners who had murdered her husband she sent cigarettes, fruit and food while she also frequently went to visit them in prison over Father's objections. (*Editor's note: It has been proposed that the religious habit designed by Ella herself had been based on those she had known from German Lutheran deaconesses who were engaged in church work in her home of Hessen-Darmstadt. She is said to have given an icon to her husband's assassin assuring him that she had forgiven him.*)

While Count Witte was Prime Minister (1905-6) there was much unrest and chaos. Madame Narishkina often informed us children about the opening of the Duma (*elected legislative assembly*) in 1906. Mother and Grandmama Marie both wept at one reception when the people marched to the Tauride Palace singing the song of revolution. She said, "Witte gave all the power to the Duma, and because of the character of this power the Duma was dissolved in 1906." But it left the most damaging results, and these effects germinated and were ripe at the opening of the Fourth Duma in 1912. Witte was still living at that time. Even during the war the Duma so jeopardized the life of the nation that finally it collapsed.

At the beginning there was a glimmer of good news from the front and people spoke of the possibility of a "short war." There was an air of industry in the atmosphere as all seemed to give extra effort to whatever they undertook to do. Father often was obliged to take calls on the telephone which he did not want to have on his desk in his study. Father's constitutionals were not immune, and many times couriers were dispatched to catch up to him with some urgent matter or other.

# IX   FAMILY HEARTACHES

**T**HE NEWS from the front was depressing. There had been serious reverses of fortune. Father was dumbstruck. The army and, moreover, the people were dissatisfied with Grand Duke Nicholai Nicholaevich in command of the Russian armies at the front. An immediate change had become of supreme urgency.

The decision of my father was to personally take over the Supreme Command of the Russian Armies in the Field. A tragic hour was at hand. Cracks of disunity began to be evident in the army, under the Grand Duke Nicholai Nicholaevich complaining continually about Father. This criticism was expressed not only to Grandmother and our aunts but also to officers of the High Command. Father thought this looming and aging relative, measuring in at 6' 4", would be better off in the more temperate area of the Persian front, especially as he was afflicted by rheumatism. The Grand Duke insisted, however, that Father was really envious of his position.

Father was now obliged to approach the General Headquarters with the task of entrusting the government to others in his absence. Of course, he hoped for the unanimous support of the Duma, but it also entailed a hard separation from the family. Mother gave him her full blessing as she was of the mind this was the right decision. The consequence of their decision, on the other hand, was that Mother was wracked with worry from that very moment onward.

Mother drove with Father to the Cathedral of Sts. Peter and Paul, then to Our Lady of Kazan to pray for divine inspiration for this task dedicating all even unto death to the undertaking. They traversed Troitsky Bridge over the River Neva erected as a memorial to the silver wedding anniversary of Alexander III and Marie Feodorovna.

Mother purported to have seen the sign of a cross in the sky (*Editor's note: much as Emperor Constantine had seen before dedicating the Byzantine Empire to Christianity*). The ensuing interpretation robbed her of happiness, as she felt it was a portent of danger for Father. Would he became the victim of a crazed fanatic such as the one who had assassinated our grandfather, Alexander II?

The risk became poignant when we went with Father to the Alexander Station to set off for Mogilev. Guards and secret police populated the waiting room. Admittance to the area was prohibited except by special permit. Only by special invitation could ministers and relatives enter. The gigantic blue Imperial train, with its double eagle crest, left the station and we espied Father standing at the broad window of his sitting room. Great comfort was afforded us when we perceived that each hundred feet of track was guarded by a soldier with the goal of preventing accidents or bombs. The exact car in which Father travelled was unknown to all. Until the train could no longer be seen the church bells of every house of worship tolled. A direct line to General Headquarters was provided by the Nicholas Railway. Roads were searched and guards were posted days before the departure. Railroad tracks crossing the Nicholas line were removed until Father's train passed as an extra measure of defense. Once he said, "I have known from my early years that I will fall a victim for my country." Nevertheless, Father disliked all the fuss.

All of us knew that Father, now being taken away from us, would carry on efficiently and with determination. Without a doubt he would miss his family, and we determined to write him often and send him packages of items he would need and want. Fruit, books, and occasionally flowers from Livadia were dispatched for him. I can still hear Mother say, as she examined the flowers while placing them in the box, "When one sees these heavenly blossoms, how can one be reconciled to this terrible war?" All contents of the packages were lovingly and tenderly packed which Father never doubted. Mother personally packed each box making a list of what she included. A jaeger (*messenger, from the German Jaeger or hunter*), an aide-de-camp, or one of our relatives waited until it was prepared. The package was usually handed over personally by Mother and taken to the undisclosed location where Father was stationed. We always included a written message keeping him up-to-date on our lives and activities. She often included her own message written in their secret romantic code which would illustrate how her profound love for Father was eternally kindled in her heart and, certainly, in his as well.

Convention as set aside when Father was at General Headquarters. His men saw him behind enemy lines at their sides, fighting with them in solidarity. Father would do all, sacrifice his all, pledge his all to save Russia based on his solemn oath of faith to protect the Motherland. He promised to do so the day he took the Crown. He said, "I shall not allow my people to be insulted and to be trampled upon by the enemy."

He was a great inspiration to his troops, imparting them happiness, assuring them that he loved them even more than his own beloved and cherished family.

News of various victories reached our ears. The end of conflict must surely be in sight especially as we learned that tens of thousands of prisoners were taken at a time. "A supreme success," Father assured us in his letters home. A few months later Kaiser Wilhem wanted to sign a peace accord.

Father wrote in Spring 1916 that he would not be able to celebrate *Pascha* (Easter) at our side. Never before had he ever been away from us on this supremely important Christian holiday, which in the Orthodox Christian religion is commemorated even more fervently than Christmas. A gift sent from General Headquarters (*GHQ*) reached Mother, a gorgeous Faberge Easter egg which he had personally designed. This precious item was made by Faberge himself due to the fact that many of his artisans were serving or had even been killed at the front. M. Faberge made a personal delivery to opened in our presence.

Mother opened the beautifully wrapped package and exclaimed, "It is exquisite. How can human hands make such a beautiful work of art?"

As she opened the unique objet d'art daintily crafted miniatures of us children were revealed in a row. Mother's declared wish to own a miniature of us children had not been forgotten by our father. M. Faberge was ostensibly very pleased as we all were. That Easter (*Pascha, The Feast of the Resurrection of Jesus Christ*) the service was celebrated by Father Vassiliev at the Feodorovsky Sobor and we all partook of Holy Communion (*preceded by obligatory fasting and confession with absolution*). Pascha afternoon was the traditional opportunity to distribute gifts to the hospital patients. Porcelain eggs and real eggs with some sweets were bestowed as presents. We children prepared strings of special china eggs. On them was painted the gold-crested double eagle with Mother's initials on one side and the Red Cross emblem on the other. A hole was located lengthwise from one end to the other so that a ribbon could be pulled through in order to place it under a blessed icon above which flickered an oil burning *lampadka*, a kind of lamp used in the veneration of holy images. Commissioned porcelain Easter eggs created at the atelier of M. Faberge were distributed by Father to the Allied Mission as well as to select others. Some of these were dispatched to Petrograd to Lady Sybil Grey (*cousin Sir Edward Grey was Foreign Secretary, and her brother Charlie served at Flanders*) at the English Hospital so that she might give them to her patients. Lady Sybil received an unique egg herself in appreciation for her exemplary work at the hospital, with one also destined for Lady Buchanan. Gold enamel bijou trinkets were given as gifts to the maids in our household as it was a custom for many girls to wear a necklace of them for six weeks preceding Ascension Day (*Editor's note: the day commemorating Christ's rising into heaven in a cloud promising to return in the same way*).

Olga had wanted to wear a pretty new frock for Pascha while Mother insisted that Olga and Tatiana wear their nurse's uniforms as usual. This was cause for a minor difference of opinion between Mother and Olga who implored her to please allow her to wear her dress. Mother would not budge in the least bit. As we were expected to do, we complied by going to our our assigned hospitals, but we sisters were of the mind that in this case our mother was in the wrong as the patients would have enjoyed seeing us in our Easter finery.

Alexei, quite perplexed, came running into our bedroom that evening informing us that "Olga was crying." He scurried to his tutor's room and then returned. We wasted no time in entering her bedroom attempting to comfort her. We bolstered her by saying that we too thought that Mother had not been just in this decision. Mother never knew how he felt about this event, and Olga, as I remember, quickly forgot it also.

> (*Editor's note: The Orthodox celebration of what is called Easter in the west is known in Russia and Slavic Orthodox lands as Pascha. Somewhat resembling the western practice of Lent, the fast before Pascha is strict, so that the celebration of the day and period after*

*it is more ebullient perhaps than in Catholic or Protestant lands. Although in Eastern and Western Christianity all foods are clean and nothing forbidden, there are forbidden foods during this time before Pascha. Even in the period outside of this Lenten fasting season, Wednesdays and Fridays are days of fasting throughout the year. Wednesday is thought to be the day that Judas hatched the plot to betray Jesus Christ for money, and Friday, of course, is the day on which Jesus was crucified. On those days throughout the year meat and meat products (lard for example), along with fish (although shellfish are allowed), eggs and dairy products, olive oil and alcoholic beverages are all on the NO list. Curiously to some, beer has traditionally been exempted and seems to be in a category all its own. The forty day fast before Pascha, however, has its own rules. In all cases, even in non-Lenten fasting, children, elderly, pregnant women, nursing mothers and the ill are free from fasting expectations. The Great Lent period, however, is considered the most stringent period. It begins with the week before Lent called Cheese-fare week. All meat and meat products disappear, but dairy and eggs are allowed all week even on Wednesday and Friday. The first week includes reduced meals for monastics and clergy. The subsequent weeks there is strict fasting every day, though wine and oil are permitted on Saturdays and Sundays. Holy Friday (Good Friday) no eating is permitted at all and laymen are encouraged to follow this tradition. After Holy Saturday liturgy some parishes break the fast with fruit and wine, and Easter/Pascha Sunday, all that has been prohibited is now eaten.)*

Mother was greatly preoccupied that Father might be lonely without his family and burdened by responsibilities and duties. Imagine our mother's overwhelming surprise, however, when Father wrote that he really had no time to feel loneliness. Moreover, he planned to take our brother to G.H.Q. with him to the front with the assurance that M Gilliard, the tutor from Switzerland, would go to so that Alexei's studies would not be interrupted. Dina Derevenko and Nagorny would be there too to watch over him. Dr. Fedorov was at G.H.Q. already, because he was Father's physician. He also gave lectures to the hospital staff there.

Mother gradually began to agree the more she thought about this idea with the firm conviction that Alexei would learn military science first hand. It would be beneficial for him to get acquainted with officers and men while learning about war in general and understanding how to deal with foreign representatives in particular. She was sure that Alexei would be the very best possible company for his Father. Little Alexei left home very teary-eyed for he had never been separated from his mother. Mother quietly entered his room every day to pray on her knees beside his empty bed. The separation from her son was also trying on her psychological well-being. As best we could we assured her that we too missed our little brother and this seemed to bring her some measure of consolation.

Mother's worries, however, continued to increase in the time that Alexei was with Father. Daily she placed calls to G.H.Q. to inquire as to the health and well-being of her loved ones. Was Alexei eating properly? Was he sleeping sufficiently? Was Father paying enough attention to him? The answer was to her liking, that they shared a room and were constantly together.

Despite Mother's preoccupation, Alexei was truly proud of his association with Father. This was apparent when we arrived in Mogilev.

With great pride Alexei showed us his bed beside Father's, then added, "We say our prayers together, too. But sometimes, when I am tired and forget, Papa says them for both of us."

Proudly he showed us photographs of himself standing beside Father reviewing troops and eating regular soldiers' rations. Russia could be proud of their genuine tsarevich, while the loving relationship of Tsar to son and to country was exemplary. This realization as of benefit to Mother as she dealt with Alexei's absence. While her son remained with Father at headquarters, Mother constantly referred to them in conversation as "her boys."

The fact of the matter was that all who were fighting for Russia were "her boys." My two older sisters went were Mother made rounds to the clinics and hospitals were the wounded were being treated. There were times, however, when the treatment areas were on the second floor which necessitated her being brought up in her wheelchair as she could not manage the stairs. This situation had the benefit of acting a symbol of courage to those who witnessed it. They remembered their own families and mothers and many died in peace after being in her presence. These long days of visitations depleted her of all energy so that she returned absolutely exhausted when the duties were done for the day. It was inconceivable that she would become inured to death, and this manner she regarded each passing as were it the death of her own son. Such personalization of all the suffering caused to increase her rejection of the deeds of Wilhelm and to seal her belief in the futility of war.

My mother was a devout Christian, adhered to religious teaching and the example of the Lord, but when it came to Kaiser Wilhelm she could not pray for him and allowed herself to feel hatred towards him. This hatred could be described indeed as self-consuming.

The suffering of sick and dying men became my mother's own Calvary. In the thick of night, she summoned the chauffeur to take her to the cemetery where she prayed grave to grave for individual soldiers and in general for the repose of their souls. At her request my sisters and I often planted flowers on their graves for she saw the dead as her children.

My mother was greatly misunderstood, yet these personal characteristics she genuinely displayed for those fighting for the safety and protection of Russia help to rectify that malicious misinformation. Often she insisted in being present at the most horrendous of surgeries. With great care and skill she provided the surgical instruments to the operating doctor. One of the older sisters would be nearby ready with needles ready to suture wounds and incisions.

A kind of self-sacrifice, of personal dedication, was given by Mother to these young men of Russia who were sons, brothers, husbands, and fathers of unknown thousands. The nurses were equally as conscientious and served heroically even while any of them were unpaid volunteers. Mother reviewed supplies for each hospital to insure that they were sufficiently stocked.

How long would Alexei remain at headquarters? Mother had mulled it over, and thought to bring him home after inspecting a hospital near to his location. Father and General Hanbury-Williams (*Sir John Hanbury-Williams. * 1859- +1946, head of the British military mission with the Russian High Command aka Stavka*) bade Mother to allow her beloved son to remain a bit longer, and we left without him at our side.

General Alexeiev was in complete command whenever Father was indisposed for any reason whatsoever. They discussed all military matters and had a wonderful working relationship. Alexei inspected Generals Ivanov and Brussilov's troops with Father with the intention to decorate with crosses all those heroes. Alexei made an impression on the troops. Dressed in a private's uniform our brother stood proudly beside Father during military reviews. His posture and expression were testaments to the responsibility he had internalized and accepted. Headquarters was within range of German armaments, but to Russia's benefit the Kaiser did not seem to know it. Fortunately the Kaiser did not know this. Food for Father and Alexei was prepared in the camp kitchen the same as it was for all the others.

Olga and Tatiana toiled to the point of exhaustion sitting by bedsides reading, praying for the sick, or writing letters if the patients were unable to do so. Olga was fastidious in all she undertook. An expert at raising money for the hospitals she was also a talented event organizer whose entertainment programs were always successful. Tatiana was physically stronger hence usually took the lead in their hospital work. Doctors praised her for her efficiency and methodic undertaking of all tasks. Mother sat with the ill soldiers for hours at a time, also giving prayer books to officers when they returned to the front. Madame Narishkina at Mother's side presented each officer a gift package of silken underwear fabricated in the "Marie-Anastasia Workshop." It was meant to protect them from body lice.

Alexei also visited the wounded at our hospital when he was home on leave. He was genuinely interested in the stories told by the patients never tiring of their tales. His humorous side was often revealed when he told them jokes and made them laugh in moments in which suffering and agony could be temporarily forgotten. When he had to leave just as the atmosphere was becoming joyful he often was not pleased.

Details of our visits, our schedules, our departures, etc. were never made public. The Minister of the Court, Count Fredericks, was in charge of all such scheduling and arrangements. We stopped at Mogilev during an autumn program of hospital visits. The deep forest camouflaged our headquarters in a train car on tracks hidden from view located at some distance from the station. Father and Alexei returned home with us after a few days. Alexei developed a nervous condition caused by many dangerous trips to the front and the sight of so much suffering among the wounded in the hospitals.

Olga was asked by Father to keep certain people hated by him out of our house, but Mother had the impression that they were of assistance to her. Olga did not care for Rasputin and forbade the uttering of his name in her presence. If it popped up in conversation she immediately changed the subject.

Once I heard her say to Mother, "Why do you listen to some of these women? Their minds and upbringing are so different from yours. Why do they come to you with all kinds of gossip? In their position; they should not be permitted to interfere with things that do not concern them."

Mother answered, "Yes, darling yet every ruler must have contact with the people so that they can gain access to the truth. That is how your grandmother, Queen Victoria, knew everything that was going on, precisely because she had confidential informants

Olga replied, "That is all right, Mother, but these people were not constantly in Granny's company. Especially we like to have a visit with Father when he is home for a short period. You must keep your public and private lives separate."

Olga was incensed with the callous and uninformed opinions offered by these people whom she deemed to be shallow and useless. They were the catalyst for later conflagrations. Marie was often at odds with one of Mother's so called confidantes.

An inspection at the front as planned for Chernovitsy, Bukovina was embarked upon by Father and Alexei. I would later spend time there after my escape. Father would not have imagined that one of his children would seek shelter here in the not distant future. Father had also spent time recently in Warsaw from which he returned with photos including one of thousands of grave crosses on Russian tombs while on the other side of the road were the graves of enemy forces.

Red Cross units were visited by Mother and Father as well as ambulance trains for the evacuation of the wounded villagers They made their way to field hospitals to say a few encouraging words to the wounded. As a group we gifted envelopes containing writing paper, handkerchiefs, sweets, fruit and desirable items. Our sisterly task was to bring these to Father. Ambulance trains were named in honor of each us sisters whose honor it was to meet the one named after us. Soldiers lay on hay covered with blankets on these trains. Many suffered from infections caused by German bullets which made jagged wounds in contrast with Russian bullets which made rounded wounds. Russian bullets had the reputation of making a clean cut. Contaminated water in the spring when snow began to melt were common as the men could not lay down. As the roads were destroyed due to heavy artillery, it was often very difficult to transport the sick and wounded. Trucks got stuck in muddy fields while rescue work often took place in the dark. The vision as heartbreaking.

Any available space had to be employed right up to the Catherine Palace in Tsarskoe Selo. Using her own money and that of Father, Mother had built many new hospitals at their own personal expense. Madame Zizi Narishkina was named as the head of the hospitals. Refugee homes for the victims of war were also established. Shelters, orphanages, hospitals and convalescent homes were constructed for evacuated villagers. As many as ninety military hospitals can be credited to Mother's tireless activities from Petrograd to Ukraine.

As men were released from the hospital many could no longer return to the front. Various of them went to work on farms or learned a trade. Others studied painting and sold their creations at various venues. Yet others learned weaving and made rugs, while some carved wood, sculpted, learned photography or book printing. With pride I can say that these opportunities were organized and made possible by my family.

Other members of the Imperial Family as well as Grandmama Marie followed suit. Incredibly she ordered camps to be built in Germany to house Russian prisoners of war. Regrettably a doctor and nurse returning from Germany reported on horrendous conditions there including abuse and substandard conditions including no sanitary facilities or heat. Many suffered from infectious sores while nurses were not allowed to treat them. Officers suffered beatings and denigration as they would not divulge information to the Germans.

The Kaiser's own son witnessed this while Russian Jews who had deserted in order to not serve in the army were treated better than other Russians who had entered the armed forces.

Under the auspices of the Red Cross, Mother sent supplies to these camps in Germany including Bibles, books, bandages and other necessities. Mother even created camps near stations in Siberia for German and Austrian prisoners of war who were sent to work on farms. She wished to showcase Russia as a place that could lead in its humane treatment of prisoners. She was routinely criticized for spending money for the cause of foreign prisoners and for saving enemy lives. They opined that some of these very prisoners had possibly killed their brothers, sons and husbands in battle.

My older sisters often returned home with curious stories from the hospitals and events they had personally witnessed. Coming out of anesthesia one young soldier sang and moved his arms like an orchestra conductor. After learning of his behavior he apologized fearing he may have used vulgarity in his utterances. Yet another soldier imagined he had received a letter from his bride to be and repeated sweet nothings as a sweetheart would write to her beloved.

Snuggling close to our mother was an event we all appreciated and looked forward to. Most often we could count on a letter from Father. Mother's ladies-in-waiting would receive them from couriers and would deliver them personally to Mother. Some parts of them were read to us by Mother and this seemed to give her some measure of contentment. It was her custom to open her own personal mail but she met others with great scrutiny and perhaps even suspicion. She often reacted with hot anger, tearing them to bits and throwing them away. She could not imagine how people would criticize her with all the suffering going on, and, on to add insult to injury would not sign their name. May the Lord forgive them for all the grief and injury they caused Mother, who often announced that the Germans were using the same kind of propaganda as the Japanese had employed in 1905.

We were not allowed by our father to discuss these moments of unpleasantness toward our mother. There was one time when I caricaturized one of Mother's critics, this at a time when Father was not with us. However, Mother promptly reprimanded me, while at the same time everyone burst out in laughter. I was successful in changing the atmosphere around us. Mother's eyes were red and swollen the next morning as she had spent hours and hours the night before reading such letters. She had obviously gone to sleep crying. All four girls composed a letter to Father and Alexei requesting they come home for a few days, which they did which renewed Mother's well-being. She doted on Father while Alexei's incessant talking made her cheery again. Her eyes became bright again. We all gather around Mother's bed in the evening and enjoyed our intimate times as a family which loved one another in harmony.

Mother wanted a small get away, a small abode where she could find peace from the world, separated from it for a short time. To be honest, there was so much love between our parents that they would have made a cozy house out of the must humble of homes. where she could have peace and quiet.

Father soon had to leave us, and would take Alexei with him, although we were so amused with Alexei and his antics that we could not bear to be separated from him again. However, Alexei would not hear of it as he so loved Father and was so proud to be at this side. Mother suffered when her loved ones made their departure. It was perhaps harder than had he not come at all. Mother continued to pray for their safe return, and although she was suffering Mother was also proud of their service to Russia.

Anonymous, critical letters continued to pour in to Mother who detested reading them as their content was so malicious. One did arrive signed, however, by none other than Princess Vasilchikova. She claimed to speak upon behalf of the women of Petrograd and urged Mother to return to Germany to leave Russia behind. How little she understood that the little Duchy of Hesse-Darmstadt had very little to do with the greater Prussia. What must this Russian princess think the Empress's children would do if their mother were to leave them?

Such communications were incited by those who to overthrow the Imperial family and its government to overthrow the old order and wrest control for themselves, which they eventually did.

An accusation was lodged against Mother alleging that she sat behind a screen behind her maple (*one assumes imported wood*) sitting room which let into Father's study where she allegedly listened to all the reports given Father on the progress on the war. According to this calumny, Mother transmitted all that she heard to Wilhelm in Germany. Such gossip was spread throughout Russia and via the press in other foreign countries. Due to Mother's heart condition she would have had to climb sets of stairs which were impossible for her to manage. She never left us alone in addition to the ridiculous nature of the story and its claim of Mother's spying. There was a personal attendant in the room next to Mother's. This was connected by a bell and was comfortable so that the maid could relax in comfort. Other employees were dismissed at 11:00 P.M. Since her marriage, the majority of Mother's staff had been with her continually except when we left for Tobolsk. Her loyalty to Russia was beyond reproach and her hatred for Wilhelm in Germany was known by all her knew her.

Another fictitious account maintained that German General Ludendorff had visited Mother. Such disinformation was freely circulation to attack the very heart of the Russian government in order to implode it. Mother's depression and exhaustion increased as the propaganda heightened. Some voices called for the dismissal of all government officials with foreign sounding names. Such a pointless demand would have necessitated the removal of staff such as Trina Schneider whose loyalty was exemplary. She too met the fate of death outside of Perm and had been Russian tutor to Mother and Aunt Ella.

She was now Marie and my governess. There were people of Scandinavian descent who had names which were German in origin, yet others had been in Russia since the time of Catherine the Great.

In Father's absence Mother felt compelled to inform him of every detail whether it be praise, criticism, advice and suggestions which people requested she relay to him. In comparison to the enormous problems facing the nation, the comments from the public were often trite and unremarkable. While eager for advice, more than a few came from people who really schemed for the destruction of the monarchy.

We began to realize that Father's telegrams and messages were often intercepted, altered and re-written to change their content. Inefficiency became commonplace and betrayals more common.

Mother said, "He must make his will felt, inspire wholesome fear through firmness and discipline. To inspire love is not enough." With her own background Mother often wished that Russia had some of the efficiency of the Germans. She thought Russia needed more ingenuity and greater economic independence.

More railroads for the transportation of troops and supplies were required, she believed, athough one Siberian line had just been completed during the war (in 1915).

Petrograd was a city of intrigue and murmurings. The rumor mill was in full swing and Mother did not know whom to trust or believe. Despite the lies and slander, Mother still wanted to be of help to Father and pass along information which she thought might be helpful. People no longer seemed to care what happened to their country and exuded apathy. Accusations of Anna and Rasputin were baseless. As far as Mother was concerned, these two were unjustly persecuted and hounded.

It was Anna who invested every last penny she had received as compensation for her accident to establish a very successful hospital where hundreds of invalids had been trained. When its success required more space, she bought additional land with her own money for its construction. What greater loyalty could be demanded? Mother was a believer in the efficacy of Rasputin's healing prayers. She was a personal witness to Alexei's healing miracle. Her only desire now was for her husband, our father, to receive divine guidance to lead Russia out of its travails. She questioned those who doubted that Rasputin had used his prescient foreknowledge which to see into a future hidden to others. Truly he had prophesied several events which later came true. He uttered a prediction that our death would follow his death and that if anyone survived they would meet their end in 1960. (*Editor's note: this would prove to be untrue once "Evgenia's" claim to be Anastasia is substantiated by DNA analysis, etc.*)

Uncle Ernie was also purported to be hiding in our palace. The last time Uncle Ernie had been in Russia was with his family in 1912, indeed at the new palace in the Crimea. That was the very last time he had stepped foot in Russia. Uncle Ernie abdicated in 1918, because Wilhelm had made it so difficult for him during the war. A number of letters had arrived from Aunt Victoria, Mother's sister in England. Prince Louis of Battenberg was her husband and was the First Sea Lord of the British Admiralty. He had to give up his position in his adopted country, one he was loyally serving, because of the nerve-wracking war hysteria. Grand Duke Constantine Constantinovich and his wife were in Germany when war was declared. He died the year after due in great part to the mistreatment he had suffered. The grand duke personally wrote to Father informing him of his mistreatment which greatly infuriated him.

His wife was also subjected to the same ill treatment. Grand Duke Constantine's death was a great loss, not only to the family, but to all Russia. He was a most brilliant scholar, poet and patron of music and drama. He wrote plays, essays, poems, using a pseudonym. He translated *Hamlet* into Russian. He wrote a play entitled *King of Judea*. It was a magnificent production, in which he took part. Even when his health was failing, he continued to promote the arts. The last production in which I saw him on the stage was *Hamlet*. He played the leading role of the Danish Prince himself. Some of his children had parts in it. Alexei sat with Mother in the front row during the last time we were present at one of his plays when he suddenly blurted out, "Mother, Mother, do you know that is Uncle Constantine! And that *there* is an officer of the Guards?" Uncle Constantine had subsidized the education of young people in music and drama. He had a theatre of his own and was renowned for designing his own stage settings (*The museum at Holy Trinity Orthodox Monastery in Jordanville, New York-USA has many artifacts concerning Duke Constantine, including an original copy of KING OF JUDEA*).

The grand duke was devoutly religious and brought up his family in the best Christian tradition. He suffered much misfortune even though he lived an exemplary life. His son-in-law died in the war shortly before the grand duke died. Prince Oleg, one of his sons, had also perished as a war casualty. A wounded German officer feigning death saw Oleg pursuing fleeing Germans on his horse and then shot him as he passed. Lamentably he passed away soon after in the hospital. In the chaos and violence of the revolution three more sons were brutally murdered, together with Aunt Ella, near Alapaevsk.

Shortly before the revolution Constantine's wife, Aunt Marva, and her children took tea with us. Deeply religious, it was their custom to cross themselves for safe driving before driving.

We were never to see them again which we could not have imagined. Aunt Marva was able to survive all the terrible fates which otherwise befell her innocent family.

Mother no longer came to the dinner table any more except for on rare occasion. She took her meals alone in her room and we would join her afterwards. Father's notes and letters were read repeatedly at these times. Alexei would often write something cute too and send it along. These brought much cheer to Mother, while we so very much hoped that she would stay cheery until she went to bed. To help dispel this pall of despair I tried to lighten the mood. Usually I was successful in making all of us laugh which was a welcome break from all other our worries and sadness.

Every time Mother's mood became dark again I intervened and tried to amuse my family. I employed a book of funny stories which I kept in the drawer of a table in the room. I poured over it to come up with material for my comedy routines. Some of these jokes were beyond my understanding, but I tried them anyway as I assumed they were meant to be funny. I tried them out on my family in the evening.

Father addressed the Duma during his last trip to the capital. He urged unity which he proposed would be the only thing possible to bring victory, a victory which was impending. People became optimistic having heard this rousing address. The nation rejoiced. This was heightened when we heard news that Erzerum, held long by the Turks, had fallen.

In theory, Father would have made sweeping liberal concessions but doubted that wartime was the right time to undertake such changes.

Sir John Hanbury-Williams was in Petrograd for Father's speech at the Tauride Palace (Duma) at which time he sas Olga and Tatiana. He afterwards said to Olga: "Knowing your Imperial Father the way I do, I am most sorry for His Majesty; so is all the High Command, for there is not one single word of truth in all the propaganda circulating. He assuredly does not deserve such malicious criticism." Hanbury-Williams thought that Father's address had been most enthusiastically accepted and provoke beneficial outcomes. On the other hand, the enemies of Russia were becoming apprehensive as victory eluded them. Father reiterated that he would never submit to Germany. Increasingly, our relative Wilhelm made Father his target. He aimed at him with traitors who spread their lies insidiously underground like the roots of a tree. A whispering campaign gathered steam against him, this after Mother had also suffered the most egregious of attacks especially for her friendship with Anna and Rasputin. Mother only became more stubborn, and no longer believed anyone around her. Her death had been marked, she believed, from the very moment she had touched Russian soil.

*(Editor's note: Alix von Hessen-Darmstadt, \*1872- +1918, full title: Her Grand Ducal Highness Princess Alix Viktoria Helene Luise Beatrix of Hesse and by Rhine, later Alexandra Feodorovna Empress Consort of All the Russias)*

# X    MOGILEV

Father celebrated his forty-eight birthday May 6, 1916. We made our way to G.H.Q the day before to be able to spend this special day with him at Mogilev. We remained on our train as was our custom. The Allied High Command and Russian officers as well as a few of our relatives arrived also to join the humble festivities.

Mother did not relish meeting members of the Allied Military Missions, many of whom she did not yet know, as she was rather retiring and timid socially. On the other hand, we did know quite a few of the Russian officers. Several friends were there who included General Keller, Generals Ivanov, Lechitsky, Dieterichs, Yanin, Resin, Kornilov, Brussilov, Father's Chief of Staff, General Alexeiev, General Dubensky, the military historian attached to G.H.Q., and Captain Nilov. General Ruzsky, who left such a bad impression in the Baltic, generally considered a traitor, was also in attendance. (*Editor's note: Nikolai Vladimirovich Ruzsky, \*1854- + 1918; He is called a traitor by her perhaps as he had resigned his position and gone to the Caucasus where other Tsarist generals were gathered until arrested by Bolshevik forces and finally executed*)

We attended Divine Liturgy in the military chapel located under the thick pines. Officers and nobility were also there to join in worship.

Flowers originating in Crimea had been ordered by Mother for this happy day. Arrangements were created by my sisters and me to decorate Father's study and bedroom. A lovely bouquet graced the icon of St. Nicholas on Father's bedroom table. Large branches of white orchids were artistically arranged on the piano located in the large hall.

About fifty guests enjoyed a sit down dinner. Russian generals with their wives sat alongside foreign guests as well as a number of the Grand Dukes who had arrived at Mogilev especially for this occasion.

Mother, Father and we children stood in the reception line as all the invited guests extended their warm wishes. White dresses with ostrich feather trimmed white hats were selected for us girls to wear on that day. Uncle Serge Mikhailovich, the Russian artillery commander congratulated Father. Grand Duke Cyril and his brother the Grand Duke Boris Vladimirovich, barely disguising their disdain for our family and in particular our mother, eventually reached Father where they wished him a happy day.

Mother sat next to Father at the dinner table and on her other side Alexei took a place of honor. Olga, Hanbury-Williams and the others sat across from them. We enjoyed a motion picture in the evening, followed the next morning by a pleasant walk in the forest in the company of our relative, Prince Igor Constantinovich. How much we reveled in the overwhelming display of spring flowers that Nature spread before us.

We inspected hospitals all the way from Mogilev to Sevastopol, Crimea. Tsarskaya Pristan (dock) in Sevastapol provided the opportunity to enjoy the greetings of sailors from Navy vessels. At every stop the people pressed forward with largely warm and friendly greetings bearing flowers, fruits, and gifts of money for the hospitals. The Romanov Institute of Physical Therapy was the site of the next surprise stop. We met Admiral Kolchak in Evpatoria. Kolchak later played an important role in fighting the Communists in 1918 with the goal of capturing Ekaterinburg in order to rescue us. In that endeavor, regrettably, he was brutally betrayed by Czech troops. Anna, who had been sent there by Mother on a special mission some weeks earlier, sat with us for tea. Sadly, Father and Alexei went back to Mogilev while we journeyed toward Tsarskoe Selo. Anna returned to the Crimea having accompanied us for several station stops.

A rumor begun by German agents purported that Mother and Aunt Ella were hiding Uncle Ernest (*Onkel Ernst*). It upset my Mother so much that she had a heart attack. The vicious lie was the catalyst for growing unrest.

This malicious propaganda gave rise to protests in Moscow, while Mother was told that Kerensky, who up to that point had shown restraint, now urged Guchkov to incite a revolution to strike while the iron was hot. It was Mother's opinion that he should be taken to the gallows and hanged for such treason. Kerensky plotted against my family in contrast with Father who was at the front making every effort to force Kaiser Wilhelm to his knees. Wilhelm was even offering a separate olive leaf with the justification that an alliance with Germany would be more beneficial for Russia that one with Great Britain.

Father ignored as senseless all such overtures, for he had already gleaned from interviews with captured German officers, that Wilhelm was losing all power in Germany. They had confided such to General Tatishchev, Imperial Chamberlain. Cousin Wilhelm could only negotiate from a position of weakness, and Father would have absolutely nothing to do with it.

Mother went with Anna to Mogilev again. The decision to travel with her friend was the catalyst for more uproar and derision. Grand Duke Dimitri Pavlovich, our own cousin, spread the vicious and untoward lies which alleged that Anna had somehow hypnotized Father with a potion that she had slipped into a drink. Dimitri had been loved by Father as were he his own son, and with a Judas-like action he betrayed his mentor and tsar. More disinformation in the form of fabricated falsehoods purported that gold was being shipped to Germany in the coffins claimed to be for German war dead.

Mother stubbornly rejected these lies and reacted increasingly vexed. Father and she would be the first to always defend any friend falsely accused of wrongdoing. We wondered how anyone could believe these falsifications lodged against Father, especially when they were definitely proven to have been false. Madame Narishkina was of the pious opinion which she shared with us that to her mind Mother's friends had brought her nothing but misfortune. She certainly had an undeniable point but others were also responsible for these misfortunes. The prevailing chaotic conditions of the war made it easy to believe in this odious rumor and deceit. One involved the tale that when the family had been in the Crimea some years before the war that Father's desk would be graced with a fresh arrangement of flowers in which a card signed "Ania" was placed.

Wagging tongues latched onto this even though it was a proven fact that Anna Vyrubova had been on the Gulf of Finland in the village of Terijoki nowhere at all near the Crimea. The intrigue escalated later when Princess Sonia Orbeliani, once Mother's lady-in-waiting, instigated an attack against Anna offering the malicious version that Anna herself had hired a gardener to place the flowers with the card.

Yet another falsehood despicably placed Rasputin entering our children's rooms via a back porch. However, there never was a "back porch" at any time anywhere. It is, however, true that on one occasion he did come upstairs to see Alexei in his sickbed. At that one unique time he ascended using the private spiral stairway from Mother's apartments. At any visit after that Alexei was brought downstairs to see the Starets. Rasputin was always accompanied by Father Vassiliev usually when the Emperor himself was also present. With focused investigation Father found that no one at all had ever seen Rasputin in the palace at unauthorized times, but had been told to say so by a certain person. Personally, I never saw the peasant in any of our private chambers. Access was prohibited as there were guards at all times at the entrances to the staircases. So many people were involved in security that it would have been impossible to go undetected.

Lamentably, this prevarication became more and more embellished with the result that Mother's reputation became increasingly more sullied. Most of these instances of gossip were generated by those who had never even seen a member of the Imperial family or stepped foot at Tsarskoe Selo. All villagers were known to the authorities and unauthorized interlopers were immediately detained and removed. All entering these private grounds had to have credentials on their persons at all times.

The originators of these fallacious tales later came to regret their wagging tongues, alas their remorse came too little too late. Many created these hurtful accounts in order to force Father to return home where he was needed.

Alexander Park was encircled by barbed wire on top of a wrought iron fence. There were regularly placed sentinels around the entire perimeter. Regular searches took place to ensure its safety. No one, absolutely no one, could enter the palace without strenuous vetting and bureaucratic paperwork. Four entrances led into the palace. Rasputin never had permission to use the main gate. Upon later rumination, this custom was probably a mistake as it made his infrequent visits seem clandestine. Always in the company of Father Vassiliev, Rasputin always entered through the side or garden gate (across from the Znamensky Cathedral) which was accessible to only a few. Even though entry this way was a bit easier, it was equally as recorded just as at the main gate. Peter the Great had created these official entrances although the Communists destroyed many of them when they invaded.

Each visitor had his or her name written down many times and paperwork on which was stated the nature of the visit, whom they were going to see and other identifying information. The exact time of arrival and entry were recorded efficiently down to the very minute. Every car or carriage was checked once again halfway up the driveway where the identity and purpose of the visitor was once again reviewed. A telephone call would have been placed by the sentry to the palace guard, so that they would be prepared for the arrival of the vetted guest. The guard on duty opened a square window reinforced by bars and the visitor was ushered into a room where they presented their calling card to the authority on duty. This officer checked the name and cross referenced it with photos in various albums kept there and around the palace. After passing such strenuous scrutiny, the visitor was escorted into the reception room and Mother received him. This was standard procedure for each and every visitor.

A record of each visitor was kept once again by a guard at the entrance of each room with the exact time of entrance and departure noted. The palace police received all of these records. In the corridors and stairways were no less than thirty-five guards at all times. All the palace staff, including the well-known Mistress of the Robes, Madame Narishkina, and the ladies-in-waiting had to abide by these stringent regulations. Even when Father or we arrived, we took part in the process. At no moment whatsoever were any of us ever left unattended. We had no idea of what privacy was as we were constantly enveloped by official staff which included our teachers, ladies-in-waiting, governesses, nurses even chambermaids who frequently entered our rooms.

Secret police continually checked every activity of everyone. It would have been impossible to enter or leave in secrecy. No doubt there was a file on Rasputin with a complete record of his visits to the minute, showing how long he had been there and whom he had seen; and the names of the officers on duty had to appear in the record, especially after it was rumored that Rasputin was a spy. The secret police were watching him; according to some it was only for his own protection. But, at the same time, his activities were being carefully scrutinized. One slip on his part would have sent him to his death.

A copy of such records was kept by the palace chief of police while yet another copy was delivered to the chief of police in Petrograd. During our arrest these records where scoured for information on Rasputin and ourselves to the very day that we left the palace. The ministers gather around Rasputin which caused many troubles, because the Starets gained a false sense of importance in their presence.

Had Kaiser Wilhelm been in our household to hear how we spoke of him, he would have known the truth about Mother who was accused of having pro-German leanings. Alexei and I created effigies of Wilhelm out of our down filled pillows, and we would use a toy gun to shoot at them. We were forbidden to even utter the name "Wilhelm" within the palace.

Olga Constantinovna, wife of King George I of Greece, sister of the Grand Duke Constantine Constantinovich, sat down to have a heart to heart with Mother about Rasputin. Father's friend, Prince Volkonsky, paid a visit to warn about him too. Aunt Ella had became so upset by these rumors that she had sent a friend and distant relative of ours, Count Sheremetiev, to deliver a message that Rasputin had been invoking the name "Romanov" for his personal enrichment while inebriated in Moscow. Having become inured to such prattle, Mother and Father even now refused to believe it. Father was obviously very distressed that the count, highly educated, could have lent credence to such a tall tale. Indeed, Sheremetiev and his well respected family had been instrumental in raising great sums of money to support hospitals. Their spacious Petrograd villa had been set aside as a clinic for recuperating officers, and they utilized their own finances to keep it running. Beyond that, two of their sons were actively involved in fighting at the front.

Aunt Ella then personally appeared at Tsarskoe Selo. She wanted to speak in private to her sister about Rasputin, but Mother pressed her asking, "Sister, you do not believe all that do you?" Ella said, "Not I, but the people, yes!." Mother insisted, "Who are these people to whom you refer? Please do not speak, as the others do. Your friends tell you nothing but lies which contain not one word of truth."

Mother was uniquely distraught and could never truly forgive Aunt Ella who implied that God might take Alexei from Mother as a punishment. Mother was cut to the quick. Aunt Ella sank to her knees the next morning imploring my parents. They maintained steadfastly their refusal to believe the story. Instead Father issued an order to his aide-de-camp: "Have a train ready for the Grand Duchess' departure."

Visibly shaken Father left at once for G.H.Q. When Aunt Ella now entered the same room from which he had departed she used her handkerchief to continually dry her eyes of copious tears. How sad it was for Mother and her sister to bide each other farewell, just as it was for us children as well. For the very last time in our lives we would kiss her good-bye. We would never see her again. As she departed she raised one of her hands while intoning: "Remember the fate of the other Empresses."

Mother, Olga, and Tatiana went with her to the station. It was divulged to us later than Aunt Ella already knew that Rasputin was to be killed.

Mother wondered quite frequently why people reached their ill-informed assessments from a place of stupidity and ignorance. They were unable to judge using the criteria of all the good we had done and wondered why. How could anyone think so errantly? The love of Russia which Mother felt so passionately led her to once declare, "I would rather die than see Germany win the war!" At the same time she was thoroughly British. Granny (Queen Victoria) had looked after her for a great deal of her life while she developed a dislike for her cousin, Kaiser Wilhelm from an early age. This was partly due to Wilhelm's disregard for their common grandmother.

Mother began to receive more correspondence than ever. Someone wrote to her of an article in the illustrated magazine Niva which depicted a dog undergoing vivisection. I could not find this edition on the table in the room adjoining Mother's where she usually kept periodicals. Mother immediately requested Mr. Shcheglov, our librarian, to find it and bring it to her. I thumbed through the pages to find the article for her when it mysteriously opened up to that very page. The helpless creature was strapped to a table on which it was undergoing surgery without anaesthesia. Such a disgusting and despicable image affected us immeasurably. Mother took the initiative to ban such cruel and inhumane practices in which no measures were taken to protect animals from pain during laboratory work.

Technicians and medical men became incensed with Mother for this action. All of us had always felt compassion for animals, especially Alexei had the habit of adopting homeless animals. He never feared them and made sure they were well fed. My precious little brother promised, "Some time I shall have a large place for all the animals who have no home. I will feed them and care for them myself." War displaced many unfortunate animals. Alexei sent dozens of stray cats and dogs to our farms. He was extremely proud of how helpful the animals were and told a farmer once, "I am positive there is not a mouse left here." The farmer readily agreed.

Mother continually received appeals for help. Mothers asked her to locate their missing sons. She appealed to the authorities to correct any wrong that had been brought to her attention. When she became overwhelmed by the enormity of it all she quickly made her way to church for religion was more than a tradition, it was truly her life.

She loved the aesthetic of the traditions which included candles, chanting and prayers. She found strength in imploring God to assist and guide her. She felt it help her to think more clearly and to trust more intimately God's will for life with ever growing humility. On the other hand, she declared that dishonesty, insincerity, friction and perfidious gossip were responsible for obfuscating her sense of Divine Will. Disunity at this time of war was treasonous to both Church and State. She fervently wished for a new kind of system so that Alexei would not be burdened in the future with the yoke of inherited autocracy.

Father had sworn solemnly that he would never sign a peace agreement with foreign enemy soldiers still on Russian land. Only a revolution could defeat Russia, and this fact was deeply understood by Russia's enemies. This was the motivation for them to spread deceit and disinformation in order to foment rebellion and negatively influence the Russian mind.

At the core of these falsehoods was the fabricated notion that Mother was increasing pro-German activities. Father was attacked in the Duma in an effort to rob him of credibility. There was an increasing number of friends who would no longer participate in the meetings of the Duma as they could not tolerate the calumny opened expressed with Father as the target.

These words are painful for me to put in writing, and I shall not further denounce these slanderers, as it would be against my Christian belief.

General Headquarters reported home that Alexei had caught a cold on the train ride to the front. Upon sneezing a blood vessel burst in his nose. Dr. Fedorov was unable to stop the bleeding so he asked Father to return to Tsarskoe Selo anticipating that the situation might take a turn for the worse. Because of the shaking and bumping of the train on the tracks, Alexei went from bad to worse, so much so that the train had to make regular stops so that his dressings could be changed. Frequently he fainted along the way so that Nagorny had to support his head the entire night. It was feared he would not survive.

Telegrams continued to arrive continually at Tsarskoe Selo informing us of Alexei's condition. Mother fretted that she may have lost her son, hence she waited all night for the wires to arrive. Anna telephoned Rasputin at six o'clock in the morning requesting prayers for Alexei's well being and cure. The Starets replied that Alexei would be better as the bleeding would cease. As if by divine design the blood did stop not long after Rasputin's message.

Anna then called Rasputin to inform him of Alexei's progress. As Alexei was brought to the platform Mother greeted them, he opened his eyes and smiled as he received her kiss. For this special grace of her son's survival Mother was very grateful. While Alexei recovered from his illness at home, Father was on his way again to G.H.Q.

Both parents agreed that as soon as Alexei's health condition improved he should return to Mogilev. He must be prepared for his future responsibilities as Tsar of Russia in spite of his compromised health. Father wanted to avoid what he himself had experienced as a sheltered youth during this reign of Alexander III, hence he wanted Alexei to be as involved as possible now.

Whenever the war might end, Alexei was to go to England with his tutors for a special course of study and preparation. All of this speculation strained Alexei and he became increasingly nervous. He once went into our eldest sister, Olga's, room at two o'clock in the morning worried sick and unable to sleep.

I was deeply moved when I was asked to share responsibility with Olga and Tatiana. It was deemed undesirable to allow Mother to be unaccompanied at night in her room while Father was away. This despite the fact that a maid was in the next room the whole time. We sisters made a schedule to take turns during the night as well as time after school hours. Alexei also wanted to help and was hurt when he was not included in the project. He demanded, "Am I not a member of the family? I am tired of taking humiliations from you. You seem to enjoy giving me orders." His responsibility, I told him, was to keep Father company and share his room when he was at G.H.Q. This seemed like a satisfactory solution to him.

I assisted Mother in any way that I could helping to keep her happy and to make her life easier by sparing unnecessary activity. I took my responsibility very seriously and was somewhat taken aback that she seemed bewildered at my sudden attentiveness. As I made her life less strenuous, Mother often called me her "little helper" which pleased me to no end. I often had to run upstairs to warn Alexei to stop telephoning Mother so frequently as was his custom. The sense of important responsibility filled me with self-satisfaction. We all worried that Mother's health might suffer due to all the strain she was under. Indeed, the condition of her heart had deteriorated to the point where she could no longer volunteer at the hospital giving direct care to the wounded.

Investigations into diverse reports about Rasputin were ordered by Father when he was at home. In one instance, he had purportedly boasted that an embroidered shirt he was wearing in public at a restaurant had been presented to him personally by Mother, the Empress. This tale originated with the man whom Father knew and had also disliked for a long time. He questioned the peasant who was taken by surprise and became frightened. Upon confessing to the deed, Father directly challenged him by asking. "How dare you?" Father stared directly into his eyes. Without ceremony an aidede-camp showed Rasputin the door. Olga confessed that she regretted that he had not been thrown out well before that.

Father never liked nor believed in the Starets and neither did we girls. Even Alexei was doubtful about the peasant's honesty. In our presence, Rasputin was always respectful and unobtrusive. Mother, however, was convinced that Alexei's life during his most severe attacks was saved by Rasputin's prayers.

Mother was impressed by the his folk wisdom and easy ways. Beyond that she held the belief that he had indeed been sent by God. Anna was the main deliverer of messages from Rasputin to Mother. Mother saw this wandering monk at Anna's residence where their conversations always revolved around God and religion.

Surely, he was a faith healer of the kind known traditionally in various Christian Churches His powers to cure were dismissed by many with the comment that he always appeared in the situation when Alexei would have recovered just the same without him. Rasputin was blamed one time when Alexei taken sick after someone had injected him with some substance in the lower abdomen causing him to suffer. Rasputin demanded the nurses and maids go to confess at the church, so it was discovered that someone else close to the family was responsible for this particular incident.

Alexei's attacks become fewer and less serious. Perhaps he would outgrow this malady my parents hoped. Alexei did think that Rasputin was a healer but was also unsure of him. "Tell me, Mommy, why is it that God listens to the peasant's prayers, but not to mine." It was easy to understand how Mother truly lent credence to the notion that Rasputin was able to save her son. Any mother would have thought the same given the circumstances.

Father Vassiliev was once as our guest for dinner. Alexei was recovering from a bad cold. He wanted to know why some people called Rasputin a saint, a question that Father thought should be handled by the priest. A theological answer was given that all who lived by the Scriptures and do good deeds could someday become a saint. "Then what shall I do that God will listen to my prayers?" Alexei wondered out loud.

Father Vassiliev of Feodorovsky Sobor was Alexei's mentor for religion. Alexei felt a deep bond with this man who was genuinely kind and was intensely loyal to his friends. Alexei was intelligent with fine facial features, a clear and light complexion and reddish brown hair. His secret nickname was "Ruchka" (the hand), but in reality he knew what people called him.

# XI      OUR LAST AUTUMN IN TSARSKOE SELO

What a lovely autumn we had in 1916. The oaks burned orange, the beech trees russet; all the elms and linden trees fused with these brilliant hues to create an artistic harmony as had they been painted by a talented artist. This was to be our last such season in Tsarskoe Selo.

Father and Alexei, again together at G.H.Q. reviewed the troops together. Father would always visit the field kitchens to try the food in order to it met the standards which had been put into place. The hospitals in Kiev were next on his schedule of planned visits which allowed him the opportunity to visit Grandmama who had made her residence in the lovely palace near the Dnieper River for the entire course of the war. She chose this spot in order to be near her daughter, our Aunt Olga.

Alexei immediately sent a message home after he had arrived back at G.H.Q. from this trip with Father. Indeed, he had perceived that our grandmother had somehow changed. He had overheard a conversation between Father and her about his illness and the role of Rasputin. Although Alexei already knew he was "Ruchka" behind his back, Grandmama did not realize it. Various other kin participated in this heart to hearts including Alexander Mikhailovich, our Uncle Sandro, who was in Kiev as the director of military aviation.

In these talks Aunt Olga favored Mother's position while her mother, our grandmother and Father's mother, made Mother the object of all her criticism. She made no attempt to inform them all that she foresaw imminent doom. Sensitive Alexei gave Mother his solemn word that he would take responsibility for his own health in order to not needlessly burden Father. When he was alone with us later on, he confessed that he no longer loved our grandmother as he once had and had cried in secret when Father was in his study.

By this time Aunt Olga was enjoying married life with her second husband who a handsome officer of the guard, Colonel Nicholai Koulikovsky.

We sisters and Mother undertook a renewed visit of various hospitals and were always received with great warmth and jubilation. Generous donations continued to arrive to help keep the hospitals financed. We had the opportunity to stop at G.H.Q. where we could visit Father. We were never to return to headquarters after that. In this particular visit we sensed immediately that Father was terribly vexed with Rasputin due to his familial interactions the last time in Kiev.

Father requested that his mother return to the Crimea to put an end to the wagging tongues which she fanned. Aunt Olga even entreated her to make her way to Crimea for the sake of God. All attempts to persuade her were to be for naught.

Uncle Sandro, Aunt Xenia's husband, made a recommendation to Father that he should announce a Constitution on December 6, St. Nicholas Day, because it was Father's patron saint and his name day. Father rejected this idea, however, saying that he had sworn on the Bible that he would never forsake the autocracy.

It had already come to our attention that there was a plan to murder Mother, Father and many of his aides, especially Prince Dolgorukov, Captain Nilov, A.D.C. Mordvinov, Count Fredericks et al in an assassination attempt. Supposedly the plan had been hatched in Kiev by Guchkov. *Granny and the Grand Duke Nicholai Nicholaevich in Caucasia supported the idea* (*boldened here as may be new information for researchers*), nonetheless, our grandmother finally confessed to Father that she had known nothing about it. Purportedly, she had been under the impression that they were only working toward an eventual abdication in favor of Grand Duke Nicholai Nicholaevich.

Mr. Pelts, former governor of Mogilev had also confided to Father that he had also learned of the plot to assassinate all those targeted but that many officers approached by Guchkov had flatly refused to participate in such a crime.

Guchov enjoyed a close relationship with the secret police, yet Father demanded more evidence of this treasonous act. Grandmama had expressed the wish that we children go to her in Kiev, but we were so frightened that our parents would be murdered in our absence that we did not go.

After the abdication and before Father left Mogilev, Granny came on her train to Mogilev. Even then she blamed the abdication on Mother. Then Father asked her whether she knew of the plan to assassinate him and Alicky, his wife. She cried that she had not known of the plan to murder but had encouraged the abdication. With these words they parted forever.

Whatever the case, it was clear that Father had been marked for suffering from the very day that the brother of Lenin had been executed and from the day the same fate had befallen Trotsky's brother. That criminal had been involved with one of the most dangerous revolutionary organizations in Russia at the time of the war with Japan.

In the governor's mansion in Mogilev Father had used an entire section of a floor with a magnificent view of the Dnieper River, set high on a forested hill. There were two large rooms set aside for Father on that floor which included a bedroom shared with Alexei. They slept in two iron beds between which was table set with a copy of the Bible and an icon. The room was furnished with a mahogany dressing table, a wash stand, a settee, and a bookcase. On one side of the room one could enjoy a view of the river, while the other side offered vistas of the the garden and the parade grounds. Father's office looked down on the parade grounds.

An enormous desk in Victorian style was set with family photos, several barometers and a floor lamp. Alexei did his school work at his own desk next to which was a settee and a bookcase. In the anteroom two portraits of Father and Mother could be viewed.

Next was a large, gloomy dining room. The entire suite had parquet floors and fine carpets. There was also a large dining room there which was rather gloomy and uninviting. There were parquet floors and Persian carpets throughout the entire suite.

Above and below Father on the other floors resided General Voyeykov, Count Benckendorff, Prince Vasily Dolgorukov, A.D.C. Nilov, Dr. Fedorov and Dr. Derevenko in charge of Alexei's health. Prince Igor Constantinovich was a frequent visitor. General Dubensky often conferred with Father. With Father was also General Dubensky. The general was a friend of the Grand Duke Dimitri, Count Sheremetiev, A.D.C. Drenteln, and others.

Father was surrounded by many military escorts including his bodyguard Dendeniev, a tall officer and Cossack who barely left his side. He was a remarkably talented sharpshooter who could hit the smallest target flying through the air with incredible accuracy never missing. Another personal guard of Father, Polupanov, was also omnipresent.

Short trips including drives to the beautiful Archayerevsky woods were part of our time at Mogilev. While Alexei played with cadets, we sometimes went for walks in the snow. Quite a ways away from the home was an Army field chapel nestled under the pine trees field chapel. The General Staff office was also nearby.

There was not enough space for everyone who was stationed in Mogilev so that government buildings and a number of private residences were converted into use by the military staff and hospitals. Wintertime luncheons were held by Father in his dining room. Soldiers home from duty on the front were invited to dine with Father at these meals. Military discussions did not take place when the soldiers took luncheon with Father. These happened in the morning at the Supreme Command. Father was not one to tarry at table after he had finished dining and he left the table almost immediately, followed by all others who had been sitting with him.

Summer luncheons were, in contrast, almost always outside under a tent under the pine trees. When we were present Father spent as much time as possible with us on our train. When we were alone he poured his own tea. On another track Father had his own train at which end there was his private study always guarded by two powerful Cossacks.

General Hanbury-Williams was present during one of our visits and happily talked to us about his family, especially his two sons fighting in the army. He was a wonderful friend to Alexei, and with General Rickel spoke to Mother about her son. They assured her that his presence helped them to forget the nastiness of war with the recommendation that she allow him to remain at Mogilev. Indeed, our little brother did remain at G.H.Q. where General Hanbury-Williams often dined with Father and Alexei.

We returned to Tsarskoe Selo only to find Princess Sonia Orbeliani (*Sonia Orbeliani-only daughter of Prince Ivan Orbeliani and Princess Maria Sviatopolk-Mirskaya, \*1875- +1915*), one of Mother's ladies-in-waiting, was critically ill. Some years before she had fallen from her horse and terribly injured her back. Her spine had now begun to cause her extreme pain and grief. Total paralysis was the outcome. A dedicated special nurse cared for her, and she continued to remain in our house. Our rooms adjoined so that Mother could easily visit her each night to make sure she was comfortable. Her presence, however, was the cause for much envy and jealous among the other ladies in Mother's retinue. Anna Vyrubova and Sonia did not like each other so that they often quarreled. Sonia was still a young woman when she eventually died. In the Crimea we sisters would take her for walks and push her in her wheelchair. It is a blessing that she passed away, before the destruction which awaited us transpired.

Father and Alexei were able in time to attend her funeral (*Editor's note: it was reported that she awoke from a fever to see the Empress at which point she thanked her for all the kindnesses that Her Imperial Highness had shown her falling then into an immediate coma and dying soon after.*)

Father's visit was to be short so that his intention was to spend as much time with the family as possible. However, Anna invited herself the very first evening. Mother was so out of sorts that she blurted, "I hope Anna can live one day without seeing me!"

Alexei and we four sisters left Mother's room early that evening with the sincere hope that Anna would follow our example. On the contrary, our mother confessed that Anna had stayed well into the night. In order to avoid Rasputin's being consulted in case Alexei was afflicted again by his illness, Father had told sister Olga that he would keep our brother at G.H.Q. after Christmas.

Father confided to us a particular event that had transpired in one of the military hospitals which concerned a wounded soldier who had received St. George's Cross for bravery. It was one of the highest honors that the Russian military could bestow on any man. As a special request, the recipient of the award requested signed photos of all us in the family which he duly received. Upon his discharge a list of German codes was found in his bedside drawer. The photos had not been for him, rather earmarked for a propaganda campaign in which leaflets with the photos on them would be dropped on Russian soldiers at the front. Other persons well known were involved; after confessing to his plot in the scheme, the soldier was executed while surveillance of his Latvian mother was undertaken.

Disloyalty was rampant in the palace Father discovered to his great dismay. Even German machine guns had been discovered hidden near Peterhof as well as at the perimeters of our farms at Dudendorff and in the outskirts of our farms at Dudendorff.

It was a mystery how any of these weapons could have been smuggled in. We were now in danger. While propaganda had failed at the front, it was rampant elsewhere. Homes, schools, hospitals, and other environs virtually seethed with it. It penetrated the essence of the

Russian mind. We found a leaflet in the palace in which the headline screamed: "Germans are killing the Russian peasants, confiscating their cattle and taking everything for themselves." The article went on to say that Mother was a spy and was collaborating with German agents. How this folder came to be placed on the table remained a mystery. Mother's real sorrow was that now Russia had begun to believe these unfounded lies.

King George of England let it be known to Mother that he wished her to arrive at Sandringham for a well deserved rest, but she refused to entertain the notion with the words: "I shall rest when the war is over," she said.

Many peacetime guards had been removed from duty at the palace and sent to the front without Father's knowledge or permission so that the palace was not sufficiently managed. Father's orders were not followed when he asked for guards to be sent to replace those who had left. Quite the opposite, revolutionaries came to take their place.

After Christmas 1916 in Kiev we were never to see Grandmama Marie again. Anna was again with us for this event. We gradually perceived that despite the feigned politeness shown to her, Ann was really held in low esteem, even disdain by more and more people.

Anna was cognizant of the fact that her friendship with our mother was really the cause of much suffering. We all made our way to the ancient city of Novgorod. we were met The Governor arrived at the station to welcome us with the traditional bread and salt with flowers for Mother which were sent by a squadron of Mother's Uhlan Guards.

The streets were crowed with military men, school children, and civilians. Handkerchiefs waved their greetings, men through their hats in the air, while flowers were strewn in front of our limousines. Having arrived at the cathedral special carpets were spread before us on which to enter while the sanctuary was teeming with the faithful, including Princes Igor Constantinovich and Andrei Alexandrovich. Igor remarked later when we sat down to luncheon, "The people most assuredly displayed great joy and devotion to you."

Mother was given a very kind reception when she visited the hospital in the afternoon. The warmth of the people encouraged and strengthened her. In a surprising turn of events, Mother managed the stairs to reach the second floor where she visited the sick and injured. Monetary donations were presented here also to aid the wounded. With music accompanying us we were transported to the station in the evening. Late that night was finally arrived home. The positive nature of the trip had been good for Mother who smiled for days as she basked in the memory of such positive experiences. The people of Novgorod had been an elixir for her.

How distinct was the beautiful Christmas of 1916 contrasted to that of the next year. When were young we we children would be taken for a long drive on Christmas Eve. As the day's light gave way to the darkness of the holy night, our children's joy grew and grew with anticipation. We would soon be at the entrance of the large room festooned for the Feast of Christ's Nativity which we would celebrate as a family.

The words and tunes of beloved Christmas carols filled the palace from a place we could not quite place. The tree glistened as the doors were slowly opened. It seemed that each year the tree was more and more breathtakingly beautiful. Family, friends with the palace staff filled the room.

All gathered around the tree regardless of their social station. No one was forgotten as a gift was thoughtfully presented to each guest. Ladies of the court with us sisters had been wrapping presents for weeks before.

The presents were so richly decorated that they seemed like glittery jewels under the tree, twinkling with the light reflected from the candles flickering on the tree branches. It is customary in Russia to keep the Nativity Fast on the day before the feast, eating no food with only a bit of water. When the first star of the evening appears the fast is broken. In the wee hours of the morning we attended Nativity Liturgy at the Feodorovsky Sobor. The trees were lit for all the gathered-officers, guards, and us. Indeed, we sisters had even decorated the trees that year.

Christmas Eve dinner of twelve courses followed the fast. The courses represent the Twelve Apostles. There was no meat this evening but many kinds of seafood and fish which all have symbolic significance. The table was laden with hors d'oeuvre, soup, mushrooms, fruit and nuts.

Upon our decision we did not take down our personal tree from the second floor of the palace until well after New Year's Eve. Not even the darkness of war could extinguish the spiritual glow of the Lord's Birth. Hospitals and orphanages celebrated with the emphasis on cheer for all patients and parentless children. Mother herself took pains to decorate various trees with white and silver ornaments. In an effort to counter the tension and sadness of the front, every effort was made to focus on happiness at this time.

On Christmas Day the tree was lighted for the Guard while the regimental orchestra played. Cossacks sang and danced. As all gathered around the tree, Olga presented gifts on behalf of Mother. They were usually simple and practical.

Christmas had been organized with all the customary tradition and expectations, but it did lack the joy we usually associated with it, because Father was heavily burdened with events at the front. To my recollection, Father had been out of sorts and worried the day before he left for Mogilev. Before his departure he spent a long time speaking with my sister, Olga, in his study. He bade her please to convince Mother to not write him her customary long daily letters.

He confided to her that he actually resented her telling him what he should do, especially when Anna added her own opinions which he felt were naïve. He actually called them *stupid.* "Everyone is issuing orders and I have to listen to them," he said. It was his express order that Mother should also not speak with her friends about matters which they could not understand. This, he added, was his business and that of his ministers. Father had even implored Mother himself to heed his request. Father's replies to her were curt which caused Mother surprise, as he had not commented on the things she had written to him. She then decided to go herself to see Father in Mogilev.

A profound thinker and voracious reader of books about natural science, religion and astronomy, she was able to solve the most challenging mathematical problems. She spent long hours reading her rare books on Indian philosophy which had been gifts from a different Grand Duchess Anastasia Nicholaevna, the divorced wife of the Duke of Leuchtenberg and later the wife of the Grand Duke Nicholai Nicholaevich himself a scholar of Persian and Indian history. Mother never wasted one minute. Her mail was enormous and she invested many hours a day going over various reports. Her skill at composing letters was well known while her correspondence was often melancholic and heart wrenching. Wealth in and of itself was of little concern to her for she cared little it. In the residences she had to abandon, namely Tsarskoe Selo and Petrograd, Livadia, and Alexandria she left behind items of immense monetary value–her platinum, rock crystal desk set, and a gold one. Not only that but she would never see again her dressing table accessories; her collection of crosses and boxes; the dozen genuine blue sapphire, gold-rimmed drinking glasses (by Bolin) gifts from Father over many years; valuable pieces of lace and over 300 Easter eggs. Count Benckendorff was to care for her things at Tsarskoe Selo.

As the holiday week approached an end, namely on December 30th, 1916, Olga rushed to find us barely able to utter: "Rasputin is missing!" The Starets' daughter had called to inform Anna that he had not been returned home the night before. Anna was greatly alarmed by this news especially as she had just seen Rasputin the evening before. She had spent only a moment with him in Petrograd in order to avoid further talk. Then Anna suddenly remembered that Rasputin had informed her that Prince Felix Youssoupoff was to call on him later that evening so that he could meet the prince's wife, Irina, at their luxurious home. It was Mother's belief, however, that Irina was nowhere to be found as she was in the Crimea recuperating from illness. Irina was Father's niece, the daughter of his sister, Xenia, with Grand Duke Alexander Mikhailovich, the grandson of the Emperor Nicholas I. He was Father' favorite cousin and his brother-in-law.

As per their established routine, Tatiana and Olga made their way to volunteer at the hospitale while Marie and I reluctantly attended lessons. When school ended we joined the rest of our family only to learn that, to our utter horror, Prince Youssoupoff was clearly implicated in Rasputin's disappearance. Not only him, but also to our own cousin, Prince Dimitri Pavlovich. The police investigated thoroughly and proclaimed that Rasputin had been murdered, thrown into the icy Neva River in Petrograd.

The corpse, now frozen solid, was found two days later under the ice. A Red Cross vehicle had been involved which was even more shocking, hence the Commander of the Red Cross, Purishkevich, must have also known about the plot. The latter was even a member of the Duma.

This was not the first time that individuals had attempted to murder Rasputin. He had been stabbed in Siberia by a lady one time, while in another instance carriage was used to run over him. Until this time he had always escaped harm.

That Dimitri Pavlovich had been involved was also a bitter pill to swallow as he had always been welcome in our house both at Tsarskoe Selo and in the Crimea. Marie, his sister, had also spent much time with us. Aunt Ella had raised Dimitri as were he her own son, because his father, a widower, had married a second time and left Russia and his children behind. He was well liked by all of us and was really a member of the family. His implication in this crime was truly inconceivable for us, although we later learned more details that his role had been only minor.

How sad we were next that General Hanbury-Williams' son died with Lord Kitchener on the torpedoed "Hampshire" which had sunk in the North Sea. How we shed tears upon hearing of this tragedy. To express her condolences Mother sent some orchids to his father the general. Alexei confessed that when the general saw him after learning of his son's death, he had embraced him sobbing. Alexei said: "My heart went out to him." The next day General HanburyWilliams once more joined Father and Alexei at dinner.

Father also now had received a telegram announcing that Rasputin had been murdered. Father and Alexei made their way to Tsarskoe Selo. Alexei was never again to see the general. Painfully Alexei described to us the last evening he had with the general. The general's woes were not to end, as he soon learned that his second son had been wounded. His losses seemed like our own so great was our empathy for him.

Father posed for a moment only for a family picture beside the tree. Then he read the report of the Rasputin murder. His reaction was: "To think that a member of the Imperial family could commit such a crime as to kill the Starets. I am ashamed to face the peasants who are fighting valiantly for Russia, and many of whom have died. And yet these boys find time for murder, as though there is not enough crime in the world."

Rather than killing Rasputin those involved should have been at the front. It was unjust to execute a man without a trial or the opportunity to explain himself. Perhaps the perpetrators had imagined themselves as patriots when they killed this man who had also prophesied about Russia's future. Father did not return home, because Rasputin had been killed, rather because the killers were members of his own family. Only Father could mete out punishment in this case. Indeed, had Rasputin been guilty of treason after all was said and done, his fate would have deserved to be much worse.

Petrograd was in the throw of great celebration due to Rasputin's demise. Champagne toasts were made, people sent each other telegrams of congratulations. Little did they realize then that these emptied champagne glasses were toasting their own deaths and funerals.

Father struggled with the dilemna of punishment for the young men. He ordered Felix to be exiled to one of his estates in the province of Kursk. It was during my escape in 1918, when I set foot there, that the whole picture seemed to come into focus before me: Mother, Dimitri, Felix. It must have been a great shock to the quiet, beautiful, young wife, Irina, who was deeply in love with her husband, Felix. (*Boldened here as it gives the reader, researcher, a clearer idea of Anastasia's purported escape route*)

Felix was an Oxford graduate thought of generally as a fascinating handsome man, one with a great deal of humor, incapable of doing such a terrible thing. Unfortunately, he believed that the murder was the solution to save Russia. Dimitri was sent to the General Staff on the Persian border to be with Grand Duke Nicholai Nicholaevich. Dimitri was blessed with the opportunity to escape the fate of his father, his half brother, his cousins, and other relatives who werekilled in 1918-1919. His relatives began an immediate campaign on his behalf, reminiscent of the event in of the well-known coronation disaster blamed on the incompetence of Grand Duke Serge Alexandrovich.

Father was particularly upset, since we all were so fond of Dimitri. He had been Father's ward, so he was more like a brother to us. Dimitri had been in Petrograd, bored with no goal in his life after he had been sent back from the front due to illness. Grand Duke Paul, Dimitri's father, expressed dissatisfaction. The relatives even resented his rather lenient sentence, hence they expressed coolness towards us. The Grand Duke Alexander Mikhailovich, Father's brother-in-law, came to see Father but was rebuffed. Father reiterated adamantly, "No matter whether it was a Grand Duke or a peasant, the law is the same for all."

A petition for the release of the two, deemed heroes by their supporters was circulated among the Romanov Family. Led by Grand Duke Cyril, Marie Pavlovna, his mother, and brothers Andrew and Boris demanded their release. This campaign infuriated my father who retorted, "They would never have dared ask such a favor from my austere father, Alexander III" and "No one has the right to commit a murder, especially in time of war and within my realm."

The Grand Duchess Marie Pavlovna (*nee Duchess of Mecklenburg-Schwerin*) had success in poisoning the family against Father and his family and hoped to use this division to somehow gain the crown for her own son. Her defamatory slander continued. She courted Rodzianko, president of the Duma. To their credit, some of those invited could no longer abide her scheming, at which moment they asked to be excused.

The plot organized by the Grand Duke Cyril to kill Mother and Father was one of the most damaging outcomes of this division in the Imperial Family. The plot had been hatched at the Imperial Yacht Club in Petrograd where my Father and all the relatives were members. Many friends also belonged to it. While others were dying in the trenches they continued to make trouble there and were ordered to cease and desist.

Upon Father's orders they were told to leave and make their way to their individual estates. Their fury was unparalleled. Now, no matter the cost to them personally, they would eliminate Father who had become a proverbial thorn in their side.

After the sad parting of the two sisters in Tsarskoe Selo, Aunt Ella's bitterness toward my Mother increased. I was told that she knew then that there was to be an attempt on the life of Rasputin, yet she did not discourage Dimitri from taking part in it; instead, she spent her time in a convent where she met one of her friends, and prayed on her knees in this convent while the murder in Petrograd was being committed. I wonder now whether she was praying for her own soul. To my sorrow her life also ended very painfully in 1918. *(Boldened as a quote because when substantiated by DNA that the authoress is really Anastasia, it will give insight into family intrigues and how they were perceived by the immediate family of Nicholas and Alexandra).*

# XII      REVOLUTION

It comes to mind that Mother had once ruminated on the notion that Dimitri might marry one her daughters to preserve the Romanov line if Alexei could not be saved. Rasputin's death was a fact now that she had to take philosophically. She was simultaneously much aggrieved that these young men could have been so misguided, especially one whom she had treated as her own child. Emperor Paul (1796-1801) had regrettably decreed that no female be allowed to succeed to the Russian throne. Personally, I think that the decree could have been modified given the political chaos in which we found ourselves. Olga would have made a remarkable Tsaritsa. Her personal qualities uniquely qualified her to sit on the throne for she was intelligent, well-read, had a kind disposition, was popular among her friends, and understood human nature. There was no truer Russian in heart and soul. Olga would not have easily fallen victim to deception. Surely she would have been a wise monarch with the best interests of her people at heart. It was this autocratic form of governance, one which Father had inherited from his father, Alexander III, which had been partially to blame for the suffering of Russia.

Although Father was still with us we saw him very infrequently, except we dined together. As soon as he had finished eating he would leave rashly to engross himself in the world of military problems and affairs of state. Nonetheless, we took great comfort in his presence at our side.

Rasputin's death had robbed the Germans of one of their most valuable propaganda tools. Hurriedly, they needed to promote an alternative theme to this end.

The new scheme involved German agents dropping leaflets into the Russian trenches stating that the Tsar was about to sign a separate peace treaty with Germany. Another malicious fabrication involved Mother who was accused of having entertained Generals Ludendorff and Hindenburg while with Father at Mogilev. The Germans used disinformation in their fairytale that Mother had been receiving letters from her brother, Uncle Ernest. Another rumor insisted that the Russian officers of the General Staff along with the Grand Dukes were debauching in cabarets, gambling and drinking while Russian soldiers were suffering and dying at the front.

Those who had seen Father's devotion in action were immune to such lies, for they knew firsthand how dearly Father loved Russia. Nonetheless, General Ludendorff and Kaiser Wilhelm continued in the propaganda campaign with increasing intensity. They knew full well that it was futile to defeat the Russian army by normal means, so they connived a revolution to implode the nation behind the front lines of battle. They employed Caesar's method of *divide, et vince*, that is divide and conquer. They aimed to poison the mind of the Russian nation with the goal of dismantling loyalty to their Tsar. There was a fear that mutiny could transpire, not because the troops were ill fed, inadequately clothed or undersupplied, rather because Father was with us at Tsarskoe Selo and not with them. Father maintained, quite the opposite, that the troops were stronger than ever even compared to the beginning of the war.

Because merchants, however, were taking bribes from German agents supplies were now being delayed. Goods were also withheld from the merchants so they could not deliver them. Ten million rubles were ultimately invested in the dismantling of Russia by means of contrived revolution. These funds had been originally destined to improve the condition of Russian prisoners of war in Germany.

Father's presence was imperative at General Headquarters. Although Alexei was mightily afflicted with fever and the measles, Father decided to go to G.H.Q. with the assurance that he would soon return. Given Mother's overwhelming preoccupation for Alexei's health, she had pleaded that Father should remain.

Given previously arranged plans for a surprise military attack, Father was unable to change his plans and he left.

No sooner had Father left when riots and strikes erupted all over Petrograd. There were shortages of supplies, but in reality there was plenty of bread even if not necessarily for sale in the shops. A number of the merchants, including some foreigners withheld the products to speculate with them and drive up the price to increase their profits. The cost of these staples rose so high that common people could not purchase meat, butter, or other essential commodities. Grain became moldy and unfit for consumption trapped on train cars, although if properly distributed could have staved off shortages.

One ominous morning our mother had entered her room only to find Father's picture lying on the floor with the broken frame glass in pieces on top of his photograph which had been taken in the trenches. The glass had broken directly over the area of Father's neck which immediately impressed Mother with superstitious nature as an ill portent of doom. Surely, there it connoted a problem that Father must be suffering at the front. Although it is possible that a servant had done this by accident or design, it was more likely than not just the wind.

Nonetheless, it was immediately assessed by Mother as a foretoken of suffering. In her anxiety she nervously recalled the large cross she saw in the sky as they crossed the Troitsky bridge a few years before. Perhaps the meaning was that Father would have his own personal cross-like burden to bear.

Another dream presented itself in which Grand Duke Serge, responsible for the coronation disaster and deceased now for some years, appeared among us, dancing with a chiffon veil all within sight of Father. As the phantasmagorical choreography ended the tip of the veil caught on Father's crown pulling it from his head. Seven of the larger gemstones vanished leaving only one. That too soon dissipated until it became as insignificant as a pebble. That too then disappeared. Would the crown be taken from Father? The thought began to haunt her. Was the little stone Alexei who would die and leave us?

Yet another harbinger soon occurred when the chain which held a cross and red diamond ring broke. Father had given it as a gift to Mother who had recently been wearing it around her neck. She had always viewed these as symbols of favorable fortune. When the chain suddenly broke, the ring fell one way and the cross in the opposite direction. She pondered the possible meaning in her heart. Perhaps this was a message regarding Father's safety; perhaps it predestined a rift between Father and the Church. Before the assassination in Ekaterinburg, this ring was taken from Mother by Voykov. He impolitely wore this red diamond as a pinky ring in our presence while in captivity. Mother and I both were mystically inclined, a characteristic which is still applicable to me. (*Editor's note: although many cultures have some element of mysticism to them, the Merovingians of yore were noted for such dream interpretation, prophecy, and foretelling of events. Thuringia, once ruled by the Franks and homeland of Queen Victoria's ancestors, hence also Alexandra's and Anastasia's, is also an ancestral homeland to this author and editor. This gift albeit custom of dream interpretation and attention to symbology is well known.*)

Mother was still not sure if Father had reached G.H.Q. safely or not. The confirmation did eventually arrive. Chaos on the streets of Petrograd commenced two days later and continued for about ten days. Everywhere there reigned an atmosphere of suspicion, strikes, riots, and accusations. Heightening the anxiety we children all had the measles. Alexei had already been taken ill before Father's departure, but now it was Olga's turn followed by Tatiana finally reaching me. Marie assisted Mother to care of us in our affliction, but helped Mother to care for us, yet the virus was not to spare her either when she soon suffered the same as we. Both Mother and I developed pneumonia and were placed in oxygen tents.

General von Grooten, assistant to General Voyeykov, Commandant of the Palaces, confided to us the gist of a conversation he had had with General Belyayev, the military commandant in Petrograd. With the assistance of Voyeykov he had been able to speak directly to Father informing him of true state of affairs in the city. Rodzianko had fallaciously wired His Majesty that tranquility was the rule of the day in Petrograd. However, the general, realizing the true nature of the critical conditions in the city, took the initiative to inform Father of the truth. Father learned that we were alive which gave him a measure of relief. He sent word to us via General Belyayev, that were to do nothing until he had safely returned home. On the other hand, we must be ready to leave with little to no notice. The fact that we were ill had reached him, but he hoped that we would be well enough to leave when he arrived. He had no idea, however, that Marie, some others and I were suffering from bouts of pneumonia.

Rodzianko placed a telephone call to us in the palace informing us that our father was fine but that we should avoid danger and should proceed at once to Gatchina Palace, southwest of Petrograd. Uncle Michael lived there while various members of the Imperial family also maintained villas in the palace park. Our security and freedom would have been greater there, because two connected parallel wings were almost entirely enclosed. The wings each had more than several hundred rooms while the park boasted a lake of some size in the center. The grounds of the estate were comprised of thousands of acres which included gardens, forests, streams and ravines.

It might have been easier to escape aboard from that vantage point. Senseless rumors maintained that Uncle Ernest was hiding in a tunnel there, obviously confusing the tunnel at the Alexander Palace with a natural geological formation at Gatchina. Following the Gatchina passage, accessed from a palace stairway into a dark narrow hall, one arrived at the bank of Silver Lake which connected to the Baltic Sea.

This spooky tunnel was cold, damp, and had a mournful echo. All these gruesome things came to my mind. I could see the statue of Paul I in front of the palace. His clothes, which were brought into his room after his assassination, remained there undisturbed as on the day he left the palace. There was a belief that Paul's ghost walked at night about the vast rooms, corridors, and terraces. Others even claimed that they had heard him calling in the tunnel, and some servants were afraid to leave their rooms when the clock struck twelve midnight. This palace was my Grandfather's favorite residence.

There existed a different type of passage through one of the park entrances in Tsarskoe Selo. The gated entry was under constant surveillance and no one entered with a pass which contained a photograph and identification. This was a way to enter for all sorts of workers such as deliverymen, repairmen, cooks, maids, gardeners and the like. The tunnel led to what was known as the English basement of the palace where there were a number of rooms exclusively organized for their use. A lounge and dining room were included in this section where one could find a dining room for officers located directly below Mother's bedroom.

The passage was traversed daily by at least five or six hundred workers. The guards knew everyone who was authorized to enter as many employees had been in our service for many years and were daily arrivals. Of all the palace entrances it was the busiest and most frequently used.

Soldiers, we were told, were breaking into storage areas becoming inebriated with stolen wine and liquor or even drunk on wood alcohol. Some died from alcohol poisoning, while their deaths were increasingly blamed on the palace guard.

For some nights in succession Mother watched over us changing her clothes frequently but always appearing in her nurse's uniforms. In order to be near us she reclined on her chaise longue. It is hard to adequately describe the trials and tribulations my mother bore during these days of disorder. As a prisoner Mother reviewed all her personal letters, burning some of the most intimate written by Father when he was courting her. Queen Victoria's missives, her own grandmother, were also summarily destroyed. Her Majesty had given her granddaughter advice when she was pregnant with her first child. Letters written by the Imperial Family were kept in chronological order following a numbering system used to archive them all. This was also a method to detect if any were missing. Ashes were found in the fireplace by the commissars appointed by the Provisional Government when they searched the palace. They accused Mother of having tampered and destroyed important evidence. They expressed their belief that she had truly destroyed even more than just love letters or those containing advice about pregnancy.

All having been burned in the all-consuming flames of fire Mother declared with satisfaction, "All is dead except my memories. No one can take them from me." Resting her arms on the mantelpiece, Mother wept over the ashes of her royal grandmother's letters which she had greatly cherished. She wept bitterly over the .flame that carried Queen Victoria's to the skies on the wings of smoke.

All remaining correspondence between my parents was now reviewed, yet nothing was found of which to accuse them. No effort was spared to lie to the public about what these letters supposedly contained. Mother's handwriting and even her signature were forged. When we viewed some of these faux letters in Ekaterinburg we realized that the handwriting falsification was indeed in great part similar to Mother's.

Hyped accusations were hurled at her maintaining that she harbored pro-German sentiments and was a spy. What would it have even matters to these traitors if she had been? The truth, however, was that she anything but a spy. They wanted to create a scape-goat to blame for the suffering of the nation. This was all done with the express goal of weakening the nation to destroy the nation. Revolution would even been used to achieve this desired result.

These allegations were all products of treason and deceit. They attempted to convince the populace that Mother and her brother were lobbying for a separate peace with Germany. The person who bore the blame in reality was none other than Princess Maria Vasilchikova of whom I have previously written. She originated from a Russian family and did know Ernest. Her family were friends with Aunt Ella. Princess Maria had known Mother for over a decade and could count among her friends members of the imperial families of German and Austria-Hungary. She happened to be in Austria in 1914 just before the war began. Officials of the German and Austrian governments convinced her in 1916 to write complimentary letters to Mother reminding her that both had been traditionally friends of Russia, a condition they hoped to renew. However, they had not given much credence to the alliance with Great Britain. We received three or four such communications, all of which were shared with the High Command, the secret police, and the Minister of War. No answer was ever penned by Father. Both Austria and Germany should have known better, he insisted. They should have taken Serbia to the International Tribunal in the Hague; instead they decided to wage war.

When Father learned that Maria had been in Germany to visit Russian prisoners of war, he was absolutely angered, because she had tried to convince them to persuade Father to agree to a truce. The report that they were being well treated was later refuted by the Red Cross which informed him that it was not true.

Maria insisted in one of her letters that all Russia would be endangered if the truce was not signed. Ostensibly, Maria understood the true goal of the enemy which was to instigate revolution. After she visited Uncle Ernst, a letter was composed by both of them. It arrived via Sweden and was delivered to Mother.

Maria and Uncle Ernest induced Mother to extreme anger, especially that they might even entertain the notion that Father would agree to such a truce. As difficult as it was for her to pronounce, she insisted she never wanted to see her brother again ever. She personally wrote the response: There would never be a separate peace treaty with Germany. Father, conversely, had never given his consent for her to write and send this letter and was greatly angered that she had done so.

Wilhelm II then sent a letter to Count Benckendorff requesting that he suggest to Father that he sign the treaty Father said, let him write such letters to all my Allies, but a separate German treaty with Russia only, will never take place. Maria persisted and wrote yet again, enclosing a note from Uncle Ernest. She requested an audience with Mother who would not think of it and, instead, forwarded the letter to the proper authorities. Her appearance in Petrograd lent credence to the errant belief that she had been there to see Mother, and this misconception was the catalyst for considerable tension and problems as the people actually believed it.

Princess Maria then wrote to Aunt Ella who also did not deign to answer, after which she proceeded to pay a visit to Minister Sazonov. Angrily he reiterated to her what she had already heard from many official sources: "There will be no separate peace with Germany." The secret police received all her communications which infuriated them all the more in that she insisted that Austria would confiscate her estate there. Mother asked curtly, "Why should Russia be held responsible because Maria's estate will be confiscated?" Father then issued an order that Maria be sent to her sister's estate. Fuming Father opined, "Wilhelm must be insane." We wondered how anyone could forget what Germany and Austria had done to steal the lives of so many Russians, destroy their property and wreak so much devastation especially in Ukraine?

It was extremely absurd for anyone to imagine that Mother would be a spy for Germany. Had she not waited so long to produce a son to fulfill the need of her adopted land? A son who would take his place on the throne when Father's time was done. She would not, she could not betray her husband, son and adopted Motherland she loved so dearly. Anyone believing such illogical and unintelligent propaganda was not a healthy thinker.

A secret panel was found in the cupboard one day when the commissars again searched the palace. It had been so well hidden that no one had found it up to that time. A number of Mother's special treasures had been secreted away there. A pleated fan with no particular value was found there on which a picture of our parents had been painted. They had received it in France upon a visit there, and it was unique in that from one angle you could see Mother and from the other Father. When it was opened one saw them both. The commissars stole another fan with a tortoise shell handle encrusted with emeralds and whose pleated lace was studded with tiny gold sequins forming the Imperial double eagle.

We wondered why Father had not arrive, especially as there were five us who were ill and recuperating. Madame Lili Dehn, the wife of Charles Dehn (*aka Karl von Dehn*), the captain on our yacht and a friend since our childhood, left her little boy with his nanny to hurry to our side when she learned of our illnesses. Ironically, she too became a prisoner in the palace upon her arrival. She informed us of plundering and clashes between rebels and the police. According to Dr. Derevenko the Liteiny Arsenal in Petrograd had fallen to rebel forces, soldiers were deserting their posts, and explosions were going off in the factories.

Former ladies-in-waiting, Princess Obolensky, Olga Butsova and Princess Dundakova, as well as the brother of Captain Charles Dehn came to help us but were not allowed to enter the palace. Mother would have been so pleased had they been able to be with us. Countess Anastasia (Nastinka) Hendrikova, another lady-in-waiting, had heard of our illness coming to Tsarskoe Selo from her residence in the Caucasus to attend to us.

Many of Mother's servants had contracted the flu as the epidemic swept the palace some fleeing in fear, including Derevenko, the sailor, Alexei's servant. He had informed others working in the palace that he was considering working for the new government. However, he was finally found to be possessing stolen property when he was arrested by the Provisional Government.

Mother was particularly perplexed that so few guards were on duty when we began to hear shouts and commotion coming from the rebels in the streets. When she telephoned the guard at the main gate there was no answer, to her horror. Calling the other entrance, she was informed by one guard still at his post that the others had deserted.

Even though a cannon had been installed on the grounds in order for our protection, Mother asked that under no circumstances should the crowd be fired upon. No one should perish because of her family. From below Mother could perceive noise coming from the officers' room below her bedroom. She took Marie with her to personally inspect the situation. Mother ordered that hot tea should be served to them as often as they came in, because the temperature had dropped to negative eighteen degrees Fahrenheit.

The arrival of Dr. Botkin was announced who entered our rooms pale and distressed. He informed Mother of a belief that Father had been shot, but she rejected this notion insisting that she did not believe it for one minute. She retired to us children, as the old world around here gradually ceased to be. Finally we five invalids had a doctor to care for us. Due to the emergency he even helped to change our soiled garments, although a rule was in place that no man could perform this assistance. Sometime after the New Year, command of the regiments in Tsarskoe Selo was handed over to Grand Duke Paul in spite of his failing health. This fact comforted and encouraged us, and we enjoyed a quiet respite for a short time.

The Grand Duke spoke to Mother at length. In the next room Marie perceived raised voices. The topic of conversation revolved around Anna Vyrobova. Mother was informed that the public did not want Anna to be with us at the palace. Her parents, the Taneevs, from Terijoki on the Gulf of Finland arrived in the meantime to be with her during her own illness, especially as she demanded so much attention. Anna's case of measles seemed to require more attention than all of five us who were ill together. Until she was well again her parents stayed with us, all to the increased irritation among the people.

One of the reasons that Anna was with us was because there had already been an attempt against her life in her own home, so that we thought she would be safer with us. Resentment grew toward Grand Duke Paul on Mother's part. He continually warned her that the palace could be overrun at any time and Anna would leave as a dead woman. Mother was indignant as she felt she had the right to have whomever she pleased in her home, impervious to the thoughts of anyone who thought differently. Mother and Grand Duke Paul parted on angry terms. Mother, henceforth became greatly agitated.

Anna learned of Mother's unpleasant encounters with Grand Duke Paul on her account. She was always the recipient of Mother's loyal and unswerving defense. There were servants who could not abide Anna, so much so that they tattled on Mother to the Provisional Government, informing it of the letters which Anna had suggested be burned. They were summarily dismissed, but asked to speak specifically with Count Benckendorff before they left. They were not permitted to do so.

It is noted that Anna's presence in our home had been the impetus for much trouble which even endangered our lives. Anna was now well, but she persisted in staying with us. When were young as children, Mother did resent Anna's presence at times when she was perceived as being intrusive.

However, after Anna confided in Mother that her parents had been abusive to her Mother felt sorry for her and became protective. Mother confessed to Madame Zizi Narishkina that her own life had been long suffering when she had to live with her brother Ernst who was then newly married. There were time she would not speak to either her brother or sister-in-law in order to avoid an argument. She locked herself away in her room for days on end until, subsequently, her grandmother, Queen Victoria, took her to England.

Anna was somewhat deceitful as she used to visit us with the ruse that her husband was absent from home, but conversely telling him that she was leaving for duty at the palace. This misrepresentation of fact disturbed Mother when she learned of them. This agitation actually caused Mother's first heart attack. If Anna's presence was causing heart attacks and Mother would not dismiss her, the physician was powerless to help his patient, so he resigned.

We children eventually learned of this from Madame Narishkina, but never from Mother's lips. All were forbidden from uttering a cross word against Anna, so it was logical that many believe that held some special influence over Mother. As we girls gradually became of the grown danger we faced, we too began to display reserved coolness toward Anna. This displeased our Mother so that she ordered us to try to be more pleasant. Her reprimand to us came despite the fact that we were in such a weakened state of health. She became angry with Olga and Marie, and said, "I will not allow anyone to criticize my friend." Olga however said; "Anna, with her petty talks has made herself indispensable to you." This, though true, so agitated Mother that we were sorry Olga ever brought the matter up. Even Dr. Botkin felt that, for the sake of the children, Anna should be sent back to Terijoki in Finland.

No one was now allowed to enter the palace without being searched. A woman guard checked the women, while a male guard searched the men.

# XIII    ABDICATION

Captain Nilov, Major General Prince Vasily Dolgorukov and others at Mogilev came to the conclusion that Father should return forthwith to Petrograd. He would then approve the implementation of the Constitution. Mother sent a telegraph that she too was of the same mind. Another wire soon arrived with the news that the revolution in Petrograd had been quelled. General Ruzsky, Commanding General of the Northern Front, was rather disturbed by this message out of fear that he and the Duma would be accused of treason. He made one last ditch attempt to bring Father into disrepute. Father's advisors and military experts all realized that the troops were well provisioned and ready for a spring offensive which would bring the victory all so deeply desired, and perhaps within three months at that.

Ruzsky did not hide his open hatred and disdain for General Alexeiev and his son. He stopped at nothing to drive a wedge betwen Father and General Alexeiev, whom Father had long known and found most capable. General Ruzsky could also not stand Count Fredericks as he sensed the latter's suspicion of him. Ruzsky wanted Father to remove the Baltic baron from his court minister post under the pretext that the people rejected German sounding family names for people in such important posts.

The Count had warned of Ruzkey's true intentions and was of the opinion that he would destabilize Father's standing with the people. Grandmama Marie also attempted to persuade Father and opined that Mother, whom she called Alicky, bore the blame for this appointment. Father was undeterred explaining that he only wished to raise the morale of the troops and make them more efficient. Grand Duke Nicholai Nicholaevich was said to provoke injustices as he was favoring certain officers over others. General Krymov told Prince Dolgorukov that the occasion of Father's taking command of the Supreme Command had initiated great rejoicing among the officers and soldiers. The specter of favoritism, they were sure, would be eradicated in the armed forces. The victories which followed illustrated the new spirit which permeated the ranks. Thousands of German and Austrian soldiers were now being captured along with ammunition in great quantity.

Thousands of soldiers crossed the frontier to seek asylum and sanctuary in Russia. The desirability of the German High Command's ordering Princess Vasilchikova to pen letters asking for a separate peace treaty was evident. General Ruzsky was beginning to come under the suspicion of officers. They were willing and ready to assassinate him, especially as they knew full well that Father would not abide murmuring, accusations, and tongue wagging.

Prince Dolgorukov would later recount that Captain Nilov had once been so furious with Ruzsky's attitude that he pounded the table with his fist uttering the words:

"His Majesty must not abdicate! He has the Army and the peasants with him. Ruzsky will destroy the Empire and the Emperor, but I will have the pleasure of killing him with my own hand."

The General's life was narrowly spared due to the rapid progression of the subsidized revolution. No one could imagine that this insignificant man who wore thick glasses for near-sightedness would turn out to be a spy? His sloping shoulders from which hanged epaulets were not those of a military man. He had full understanding of the prevailing situation in Petrograd which led Father to exclaim: "I can never forgive Ruzsky because, as a Russian general, he committed the most terrible crime against his country."

General Ruzsky was at Mogilev one time when we were there. He refused to look Mother directly in the eyes which implied that he was suffering from a guilty conscience. A telegram arrived from Grand Duke Nicholai Nicholaevich in the Caucasus urging Father to abdicate.

Father was devastated by this message but inherently understood that it was nothing more than an act of revenge for having relieved the Duke from his position as Supreme Field Commander. Father had simultaneously relieved Prince Orlov (Fat Orlov), Director of Chancery, of his position and had sent him to the Caucasus with the Grand Duke. While Nicholai Nicholaevich was in Tiflis (*now Tiblisi capital of Georgia*), his enormous height and his thunderous voice impressed the people. He enjoyed a modicum of popularity due to his great strength, exuberance and prowess in horsemanship.

General Ewers and General Ivanov had prepared to send troops to Petrograd to crush the riots. Ruzsky, however, wired Rodzianko with the request to take no action. (*Rodzianko was related to Prince Youssoupoff by marriage*) The Litovsky and Volinsky regiments consisting of recruits had just then capitulated to revolutionaries which was another blow which Father had to endure. The last salt in the wound was the misinformation that Mother had died and that we were all in grave danger. Father was to go to Petrograd and there grant the Constitution. However, by direct order of the Duma and with the collaboration of Ruzsky and others, Father was prevented from arriving on time thereby allowing the Revolution to take deeper and more noxious root.

Before leaving Mogilev Father wired General Khabalov with the order to crush the riots in Petrograd which were intolerable. Lamentably, the General informed Father that there was not action which could be taken as the die had been cast; all was for naught, and the situation was beyond hope. The barracks were already deserted. Two companies of Life Guards, commanded by my paternal cousin, Grand Duke Cyril Vladimirovich, were marching through the city. None other than the Grand Duke was leading the manifestation adorned with a red armband and a crimson rosette om his chest. The revolutionaries took much encouragement from the fact that a member of Father's own family had betrayed him. Cyril imagined that this was the moment of truth in which he could employ the assistance of others in the Imperial Family to usurp the Crown.

Grand Duke Michael (Uncle Misha) was detained at this time at the Duma which was located in the Tauride Palace. He understood exactly what Cyril was attempting and refused to grant him an audience. Uncle Misha was in talks about becoming the acting regent, a decision made more problematic because Alexei's health was fragile. Grand Duke Michael found it difficult to accept, because the condition of the country had deteriorated so much by that time added to the fact that he had never been prepared for such burdensome responsibilities.

Cyril Vladimirovich sought to establish good relations with the new government. Rodzianko began to doubt the Vladimir family. Grand Duke Paul Alexandrovich informed Mother of all of this on his own accord. The troops under his command were handed over to the Duma by who would now be under the direction of the new regime. He had exacted his revenge against Mother. Cyril and his German mother, Marie Pavlovna, the elder (*nee Duchess of Mecklenburg*), Grand Duke Vladimir's widow, had always spoken highly of the former German ambassador to Russia, Bismarck. Not only that they had also praised Kaiser Wilhelm despite the reality that the two countries were at war. The Grand Duchess's true affinities were common knowledge with no pretense of disguising them. Cyril and she had hosted lavish parties to which they had invited influential people. Among them were supposed to be General Ruzsky, Princess Radziwill and Sir George Buchanan, British Ambassador. Revolutionaries were also on the guest list, and surely they perceived much confidential information while they co-mingled with the upper echelon of Russian society. After our arrest in Tsarskoe Selo this was brought for the first time to Father's attention. . Even the invitations to these events were extravagantly printed. They had employed the Imperial double eagle and the crown which they had embossed in different shades of green, yellow, and blue with sheets of real gold or red and blue enamel. All of these were artistically pressed into the finest grade of costly paper.

Marie Pavlovna (the elder), the main conspiratrix, possessed a most charming personality and was known to be an excellent conversationalist. With evil intent she did all within her power to sully my parents' names.

Cyril was married to Princess Victoria Melita of Saxe-Coburg and Gotha, Queen Victoria's granddaughter, who had been divorced from Mother's only brother, Grand Duke Ernest of Hesse, also a grandson of Queen Victoria. (*Editor's note: an example of endogamy, intermarriage within family groups*).

Mother had truly suffered when Victoria married Ernest due to her jealous disposition. No other option was open to Mother at that time, so that she was obliged to take up residence with the unhappy pair. Her goodly grandmother, Queen Victoria, finally spirited Mother away to Great Britain. With the object of her derision no longer there, Victoria had begun to turn her malevolence on Uncle Ernest so that the marriage ended in divorce only a few years later.

Now a divorcee, Victoria had wed Cyril which generated a ban of their presence in Russia. However, they had returned just before World War I . When we sisters were born one after the other, Cyril indulged in what is called *Schadenfreude* (*the perverse pleasure in someone else's perceived misfortune*).

Cyril continued with this despicable talk even after Alexei was afflicted with haemophilia cognizant of the fact that Alexei might die young opening up a pathway to the throne. Cyril's hopes for the Crown were quickly re-intensified, because his mother was holding something akin to her own royal court. redoubled and his mother held, practically, a court of her own. These relatives lived long enough to see the catastrophe that their country had become.

Upon realizing that Alexei was so ill Cyril's mother, after thirty years of indecisiveness, decided to convert to Russian Orthodoxy in order to strengthen her son's claim to the throne. The Church, however, would never consecrate a man whose first wife was still alive, so all this maneuvering was really in vain. Another disqualifying factor was that his wife was a divorcee.

Von Grooten, Prince Putiatin, and her secretary, Count Apraxin, had stood by Mother through thick and thin. Apraxin had even trudged through the snow from Petrograd to inform Mother that Father was to arrive the next day. Now she listened intently to their recommendations and counsel. Count Adam Zamoyski, A.D.C., and General Dobrovolsky were also held in esteem by my Mother. She followed their suggestion that she descend to the troops gathered in the courtyard and address them. Mother, Marie, Count Beckendorff, and Count Apraxin them and thanked them for their service.

Mother noticed the men were in no way changed in their behavior from earlier times. Count Apraxin had been a long time devoted friend of Mother and Father. A deeply religious man, he also encouraged a culture and the arts. He had a deep understanding of the conditions in society.Preceding the abdication, an ukase (proclamation) was signed by Father by which the old Cabinet was dismissed and Prince Lvov was named Prime Minister. Grand Duke Nicholai Nicholaevich returned also to his position as Commander-in-Chief of the Army.

All the old ministers were arrested by the Provisional Government, despite the protestations of the Prime Minister. Kerensky, Shulgin and Gucbkov, the latter a sworn enemy of Mother's, exerted this pressure. Gucbkov was rumored to be influenced by traitors from abroad. An epidemic of measles, flu and pneumonia raged throughout the palace. Additional doctors were permitted to attend all who were ill twice a day, but officers shadowed over their shoulders during all of these examinations.

Patients found it embarrassing to have these strange men in their bedrooms. Count Benckendorf asked that the guards stay in the hall which he requested directly of the commissar. Extra nurses were not permitted to attend those who were ill. We heard that Countess Fredericks had contracted pneumonia and been taken to English Hospital under supervision of Lady Georgina Buchanan (nee Bathurst, *1863- +1922). Her father had been the Ambassador to Russia and had known Uncle Ernest and Mother for years. He had been a frequent guest in our home. Together we would view newsreels of events from the war. Sir George Buchanan, however, ordered that Countess Fredericks be removed from the British Hospital, because she had been associated with the old regime, and he believed in the new. She was taken out of the hospital into the freezing cold. A Good Samaritan gave her needed refuge, while her crippled daughter named Emma was made to appear before the Duma. There they confiscated her jewelry. The old count had been the target of the intended arrest, but he was not Home when the government sent officials there, so they set it on fire. Not only was his home destroyed but also his valuable art collection. Ironically, Sir George enjoyed and genuinely liked our family on a personal level. He admired many of the women who appeared in our house as well, and as a middle aged man he too was admired by many of them.

Common lore had it that he was open to the hospitality of women from all strata of society from the highest to the lowest. He became hated by husbands at war who became jealous at hearing of these dalliances. He came to regret his mistakes only to praise Father's loyalty to the Allies.

Father learned that Sir George had said he did not care if Germany were to invade Britain. This disturbed Father greatly. Another point of contention was the fact that Sir George had been instrumental in spreading untruths about our mother. This was unsettling to Princess Victoria of Battenberg, Mother's older sister who summarily wrote her a disquieting letter. Father wanted Sir George recalled from his post and to return to Great Britain, hence he requested the Grand Marshall of the Court, Count Beckendorff, to write on his behalf to King George to request the same. Peter Bark, as stipulated by Father, was to withdraw all his money from banks in Britain, but the mercurial evolution of the revolution made such transactions impossible. (*Editor's note: Sir Peter Bark, aka Pyotr Lyvovich Bark, Minister of Finance to the Imperial Russian Government, *1869- +1937*)

Sir George's wife, Lady Georgina, distinguished herself nonetheless as most energetically dedicated to her war work. As a result, Father presented her with the Order of St. Catherine. In the Embassy the sewing group was under her supervision as was the Anglo-Russian Hospital on Nevsky Prospect. In addition she was the directress of the British Convalescent Home.

General von Grooten, Commandant of Tsarskoe Selo, was sent by the Provisional Government to prison. Colonel Girardi, Chief of Police, General Resin, once the Commandant of the Combined Regiments, and Prince Putiatin were also placed under arrest. In an attempt to negotiate with Rodzianko, Mother asked A.D.C. Captain Linevich to try to reach some concession. He was never seen again. We were told to be ready to leave Russia at any instant and that our bags should be packed in anticipation of this fact. Our luggage was placed upstairs having been removed from the storerooms.

When she was not involved in her sewing projects, Mother selected the most essential items that we were to take. However, every item was reviewed by our new jailors later on.

It came to our attention that two divisions of revolutionaries were marching toward Tsarskoe Selo riding in tanks and armored vehicles. They would storm the palace we heard. The inclement winter weather thwarted this plan as they could not reach the village. Soon after this event we lost electricity for twenty minutes one night. The courtyard, the park, the gates, and entrances were not illuminated so that we could see nothing. We were later deprived of water which was shut off and then restored. The elevator, which we called a lift, was out of commission which made things difficult for Mother. During that time she was carried up the flight of stairs to the second floor.

We found ourselves in a constant state of apprehension fearing for our well-being, suspecting that at any moment revolutionaries would invade. The Provisional Government, we had heard, had ordered Rasputin's body to be removed from the grave. They did not know its exact location and errantly disinterred the corpse of our elderly butler. The two had died during the same time period. The remains were burned in the Pergolovo Forest, but they had confused the identity of the deceased and turned to ash the body of the butler who had faithfully served my great great grandfather Alexander II in the Winter Palace the day he was killed. He continued his service to our family for a long time after that until he became too feeble to carry on. (*Editor's note: the fact that the Provisional Government had burned any corpse at all illustrates its opposition to traditional Russian values and norms, Christian Orthodox teaching does not allow cremation to the point that a priest will not offer prayers for anyone who has been reduced to cremated remains.*)

A rumor persisted that Mother was responsible for burying Rasputin's body in the park at Tsarskoe Selo, which was totally without merit. She had no part in any burial arrangement, suggesting rather, that his body should be shipped back to his family in Siberia.

Anna Vyrubova, on the other hand, had wished to bury him on her own property near the woods on the high road heading toward Viborg. This spot was on the other side of Alexander Gate and Alexandrovka Village. Anna was of the mindset that Rasputin had been instrumental in saving her own life, so she paid his burial expenses in a service officiated by Father Vassiliev. People believed that we had signed an icon placed with him in his casket. In reality we had an icon to be placed in the coffin of a son of one our tutors who had been killed while another was signed to be placed in the coffin of the beloved butler.

The history of untrue rumors concerning Rasputin had their origins many years before. Supposedly Christians had been persecuted in Persia by a government official there. Father, the Defender of Orthodoxy, and used his influence to have the persecutor removed from his post. influence to have this instigator removed from his diplomatic post in Persia. This person had then sought to seek revenge striking back at Father and the Imperial Family. With the help of a ghost writer he published a most vile and denigrating book based on various falsehoods. They both tried to extort the equivalent of $60,000 from Mother to keep the book from going to press. Mother refused and ignored their threat. However, during the war the content of the book was circulated throughout the land which had a most sinister effect among the people. Now the same protagonists began a propaganda campaign against Father which only served to embolden the Bolsheviks, although neither authors had ever known Father personally. Their publication was based on total fabrication.

At home a crowd once gathered upon believing a rumor that Alexei had died, and they demanded to see for themselves. Mother, Marie and Count Benckendorff appeared on the balcony where Mother responded. In a voice, clear but weak, she said; "I hear you want to see me and my son, but why? My son is critically ill, and he must not expose himself to cold. To see him is impossible at this time. For myself I am only a mother who is nursing her sick children. ·They left without a single word.

In the evening of March 13th Marie became feverish with sickness. She was put in the infirmary with the kind help of Baroness Baroness Buxhoeveden, Madame Dehn, Dr. Botkin, and several nurses and maids. Meanwhile, Mother accepted responsibility for the care of all other patients in our home.

News of Father's abdication came amidst this chaos and disorder. Grand Duke Paul arrived later that day too. He brought with him a printed bulletin with the announcement of the abdication. He felt great sympathy for our situation and urged us to leave Russia as soon as possible, upon which Mother lost her composure with the words, "Russia is lost; Russia was betrayed." Alexei was to hear this news from M. Gilliard, because Mother did not have the heart or energy to do it herself. He was incredulous asking, "How can that be? Father promised Alexander III that Russia would always remain an autocracy, and Father had to swear to uphold this type of rule."

It never dawned on him that Father no longer was the Emperor and he was no longer was Tsarevich. He never dwelt on his own troubles yet thought selflessly of Russia not selfishly of himself. Boxes containing Father's various documents, including the abdication papers and the speech he had delivered to his beloved army, began to be delivered at the palace. Both Mother and Father had suffered e emotional agony thinking that the other had been shot and killed. Father was soon to be with us in Petrograd, but an odd event had caught his eye in Mogilev. Indeed Ruzsky had warmly received Shulgin and Guchkov when they arrived, unveiling the truth that they had been intimate friends the entire time and that Ruzsky had been a spy.

Indeed, there were six specific men, on orders from the Duma, who had delayed Father's arrival in Petrograd where he would have granted the Constitution. Hence his train never arrived on time. All this was organized to enable the revolution. In Petrograd Kerensky handed out orders, while Guchkov, Kalenin, Gribushchin and Shulgin were on the train with Father. General Ruzsky, Commander of the Northern Front, was located in Pskov. Mother responded; "I urged Father to close the Duma long ago. Before Papa left for G.H.Q., he was discouraged with the Duma and left a signed order with the Premier, Prince Golitsyn, to dissolve it at once, but the Premier failed to carry out his orders."

General Count Keller and General Khan of Nakhichevan, old friends of Father came to visit him after his abdication. Generals of the Guard they had known Father for many years. They wanted to send their troops to Petrograd to put an end to the revolution. Father felt the same way, but was no longer in a position of power. Instead, he suggested they approach the Provisional Government with the plan. Surely, Ruzsky himself received word of this planned action and it was never acted upon.

Father's train returned Mogilev from Pskov so that he could say good-bye for the last time to his beloved troops. General Count Keller came to see Father kissing him with the assurance, "Your Majesty, I would rather be dead, before I would serve any other government." It came to our attention that he was later shot or committed suicide.

General Alexeiev in Mogilev with Father now imprisoned him, although they had always been friends. There were also representatives of the new government and generals present.

Several grand dukes could be seen there including Boris Vladimirovich, Cyril's brother. Boris expressed a desire to see Father in person but was denied this wish by General Voyeykov.

Right after Father's farewell address the General Staff swore a loyalty oath. However, the new regime ordered them to remove Father's initials from the epaulets which they did not want to do, and they actually refused to comply with this order. They would have rather killed the traitors than do such an ignoble thing. To this, however, Father declared, "Now, it is too late."

We heard later from Prince Dolgorukov that Father turned his head from the train window which faced the parade ground to hide his copious tears which he shed at that moment. It was impossible for him to view this reprehensible moment for his army. It came to Father's attention, still at G.H.Q., that Grandmama Marie, his mother, was on her way to see him at Mogilev. He was not looking forward to this encounter as she was the cause of much distress for him. She was more formidable than all of his ministers put together. She came to him on the train where she blessed him. Upon their parting they were never to see one another again.

Father finally reached Tsarskoe Selo, on March 9/22, 1917, at 11:30 am, after several days journey on the train. His travel companions left him here. They had included many of Father's lifelong friends among which were his trusted officers and his favorite aides-de-camp.

Historians will never know for sure, but we had heard that they were informed on the train that if they did not leave immediately after their detraining, that they would be immediately shot by the Provisional Government. "They deserted me in my saddest hour," lamented Father. Those who would not, or could not, remain at his side included Cyril Narishkin, chief of his mobile secretariat, son of our dear Zizi Narishkina, the Mistress of the Robes as well as Count Grabbe, an A.D.C., whom we had known since our childhood. How sweetly I remembered how he accompanied us sisters on long walks on the shore in the Crimea. I had even poured sand down his neck in one my mischief making moments. The Duke of

Leuchtenberg and our friend A.D.C. Mordvinov (whose daughter I knew and liked) and Sablin, once a lieutenant on the "Standard" were among those who did not remain at his side after arriving at Tsarskoe Selo. Captain Drenteln, a cherished friend and commander of Father's own Preobrazhensky Regiment, also disappeared.

Father made his way without haste upstairs to Mother. Marie and I were seriously ill, and I was fading in and out of consciousness. In this state of delirium I was sure I was only dreaming that he might be there. As I realized that I was not hallucinating in my fever it dawned on me how drawn and exhausted he seemed. He was emaciated with sunken sad eyes. A nervous shake was noticeable in his left shoulder, more than it ever had. Prince Dolgorukov informed us at a later date about the disturbing shock Father had experience upon reaching Tsarskoe Selo. His chauffeur was clad in civilian clothes. He was further rattled as the guards on duty, who knew of his exact arrival time, demanded that the chauffeur tell them via telephone the exact identity of the occupants of the car. When he replied that it was "His Majesty" they replied with disrespect, "Let Nicholai Alexandrovich pass through." Father was furious at such improper protocol, while he also noticed that he hardly recognized anyone in the packed antechamber. He never said a word as he passed among them.

Mother hurried breathlessly down the long corridor to collapse in Father's arms, and they went upstairs together. Representatives arrived later to interrogate Father to great extent. They ordered Father's badges to be removed from all staff uniforms without Father's permission. We were all now placed under immediate arrest. Mordvinov was forbidden to arrive at the palace, although he had wanted to do so.

By reading Father's copies of his abdication speech we could more thoroughly inform ourselves of how it had transpired at 3:00 pm. on March 2/ 15, 1917 in the study of his private train at the railroad station in Pskov. Upon consultation with Dr. Fedorov, Alexei's physician, Father decided to abdicate in favor of his brother, Michael, instead of Alexei who was really too ill to sustain such pressure. Father understood the ramifications as he was well aware that the Holy Synod of the Russian Orthodox Church the Holy Synod as Heir to the Throne. He reached this untenable decision, nonetheless, in a valiant effort to avoid the bloodbath that a revolution would unleash. Those who had accompanied Father on the train divulged to us that Ruzsky had even demonstrated the audacity to direct a threat at Father. Reportedly he stated, "If the Emperor will not sign it now, I would hate to say what may happen to his family." Our eyes moistened as we read and listened to his heartfelt plea to the people to support the Provisional Government and to try to be loyal to it.

*Farewell Address*

I address you for the last time, soldiers so dear to my heart. Since I have renounced in my name, and that of my son, the Throne of Russia, the powers I exercised have been transmitted to the Provisional Government which has been formed on the initiative of the Imperial Duma.

May God help it lead Russia on the path of glory and prosperity.

May God bless you also, glorious soldiers, to defend our native land against a cruel enemy. For two and a half years you have in every hour undergone the fatigues and strain of a wearing campaign, much blood has been spilt, great efforts have been crowned with success, and already the hour is at hand when Russia with her splendid allies will finally crush by one joint and daring effort the last resistance of the enemy.

A war such as this, unknown in history, must be continued to the final and definite victory. Whoever dreams of peace or desires it at this moment is a traitor to his country and yields it to the enemy.

Carry out your duty, protect our beloved and glorious country, submit yourselves to the Provisional Government, render obedience to your chiefs, and remember that any slackness in your service means a gain to your enemies.

With the firm conviction that the boundless love that you have for our great country will ever remain in your hearts,

I pray that God may bless you, and that St. George the Great Martyr may lead you to victory.

> (Signed) Nicholas
> (Countersigned) Alexeiev, C.G.S.

To hear Father read such a statement shocked the troops as were it a bolt of lightning. Indeed, one of his personal guards suffered a heart attack while he listened to the speech. Father exhorted the army to fight until complete victory had been attained. He honestly felt that Russia would crush the enemy completely. The support needed for this last valiant effort to secure victory for Russia never materialized as there was a lack of unified approval among the upper classes in Petrograd. They did not heed Father's plan to win the war within three months as he had promised in his speech before the Duma. Indeed, it was not "Father's War" but "Russia's War." Father would have returned to G.H.Q. even given Alexei's weakened state of health.

More and more political leaders lent more credence and importance to malicious rumor mongering than to reality. Later these same politicians claimed Father had only abdicated in order to spare us, his family, from being killed. Had they not spread rumors and falsehoods, and had they not supported traitors, then the problem could have been solved that way, not by killing the Imperial Family.

I permit myself to ask before the Russian people what sin we children could have committed that we should perish, from the eldest to the last born, even after we had dedicated our life energy to the war effort in the service of our country. Why did we have to die in the end as a penalty, a penalty for what? Why could the traitors who hatched and carried out the revolution not have taken up arms to defend the nation rather than to tear it down and subject it to tyranny and godlessness?

My sisters, whom they had never even seen, were beyond reproach. Whatever their comments and complaints about my mischievous nature were of little importance to me, for they were my sisters and could say whatever they wanted.

Tears welled up in Dr. Botkin's eyes as he listened to Father's farewell address after which he exclaimed, "Only His Imperial Majesty could speak such deep words." Father then recited the words of Tsar Nicholas I: "Ode raz podniat Russkii flag, on uzhe spuskatsia nedolzhen." (*Where once the Russian flag is raised, it shall never be lowered.*)

Details of the abdication began to trickle down to us. We learned that Father had at first abdicated in favor of our brother but that after the doctor's advice, he had changed this to his brother, Michael who was to make his way to Petrograd from Gatchina to take the oath of office. The Provisional Government pressured Uncle Misha to abdicate quickly after he had ascended to the throne which disappointed Father greatly.

Many ministers and high officials were placed under arrest by the new regime only because they had refused to sign the loyalty pledge to the Provisional Government. Father had had no idea about the goings on in Petrograd until he had arrived home.

In order to obfuscate their crime General Ruzsky hyped the lie that Father had been drinking before he abdicated. Father was not the only one to suffer this ordeal, for on the train were others whom he held in high regard including his friend, the Minister of the Household of the Court, Prince Vasily Dolgorukov, the Flag Captain Nilov, A.D.C., General Voyeykov, Chief of Administration of the Palaces in Tsarskoe Selo, Count Vladimir Fredericks, Father's Chamberlain as well as the latter's assistant, General Mossolov. Other travelers on the train of abdication were A.D.C. Count Grabbe, Commandant of an Escort, A.D.C. Captain Drenteln, A.D.C. Cyril Narishkin, head of the Chancery, Colonel Mordvinov and General Dubensky. The Provisional Government had a representative onboard also in Kerensky's friend, Vershchinin, and others.

Prince Dolgorukov assured us that the only thing that Father drank while pacing around the study on the train was tea. Father's butler and valet insisted to Count Beckendorff with tears in their eyes, that a great sin was being committed against Father by the dissemination of such slander. Father stayed up all night that last evening on the train sitting in his study. One of the engineers requested an audience with Father at midnight which was promptly granted. He had made many trips with Father. Upon seeing Father he sank to his knees and kissed his hand, crying and revealing to his Tsar: "Your Majesty, I will never serve these bandits. It is the end of my life." After the train reached the Tsarskoe Selo train station at the moment Father was getting into the automobile returning the salute of his officers, he heard a shot and the engineer fell dead.

(Editor's note: the juxtaposition between the humility and loyalty of the engineer and his immediate and cruel execution or suicide heighten the sense of the radical nature of the Provisional Government which illustrates its lack of commitment to a new and better Russia based on high ideals. In contrast, it seems to show readers, at least this reader, that the Left was interested only in the rhetoric of necessary change in order to gain power and impose its will. Surely the Tsar prayed for the engineer's soul when he realized he had died for his loyalty to the monarch. The engineer's demise foreshadows the Tsar's.)

\*

# PART III

# *Arrest And Exile*

———————————————————————

# XIV    ARREST

Mother was to be separated from the rest of us children much to Father's objecting that such an event would be cruel to their children who were still ill. Finally an agreement was made that Father would stay downstairs, but that Mother would stay with us on the second floor.

Due to the fact that we were all now under arrest, Mother was allowed to stay with us but Father could only join us at mealtime. However, a new rule had been imposed that we were only allowed conversation in the Russian language. The new guards in our private living space were a different kind of guard than we had been used to. Indeed, they were noisy and gruff. I was told that our private wing of the palace was strongly guarded by a new kind of guard. Mother admonished to show them courtesy at all costs.

Father would have insisted that we go to England if it had not been for our illness, at least he would have insisted that we children leave even if Mother had refused to go. We gathered from later conversations with him that Father would not have gone either.

Kerensky placed his Communist friend Korovichenko, whom he dubbed his "governor" as a kind of commissar over us. Korovichenko was a repulsive creature- rude, dishonest, cunning, insulting, ignorant and quarrelsome given to annoying us at all hours of the day. The guards were chosen with the goal that they would behave exactly as their supervisors and carry out orders in the same way. When General Kornilov replaced this reprehensible man with Colonel Kobylinksy and Commissar Makarov we were truly grateful.

During this time I could not fathom all the changes which were transpiring as I had been totally bedridden. Upon being able to sit up and look out the window, I noticed that the old order of things had been replaced by the new and undesirable. The way the soldiers acted and the way they looked were totally in contrast to the Imperial guards of yore. Blessedly our health improved more and more. As Tatiana had temporarily lost her hearing she had to resort to paper and pen to compose her messages to us. Alexei was still very much under the weather. We attempted to play games which were not strenuous such as word games, puzzles and listening to French read to us by Mlle. Schneider.

At the sound of the name "Kerensky" fear entered our hearts, and we had just learned that he was on his way to visit us. He seemed to be the instigator behind Father's ill treatment. His visit was a dreaded event. When the time of his arrival drew near, we were filled simultaneously with trepidation and repulsion. We understood that this maniac of a man, Kerensky, and his Communist "comrade" had ordered all employees to gather in the large hall. Unceremoniously, Kerensky informed them that they were now employees of the Provisional Government which paid their wages they were forbidden from taking any orders from Father or Mother. What Kerensky and cohorts were doing was appropriating Russian money and our own money. While they made everyone's life difficult, they allowed themselves a luxurious lifestyle which one only reads about in fiction novels.

Among our servants were paid spies who were to inform on us including on Anna. Some of them so detested Anna that they immediately went to Kerensky to let him know that Anna was recuperated now from her illness. In a fit of anger, Kerensky ordered her to get dressed whereupon she was taken into custody and imprisoned. Unaccustomed to such uncouth behavior, Alexei asked his tutor with a nervous voice, "Will he kill us?"

Those two cronies were not only to blame for upsetting our family but for disturbing everyone associated with us. I saw both of them passing by on their way to the classroom with the intention of seeing my parents. Kerensky was brought into the room where he made the acquaintance of "Big Pair," that is to say my two older sisters. Without flourish Father succinctly stated, "My daughters, Olga and Tatiana." Marie and I were still in bed only now somewhat recuperated from our bouts of illness.

When I first caught sight of Kerensky, a man of medium height, he seemed to twist his finger nervously. The pale, ugly face hosted two small greenish eyes which together composed a rather peculiar looking head. The cut of hair on his flat head stood up brown and rigid not unlike General Ruzsky's. I now experience an unpleasant sensation whenever I espy anyone who resembles these men.

Soldiers and sailors, allegedly, were in the hallway behind Kerensky, while in reality they were nothing but thuggish convicts, ne'er do wells who were untidy, unkempt, and uncouth. To make matters worse they were armed with daggers and hand grenades. Of course, we were frightened, and I had the sensation that it was due to my fever that I was envisioning such horror. Foreign spies and traitors assisted Kerensky with his new coterie to crack the morale of the people. First they told the soldiers that the land would be divided amongst them on a first come first served basis. There were mass desertions now of the armed forces since capital punishment had been abolished. The government took over many manufacturing plants and factories including those making munitions, upon which fires broke out at these locations. Without supplies, the soldiers were compelled to leave their posts.In the meantime the munitions and other factories fell into the hands of the new government and many were set on fire. So the soldiers, lacking supplies, had no choice but to desert their posts. The downfall of the army was orchestrated by Kerensky and his cadre. As the people began to learn of our arrest, especially of their Tsar, our father, the army also suffered emotionally. Even Father's own military escort, fearful for their lives, sported red ribbons. To implode the public order, criminals were now freed who then broke into private wine cellars, became intoxicated and wreaked havoc.

The new leaders did not seem to be concerned with snow removal during that unusually harsh winter. They left but a narrow path upon which for Father and others to walk. This turned out to be an unintentional blessing for Father who used the activity of shoveling snow to maintain his physical fitness. Each day from the window I observed my father engaged in shoveling snow. This helped him to maintain not only his body but also his mental facilities in every way.

During the initial days of establishing an exercise routine, Father experienced a rather unpleasant action when a soldier to whom he had extended his hand had refused to shake it. It was at that moment that it dawned on Father how extensive the propaganda campaign against him had been. Father, took all with aplomb which actually made him seem even more heroic in my eyes.

To us children, Kerensky was a fire-breathing dragon waiting to devour us whole. His frequent visits did nothing but terrorize us. Initially, he imagined that he could enter the palace whenever he wanted and wander around at will without Father's consent. Kerensky never failed to come accompanied by the Marshal of the Court, who was followed by a messenger. Father would receive them in his study, always courteously at that, in order to facilitate all undertakings of the new government. Kerensky began by not understanding or acknowledging Father's courtesy though with time he did notice Father's collaboration and became quite human. With that we children began to feel somewhat more relaxed in his presence, while our parents too felt a bit more confident with him having conversed with him at length. However, Mother could not forget the recent injustice she had undergone making her wish for rectification of her reputation which she felt had been unjustly impugned. Kerensky, on the other hand, had no intention of informing the public of the real situation at the palace, and, beyond that, he was the one responsible for Anna's arrest. Mother would never forgive him. To add insult to injury, Mother said that Anna had been still too ill to move when Kerensky carted her off to prison. Madame Lili Dehn was forced to leave at this time as was Madame Zizi Narishkina who suffered now from pneumonia. In that case, Mother felt that she would be better attended to in a hospital rather than with us. This wise little lady was cherished by Father as he known her since his own childhood. In turn she had been like a mother to our mother treating her with simplicity and kindness, characteristics that emanated from her gentle face. While she truly was a princess in all honesty, she wished to be called by the moniker "Madame." When were among ourselves, she called Father Nicky. Even though she was aged she had suffered unfair criticism as well. However, in this case, there was so much resentment among the public because of these tall and vindictive tales, the newspapers were forced to retract their calumny.

Aunt Olga, who loved peasants, had invited condemnation due to her visits to the people in the countryside where she gladly accepted their hospitality. Our house arrest was highly controlled and regulated; only two periods a day were allowed for to walk outdoors-11am to 12 pm and later 2 pm-5 pm. We very much enjoyed these chances to be outdoors and we prepared ourselves eagerly before each outing. When the clock struck 11am, all the staff came together in the semi-circular room with the guards who would accompany us.

We had to wait sometimes for their arrival as they would invariably arrive late, a fact that would shave half an hour off from our outdoor time. A sense of violation arose in that we felt cheated only exacerbated by the fact that Father was incapable of doing anything to make things better. It was a kind of psychological torture, we realized, as the more we fretted the longer they made us wait. The door was locked tight which led to the circular room, as was the case with the other rooms and the balcony area. The only key was held by the commissar on duty. Until the commissar released the key to the commandant who arrived to unlock the door, we were sealed inside. Korovichenko had the custom of sunbathing outside so this was another reason for the tardiness. We had the sensation that even the guards did not care for him. When we were finally allowed out, we walked at a fast clip to make up for lost time.

The area around the bridge over the ravine was more private so we preferred it for our constitutionals, but our afternoon walks were gradually scheduled for later due to demonstrations we were to avoid. M. Gilliard helped us in the garden for which we were very grateful.

No news from our relatives arrived at the beginning of our incarceration. With great joy we finally received letters addressed to Father and Tatiana from Aunt Xenia at Ai-Todor in the Crimea. This post was the only joy we had experienced since the beginning of our arrest, yet the Provisional Government censored the mail and inked out entire sections.

Aunt Xenia certainly recognized that our letters were rather dull and lacked enthusiasm, because we had become reluctant writers still reeling as in a daze due to all that was befalling our country. We did take satisfaction in the fact that Grandmama Marie was in the Crimea also. She had not stayed there until this point since the death of her husband, our grandfather, Alexander III. We tarried in writing her fearing there would be repercussions if we did.

Replies to our letters stretched into months. When we sent ours they were left in unsealed envelopes for it was understood that they would be read first. How we longed for a reunion in the Crimea. Father read the newspapers daily, but even these had been censored for his consumption. All too often the papers were withheld altogether. Reading between the lines for some glimpse of the truth became the Father's standard mode of trying to glean truth from media fabrications. At times, all too often, no papers at all were given to him, so that the only source of truth was from the mouths of various household workers. Their access to information was also to be curtailed when they were then forbidden to leave the palace too. Guards were placed in the small garden beneath Mother's window and at the garden gate which was across from the Znamensky Cathedral close to Mother's balcony. She began to not look out her windows as she knew that there were men outside watching for a glimpse of her through the panes of glass. It was during this time that we clearly saw someone drive in and out of the courtyard in Father's favorite Packard. Kerensky made himself at home appropriated our private property including cars, chauffeurs and horses.

Several revolutionaries led by the Pole Mstislavksy arrived from Petrograd came after midnight one night to begin a campaign of bullying. This included cutting telephone and telegraph lines to the Palace leaving us totally disconnected. The guards would not let them enter at which point a loud verbal fight ensued, but when the Pole and his conspirators lost their patience they blew open the gates with their artillery. People gather in the avenue due to the incredible rumble the attack caused. We were all woken out of bed. The armed thugs confronted the guards with the menacing words, "Shoot us or we will shoot you."

Count Benckendorf and Prince Dolgorukov came downstairs to inform Mstislavsky and his companions that they would not be allowed to speak with the Emperor as they would have had to possess a special permit from General Kornilov who commanded troops in the area. The officers on duty retorted, "You arrest us, or we will arrest you." Impervious to resistance, the revolutionary hooligans made their way upstairs to the gallery room to find Father walking straight towards them. They suddenly ran away in fear. Subsequently we learned that this revolutionary Mstislavsky had ordered the execution of many innocent families which he felt were impediments to his goals. These killing sprees afforded him and his fellow thieves the opportunity to seize anything of value which they fancied. Suddenly it was evident that all escape routes were now blocked.

We did take some measure of satisfaction when Korovichenko was transferred, a fact which gave us a modicum of hope. His position was now filled by Colonel Eugene Kobylnsky, an officer of the Imperial Guard. General Kornilov was to be thanked for sending this wonderful man, one who had served our family faithfully in spite of many dangers to his own life. Sincerely he wanted to ameliorate our current condition determined to save us. The number of guards made all such attempts to help us futile, as any helpful action would have created immediate suspicion of him. He spent four days with us at Tobolsk right up to four days before our departure, and had to leave as he had become seriously ill. We were never to see him again before our departure for Ekaterinburg.

Commissar Makarov was another very intelligent and cultured person known for his tact and being a polyglot. He had killed a policeman so had a police record having spent fifteen years behind bars. He accepted his punishment as being commensurate with his crime so that he had not become embittered to his imprisonment. It had not robbed him of his gentle manner and kind manners.

Colonel Kobylinsky tried to have the guards who had known us all our lives accompany us during our walks as they would do all they could to assure that we were not victims of abusive actions. He could not defend us out of fear for his personal safety. The Provisional Government had come to the conclusion that Father harbored no desire to make trouble for them. Father was not happy about the way the war was going and he followed whatever news he could access with the burning desire to be of service, even if he had to go to the front as a private.

Secret messages urged us to escape to Germany, but father answered adamantly, "No, we shall not escape like convicts." It happened one day that a large enclosed car approached

Father and Alexei who was nearby with his dog, Joy, shouting at them to get in and escape at once. Father refused stating, "Go at once." More guards were soon posted.

Cabbage and carrots were soon becoming tiresome for us to eat. How we wished for something different, something green, but the greenhouses no longer produced any vegetables. Father immediately realized that the fields were fertile and could be the source of daily vegetables. He suggested a vegetable garden in the spring. The area where some trees had been cut down would serve as a garden spot, and we all looked forward to some exercise. Count Fredericks discussed the idea with Colonel Kobylinsky who gave permission to proceed with the undertaking. We became enthused with the notion that we would have access to fresh vegetables.

Father eagerly began with the garden work, and Mother now wanted to go outside which she had not done for quite some time. She went outside in her wheelchair in which she sat under a tree near a stream. While she sat there guards paced back and forth across the bridge. Mother walked less and less these days. We planted and watered and tended our little garden. During my garden work the simple words of a beautiful Russian song came flooding into my memory:

> *"The Christ had a garden, where many roses bloomed, He watered*
> *them thrice a day to make a wreath for himself."*

We now went outside later and kept working until about 8 pm as the demonstrations had caused our schedules to change. We sewed or knit in the evening, while Father read to us. Soon the first green seedlings sent up their shoots and in a month we were eating green salads. Other seedlings transformed into full scale plants, and their tiny blossoms became beans. Within a week or so we would begin harvesting from sixty beds in their verdant splendor. Spring, a special time for Russians, was both beautiful and sad at the same time for us.

*(Editor's note: Anastasia's memory of a Russian Christ-centered song while she works in the garden heightens the fact that the Bolshevik-Marxist-Leninist "revolution" was not only an economic paradigm shift but also a type of culturicide. Before the Communist takeover salutations were often reiterations of Christian faith. Christ is Risen-Khristos Voskrese- traditional at Pascha, was also used throughout the year especially in the countryside. The Communist yoke made this impossible. This fact was highlighted recently by a paternal relative born in post war, communist controlled Slovakia, who explained that greetings and departures were formerly Christian based phrases as the Christian faith and the general culture were inseparable. In the then new leftist reality, these faith centered phrases were banned in an attempt to separate the people from their faith. The lessons for our current era are clear.)*

# XV     SUBJUGATION

The beginning of July was marred with new incursions into personal liberty. This time of year is full of light. The day and night sometimes indistinguishable as the night still has life with its hazy white glow. Now this glorious beauty was punctuated with the gleam of bayonets which emerged from the trees and bushes. We were now under surveillance even at our windows bushes. It is difficult for me to think and speak of it now. Russia has so much promise, but its soul has been reduced to a heap of rubble and debris. How painful is the deep love I have for that land.

When the leaves on the trees had not yet budded, we used to go to the area of the greenhouses where we imagined we would not easily be seen. They were in a state of utter neglect. As the gardeners had been dismissed, the plants were no longer tended. The Provisional Government deemed their talents best used elsewhere. Rare and costly bushes surrounding the colonnade had been cut down against our objections. Kerensky had given this order which provoked Father to tears.

The iron fence which had once protected us from the outside world was now meant to imprison us within. The driveway upon which many a happy visitor had arrived in the past had transformed into a source of fear. Spies hid in the bushes and trees which added natural luster to the palace grounds. We had been used to guards and protection in the old world, but the presence of these unfriendly and rude sentries was the cause now of ever growing depression.

Even the swans wailed in mourning during this time, sensing that we were inside and that the natural order of things had been turned inside out. We no longer visited them to talk to them and feed them. They felt our absence and their neglect. These majestic birds intuited that…

Never before had our food been so very cold. The kitchens were not located in our building but separated from us, so that the food was wheeled on cards through a long tunnel and subjected to inspection various times along the way. It may have started its journey warm, but had cooled off completely by the time it reached us.

"Children's Island" was an area on which we could play at times. Alexei would take his small rowboat to play on the water with his toy sailboats. The four room playhouse, however, in which he had once frolicked with his cousins and young cadets was now off limits. Our captors had now locked it up and taken away his source of joy, the rowboat. All this caused him great unhappiness.

We occupied our time in various ways. Father and Alexei rode their bicycles while we girls followed on our velocipedes. Mother was not able to join us in such merriment so she sat under a tree in the woods with her needlework replicating the motif of the pattern on her Hepplewhite chair. At times Father and his officer friends cut down trees and we children would stack the kindling and future firewood to dry during the summer months.

Our friend Captain Nilov, "the little admiral", former commandant on the "Standard" and later at G.H.Q. had now been arrested by order of the odious Kerensky who shot him without benefit of trial. Obviously this was an act of vengeance as Nilov had once proclaimed at headquarters that he "would kill General Ruzksy." Nilov never had the pleasure of doing so which was to Ruzsky's benefit. It was common knowledge to Nilov that Ruzsky was nothing but a traitor to the Russian Motherland.

Fresh vegetables now began to grace our table. Until now we had taken such abundance for granted, but it all seemed different, more praiseworthy now that we had grown them ourselves. We lingered and feasted our eyes on the beauty of nature which until now had been taken for granted. Alexei, not yet thirteen, amused himself happily by taking off his boots to wade in the water up to his knees. Some moments were still so simple in these increasingly difficult times.

So young, Alexei wished very little from these godless captors than to be left to enjoy God's creation in nature without their needless interruption and cruel malice. We are fortunate as human beings to be able to use all our senses to appreciate the beauty which the Lord has created for our benefit on this Earth. How cruel too when men deny this privilege to their fellowmen!

Reminiscing in Tobolsk, Alexei recalled the Children's Island yearning for the day that he might be able to return there and wade in its waters anew. Gleefully he remembered out loud his playrooms, his small cars, and other pleasantries. That is until he understood that this would be impossible. The painful reality was more than he could bear, and he never uttered another word until the end about his favorite place to play.

We began to witness guards driving people away from the fence around our enclosure. As the people knew at what hour we would go outside, they gathered hoping to catch a glance of us. They even climbed to the tops of their carriages and carts to be better able to peek over the top to watch us. Sundays were especially busy with people peering through the rails to observe us.

Familiar and friendly faces appeared in the crowd, yet we did not want to openly recognize them and jeapordize any of us including them. I was sure that some of the Tolstoys had appeared there too, in particular Marie and Elixabeth with Pasha and her brother. During the course of time Mother had met various of the Tolstoys from abroad. Nurses from the Tsarskoe Selo hospitals and friends from Petrograd also appeared at the fence to make their silent presence known.

At the time near Pascha (Easter) we became distressed when we learned that eighty workers at the palace were to be fired and discharged from their duties. Some of these loyal workers had been with us since Father's and Mother's marriage. We were naturally worried what they would do to maintain their families without the income from these jobs. Before they bid us good-bye, Mother and Father presented them with silver or gold medal. Count Beckendorff as well as all of Mother's ladies-in-waiting were ordered to leave. If they wanted to stay without remuneration, however, they were allowed to do that.

The private chapel was where we were allowed to have our Lenten services, but the priest, Father Vassiliev could no longer, by order, invoke Father's name during the ritual and prayers of the Church. As he approached the customary section of the liturgy in which he would have normally exclaimed, "Long Life for the Imperial Family" his voice began to tremble, but he was able to get through the section with the new omission. Father Vassiliev became ill and arranged, after negotiations with the Court Minister, Count Fredericks, for Father Belyayev, a deacon and four choir members to serve in Divine Liturgy at the palace.

We had commemorated Palm Sunday on the ground floor chapel at the fourth entrance of the palace. During the services we were scrutinized spying guards who hid themselves in the draperies and even behind the altar (*Editor's note: where only clergy would have normally been allowed behind the iconostatis near the Holy of Holies*) Father Belyayev broke down in an emotional collapse upon witnessing the sacrilege, so much that his vestments were stained with his tears.

Our souls were quickened during Holy Week with two services a day. Father had once given Mother a lovely screen of glass with a hue created by a mixture of purple and blue c crystal glass. It was her custom to stand behind this during the service. Behind the screen was a *prie dieu* upon which was placed a Psalter. On the right wall were paintings with religious motifs which Mother had inherited from Alice, her mother, and her grandmother, Queen Victoria. The guards had the audacity to inspect the Psalter when it was brought in and when it was taken out each time. There were Bibles in a room connected to the chapel to the right. Mother was greatly dismayed when a guard stood to her back during the liturgy. "Even in this holy place," she said, "one is deprived of a moment of meditation."

On the day of the Lord's Crucifixion (*that is Good Friday*) the revolutionaries attempted to illustrate their triumphalism over Christianity by burying their own dead. Red flags fluttered in the breeze while a band cranked out the *Marseillaise* and Chopin's *Funeral March*. The funerary procession progressed underneath the linden trees (*Editor's note: sometimes referred as lime trees, though not related at all to the citrus version, basswood and tilia*) . By design they stopped across from the circular balcony to with the dead they had taken from the cemetery including those who had died drunk in the cellar. It was the very cellar they had set fire to during a drunken bacchanal they had participated in some time before. Their insolent commemoration to counter the most solemn of days on the Christian calendar came to an end seemingly planned by heaven: angry black clouds form from which a ferocious storm was born raining down hail with fierce winds, breaking branched, and pelting the metal roof of the palace. We lit candles for light so that we could see, but when the daylight appeared we could see that the courtyard was flooded with ice floating it in. God had now sent calm.

The increasingly irritating *Funeral March*, traditionally reserved only for the deceased, was now played every day. Even the sentries found it irritating, evoking whistles of irritation as a sarcastic response when those demonstrating to the co-opted music appeared. I even heard this abhorrent *March* in my sleep.

At Pascha Vigil, Holy Saturday in the evening, the staff, servants and several hundred others gathered at the traditional midnight service in our private chapel. This service went into the wee hours of the dawn and included a procession headed by the priest with an icon and lighted candles. We went room to room and exclaimed that Christ had risen (*Khristos Voskrese!*) This gave us hope that the darkness clouding our lives might be lifted.

This Pascha was not happy and rather sad, but one much worse was yet to occur. Blessed bread was to be broken together on this Easter morn with staff, chief of guards, ladies-in-waiting and others assembled in Father's library. Those working later that day would receive Mother's blessing later in the afternoon

In a decision meant to denigrate Christianity and to denigrate us as a family, our relatives, military officers, ministers and representatives of foreign countries were not allowed to visit and exchange greetings on the holiest day in the Christian calendar. Queen Olga of Greece, the sister of the Grand Duke Constantine Constantinovich, had miraculously been able to enter the grounds but although she was banned from entering the palace. An officer did deliver her sweet message to us along with an Easter egg. Others tried to gain entry but were rebuffed at the gate.

Several birthdays were celebrated during our short time at Tsarskoe Selo. My father's was first of all. A long liturgy was held in the chapel on this day. However, the phrase "Long Life for the Tsar" were still missing which threw a pall over the day. Mother's followed with Tatiana's next and on Old Style Calendar June 5 on the Russian Calendar (*Editor's note: Gregorian calendar June 18, which is the date on the grave cross of the woman known as "Evgenia Smetisko" who claimed to be Anastasia and who then passed a thirty hour lie detection, polygraph exam with the renowned CIA operative, Cleve Backster, who declared that she was telling the truth*), I turned sixteen and would have been officially presented to the Russian Court. This year I would not be a debutante, nor did I care. Divine Liturgy was held in the chapel and all congratulated me.

A year earlier a design made by Faberge for my lavalier (*pendant*) had been approved by my family, to be made of diamonds and pearls. I was to receive it on this day. Instead, these sixteen diamonds and sixteen pearls, one for each birthday and one for each name day, were sewn into my clothes when we left for Siberia. Marie's was not long after mine and then Alexei's just before we were to leave Tsarskoe Selo.

Here I will inform you a bit more about our imprisonment. Mother's health did improve some at first but her heart took a turn for the worse during the heat wave in July. Commensurately, she was forced to lead a retiring lifestyle. Our daily life became very routine. All the time that we were ill we had had no lessons. Some of our teachers were from the outside and were teachers at the Gymnasium and other lyceums and schools. gymnasium and in other schools.

These former instructors were no longer able to teach us lessons. Monsieur Gilliard spent most of his time with Alexei, while he also reorganized the household because many were not capable of coping with the great changes taking place. Our collection of books was unrivaled while we also had several pianos on which to practice and take lessons. Once again we took piano lessons but this time with Anastasia Hendrikova who replaced Mr. Konrad It was he himself who began teach us history, geography and natural science. Mother taught us while Baroness Baroness Buxhoeveden gave us lessons in English. Our lessons in Russian language and literature were conducted by Dr. Botkin and in French by M. Gilliard. Our math teacher was Mlle. Schneider. All of our subjects were covered but one thing was sorely missing and that was inspiration.

Kerensky was known for barging in on Father without as much as a notice which disgusted the Court Marshal. Kerensky demanded to know of Father if he would go to Germany if he were extended an invitation by Kaiser Wilhelm. Expecting a different answer, Father gave him an undesirable answer assuring him, "I shall never set foot on German soil. I have already previously rejected the invitation." The car which had been set aside to carry us over the frontier crashed into the fence as it attempted to enter into the palace gate. Even if such a move had been possible, there were too many bonds to Mother Russia to ever make it a reality. Another scheme was to have us exit Russia via Murmansk, but Kerensky informed the revolutionaries, but it must be said that that plan would never been acceptable either.

Kerensky wanted General Kornilov's resignation without any warning, although the general would not agree to the demand. Kerensky portrayed Kornilov as a traitor to Father. What was Keren sky up to? What and how was he really? In retrospect, I wonder now if the General was not in Kerensky's way! Kerensky also was also opposed to Captain Count Kotsebue, the Commandant of the Palace and in former times an Uhlan Guard officer. Kerensky got rid of him in order to install his Communist conspirator, Korovichenko.

A new guard once stopped Father from entering the palace after one of his walks. Alexei had view of the situation and began to cry bitterly at seeing such degradation. Guards also stepped on Father's heel as they were too close behind him one afternoon while he was walkng with Prince Dolgorukov. Father hit him severely with his walking cane, making the guard double over in pain, after which time none ever dared to impose upon him this way again.

I distinctly remember that by serendipity I entered into a conversation with a former Russian officer who opined, "Your father should have prayed less but worked more" to which his wife quickly retorted, "What kind of officer were you? When you became ill with appendicitis you carried on like an infant! Is that bravery?" My Father was a devout Christian who not only prayed and worked but possessed the bravery of a hero. Not a day went by without his spending ten to fourteen hours a day at his desk. No other ever was as determined or as dedicated as he.

We would have been fairly comfortable if we had had enough heat and the right food for the convalescents. Our old and familiar rooms brought us comfort but were also somehow disturbing. Our treasures and household possessions were no longer ours. Many were immediately confiscated by the Provisional Government which even took my mother's own silver sets. They consisted of heirlooms from Queen Victoria and wedding gifts. Trays, platters, urns, gold plated, gold tea glass holders, spoons and over five-hundred place settings were taken by Kerensky and co-thieves. They even appropriated Mother's imperial jade figurines and crosses by Bolin, the most famous jeweler in Petrograd. They took both secular and religious items, including icons with gold *oklade* embellished with gemstones of untold value.

Alexei's jade and rock crystal collection of animals was taken away from him and even portrait miniatures and his icons. These articles of religious veneration were very meaningful to him, because faithful Christians had prayed for his health kneeling before them. They were presented to him in 1912 in Spala during one of his severe attacks. Upon Alexei's birth in 1904 the Persian shah presented him a marvelous woven carpet with a religious-historical theme which measured 12 feet by 16 feet. It had taken twelve years to create. To my recollection, Christ's face was in the middle surrounded by figures of historical importance up to the year 1900. An excellent likeness of George Washington was even included.

Olga and Tatiana had saved enough money to be able to retrieve some our tea sets at least, also a few place settings and some gold tea glass holders. Fine Persian rugs had covered our floors in the palace alogn with furniture by the Chippendale like Hepplewhite furniture. The art gallery boasted priceless paintings by the world's finest painters illuminated by the light of chandeliers dangling with fine crystals.

When Father read that capital punishment was now banned in Russia he felt it would be detrimental to the nation. He composed a detailed letter to the Provisional Government explaining how it would not be of benefit to the Army and Russia in general.

Father again had been prescient. Precisely, because there was no longer a death penalty, Kerensky carried out the murder of hundreds of young cadets after torturing their superior officers. He did not fear paying with his own life as a consequence. We had known of the victims of this ungodly deed. They had been bound, covered with straw and then set alight in front of their horrified families.

Kerensky was eloquent and known for his mellifluous manner of speaking which was useful in hoodwinking his audience into believing that he was honest in his deeds. However, all of the people could not be fooled all of the time, and people began to doubt him. He spoke of freedom and many exciting ideals poured from his rhetorical lips. He promised that when his idealistic ideals had been put into effect, that the outcome would be prosperity for Russia, yet the reality was anything but positive, in fact it was the opposite for Kerensky's action brought nothing but tragedy.

Kerensky's absurd promises were never kept and always broken. He became known to many as an unabashed opportunist. He fabricated stories to tell us including that we had received an invitation to go to England, but soon he said it had been cancelled. While we were perplexed, we felt compelled to believe him just a bit longer. Father at first was of the mind that Kerensky was the right man to be in charge of the government. While more and more people began to doubt Kerensky, we were not in a position to openly repudiate him. Kerensky's regime was mercurial; it came and went quickly and when it did it ended in rivers of blood.

Not unlike Caesar he was betrayed by those closest around him. He went headily to General Headquarters but was met with derision by people who uttered, "A Napoleon is now on the march. With a snap of his fingers, he will sweep on to Berlin and secure the keys to the city." Marching with the thieves and murderers of Russia, Kerensky imagined he could win the war and become popular with the people. His followers carried the red flag and sang, "My poidyom vperyod i vyigrayem voinu s krasnym flagom-We are marching forward and will win the war with the red flag."

Kerensky miscalculated in that he kept gifted officers under arrest, left to rot in prison, who could have been of assistance at the front. His psychological state of mind wanted complete power over every aspect of society. As a result Prince Lvov, Rodzianko (once his friend) and Generals Alexeiev and Kornilov, as well as many others, resigned their positions.

Kerensky now acquisitioned part of the Catherine Palace, once occupied by Father's A.D.C., where he indulged as a nouveau riche in luxuries to satisfy his most worldly whims. Rare flowers and special vegetables were cultivated for his personal delight, a man with an unquenchable thirst for luxury. He left behind only blood by which Russia would remember him.

Alexei somehow believed in Kerensky to a certain point, asking him once if Father could abdicate for him too. Kerensky replied, "Yes and no, but in your case I think, yes." Father was taken aback and was surely puzzled by the whole notion of abdication. Obviously, he wanted an independent answer from someone other than Father.

# XVI    DEPARTURE

We sisters had partially lost our hair due to our recent sickness. The doctor had suggested we shave our hair after Marie had lost half her hair. We did this right before our departure for Tobolsk. As bald sisters we resembled one another so much that it was difficult figure out who was who. We wore turbans when outside especially in the vegetable garden which was now established.

Uncle Michael had received permission from Kerensky to come to the palace on Monday, July 31st, 1917 calculated on the Old Style, that is Julian calendar. Father felt this was a kind gesture on Kerensky's part and appreciated the courtesy. Uncle Michael was also under arrest at this time. The joy was mixed with pain, as only Father was allowed to see our uncle and no one else. At each visit, Kerensky and Colonel Kobylinsky had to be present in Father's study. There was no privacy allowed for the brother, although neither thought it would be the last time for them to meet. Given the circumstances, neither brother could confide in the other. Father did say, on the other hand, that had he known that Michael would abdicate too, that he never would have done so in the first place. We understood that our uncle, Father's brother, had actually abdicated because the Provisional Government was forcing him to do so, and Kerensky was the only one responsible. Father also asked Michael about their mother in this meeting, to which Michael replied, that he was not able to see her. Father suggested, "Why not send Mr. Johnson (Uncle's secretary) or contact General Ivanov." Father wanted Uncle Michael to have Kerensky allow and organize for us to proceed to the Crimea where Grandmama Marie was now for the first time since the death of her husband, Alexander III. Aunt Xenia along with Aunt Olga and her newborn were there.

All of us were fearful that something would befall Alexei on his upcoming thirteenth birthday. Although we sensed that that our departure date would eventually come, we had no idea that it would be on such short notice. Honestly, we sisters did harbor a superstition about the number thirteen as there had been so many incidents we knew about associated with it.

The three hundredth anniversary of the Romanov dynasty was celebrated in 1913. On March 13th, 1917, Marie became deadly ill with measles and pneumonia. On Sunday, July 30th (August 12th), 1917 Alexei became thirteen years old.

Again another odd coincidence was to occur. Right after the singing of the Te Deum in our chapel we all congratulated Alexei on his birthday. Suddenly Count Benckendorff informed us that we were to leave the very next day. Our hope of hopes was that the location would turn out to be the Crimea. We waited with trepidation.

Our destination was a secret to us. Kerensky did not share it with us although he knew exactly where we were to go. Father was assured by him that it would be safer than our current location, but that we should take our warmest clothes. Evidently, the destination could not be the temperate Crimea. Our trunks had been packed for weeks in anticipation, but we were now informed that we should pack additional essential things, but only those which were actually needed. I laid aside many things which finally had to be abandoned. I felt like a traitor. At last, I finished sorting.

For the first time in my life I packed my own luggage. We no longer had access to our vaults within which were treasures given to Mother by Father and by her own family. She carefully wrapped and packed some of her precious icons, but only those which had been given to her by loyal friends who were above reproach. We children also took some from our own rooms.

It had initially been our intention to "travel light," instead trunk after trunk was sent to be transported with us. We wished to have as many things as possible with us if we were ever fortunate enough to reach Great Britain.

Anyone of our household staff who wanted to go with us was given permission, but anyone not going was ordered to immediately leave the palace. Father said that only those without family responsibilities should go, and many who did not want to be separated from their families had already departed. There were those who did have families they left behind in order to go with us. Such a decision required great courage as no one knew exactly where we were going. We never questioned the loyalty of those who had not wished to go with us. The vegetables from the garden were given to those loyal workers who had stayed with us up to this undefined end. Count Benkendorff would remain at the palace to oversee Father's private business affairs. *Before we left, Father reminded Count Benckendoff that he, through Count Rostovtsev, Mother's secretary who was in charge of our <u>private fortunes</u>, and through Mr. Peter Bark, whose responsibilities related to <u>family private interests abroad</u> including <u>insurance and investments</u>, should pay, respectively, all our bills at home and abroad. One of Count Benckendorff's stepsons, Prince Valia Dolgorukov, was to go with us. We heard later that Kerensky went back to the palace, after taking us to the station, and ordered Count Benckendorff to leave our home at once. (Editor's note: boldened and underlined by the editor, because this indicates finances beyond Kerensky's reach which may have later come into Anastasia's, albeit aka "Evgenia's" control, research about which continues. We do know that the woman known as "Evgenia" has left a sizeable annuity in perpetuity to a monastery museum due to only partially understood investments.)*

Father was allowed to choose one general to accompany him so he chose General Tatishchev. The general was was independently wealthy and well thought of. A tip was given to the several hundred men who carried our luggage downstairs for us. We witnessed one soldier kiss a three ruble note which had been given to him. We knew he was crying from the way his shoulders trembled. Some of our trunks stayed in the palace and were delivered later to Tobolsk. Several of our pet dogs were also allowed to go with us, so I took "Jemmy" who was small and did not require a lot of food.

We sisters placed our dolls in the playroom with their arms outstretched as though they were calling out to us. Alexei cried as he put his teddy bear against the door to protect his possessions. We tried not to look at each other in the halls as we prepared to go. Those servants who were not going with us cried and embraced us. This forced evacuation was emotionally very distressful. With all due reverence Marie and I knelt in front the space where our icons had once hanged, but which we had now packed to take with us.

Although we had tried to put on a brave face, we were reduced to sobs at the end. Dr. Botkin had just returned from nursing his own ill family. We were given drops of Valerian to sooth our nerves. No one could know or understand the inner machinations of Mother's and Father's hearts. It was so disquieting to leave our familiar environs to leave on a journey the end of which was unknown. My memory flashed back to my young childhood. As we children descended the private back stairway, I could remember vividly trying to run up and down the stairs two at a time. I was now blind to it all as my eyes were swollen to which I held my handkerchief to dry them. We went past Mother's private chamber at which time she also appeared, having finished a prayer of thanksgiving. We could not bear to look at her.

Surely the palace was full of the spirits of the Tsars for Father, who he felt were looking down at him from their looming portraits on the walls condemning incontrovertible surrender of autocracy. Father gazed upon a life size portrait of Mother at a young age painted in 1903 by the well known Kaulbach. He examined it one last time as never before. In Mother's mind, *sans doute*, she was ruminating on the last words that Aunt Ella had uttered to her: "*Remember what happened to other Empresses!*" (*editor's emphasis*)

Perhaps Mother was also remembering the portrait of Queen Marie Antoinette and her children by Mme. Vigee-Lebrun, a gift to Mother by the President of France. Were they now sharing a common fate? Or perhaps she thought of the words of Emperor Joseph II, Marie's brother, as he shared a prophetic word with his lovely sister "In very truth, I tremble for your happiness; the revolution will be a cruel one and perhaps of your own making."

In contrast, this revolution had nothing to do with my mother, but rather was the making of revolutionaries. Why was Mother so taken with Marie Antoinette was a question I often pondered. She was really so different from Mother in many ways and in her education. Olga's and Tatiana's christening gowns were exact replicas of those worn by the children of Marie Antoinette. Mother also had a collection of replicas of Marie Antoinette's dresses which were fashioned in Lyons for Mother when she had visited there one time. None of us understood Mother's fascination with this tragic queen of France. At midnight on August 13 (New Style, that is Gregorian calendar) we were scheduled to depart. We were served tea just before beginning our journey. After one in the morning we assembled in the hall designed in a half circle. Count Benkendorff informed us that General Tatishchev would meet us at the station but would not be allowed to meet us at the palace.

Although books and periodicals were brought to us, none of us were in the mood to read anything at all. How I remembered how Mlle. Schneider had read aloud to us while we were recuperating from our sickness. I also recalled at that moment the large painting of Marie Antoinette in an imposing hat, seated with her children and a long haired dog. This portrait was heavily framed with gold leaf and measured about six feet in height. The portrait set the tone for the room in its domination, but below it was a very simple inlaid console table with Cousin Wilhelm's red enamel French vases which I had wanted to break during the war.

Father was well versed on the French Revolution having read the most important books about it. He reread them many times. Olga and Tatiana had also read them, while Marie and I, because of our weaked sight, had only read bits and pieces. Kerensky and the traitors, no doubt, had read them too as they seemed to be replicating the same pattern. There were so many similiaries and comparisons between the Russian and French Revolutions.

Now I fully realized the full and deep meaning of the French Revolution. Disasters happened during the celebration of the coronation of Louis XVI and Marie Antoinette just as had happened during my parent's coronation festivities. At the time that France's economy declined and conditions were bad, only 35 per cent of the land was held by the French peasants; the rest was in the hands of the Church, the nobility and the crown. However, Russia was still economically strong inspite of the war and the devastation of its western provinces.

Marie Antoinette had eighty attendants at her service when her daughter was born. We are led to believe by the depicitions of historians, that Marie Antoinette was carefree and demanded extravagant luxury. Books reported that she had purchased an expensive jewel just at the time that her country was suffering. Later it was proven that this was not true, but it was all too late.

That Mother and Father were "extravagant" in the same manner as Marie Antoinette would be difficult for Russians to believe. *As Father commented, when the revolution broke out 75 to 80 per cent of Russian soil was in peasant hands. (editor's emphasis)* We had only several attendants whenever a baby was born in our family. Mother, in contrast to the French Queen, was not keen on gaiety or luxury. We all mended our own clothes and made our own beds in the morning. Just as Louis XVI had been betrayed by Mirabeau, so was the case with Father and the Allies, followed by the Duma and miscreants such as Kerensky, Ruzsky, Lenin and Trotsky with other foreign operatives. Foreigners had encouraged revolution in Russia, while the horrors of France replicated themselves in Russia. Marat was responsible for a quarter of a million lives in France, while Trotsky, Lenin, Apfelbaum and others of the devilish clique exacted more than fifteen million. Many of the Russian educated classes, millions of peasants, and forty thousand Orthodox clerics were put to death.

Many of these revolutionaries were shipped to Russia for the purpose of inciting the plundering, robbing and strangling of Russia. They were supported by the prisoners of war, mostly Austro-Hungarians and Germans. They were helped by a powerful branch of the Christian church, who were apparently desirous of detaching our people from the Orthodox Church. Fortunately the Russian people were and still are very devoted to and proud of their own religion which they consider to be the true exponent of the Christian faith as delegated to us by the Apostles and particularly by the Apostle Paul. (Read M. Pierre Gilliard's book, *Thirteen Years at the Russian Court.*)

Would the same fate as that of Louis XVI be ours as well? In the French Revolution the catalyst for the overthrow of government was a rumor about the supposed purchase of a jewel; in the Russian Revoltuion Rasputin filled this tole. Were our royal relatives around Europe or any others planning to assist us? Tea was served once again at 4:00 am. Breakfast was planned for 5:30 am as the sun began to fill the palace and the lights were turned off. By some error or design, breakfast for us children and the governess was served upstairs, but we were forbidden from going there. In reality, we did not want to go there again in any case. The men who were guarding us were confused and in a tizzy knowing that our morning meal was in a place where were not allowed to be.

Kerensky was on his way to us was the message which Count Benckendorff brought to us. People crowded in the room to take their leave and bid us adieu. There was a long line of sentries forming down to the waiting vehicles. A group of people had waited the entire night near the fence to be able to see us off. It would be their last chance to say good-bye to their Emperor. They rushed toward the gate as we made our way down the roadway. The guards pushed them away from our cavalcade. The blue domed church was next with its golden cross with double eagle.

We observed the iron gates which had become the gates to our emprisonment. As we left, they creaked open and then slammed shut. As they closed, so did our hearts. No church bells chimed to wish us well; no regiments of Cossacks cheered as we were driven away; no retinue of horses accompanied the Tsar this time. How I missed the tall caps and coats of red and blue. Our car sported no yellow flag on this exit from the palace. A flag atop the palace traditionally always fluttered in the wind when were at the palace, but it had long come down before our departure. Instead of a royal progress, our procession seemed like a funeral cortege.

Representatives of the calvary delivered us to Alexander Station. Ironically, the air was fresh as we prepared to leave. The sky was golden with the morning light. Strain as we might, the traditional wish, "I shall light your way wherever you go" would not be heard this time. Tsarskoe Selo did not seem the same at all. How the new leaders had changed the peaceful and charming nature of the village. It inspired fear and made us depressed.

Our motor vehicles stopped close to our white station which was close to the public one. We crossed the track by walking. As we boarded the train, Kerensky took Mother's hand, which she had offered him, and kissed it with the wish that her trip would be pleasant. She had difficulty in managing the high first step as there was no landing step for her to support her legs. Our luggage, laying in a heep down the platform, was still being loaded on the train. When we reached our compartment Mother sprained her ankle and finger, because she had lost her breath and collapsed before anyone could catch her. She was given a sedative by the good Dr. Botkin, but the heat made her recuperation slow, so that it as several days before she felt well again.

What a sad event to say good bye to our friends and to see the officers bow their heads with their hats in their hands. At the windows of two compartments all of us blessed those good souls who waved good-bye to us. Some of the officers entered our compartment where they began to fall to their knees before Father who would not allow them do so. Insteadt, they placed their heads on his shoulder and he embraced them. Two that I remember were among the group, one named Kushelev and the other a name I do not wholly remember but something sounding like Artsalev.Father encouraged them with the words: "Be loyal and help your country; they need you now more than ever." Suddenly all the shades of the car were drawn by order of Commissar Kozmin.

Our restricted confines could not hold the agony which Father began to experience deep in his soul. He had not abdicated for any selfish reasons, but rather to prevent the blood letting which he know would have probably occurred had he not. The secrets of the dynasty were now carried into uncertainty by our family.

Suddenly the train began to lurch and move down the tracks. Its screeching filled us all with fear. The journey now began at 6:30 am. Would the train go west or south as we wished? It did not take long, however, for us to realize that we were travelling eastwards.

Ironically, Father had indeed once promised us that he would take us to visit cities in Siberia. However, this promise was now being fulfilled spontaneously without any planning on our part or knowledge. Cowardly Kerensky later placed the blame at Mother's feet, purporting that it had been she who had requested Siberia. To be honest, the moment we knew we were headed to Siberia, Mother had asked, "Of all places, how could he think of Siberia?"

Father had asked us all to write our names on slips of paper and place them in envelopes in our rooms before we left Tsarskoe Selo.

(Editor's note: Interesting to note Alexandra's supposed fascination for Marie Antoinette of France. She surely would have found of interest an altar frontal at the Cathedral (Episcopal) of All Saints in Albany, New York-USA, which boasts lace from the collection of the French Queen. Purchased at auction after the French Revolution the bolt of hand crafted Belgian lace became property of Mary Parker Corning, daughter of Amasa Parker (a plaque to whom is in the Cathedral), wife of Erastus Corning, *1827– +1897, and mother of Edwin Corning, former Lieutenant Governor of New York. Meant to be used in a gown for Lincoln's second Inaugural Ball it was stolen before being turned into haute couture. Pinkerton guards were dispatched on a tip to New York City where the material, now cut into three pieces, was found at a fabric merchant's shop. Mrs. Corning donated it to the Cathedral where many of the city doyennes worked together to fashion the museum worthy altar frontal.)

# XVII   JOURNEY

With shades drawn and the lights burning in our compartments we could hardly know that the day was sunny outside. We were exhausted, so much so that we sat without speaking for quite some time before taking breakfast. We were absorbed in our own thoughts, not knowing what the other was thinking. We were all terribly tired and we sat quietly for some time before having our breakfast. Our hearts were heavy and there were tears. Mother gathered us with her eyes. "We are together," she said. "You are my wealth and I am rewarded by the Lord for giving me such a good, family."

Four or five compartments comprised our train. The family was one, and next to our was that in which Prince Vasily Dolgorukov, General Tatishchev, Mlle. Schneider, Countess Hendrikova, Dr. Botkin, M. Gilliard, and Colonel Kobylinsky travelled. Commissar Makarov, Vershchinin, and another whose name I can not recall at this moment, were also in that car.

Our household staff and the guard were in the other cars. How thankful we were that they had stayed with us. Kerensky had allowed Colonel Kobylinsky and Commissar Makarov to accompany us.

Our spirits were somewhat lifted after we had been served some coffee. Aside from making our way for meals to the dining car and back we barely left our quarters. Mother and Alexei took their meals in their own compartments. Before we reached the part of Russia in Asia, it had been extremely hot, dry and even dusty.

Frequently the train stopped somewhat removed from the station in order to take on water. Sharpshooters guarded our train and we were continually under surveillance. Colonel Kobylinsky was their commander. The atmosphere of the ride was glum, yet at the same time Kerensky had convinced Father that we were going somewhere where we would be safer.

The city of Perm was within sight on the third day, and then a river. How quaint it all seemed, so quintessentially Russian. The difference in the air was immediately noticeable as we left the European side of Russia to enter the Asian once, passing through the Ural Mountains. This suddenly coolness in the air was beneficial for Mother who might have otherwise suffered from heart failure had the heat continued. Out train passed through the two stations of Ekaterinburg, one on each end of the city. Who would have ever imagined that this Siberian city would be come the scene of one of the century's most horrific crimes a mere eleven months later.

The times that the train would stop for any reason, we sisters saw it as an opportunity to stretch our legs. Under the every watchful eyes of the guards, we four would pick flowers along the track.

Father had been in Siberia in 1890-1891. He knew Siberia well, not only the cities, but the locations of different industries and the mining regions, because he had personally visited them. Indeed, he had been sent to Siberia by his father, Alexander III, in order to be acquainted with the local industries such as iron works, paper mills, gold and copper mines. His companions on that journey were the engineers leading the committee to design and construct the railway which would connect European Russia with the Pacific Ocean.

Alexander III had entrusted Father with the completion of this project which he undertook when he ascended the throne. In March 1915 the Amur Line was finished, two years exactly before the revolution. The initial stone of the Ussuri Line had been laid 1891 in Vladivostok when he returned from the Far East. The Far North of Siberia had also been visited by several Romanov uncles. During the reign of Alexander III the inauguration of the University of Tomsk had taken place. A large portion of the Numismatic Department of the Ekatinerinburg Museum consisted of a gift of rare coins from Father. The Ural Mining School in Ekaterinburg had also received generous donations from Father. Our uncle, Grand Duke Michael Alexandrovich, was the patron of the The Ural Society for Natural Sciences. The Imperial family itself were the owners of the The Imperial stone cutting works and the Gold Melting Department in Ekaterinburg where our fate would later be sealed.

Alexander III had built the Alexander House for the Poor and other civic institutions, while other friends had industries in those areas. Among them could be counted Count Vorontsov-Dashkov, Countess Stenbock-Fermor (*probably Nadezhda Vladimirovna Bezobrazova, née Countess Stenbock-Fermor*), General Tatishchev, Prince Dolgorukov, Count Ignatiev, Prince Demidov, Baroness Meller-Zakomelsky (*née Duchess Natalia von Leutenberg, her ranked was lowered to Baroness when she married Baron Vladimir Meller-Zakomelsky*), Count Muraviev-Amursky, Count Stroganov, and others. We knew who all of these people were, in fact General Count Tatishchev, with us on the train, shared many historical facts about Ekaterinburg with us along the journey. Indeed, his family had built this city in honor of the Empress Catherine the Great.

Ekaterinburg is located at the junction of various railroads which connect the main Siberian main line with Tiumen and Cheliabinsk via Perm. Old Style (*Julian calendar*) November 14th, 1894, the date on which Mother and Father had wed, had donated a library and free reading room to Cheliabinst, followed by an annual set of books for every wedding anniversary. There was a tea business there which he described to us, and informed us that many of our grey horses originated there.

The path to Tiumen allowed us the chance to view feeding stations, medical shelters, railroad car churches and portable schools. They had been built for the convenience of the settlers.

Almost every city could boast a school or hospital built with the personal funds of our grandfather, Alexander III.

The train climbed in altitude to finally pause near the town of Bazhenovo. There were peasants who had seen us who immediately approached, but they were rebuffed by the guards. They reported that the wineries and distilleries which had been closed during the war, had been breached and that those vandalizing them were getting drunk.

Another report informed us that the men who had been let go from the emerald mines also closed in the way were among those becoming intoxicated with looted spirits.

We arrived in Tiumen at midnight of our fourth day of travel. From there we were to change our mode of travel to a boat, on which our trunks and baggage were loaded. We needed to cross three sets of tracks by foot, which made it necessary to walk for a few hours on the dimly lit streets in the chilly air of Siberia. Looking around the bend in the river, we could make out the twinkling lights of Tiumen.

Soon we climbed on board the two-decker steamer "Rossia." Father and his friends tarried on the deck into the wee hours of the morning. We girls had wanted to see the city in the distance so we got up early, however, the boat was already on its way escorted by two smaller boats, "Kormilets" and "Sibiriak."

On our way the boat passed many small rivers, swamps, and lakes covered with reeds and millions of red flowers. Mother called them *saltwort*. (*Editor's note: known as land seaweed*) Red fox, white partridges and swans appeared along the way. Some of fowl were unknown to us while we recognized others.

Father informed us that Godunov, Volynsky and Prince Bariatinsky had contributed much to the progress of Tiumen. Tsar Alexei Mikhailovich had founded Tiumen in 1664 visiting this frozen land himself. Alexander II had constructed hospitals while Father had later sponsored shelters, feeding places and medical centers for exiles on their way to the settlements.

While on the topic of exiles in Siberia, the first to the Tobolsk Government had begun at the time of the murder of Tsarevich Dimitri in 1591. Two Romanov brothers, Ivan and Vasili Nikitich, Yuriev-Zakharin along with Prince Beloselsky had been banished by Tsar Boris Godunov in 1601. Sheremetiev and Prince Dolgorukov had also been sent away there to Tiumen and Tobolsk. The members of the families for which the two were ancestors were close friends over many generations. It is also worth noting that the first Romanov tsar had visited Siberia while the last was to die there. Among the people there was a belief that Ivan the Terrible had been responsible for the prisons established there.

However, vicious propaganda tried to falsely "reeducate" the populace with the prevarication that it had been Father's doing that prison camps had been opened. It is safe for me to say that this was nothing more than unmitigated Bolshevik false news.

Late in the afternoon we approached the juncture of the rivers Tobol and Tura. We went by the village of Pokrovskoe where Rasputin's house looked down on the village from a place on a high bank. The Tobol was met then by the Irtysh River which became wider and which we continued our trek. Late in the afternoon on the second day we arrived at Tobolsk. The city was seemingly constructed on a hill which loomed over a lower one. A stone wall was visible near the uppermost level. The wall, we heard, was a remnant of a 16th century fortress which was supposed to have protected the new settlements from tribes of the the Kirghiz, Kazak, and Kalmuk peoples.

The wharf was filled with people who had come to catch a look at us. We were to stay at the governor's house which was inspected by Dr. Botkin, Colonel Kobylinsky, and Commisar Makarov before we entered it. The house was undergoing a renovation and redecoration was not yet ready for habitation which necessitated that we remain on board for a few more days. The beds were not sufficient for our parents, while the furniture was scarce. The three scoured the village to purchase beds to place in the house. Makarov even purchased a piano with part of his own money. Little trips on the river took place during the day. We disembarked to stroll on the shore a number of times visiting the Abalak monastery which was around the bend of the junction of the Irtysh and Tobol Rivers.

The monastery lent us a carriage for Mother's use, while the rest of us preferred to walk up the hill along the narrow path on foot. Not far from the landing place, the monastery rested on lovely grounds. When the people on the other side of the monastery church saw us they began to cry. In front the of the icon of the Holy Theotokos, the Ever Virgin Mary, Mother of the Lord, we prayed. In this painting the Virgin's hands were raised from her elbows with the Christ Child resting within the folds of her robe. Her crown was embellished with pearls.

This icon of the Mother of God was later brought to Tobolsk. In front of it we had our spiritual peace, because our prayers were undisturbed there. We found strength in our prayers along with hope and courage. Byzantine icons made up the lovely iconostasis which outshone the one at Tsarskoe Selo. We were elated to finally visit this monastery of which we had long heard. Our gratitude went out to Colonel Kobylinsky and Commissar Makarov for this wonderful opportunity.

The steamer anchored later that night in the middle of the river in front of Tobolk. We would now be allowed to occupy the governor's residence. Alexei and Marie accompanied Mother who went by car to the house, while the rest of us walked along Tulyatskaya Street, leading from the dock, to our new home. Mother's group had passed by the local Lutheran Church at which time her eyes filled with tears. She told Marie and Alexei: "It reminds me of the day after your Grandfather's death. I was baptised in the old chapel in Oreanda in the Crimea." It was the day she was converted to the Russian Orthodox Church and given the name of Alexandra Feodorovna with the title of Grand Duchess of Russia and the style of Her Imperial Highness.

(Editor's note: Alexandra's conversion from the Lutheran faith to Orthodoxy was not unique. Dowager Empress Marie had been raised in the Danish Lutheran faith and Empress Catherine had been baptized in the German Lutheran church. In early Tsarist Russia Lutheranism was a minority faith, practiced by those Germans who had begun to arrive in Russia under Ivan, dubbed "The Terrible." The first Lutheran church in Moscow was the Lutheran Church of St. Michael in Moscow dating from 1576. A Swedish-Finnish Lutheran church was erected in St. Petersburg with the approval of Peter "The Great." When Latvia and Estonia were incorporated into the Russian Empire Lutheranism became more pronounced within the realm due to its majority status in those lands. According to East West Ministry Report (eastwestreport.org): "By 1914 the Evangelical Lutheran Church in Russia (except for Finland and Poland) included 1,828 churches and prayer houses with a membership of

| | |
|---:|---|
| 1,293,000 | Latvians |
| 1,100,000 | Estonians |
| 1,098,000 | Germans |
| 148,000 | Finns |
| 12,000 | Lithuanians |
| 4,000 | Poles |
| 1,000 | Armenians |
| 4,000 Other nationalities | (including Russians) |
| 3,660,000 | Total" |

✳

# PART IV

## *Tobolsk*

# XVIII  ORIENTATION

𝔍 was filled with lonely sadness when I finally viewed the house being enclosed with a high wooden fence still under construction. Indeed, I had imagined it in the midst of a forest. The gate closed behind us after we approached on the dilapidated wooden walkway, and suddenly were were prisoners. Quite the irony that the street was named SVOBODA (Freedom). Our faithful friends General Ilia Tatishchev, General Valia Dolgorukov, Dr. Eugene Botkin, M. Pierre Gilliard, Countess Anastasia Hendrikova and Mlle. Ekaterina Schneider; also Miss Alexandra Tegleva, a nurse and her assistant, Elizabeth Ersberg, and the chambermaids, Miss Tutelberg and Anna Demidova; Father's serv ant, Terenty Chemodurov; Mother's servant, Alexei Volkov; and Ivan Sidniev, the servant of us four sisters shared the same residence with us. Alexei's personal attendants, Trup, Ivanov and Markov, his male nurse, Klementy Nagorny; a writer, a hairdresser; several cooks including Kharitonov and his helper, Leonid Sidniev were among the retinue as well.

Mr. Sidney Gibbes, our English tutor, and Dr. Derevenko, were finally permitted to join us and resume their duties. At a later date Baroness Buxhoeveden, a lady in waiting, joined us on the boat the day we departed for Ekaterinburg. In addition there were close to four hundred military personnel surrounding us. The current house was pleasant enough, although our rooms on the second floor were not as spacious as the ones Our quarters on the second floor were smaller and more crowded than those we were used to.

Three bedrooms in all were at our disposal including one solely for Alexei, another for our parents and one for us girls. There was a big hall on this floor which sported a pianto and a comfortable sofa with other pieces of furniture. Alexei's male nurse had a room next to Alexei's bedroom There was a corner room at the top of the stairway which served as Father's study. We had a balcony which we found incredibly enjoyable especially when the sun shone. From its vantage point, Mother could watch us as we took walks in the small yard. The sun here seemed somehow brighter than in St. Petersburg.

The arrangements of the first floor were the same as on the second. The rooms opened on both sides of a long corridor which ran from the front to the back of the house. The closest room to the vestibule was occupied by an orderly officer on duty. M. Gilliard's room and the dining room were on this floor, as were the remaining quarters used by our household. But later the larger rooms had to be divided by partitions to make two rooms out of one, in order to accommodate every one possible. Almost all the rooms had parquet floors, and on the second floor we had some of our fine Persian scatter rugs and others, all sent to us from

Tsarskoe Selo by Makarov. Most of the remainder of the staff was housed across the street in the large residence which belonged to a rich merchant named Kornilov. Extra maids had accommodations in town.

Our walks were not exciting, because of the limited space, which consisted of a small garden, where there were some Siberian irises, and a part of the street and a part of a square joined to the garden by a high wooden fence. This space was always guarded by a dozen or more soldiers on the outside and by that many more inside. In the back of the house there were the temporary barracks built to accommodate the guards. From here they could observe all our activities. We played ball or tug of war among ourselves; and occasionally other games with the guards. Father was always present at these games.

We began to feel almost natural in our prison house. The small quarters took the form of a home and we settled down into a peaceful routine. From the absence of shooting and rioting, it was evident the revolution had not reached this part of the country. In fact, everything was so quiet it was hard to believe it could be Russia.

One of Father's complaints was the lack of news. We were completely isolated. We did receive a locally published news paper containing mostly hearsay. No first hand information freshened its pages, nor did it contain any foreign news.

Now and then Commissar Makarov and the guards inadvertently dropped some news. Our friends from across the street were at liberty to enter the governor's house and resume their duties. They even were permitted to see the town, b t we could not go out. Thanks to Colonel Kobylinsky, our first two months at Tobolsk were quite pleasant. The house came near to being the kind of home that Mother had always longed for-one in which we could be close to each other. No exter nal duties claimed any of us, not even Father-a situation that made him restless.

There were many guards everywhere, but they, like Colonel Kobylinsky, had come with us from Tsarskoe Selo and knew us as submissive prisoners. They became our friends and we chatted with them freely. The colonel was very kind; Father nicknamed him "our friend." There was no friction because we complied with every demand. They trusted us but still they watched us as they were ordered to do.

Our food was simple but nourishing. Our own chef, Kharitonov, and his helper cooked to our satisfaction. In living this simple life, Mother became much stronger. She ceased to fret over the wounded soldiers, whom she could no longer help, and she found compensation in her writing, painting and re ligion and in our close family life. At least, we were all under the same roof. She had her one wish: the right for us to belong to each other. Our being together went a long way to soften our captivity.

At first it was very difficult for Mother to adjust herself to the new experience of housekeeping, managing personally and coming in direct contact with the attendants. The sudden change from many servants to a few was very confusing to her. She had not kept house for some years; even while living with her Granny she had devoted her time to her studies. Since these servants had to assume duties which were strange to them, we sisters helped Anna and Tootles in their daily work. Operations were not always smooth but the servants were willing and adaptable and above all loyal. After a while Colonel Kobylinsky gave permission for several maids from Tsarskoe Selo, who were willing to come, to join us. But the sudden changes in Tobolsk kept them waiting there for weeks and in the end they never were able to enter the house.

At this time we had a few letters from different friends but nothing from our relatives in the Crimea. The latter were constantly in our minds and we wished so much to be near them in that beautiful country, among all those flowers and near the blue-green sea. Then, as if by mental telepathy, Colonel Kobylinsky arrived, his pale face beaming with excitement, and handed a letter to Father from Aunt Xenia in the Crimea. It calmed us, but at the same time left in our hearts a painful and lonely feeling which stayed with us incessantly. Later a number of letters came from that distant land. One such letter took six months to arrive. Father wrote short letters as there was always the fear of bringing trouble to the recipients.

When shortly our English tutor, Sidney Gibbes, arrived in Tobolsk, he brought us first hand information on the happen ings in the Crimea and the conditions in Tsarskoe Selo and Petrograd.

The older men who came with us from Tsarskoe Selo, especially of the First and the Fourth regiments became our friends. They were kind to us and could not understand why we were held prisoners. These men loved Alexei, and to them he still was their Tsarevich. Those good fellows brought him gifts, which they proudly presented to him with loving smiles and touching words. I will never forget the time when one of these men spent many evenings carving a puzzle out of white soft wood. It was chain-like and every turn made gave it a new design. Another man made for him a set of wooden Kalmuk toys, from the great-grandfather to the tiniest baby boy. They fitted into each other so skillfully that when all together they formed only one big great-grandfather. Alexei was touched by these gifts. We knew all these men and the families of some of them. Knowing their financial condition, we felt sorry for them.

The soldiers of the Second regiment, who at first were un pleasant, had by now become actually insolent. They formed a Soldiers Committee under the direction of a man called Arnold Goldstein who came to Tobolsk about a month after our arrival and at once started to poison those men. All other individuals who came to Tobolsk were at once arrested but this man was allowed to stay and make trouble. The committee asserted its authority over the officers whom Kerensky had sent when we first arrived in Tobolsk. The friendly spirit that prevailed in our prison was reported. Stern orders bounced baek. Our kindly guards had to step aside, and radical ones took their places. Colonel Kobylinsky tried to resist but, alas, it was a losing fight.

Shortly after we reached Tobolsk, the young townspeople had a dance on the street, called "Krugom." The girls were dressed in handsome embroidered red babushkas and the boys in high boots and pleated trousers. The dance starts when one of the girls calls her boy friend by his name, saying please come. He takes off his fur cap and the couple dance in the middle of the circle while the balalaika and accordion play and the participants sing a song-the words of which usually center on water, birds, the moon, etc., all taken from nature. The boy then kisses this girl, the girl of his heart, and asks her to dance with him. The girl then calls another man who in turn invites his own girl. The first couple drops out and the procedure is repeated.

Father liked the Siberian climate and the fabulous splendors of the sunrise and sunset over the mountains and the soft clouds hiding the distant hills. We too found it agreeable and peaceful after the turbulent months we had just gone through. But these tranquil few weeks came to an end all too soon. We shortly learned that one of our former ladies in waiting, Mlle. Rita Khitrovo was in Tobolsk. Her unannounced arrival caused us a great deal of apprehension. We felt that our Russian teacher, Mlle. Bittner, in whom Colonel Kobylinsky was interested, might find an opportunity to exaggerate the reasons for Mlle. Khitrovo's presence in Tobolsk and thereby create an incident which would have serious repercussions. Once Mlle. Khitrovo was seen talking to a member of our staff across the street, and making a cross with her hand toward the balcony on which we were standing. Immediately after that she was arrested and sent away. The letters she had brought with her were seized and were not delivered to their owners until after they had been censored. Following this incident Kerensky ordered that all persons coming to Tobolsk must be registered.

As a result of this incident Commissar Makarov who knew of Khitrovo's coming was relieved of his post and replaced by Commissar Pankratov and his deputy, Nikolsky. Pankratov, despite his prison record, was kind to us. His knowledge of languages and his taste for art and literature betrayed his cultural background. This middle-aged man often used to tell us sisters about his experiences in prison. Yet never once did he complain. Instead he admitted his guilt. He was a man of fifty with dark hair. He made a notation on every letter received and often delivered our mail, most of which was addressed to him, saying that he was glad that our friends had not forgotten us. Once he told Marie that no harm would come to us while he was there.

Nikolsky was a Pole of disreputable background. He was rude and fanatic and had an uncontrollable temper and hatred. He immediately ordered everyone to have his picture taken and to carry a card showing the name, age and day of birth, because he had had to have his picture taken and carry a card while serving a prison term for killing two men.

Our schedule for the week was made up by Olga and M. Gilliard. Our friends were the only gleam of light in our daily life. To change the atmosphere it was decided to stage some plays in which the staff and we children could take part. A stage was put up in the big hall on the second floor, which also served us as a school room and later as a chapel. All our friends from across the street were asked to these performances to share in this diversion. Olga was in charge of the music, if such was needed. Alexei was not very keen about taking part in the plays and often begged for someone else to take his role. There was always an officer present at these performances. But soon rapidly changing conditions no longer permitted us these recreations.

Our day began at eight in the morning with breakfast served to us and our friends in the dining room downstairs. It con sisted of tea or weak coffee. Olga had hers with Father in his study, and Alexei his with Mother. At 9:00 A.M. we younger sisters took our lessons in the big hall, but during the cold spell, before the house warmed up we started the first lesson in bed with Mother. We wore in the house our woolen leggings or boots and were bundled in warm cardigans. Our instructors were M. Gilliard, Mlle. Hendrikova, Mlle. Bittner, once a teacher at the gymnasium in Tsarskoe Selo. Father continued with the history and geography lessons. The classes lasted from 9:00-11:00 AM. Alexei had his lessons in M. Gilliard's or his own room. Afterwards we went out into the yard for a half hour's exercise before our luncheon at 1:00 P.M.

Father and Olga ate luncheon with us in the dining room. Mother and Alexei had theirs upstairs. Our luncheon consisted of soup, meat or fish and sweets. From two to four we went out again and helped saw wood behind the greenhouse. Mother seldom went out with us in the morning. Alexei joined us in the afternoon after his rest and, when the weather permitted, Mother sat in a chair in the sun, sewing, knitting, writing or painting. When indisposed she stayed upstairs. Sometimes she played the piano and sang, mostly religious pieces. From 3:45 to 4:00 there was a short break for tea, for the family only, during which Mother poured the tea herself. The lessons started again at 4:00 and lasted until 6:00 or 7:00 P.M. Dinner was served at eight; the menu was the same as that served at luncheon except that we had no dessert. Mother always was present at these meals. After dinner, coffee was served upstairs. While Father poured, all stood up except Mother. We could not help noticing that usually there were thirteen persons at the dinner table, seven from the family, and six from the staff. Occasionally Dr. Derevenko and his son were asked to dinner, also Colonel Kobylinsky and Mlle. Bittner.

During the first few weeks the food was satisfactory; this did not last long because many products became scarce and prices went sky high.

It was decided to raise our own food. Within a month we had many chickens, turkeys, and ducks that enjoyed swimming in their little pond which we had made by diverting a small portion of a brook which ran through the garden. The horse stable was used for pigs and even the greenhouse was converted into a chicken coop.

Soon the people learned of the hour of our walks. They tried to get a better view of us through the cracks between the boards, and many of them kneeled down in prayer for us. Even Kalmuks who are Mohammedans raised their hands and prayed to Allah for us, without being afraid to do so. To many millions, the Emperor and Empress were still the Father and Mother of Russia.

In October before navigation on the river stopped for the winter, and after his enforced return to Tsarskoe Selo, our friend Makarov sent us from there some warm clothes and rugs, curtains, linens and other needed items as well as some provisions.

During Kobylinsky's administration we were permitted to go to church on Sundays and holidays. The church services were held at 8:00 A.M. when it was still dark. We assembled in the yard and proceeded to the church flanked on each side by sentries. The church was a short distance from the house and in getting there we had to cross the street, pass through a park and onto another street.

Father went into the church first, followed by Mother, Alexei and then us sisters. Some of the guards entered the church and stood behind us while the others remained outside, waiting near the steps. On our return, after the service and as a mark of honor, the church bells kept ringing until we entered the house. This procedure however was changed by Nikolsky who, in a childish show of authority, ordered that the ringing of the bells be stopped before we reached the gate. Church services for us were strictly private and the public was not permitted to par ticipate in the services while we were there. Instead they waited outside, and as we left the church they kneeled and kissed the ground after we passed as a sign of their love for the family.

When Dr. Derevenko came to Tobolsk with his son Kolia, it was a joy for Alexei. The two boys played together, read and wrote little stories. Alexei was happy to have a friend to play and eat with. But this did not last very long. One day Nagorny carried a letter from Alexei to his friend Kolia. It was nothing more than childish play. Nikolsky searched Nagorny and found the letter. He immediately went to Pankratov with it, saying, "You see how easily they can smuggle letters out and who knows what else?" Kolia was forbidden to come into the house, and only occasionally were they permitted to play outdoors under the watchful eyes of the guards, provided they kept at a distance from each other.

For weeks Mother had been suffering from neuralgia. Now her teeth caused her a great deal of pain. Everyday she waited patiently for her dentist, who was to come all the way from the Crimea. I never knew of anyone who suffered so much and still had so much patience and never complained. On the arrival of Dr. Kostritsky, he repaired Mother's false tooth and one of my front teeth which had been damaged. He brought us news from Granny and both our aunts who were in the Crimea. From a previous letter we had learned that Grandmother was ill and was complaining about the shortage of food and the fact that her belongings had been taken away from her, news which distressed us considerably, especially my Father. We had also received a charming letter concerning Aunt Olga telling us about her baby son being driven in a carriage drawn by a small donkey. I remembered when I was a little girl I rode n a small wicker chair strapped on the side of a pony. The news brought by Dr. Kostritsky was cheerful on the whole.

Finally Dr. Botkin's children, Tatiana and Gleb, arrived in Tobolsk. We hoped that they would join us in our class work, but even that was denied us and we could only see them from the second floor window. The situation was gradually getting worse. Nikolsky was stirring up more hatred among the soldiers and poisoning their minds with false doctrines.

Dr. Botkin spent several hours with Father, telling him of the conditions in Tsarskoe Selo and Petrograd. We now had a fairly good idea of the existing situation in our country. We heard that Pravosudovich, head engineer of the Imperial personal train, had been shot; also that Kerensky, his relatives and his friends were splurging at the Catherine Palace, indulging in all kinds of luxuries, of which we had deprived ourselves at all times, especially during the war. Kerensky and his friends were driving in our cars and carriages, and even some servants lay at his feet. Within a short time this man who not long ago had appeared on our threshold in Tsarskoe Selo, with men whose past was steeped in crime, was now enjoying all the luxuries of which he deprived the original owners. We had several letters from Anna Vyrubova and even some packages. We gathered from her letters that Anna was having a terrible time, though her language was cryptic. She was forced to assume her maiden name in order to avoid persecution. All our mail that came through the regular channels was censored and the contents were known to Colonel Kobylinsky. Father tried to discourage the sending or receiving of mail secretly. He even asked his own relatives to address their letters to Commissar Pankratov, in order to avoid any mis understanding. Father wrote only a few letters, primarily to his mother and to his sister Xenia.

We had news from the English Sisters of Mercy in Petrograd, and from the hospitals in Tsarskoe Selo; also we heard from Countess Orlova-Davidova; from Shura Petrovsky, whose husband was one of Father's aides-de-camp, and from Liuba Khitrovo, sister of Rita Khitrovo who had been arrested in Tobolsk. The news we received indicated untold tragedies. Many officers were shot after they recovered from the wounds. The Provisional Government cared little for these helpless men.

We heard that the people wanted their Emperor back and that the Army was hostile to the new Government, refusing to take orders from the former convicts, spies and invaders, and that it wanted to get rid of Communist agitators around the country. Again Kerensky refused to sanction this proposal, because he wanted to retain all power in his hands, even though it would mean the destruction of Russia. Father knew then that the country was lost. We heard all kinds of stories. One concerned a boat caught sailing in the dark on the Volga River without the permission of the authorities. On the shore, it was discovered that this boat carried six bullions of gold, each worth a fortune. When asked where they were taking this loot, the persons aboard replied that they were taking it to the village of one of the leaders.

Kerensky made many blunders. He prevented the Army from crushing the revolution at a time when it was ready and willing to do so. The soldiers of our regiments, who came with us from Tsarskoe Selo, complained to General Tatishchev that they had not received the allowances that Kerensky had promised they would receive while they remained with us. As a result they were discontented. Many of these men had to meet their family needs. Some of them were able to obtain extra jobs, but those who were not able to do so became angry, which strengthened their sympathy for Bolshevism.

A few weeks before Christmas came the shocking news that Kerensky's Provisional Government had fallen and that the Bolsheviks had taken control of the country. He was now receiving a dose of his own medicine. The persecutors were more lenient and less cruel toward him than he was toward his Emperor and his family. General Tatishchev told us that when Kerensky was betrayed by his colleagues-the Bolsheviks-he jumped from the second floor of the Winter Palace in order to save his life and in his haste to do so left the belt of· his tunic behind. It was said that Prince Volkonsky was an eye witness to this heroic performance. A brave man, indeed. An Emperor without portfolio, a minister, a lawyer, an orator, and Napoleon, all in one.

There was talk that if the Ukraine were to go to Germany, Father would be placed on the throne by German help. Father said, "Never will I or my son accept the throne with the help of the enemy."

We learned that the Winter Palace had been plundered and that many of its treasures were in the hands of foreign bandits from both hemispheres who came to our country to rob, take and plunder. They pulled down our tricolor flags-white, blue, and red. White stands for snow, blue for the heavenly sky and red for the blood spilled in defense of our country. They hoisted their own flag over the Winter Palace. They removed the double eagles from the buildings and were burning them on the streets before the eyes of respectable citizens. They emptied the historical treasures preserved for generations by our forefathers, the pride and wealth of Russia when she was in her glory. These treasures were sold abroad. The wine cellars of the Palace were broken open and the mob drank so much wine that some of them literally died from it; the rest of the old wines were poured from the bridge into the Neva River.

The secret police still was working at the time of our arrest. Before our exile the names appearing below were given to my Father which he remembered and made us remember. When some of these men found it necessary to escape from Russia for their lives, they were given sanctuary by other countries, instead of being tried for their crimes against the Russian people. These men dared to look into the eyes of Russians knowing what they had done to them, and how easy the Russian people had forgiven them all the wounds they had inflicted upon them.

Communism was founded and organized by these men whose real and assumed names follow.

*Original names . . . . . . . . . . . . . . . . . . . . . . . . . . . . .Changed to*
Bronstein . . . . . . . . . . . . . . . . . . . . . . . . . . . . . . . *Trotsky*
Tsederblum changed to Ulianov then to . . . . . . . *Lenin*
Apfelbaum . . . . . . . . . . . . . . . . . . . . . . . . . . . . . . .*Zinoviev*
Rosenfeld . . . . . . . . . . . . . . . . . . . . . . . . . . . . . . . .*Kamenev*
Goldenberg . . . . . . . . . . . . . . . . . . . . . . . . . . . . . *Mikhovsky*
Krachmann . . . . . . . . . . . . . . . . . . . . . . . . . . . . . *Zagorsky*
Hollender . . . . . . . . . . . . . . . . . . . . . . . . . . . . . . . . .*Mieshkovsky*

Tsederblum II . . . . . . . . . . . . . . . . . . . . . . . . . . . . . . . *Martov*
Himmer . . . . . . . . . . . . . . . . . . . . . . . . . . . . . . . . . *Sukhanov*
Goldmann . . . . . . . . . . . . . . . . . . . . . . . . . . . . . . . *Goriev*

We were told that Tsederbaum (Tsederblum?), Lenin's father, was arrested for murdering a policeman; his sons were very young. One son was brought up in Simbirsk by a well-todo half-Kalmuk and half-Christian family by the name of Ulianov. The other sons were with Lenin's uncle, Tsederbaum. While in college both boys met secretly with other boys and inspired them with revolutionary ideas, such as the derailing of the train in which the Emperor and his family were riding; as a result many people were killed. One brother was hanged; the second, Lenin (Ulianov), ran away; and the third was in hiding in Russia until the revolution when he reappeared. There were two brothers who are mentioned above in my list which was given Father while in Tsarskoe Selo. Later in Tobolsk and more so in Ekaterinburg, additional names were given to us to remember, the names of men with whom we actually had contact. Unfortunately I can only remember now the names of about twenty-five out of a total of approximately one hundred. One morning Colonel Kobylinsky arrived in Father's study.

With tears in his eyes he informed Father that a peace treaty was to be signed, but that prior to the signing the old Russian Army would have to be demobilized. Father said that this terrible move by the Bolsheviks was dangerous not only for Russia but also for the world; that this move on the part of the traitors should now make the Russian people realize that they were being deceived. I cannot describe the feeling it left on us. Father was a prisoner, trapped like a lion in a cage, thou sands of miles away.

But going back to Kerensky, it is significant that when he was in danger, he did everything to save his own life. But he never stopped to think that he was the one who had sent the Imperial family to the distant, frozen North. Did he give a thought to the fact that the unfortunate victims were trapped by the traitors and by the bribed convicts, and not by their own people? Now we could see why he had ordered the ar rest of everyone who came to our aid and who was willing to·risk his life, as well as ours, to save us. Kerensky had given his word of honor to Father that he would protect us. He knew what these men were like and what they were doing. I often ask myself the question: did he do it intentionally? Will one ever know?

If Kerensky was sincerely interested in protecting us, he could have ordered the train in which we were traveling, under the Japanese Red Cross flag, to proceed to Vladivostok from where we could have gone to Japan whose Emperor was quite friendly with Father and would have given us the protection of his country. During the war we had a visit by two young Japanese Princes who brought beautiful gifts for Mother and us from the Empress of Japan. They also visited Father in Mogilev.

Now the Russian people were helpless, numb as from paralysis. With stunned eyes they watched the nightmarish happenings in their country, the wiping out of their possessions, and the tragic end of their families.

(Editor's note: Anastasia gives here insight into Kerensky's true motivations which seem, with this assessment, to be closer to that of the Chekas under Bolshevik albeit Lenin orders. One has the sense that Tsar Nicholas II and his family would have suffered a similar fate had the Provisional Government been successful. Had Kerensky truly had the family's safety at heart, Japan would have been able to keep them safe and preserve their lives.)

# XIX  WINTER

The days passed rapidly as winter approached, the cold was relentless. We were glad of the warning to bring warm clothes. December was very cold and it continued through the months of January and February. The house was unbearably cold and our bedroom was like an ice house; even a glass of water had frozen solid overnight. Our rooms were large and each had only one tile stove, providing scant heat against the raw winds that forced themselves right through cracks in the windows. Even Mother, who always preferred cool rooms, complained of the cold. The only time the house ever felt warm to us was on coming in from the icy outdoors.

Mother's arthritis began to give her serious trouble, her joints and fingers became swollen. She suffered a great deal of pain and was not able to write or paint as much as before. Tatiana had a gift for nursing. She knew how to care and comfort the sick. She massaged Mother's frostbitten hands in a bowl of warm water. Mother's eyesight troubled her, too; her glasses no longer helped, since she needed new ones. The cork on the bridge of her frame had broken off and she felt this increased her sinus condition which bothered her to the very end. After a long debate a doctor came and she at last had her new glasses. Now she spent a great deal of time in theological studies and writing in the old Slavonic language.

Father's joints were swollen also, but my saintly Father never complained lest he might worry us.

We all were supposed to keep our diaries. Alexei made only occasional entries. Whenever he was encouraged to think of something, he wrote "The same old thing." I too lost interest, for fear that writing what took place in our daily lives might cause us trouble. Olga and Tatiana wrote a great deal, but right after our parents left, General Tatishchev suggested that they burn all unnecessary papers. Olga's poems and Mother's poems and paintings all went up in smoke.

Our dogs always went with us on our walks. They were our constant diversion; they saved these outings from complete boredom. We envied their retrieving sticks we threw and jumping happily, since we ourselves felt cramped. Every morning my own dog Jemmy announced her arrival by scratching frantically at the bedroom door. Her happy mood made us forget our troubles. I carried her up and down the stairway, because her legs were too short to climb the stairs. Her long silky ears got into everything. Her long tongue was always out. The poor animal did not know that a few months later her happiness would end in Ekaterinburg.

For months before Christmas we worked on gifts for everyone who came with us from Tsarskoe Selo. We had some yarn on hand and some was sent to us by our friends. Mother made waistcoats, mufflers, mittens, socks and wristbands. We tore apart old blouses and fashioned them into handkerchiefs and then embroidered initials on them. Pieces of silk were made into fancy bookmarks, some of which we painted and some we embroidered. We wanted to surprise our friends with these gifts, in appreciation of their loyalty to us.

Mother, however, seemed to have a premonition of trouble. First, she was worried about Anna, who, she thought, might be in trouble for sending letters and packages to us. Mother warned Anna to be careful about sending people with messages. She feared they might betray us. And so it happened. The least suspected person was Soloviev, husband of Matriona, Rasputin's older daughter. Soloviev came to Tobolsk several times with letters and packages. Even Olga and Marie called the situation to Mother's attention, and suggested that Anna should let the officers handle matters and not the Yaroshinsky Soloviev clique; but Mother said that Anna would die before she would betray us.

In the evening we gathered in Father's study which was smaller than our other rooms. Father read to us and we sewed·until our fingers became so stiff we could hardly hold the needles. But there was a richness in that room that made us reluctant to complain. Sometimes we played dominoes, bingo, or durachka, a card game (resembling five hundred) which Father disliked. Tatiana played bridge best of all, while Mother's favorite was bezique. (*A two player card game, Bezique originated in France in the early 19th century as Bésigue*) Ten o'clock was bed time for us younger girls, but Alexei used to retire at eight. Later on when life became monotonous, Mother asked our friends to join us in the evening. Some played games and others read. Father also brought with him his diaries and his letters. These had been confiscated in Tsarskoe Selo but were returned to him when nothing incriminating was found in them. We sat around Father in the middle of the room, away from the draft of the windows, listening to his reading aloud. I am sure his heart felt sad as did our own. We learned many interesting events that took place before and during Father's reign. Father wanted Olga or Tatiana to write a history of present events as soon as we were free, and for that reason he wanted us to remember every event that took place before andafter our arrest and during our life in Tobolsk.

Our letters to friends were harmless; some went through Colonel Kobylinsky's hands and were read by him, but some were not. Later, when we were in Ekaterinburg, we were shown photostatic copies of these letters carried back and forth by Soloviev. Then we realized he was a spy. Once in Ekaterinburg, Mother in her dark hour said, "I warned Anna again and again to be careful of what she was doing, and now she has made another mistake." After this Mother never again mentioned Anna's name. I hope she did not leave this world with this bitterness in her heart toward her friend, who unfortunately brought one serious trouble after another not only to Mother but to the whole family. Olga and Marie always opposed Anna but Mother resented anyone saying anything against her friend.

It had been promised that when Baroness Buxhoeveden arrived, she would be staying with us. We fixed her room our selves and the final touches were approved by Mother. It was Christmas week when she reached Tobolsk. The day she was supposed to come to the house, Colonel Kobylinsky notified Father that he wished to speak to him. He informed Father that the Soldiers' Committee decided against her joining us. Not having money Iza and her English assistant organized English classes in town and found many people enthusiastic to study this language. She met us only on the boat when we left for Ekaterinburg.

On two occasions, the icon of the Image of the Holy Virgin was brought from the Abalak Monastery to the Church of the Annunciation for services which the family attended. The first time was November 14th, old style, the anniversary of my parents' wedding. We had prayed before this icon in the monastery and were deeply moved to be able to do so again. The church bells rang as we left the church and continued until we reentered the house.

The second time was on Father's name day-December 6th, Old Style (*id est Julian Calendar*). No one was allowed to enter this holy place while we were there. At the end of the service, as though nothing had changed, prayers were offered, ending with a Mnogoletie ("Long Life for the Imperial Family") as had always been done before the revolution. We were surprised at the priest's courage. Father's face turned white and we all glanced at each other. Olga's pale face turned faintly red, and she wiped her eyes. We wondered if there was going to be trouble ahead. There was. They promptly demanded the death penalty for Father Vassiliev, but he was saved, though not for long. He was sent away by Bishop Hermogen and was replaced by another one. The nuns too were taken away.

We were now forbidden to attend church services, but after hours of pleading with the Soldiers' Committee by Colonel Kobylinsky, we received permission to attend church services but only on the twelve principal holidays. From now on the restrictions became more severe.

Finally Christmas Eve arrived. Mother presented everyone with one of the gifts we had been working on for months. The villagers too were thoughtful. They sent us two Christmas trees, one of which we sent to our friends across the street, with whom we shared some delicacies that were sent us by the Ivanovsky nunnery and by the head people of the local museum. In the evening, vespers were held in the big hall and we were grateful that there was no interference. We looked forward to the Christmas morning services at the church.

Somehow I felt a sadness as we walked along the path packed with snow. It was cold and dreary and at eight in the morning still dark. The sky overhead was heavy. It gave me simultaneously a feeling of loneliness and apprehension. It was so quiet that only the crackling of the frozen snow under our feet broke the stillness. We did not speak to each other; each one was occupied with his own thoughts. It is quietness like this that awakens one's heart to fond memories of the past. We crossed the small garden and with my mind's eye I could see the museum, the little park, and in it the proud obelisk dedicated to Yermak, the conqueror of Siberia. A short walk, but my thoughts covered thousands of miles behind the frozen plains of Siberia. I could see our Grandmother, our aunts and their children, and our friends, and I wondered if they had forgotten us. Above all I thought of our old homes, where I had spent sixteen happy years of my life. All seemed so cold and so far away.

My thoughts came back to Tobolsk. Only recently we had discussed with our friends here the historical background of this town. It frightened me. I thought of the chapel adjoining the Metropolitan's residence where the Bell of Uglich was formerly hung. This bell summoned the people of Uglich when Prince Dimitri, son of Ivan the Terrible, was murdered in 1591. By an order presumably given by Boris Godunov, this bell was transferred to Tobolsk, where it was damaged by fire and re cast. We too were transferred to Tobolsk, by Kerensky.

Father realized what the prison life had done to his family. We once overheard Father saying to Prince Dolgorukov, in the presence of Colonel Kobylinsky, that his heart was aching for his little family whose life which had just begun was about to come to an end. He continued, "During my whole life I tried to serve my country faithfully, and if I have done wrong I am willing to suffer for it. I am not sorry for myself or my wife, but for the children. It is a crime to punish these innocent youngsters. They are so pure and so good. They are the children of Russia."

On New Year's morning we went to church. It was one of the twelve holidays on which we were permitted to attend services. The new priest officiated but he appeared nervous. Then we heard that our former priest, Father Vassiliev, who had officiated at the previous service, had been taken away from the Abalak monastery. He was then tied, beaten and thrown still alive into the Tobol River in front of the monastery. It was very cold that morning. The temperature often went down to 25°-35° below zero. The church was unheated but dimly lighted, and we could offer only one candle apiece. Although we were provided with rugs, even then our feet were numb from the cold, but our hearts found comfort, warmth and hope ahead. Due to the extreme cold, my sisters and brother became ill again with the German measles. This time, however, they were not so seriously ill as the previous year.

Through General Tatishchev Father was informed that we could not go to church on Epiphany Day (*Theophany*), commemorating the Baptism of our Lord, which falls some twelve days after Christmas. It was decided to build a movable altar in a corner of the big hall on the second floor, where we took our lessons and gave our plays: Mother busied herself by supervising the placing of the icons in their proper places. The priest and the four nuns came to the house for the Divine Liturgy and the Blessing of Water. Father and we children sang with the choir which consisted of some members of our staff, including Nagorny, Alexei's servant, who had a very fine voice. At the end of the service, according to custom, the priest dipped the cross into the water and with it sprinkled the water in the air in the shape of a cross. We all kissed the cross but when Alexei's turn came to kiss it, the priest bent over and kissed his forehead. It touched Alexei deeply. This kindness meant so much to the little, frail boy. To the last he never forgot this courtesy, nor did we. We "broke bread" with our friends in the dining room downstairs.

It was on this day that Prince Dolgorukov and General Tatishchev pleaded with Father to have his epaulettes removed. For the sake of his family, finally Father gave in. Right then and there something died within him. He did keep his St. George's Cross and the French Croix de Guerre. He was very proud of them. Father told his valet, Chemodurov, that Gen eral Tatishchev should remove the epaulettes before brutal hands touched them. With a painful expression the general removed them. I remember when the St. George decorations were given to Father and Alexei. General Ivanov sent Father's friend Prince (Toly) Bariatinsky to present these decorations while Father was home for a few days.

Practically buried·by snow, we were permitted to make a mountain. Hundreds of shovelsful of snow were carried up and covered with water, which froze immediately. The process was repeated until a good sled course was built. We helped our friends, Prince Dolgorukov and M. Gilliard, as well as the soldiers, until we were exhausted.

January 12th/25th was Tatiana's twenty-first name day. After the Te Deum, which was held in the house, we all extended to her our congratulations. Even the soldiers of the Fourth regiment presented her with various blooming plants and flowers. Except for Mother, we had no gifts for her.

We heard that Felix Youssoupoff was killed. Mother said, "God forgive his mistakes." Later the rumor was denied.

We had a swing in the back yard, but Nikolsky's men at night wrote vulgar words on the wooden seat board. We were forbidden to go near it until Dr. Botkin, Colonel Kobylinsky or Pankratov had examined it. Our outdoor exercises were limited to the small space allotted to us. Each day they found something new to accuse us of. One afternoon Alexei was on the front steps before the house, which were protected by a wall about 2-3 feet high on either side. He heard some children on the street and climbed on top of this wall which was about 35-40 feet from the fence. Nikolsky saw Alexei from the window, and like a bullet ran out of the house and loudly reprimanded the little boy, who had done no harm. From then on we feared him.

From the window, hungrily, I watched the children romp and play all wrapped up like little bear cubs in bright red felt boots. They rode around in bright colored orange or red sleds, or were drawn by plucky little horses which reminded me of the Crimea. These ponies looked so warm in their winter "coats" and so alive as they tramped over the packed snow with their bells ringing and jauntily pulled their sleighs behind them. I pressed my face against the window. The jingling bells outside and the icy cold of the window cutting into my cheek inside were cruel substitutes for my great desire to go sleigh riding myself.

Nikolsky taught the soldiers all kinds of communistic doctrines which he called Yurovsky's teaching. At that time we did not know who this evil Yurovsky was. The hatred Nikolsky taught to the men, he was to experience himself. Soon afterwards the soldiers drove Nikolsky out. Unfortunately, old Pankratov had to go too. His going was a loss to us because he always defended us. From what we heard in advance about the new commissar who was coming from Ekaterinburg, we were apprehensive.

There were many repercussions in store for us. All the old soldiers of the Fourth and First regiments, who had come with us from Tsarskoe Selo, were ordered to leave. Before they did so, however, they came quietly one by one to Father's study to say good-bye. Almost all of them cried as Father embraced them and thanked them for their loyalty to us. One of them brought a small body icon for Father to remember him by, and another one brought with him a small notebook which he asked us to autograph. Two men from the Fourth regiment refused to leave the place, saying that they would stay to guard their Emperor. At the point of a gun they were taken away and later we heard that they were shot, near the river. When the last several hundred men were leaving, they assembled on the street behind the fence in front of the house.

We all, even Mother, went part way to the snow mountain to see our friends depart. We were never to see them again. The whole family and all around us were crushed by their going and, as they went, our hopes left with them.

We derived a lot of pleasure out of tobogganing on the snow mound we had worked so hard to build. But our pleasure lasted only one month. To the guards the snow mound was a sore spot and we tried to pacify them by not going to its top, so as not to attract the attention of passers-by who often gathered on the other side of the street to watch us. Notwithstanding, the Soldiers' Committee decided to have the mound demolished. We soon heard heavy chopping and pounding in the garden, and we knew then that the snow mound was being destroyed. They cut deep notches across the mound so it could not be used for tobogganing and in order to prevent us from looking across the street. We showed no resentment at what they did, although in our hearts we felt differently.

Now we had even less space for exercise than we had had before and we tried to amuse ourselves as we elbowed each other in the yard. We looked at each other understandingly even though no words were uttered.

More bad news reached us, that agents of the underground, friends and relatives of the men listed previously, continued to pour into Russia from foreign countries by the thousand, fol lowed later by Generals Pilsudski and Ludendorff and Count von Mirbach, the German Ambassador. We were told that all the buildings in Moscow including all of the Imperial quarters in the Kremlin were taken over by these intruders. These men ordered that the Russian Army be disbanded and that all German and Austro-Hungarian prisoners of war be released from the camps. These camps were scattered on the important railroad lines and mining regions throughout the territories of Omsk, Tomsk, Tiumen, Ekaterinburg, Cheliabinsk and other cities.

Up to now Father had refused to allow himself to be depressed. But this time he no longer was able to hide his feelings. He suffered painfully, because he believed his Allies, in whom he had had faith, had failed to help him in these difficult times. They could have prevented these men from coming to Russia. Instead, passports and other documents were issued to them. Father said again that fifty years from now there would be no democracy left, that when Russia falls the whole world will fall with it. A year later, when I recalled these words, in 1919, I wrote in my notebook, "Only the fu ture will tell."

Father was so distressed that he often sat up at night with only a little flickering lamp in the corner of his study. Mother knew that Father could not sleep. We heard the cracking of the floors which were more pronounced at night. She had left her bedroom and gone to him. We heard her say: "Nicky, are you not tired? Can you not sleep? I came to keep you company, dear." Said Father: "No, Alicky, I am not tired. I thank you for thinking of me." Such words of devotion and understanding always rang in our ears.

The only joy we had at this time was whenever we heard from our family or our friends. We longed so much to see our aunts, especially Aunt Olga's baby. Aunt Xenia's letters de scribed to us the little man so charmingly that we felt as if we knew him.

# XX    DANGER

After Nikolsky and Pankratov left, Colonel Kobylinsky brought back the key to the balcony which Nikolsky had taken away. Now Mother was again able to sit on the balcony in the sun. For several months we lived quietly and peacefully. But when the new guards came, our lives saddened.

One day Olga was found crying. She had been unhappy. She said that she had been observing the developments and believed that we were doomed. Father sent for Colonel Kobylinsky who admitted that danger was creeping upon us. Prince Dolgorukov and General Tatishchev believed she was right and thought we should escape before the new commissar from Ekaterinburg arrived. But our parents refused to leave Russia, and would not think of separation. We humbly bowed our heads and accepted the inevitable.

All of a sudden a change came into our lives. The Bolsheviks turned their binoculars on us. One day Colonel Kobylinsky informed Father that the Imperial family must go on rations, because keeping us was too heavy a burden on the Communist regime. Each one of us was to receive 600 rubles per month, the same as the soldiers. Father knew nothing about the cost of the operation of our establishment. He asked M. Gilliard, who was the most practical of all, to set up a budget and Prince Dolgorukov and General Tatishchev to help him. When they came with figures, it was concluded that ten servants had to be discharged. My parents became terribly distressed and made all kinds of excuses: this one had a sick mother, another had an invalid son, a third was the sole supporter of his motherless children. What would happen to all these families who came here from Tsarskoe Selo? It went on and on.

At last "Gillek" (M. Gilliard) and General Tatishchev made their own decision, and ten servants came to thank us for treating them so kindly in the past. It was sad losing them, though we could not foresee how fortunate they were. The new commissar from Ekaterinburg arrived and we heard that he had brought with him about one hundred men·, all fanatical Marxists. He was a red-faced brute by the name of Zaslovsky, with a bad reputation.

No sooner had the new young men arrived than trouble developed between them and the old soldiers who had refused them entry to our residence. They became angry and threatened to storm the house. Colonel Kobylinsky and Zaslovsky were bargaining all night downstairs. We dressed and sat up expecting trouble. Long after midnight we heard familiar voices in the corridor. Colonel Kobylinsky sent for more guards to insure our safety. We heard some foreign voices coming from outside the gate, then a loud voice saying, "I am following the orders of Colonel Kobylinsky. I cannot let you in. Then speak to him." As a result of this incident Colonel Kobylinsky wanted to resign but Father persuaded him to stay with us. We felt that his presence was helpful to us, even though we knew that he had no power over the new soldiers. Father believed that at least ten of the new men were disguised former officers. However, if they were former officers they were helpless, because Zaslovsky ordered more men from Tomsk. These men boasted that they had killed the director of the Cadet School and destroyed the headquarters of the Fourth Siberian Army Corps stationed in Tomsk. They said that they had burned the house on Father's estate in the town of Bernau on the river Ob and had killed the superintendent in charge. Father had inherited several big estates with large milk and cheese plants in Siberia. Tons of these products were distributed every year to different charitable institutions.

Father had visited his estates during the construction of the Trans-Siberian railroad. Zaslovsky bragged that they had already destroyed the gold smelting works and had taken away all the available gold. They also tried to plunder the monastery at Tomsk but were driven away by the monks. This is the monastery that was referred to previously.

Zaslovsky brought us much misery and inexpressible horror right from the start. He ordered us to keep from five to six feet away from the fence, and to go out only under guard and only for thirty minutes twice a day. Our outdoor exercise consisted mainly of cutting wood. We performed this humble work in the back of the building cheerfully and without complaining, and by so doing we helped members of our household whose duty it was to supply the house with wood. Zaslovsky had our house searched and several items belonging to Father were taken away.

Each day brought some new deprivations or restrictions and some fresh heckling by the guards who took pleasure in humiliating us. In return we acquiesced in their demands, disarmingly, at least outwardly. Following Father's example we accepted everything. Among the soldiers only a few good men were left. In the past, each relay of guards had started out to be severe, then gradually softened. But not these men. They were a dangerous lot. In order to avoid trouble Father and his friends-all of them understood carpentry-had earlier built a ladder which led outside to the top of the roof of an unused greenhouse, which had already been converted into a chicken coop. They also built a platform where we could sit in the sun without being seen from the street.

More restrictions were put on us. The last two days before Lent are by custom days of merriment during which the people enjoy themselves at concerts, balls and in many other ways. Zaslovsky, fearing riots by the people, forbade us to leave the house during those two days. The schools were closed and there was a constant flow of students from the gymnasium.

They were gay; we heard the bells ringing; the children were expecting to see the monkey and to hear the organ grinder, who had stopped before the house for Alexei to witness the spectacle and to hear the children sing and play. But Zaslovsky had locked the balcony door and had taken the key back to the office. We heard loud voices outdoors; the guards were driving the students and the youngsters away with the butts of their rifles. The youngsters ran and the students cried: "Go back from where you came, you unwelcome guests." Zaslovsky said he would shoot anyone who came near the fence. In spite of the warning, the passers-by continued to walk past the house, even more than before. When the people saw us in the window, they always removed their caps and bowed low. Sorrow and dread were our constant companions. We woke up with sadness, and went to bed in sadness. Father tried to read to us, but the silent interchange of fear muddled the thread of the story he read. He tried to make his voice firm and hopeful but it did not have the ring of former days.

Up to now we were able to send and receive some letters from our relatives in Ai-Todor in the Crimea. Now we heard that the mail service was being discontinued. However, we continued to receive some letters. Since Zaslovsky's arrival we had stopped writing letters as we knew that they would not be mailed. The last letter we received from the Crimea told us that the family there had been separated. Aunt Xenia with her family and Grandmother had been moved to the chateau of Dyulber, belonging to the Grand Duke Peter Nicholaevich. Though they were not far from the Youssoupoffs at Koreiz, still they could not see each other.

A few weeks before our departure for Ekaterinburg we received a letter from the family through a peasant woman from the Crimea. She had carried this letter: surreptitiously thousands of miles. Through her, in return, we sent a letter to the family in the Crimea, together with a photograph of the family-one of the few we had taken in Tobolsk. It was our last link with Granny and our aunts. The very last letter we received came from Irene Tatishcheva. A few of our letters were returned to us undelivered.

We huddled closer together, not so much for warmth, as to feel the strength of each other's presence. In the evening we dreaded to think of what the morning would bring. Morning returned with the same overhanging fear. Mother's first words were: "Thank God for the night just past and for the breaking of the new day. Also for giving me such a good family. The Almighty is watching over us." Then Father read from the Bible some reassuring message.

Our brief walks around the yard brought us no inspiration. They were cut shorter. Mother assured us that God was with us even in our trials. No harm could come to those who had faith in Him. He is putting us to the test. What good is our religion if we are not victorious over suffering? So we continued to endure, brightening the darkness in our hearts with the trust that in time God would lead the way to our safety.

Not being able to attend church was our hardest punishment. Mother especially missed this spiritual support. It had helped us. We had found there the answer to our prayers, and temporary relief. Tatiana made her decision to sacrifice her life in search of theological subjects. She became stronger and firmer in her belief and spent part of the day in reading the Testaments. Mother was a tower of strength to us. She was full of resourcefulness and hope, continually replenished by faith. We felt sure our fate was in the hands of God. This trust in Him made Father calm and resigned. He was one of those who had the truth within him. He carried his grief silently and maintained his high spirits for the sake of his family. We shuddered at the thought of being separated and clung closer together.

Suffering had made Mother meek and more tender and her soul had grown stronger. Under Mother's influence Olga composed a prayer which follows:

> *Give patience, Lord, to us Thy*
> *children, In these dark, stormy*
> *days to bear*
> *The persecution of our*
> *people, The tortures*
> *falling to our share.*
> *Give strength, just God, to us*
> *who need it, The persecutors to*
> *forgive,*
> *Our heavy, painful cross*
> *to carry And Thy great*
> *meekness to achieve.*
> *When we are plundered and insulted,*
> *In days of mutinous unrest,*
> *We turn for help to Thee,*
> *Christ-Saviour, That we may*
> *stand the bitter test.*
> *Lord of the World, God of*
> *Creation, Give us Thy Blessing*
> *through our prayer, Give peace*
> *of heart to us, O Master, This*
> *hour of utmost dread to bear.*
> *And on the threshold of the*
> *grave, Breathe power divine*
> *into our clay*
> *That we, Thy children, may find*
> *strength In meekness for our*
> *foes to pray.*

Zaslovsky hated everybody. He even kicked our friendly dog Lisa, because the dog wanted to make friends with him. He also beat the dog in the yard and stepped on our cat with out any reason. He said that before he left he would do away with all our pets. We suffered and our animals clung to us. When they heard his loud voice downstairs, they all ran and hid under Mother's chaise longue. Eventually the soldiers drove Zaslovsky away and he went back to Ekaterinburg.

In the meantime our finances were getting low and Anna Vyrubova made an arrangement with a banker named Yaro shinsky to send us some money through Soloviev, the husband of Matriona, Rasputin's older daughter. Marie and I knew Yaroshinsky from Tsarskoe Selo. He had financed Marie's and my hospital and we had seen him occasionally. He spoke poor Russian with a Polish accent. He told us once that he had an uncle who was a cardinal in Italy.

Soloviev was entrusted with several thousands of rubles and some letters to be delivered to us. We did not know Soloviev but knew that Anna trusted him and that he had delivered some letters to Tobolsk previously. We received only thirty thousand rubles out of the three hundred thousand that were sent to us by Anna. Later in Ekaterinburg we were shown copies of all letters and records of the money, which Soloviev took as a payment for spying on us. Because he was the husband of Matriona, Anna had confidence in him in financial and other matters. Dr. Botkin told Father that Yurovsky said that Soloviev and Yaroshinsky were friends of General Pilsudski, Lenin, Trotsky and of Voykov (who later, it seems, signed the death verdict of the Imperial family).

We still had about 35-40 employees whose wages we were unable to meet. Food became a problem. We had no sugar, coffee or butter. When the good people of Tobolsk learned of the conditions in the Governor's house they sent us whatever they had. Some of the merchants and the heads of the city had met Father in 1891 when, on his way home from Japan, he had made an extensive tour throughout Siberia. At that time the museum of Tobolsk was established and Father deposited a great deal of money in the Imperial banks for the upkeep of this museum. Magazines and articles were sent to us and we read them with interest. Incidentally it was twenty-seven years later, in July also, when the murder took place in Ekaterinburg, July 16th-17th, 1918.

One morning we awoke to an acute misery; Alexei was ill. The dreaded disease had returned. And now our previous deprivations seemed insignificant. The youngster's resistance had been lessened. He was thin and unable to take the food offered him. As always Mother nursed him. Her care for him was the same but her affection for him had changed. My heart tells me not to say that, but conscience tells me otherwise. Alexei sensed it. I remember how much Mother loved her precious "Agoo" and wanted to have him close to her on the chaise longue.

I can still see this little boy under a blue silk and lace cover lying on her chaise, or later, his hand in her hand, going into his bedroom to say a prayer. M. Gilliard and all the others knew of the change on Mother's part, and they gave Alexei more love now to make up for the loss of a part of his Mother's affection. We sisters became much closer to him, and our hearts formed as one and this one we gave to our unfortunate brother and to our Father who suffered so much.

Following the incident when Nagomy was caught carrying a letter from Alexei to Dr. Derevenko's son, the Doctor was not permitted to come to the house. But now his services were needed and he, at last, was allowed to see his patient.

When the conditions became dangerously bad, following Nikolsky's departure, Father wrote an important document about the war, which was placed in a safe place until a change in the Government should occur. At that time it was to be released to the proper authorities. It was left in care of four men and it was endorsed and countersigned by at least four persons.

A treaty between Bolshevik Russia and Germany was now in the process of being signed. We were told that one of its provisions was that the Imperial family was to be brought to Moscow unharmed. Evidently the Germans suspected that our captors were dangerous and would not spare our lives. Father feared if the family went to Moscow, he might be forced to sign the treaty in order to save his family's life. He said: "Now the people know who are the real traitors to Russia. All these years they have been accusing Mother for being a spy and wanting to sign a separate treaty with Germany." Father blamed the downfall of the Russian Army––our national pride––on Kerensky, Guchkov, Ruzsky and Shulgin. He said that now Germany would get all kinds of concessions, which would reduce Russia to poverty, but that Germany would not enjoy these concessions. The treaty was prepared in advance by Tsederbaum, Bronstein, Apfelbaum, Rosenfeld and others-better known to the world today as Lenin, Trotsky, Zinoviev, Kamenev. Not many Russians among them, but traitors. I well remember that as we sat one evening, Father said to Prince Dolgorukov, "Valia, you remember the time when I refused even to consider a separate treaty with Germany. I would not accept any appeasement after the loss of thousands of lives and all the property damage. I was determined to bring Germany to her knees. Even if I had signed a separate treaty, Germany would have paid for all the damage done, and now she is going to get from the traitors anything she wants." Father went on, "Germany will not enjoy the things she has done to us, and our Allies will not either. They are digging their own graves and soon they will be buried in them. If Russia falls, the whole world will topple with her, and within fifty years from now there will be no democracy left, believe me, Valia." I remember the last words as though they were spoken only yesterday.

By betraying his country he would have bought freedom for himself and his family. Every soldier knew that Russia was betrayed and that the propaganda about my family was totally untrue. But they were helpless. Father never lived for himself but for his people; they sinned against him and still he loved them. Mother said the time would come when they would stand before Him to answer for murdering our country. The Bolsheviks had every reason to remove Father and all male Romanovs, because by so doing they would eliminate all inter ference with their plans, and no emperor would ever be in power again.

Lenin had a personal hatred for the Imperial family. He waited for an opportunity to get his revenge. When Father was a young man, he and his parents were on their way to the Caucasus when the train in which they were riding was derailed and eighty people lost their lives and many more were injured. The roof of the Imperial car was on the verge of collapse when my Grandfather, Alexander III, held the roof on his shoulders, preventing further disaster. Six years afterwards he died as a result of the injuries he suffered on that day. The conspirators who caused this derailment were Lenin and his brother. Lenin's brother was caught and was executed. Lenin himself escaped abroad. The Russian people did not know that Lenin was one of the Ulianov-Tsederbaum brothers. Later it was established that Lenin himself was the mastermind in causing this accident. Little did the people suspect that he was later also an agent of the German government. Trotsky's brother was also a revolutionary; he was hanged in 1905. Lenin and Trotsky came to Russia shortly after Father's abdication. Once my Granny told me if Grandfather had not held up the roof of the railway car they would all have been crushed.

Aunt Olga suffered an injury to her back, and Granny to an arm. From the life-size painting which hung in Father's billiard room, I judge my Grandfather to have been enormous, with broad shoulders and colorful, healthy cheeks, a handsome specimen. I would not be surprised if his voice was a deep baritone, like the voice of a lion roaring throughout the vast rooms of the Gatchina Palace. That kind of impression my giant Grandfather made on me.

Father was emphatic about two things: He would accept nothing from Germany and would not permit the family to become separated. After seeing what these people had done to Father, we sisters, though we longed for freedom and an opportunity to enjoy our life, young as we were, were ready to sacrifice everything and even die to save our country.

A new detachment of guards arrived from Moscow under the supervision of a man named Yakovlev. He had been in Tobolsk for several days and no one knew the reason for his being in town. Before the thirteenth day of each month approached we feared some kind of trouble, and the 13th of April was no exception. On this day Yakovlev put under arrest General Tatishchev, Prince Dolgorukov, Countess Hendrikova, Mlle. Schneider and Mr. Gibbs. They were ordered to move into our house.

After all the rooms had been searched, Yakovlev, wanting to be sure that Alexei was ill, brought in a doctor from the outside, who soon verified the boy's illness. I remember a conversation one evening with Count Tatishchev. Prior to the war he represented Father at the German Court and spoke German fluently. During the war he questioned German prisoners who told him that their officers were dissatisfied and that even Von Moltke, the German Commander in the field, was disgusted the way things were going by 1917, and was in favor of putting the Kaiser under arrest; that virtually the Kaiser was a prisoner at his own headquarters and no longer had the power to do anything about the situation. Besides, it was further said, Germany was at the point of collapse.

Ludendorff was then master of the Army and the Empire. It was the Russian revolution which was so skillfully promoted by the traitors who had settled for a while in Switzerland that saved Germany. Had it been delayed even by as short a period as three months, victory would have been ours.

Another evening the subject of discussion was the treaty which was about to be signed. As usual we were gathered in the big hall. With us were Prince Dolgorukov, General Tatishchev, M. Gilliard and Mr. Gibbes; also the two ladies in waiting, Mlle. Hendrikova and Mlle. Schneider, both of whom were later killed outside of Perm. Father turned to General Tatishchev and said: "General, do you remember the letter that Wilhelm wrote to me in which he said that he wanted to sign a separate treaty with Russia, after which the whole affair would be forgotten and the two countries would be friends again?" Across the face of that letter Father had written: "Our friendship is dead." There was a second letter, this one to Count Benckendorff, in which the Kaiser asked the Count to speak to Father about a treaty with Germany.

We all knew about these letters as we were at General Headquarters at the time. Father showed these letters to Sir John Hanbury-Williams and the other members of the Foreign High Command. His own reaction (which may have been sent to Berlin by Count Benckendorff) to these letters was, "If the Kaiser wants peace, let him make his proposals to all my Allies; a separate treaty with Russia alone is out of the question. No treaty without indemnities to my country and my Allies."

Prince Dolgorukov said to Olga, "Knowing how honest His Majesty is, he would and could not break the promise he made when he put his hand on the Bible, assumed the purple and was crowned, and received the Orb and the Sceptre. At the same time he kneeled in prayer to guide him in his service as Tsar and Judge of the Russian Empire and to keep his heart in the will of God asking for His guidance to help him in his task to rule wisely and be a true father to his people, in order that on the Day of Judgment he may answer without shame." During the proclamation of war Father again swore with his hand on the Bible never to make a peace with the enemy as long as one enemy soldier was on his soil.

Father would never have betrayed his Allies. However, the Allies did not recognize his loyalty to them and his unwillingness to sign a separate treaty with the Central Powers. Because' of his loyalty and their failure to recognize it, he underwent great spiritual suffering, particularly because he knew that it would mean the end of Russia at a time when he so needed the support of the Allies which they failed to give. Even the Bolshevik leaders feared that the stubborn Emperor might be a threat to them, and decided that the only thing left to do was to kill him. Father might still be alive today, if he had been willing to betray his Allies. It was known that Wilhelm had more confidence in Father for keeping his word in honorable dealings than in his other cousins.

# XXI   SEPARATION

At this time the new commissar informed Father that he would have to leave Tobolsk within twenty-four hours; and that, because he could not take along the entire family on account of Alexei's inability to travel, he could take with him any other member of the family who wished to accompany him. That meant separation, the thing we dreaded most. Mother was caught between two tortures, at Yakovlev's mercy. If she accompanied her husband, she must leave behind her sick boy, who needed her above everything else. But should Father face whatever was ahead alone? Suppose he was to be 'tried and questioned, would he not need her support? Might they not try to force him to sign the shameful Brest-Litovsk treaty, by threatening to kill his family? Yet Alexei might die without Mother. And what about Father? Did this mean death for him? We knew that all this was surging through Mother's tormented mind, just as it was through ours.

General Tatishchev wanted to go with Father and said: "Your Majesty, you will not sign anything. They will have to kill us both."

Olga was like a mother to Alexei. With Gillek, our loyal friend at his side, and Dr. Derevenko across the street, Alexei would be well cared for. At last Tatiana spoke up. She suggested that Mother and Marie go with Father. We knew that was the right suggestion. We knew also how Mother and Alexei would grieve for each other. In the midst of this discussion Father, as was always his habit, went outside in the yard to be alone and not show his agony to others. He had always found the answer to his problems when alone, but this time he had none.

Father was supposed to leave at night, but it was decided to wait till morning when it would be safer to travel on the river. If only they could wait a few days, perhaps Alexei would be able to go with them. It was decided that General Tatishchev should stay in Tobolsk while Dr. Botkin, Prince Dolgorukov, Chemodurov (father's old attendant) Sidniev (our footman) and Anna Demidova, Mother's maid, would go with them. Colonel Kobylinsky selected eight soldiers of our guard, under the supervision of eight officers, who would accompany them on this trip.

All day we moved about in a daze, as if we were under hypnotism. Mother ordered her most needed articles to be packed. Tatiana with trembling hands placed them in the suitcase. She swallowed fast to turn back the tears but in spite of stoical efforts more than one tear dropped on the articles and sank deep out of sight. Alexei cried incessantly. With him was *Gillek* (Gilliard), his faithful tutor. Alexei called for Mother for hours but she could not go to him. She could not hide her tears. At last she found strength to see him. When Gillek left the room, Mother threw herself on her knees in front of his bed and her face next to his, though she could not control her emotions. Her arms around Alexei's thin body, she wept bitterly over the sick boy, "We will be back in a few days. We will soon be together." A few drops of valerian were given him. While she sat in a chair, holding his hand, Alexei fell asleep. Then Mother bent over him and kissed her sick boy. He woke up and started to cry again. We could all see that she had prepared herself for this ordeal.

Mother understood the seriousness of this trip, that it might mean the death of all three of them. They all accepted it stoically in the hope that it might save their country even though it could lead to the loss of their lives.

The presence of new guards produced another problem, but Colonel Kobylinsky promised that he would see to it that all who remained behind would be cared for by him person ally and that he would have the few remaining old soldiers on guard in the house and watching over us. Countess Hendrikova and Mlle. Schneider were to move in with us.

When all the business was finished, late at night we all assembled in the large hall. All the employees, with tear-stained eyes, came to say good-bye to those who were leaving. Mother embraced all the women and Father all the men. After tea our friends from downstairs departed. The family did not go to bed; our friends also stayed up all night. At 3:30 A.M. tea was again served to the travellers. All changed into clothes for the trip and took with them a few valuables which could be sold, if necessary. But upon their arrival in Ekaterinburg, Mother's and Marie's handbags were searched and the con tents confiscated.

Mother drew us daughters into our room. We gathered around her. Then and there I suddenly realized what Tobolsk had done to her. Mother's hair was partly grey and her eyes were sunken deep in her head. Her beautiful skin was lined and transparent, and her neck thin and drawn. Her clothes hung on her wasted frame- she cared little how much she had aged. She was speaking slowly as if the choke in her throat would not let the words come through. "My only desire," she said, "is that should we ever be scattered outside of Russia, I hope none of you will ever choose Germany, and that you will never do anything to disgrace yourselves. There will be some people who will try to put you in a compromising position to take advantage of your youth. Always keep respectable. Never marry for wealth or power, only for love and devotion. The greatest happiness I can ask for you, if ever you will marry, is that you will love your husbands as I do mine, your dear Father, and we are thankful, for He has rearded us by giving us such an understanding family."

We fell on our knees while she prayed for our safekeeping. Then she drew each one of us to her and kissed us feverishly. She embraced us together, then tore herself from our clinging arms and started toward the door. Suddenly she was back again to hug us once more. Again and again she tried to leave. Each time she came back.

Until the last moment we could not believe that God would let this separation take place. Not only that we feared what would happen to them when they reached their destination, but there was the dangerous river to cross for which one closed carriage and several *tarantasy* (Siberian primitive open carriages) were provided, now that the ice was thawing.

The night was dark and cold. It was safer to start early in the morning, because the river freezes overnight, and they had to travel in the middle of the river where the ice was thicker and safer. Without a word, Marie clutched my hand; my arms flew around her. With burning cheeks our lips met. Then and there I felt that a great part of my life was gone. Marie was my other half.

Father was the most possessed of us all. He was so brave, parting from him was the hardest, for we might never see him again. Mother was gone. We stood there motionless, not yet believing, staring at the door she had just passed through. She was heading for Alexei's room. We knew that she wanted to be with him alone. We could see into the room. She found him crying with his head buried under the covers. He always thought it was bad taste to cry before others.

Through the mist in our eyes we saw Father standing. He was white, but with a faint smile on his face, he said: "Come now, children. We will only be away for a short time. Hurry Alexei's recovery so that he will be well enough to travel." Somehow we passed the intervening hours with the servants, those faithful few who had given us their all in their desire to lessen our suffering, friends whose loyalty had lightened our burdens. Now these friends were pouring out their love and devotion we so needed, all the time assuring us of their watchfulness over Alexei and ourselves. Nothing would happen to him or to us sisters. We never could have gotten through that night without our friends.

Each moment we thought to be the last, yet each moment was filled with the hope that the trip would be called off. The minutes passed into hours. Midnight, morning, each second was filled with listening dread. Then came the guards, and Colonel Kobylinsky and Yakovlev. Mother went again into Alexei's room as he was still crying. Almost gayly she assured him she would be back soon. Father made a cross over us, gave his blessing and kissed our wet cheeks. "All ready," a voice came. "Certainly," Father answered. We followed our parents out of the house and stood on the steps to see them seated in the waiting *tarantasy*. In one a mattress had been rolled to make a seat; it was covered with a blanket. This vehicle, drawn by three horses, Mother and Marie occupied. The other one had a bundle of straw to serve as a seat, which also was covered with a blanket. Father and Yakovlev got into this one. There were also *tarantasy* to carry the others, all the luggage and three folding beds. The guards stepped aside; the gate opened and closed. They were gone. Prince Dolgorukov, Dr. Botkin, Chemodurov and Anna Demidova were with them. The officers and soldiers were following on horseback. The gate closed at 4.00 A.M., April 26th, 1918, new style, leaving us standing there in tragic silence, confused, frightened, bewildered as to our future.

We ran to our room, threw ourselves on the beds and sobbed until we could cry no more. Our dear friend Gillek was with Alexei. We could not get to him. He understood. Thank God, for our loyal friends who defended us. How much they suffered on account of us! And how many good people lost their lives to save us. God give them everlasting peace.

Alexei was calling. The room was full of his calls, pitiful calls for Mother and Father. Tatiana bent over him tenderly with both arms wrapped around his frail body. From utter exhaustion his cries grew fainter. She pressed him close. At last he quieted down and fell asleep in his new mother's arms. After the parents left, we sisters assumed additional duties. I, being of a restless nature, was given the task of entering all bills and receipts in a big book at the end of each day. The first time I opened the book I found inside many bills and copies of receipts and promissory notes that were given to merchants by Prince Dolgorukov and General Tatishchev. On inquiry we found out that when the expense money which had been promised to Father by Kerensky and which was to be drawn from our own funds, had failed to come, our household bills had been cared for, unbeknown to Father, by Prince Dolgorukov and General Tatishchev. When their own personal funds were exhausted, these good friends of ours gave the merchants their own personal notes guaranteeing payment of these debts. This fact was kept secret from Father.

The same railroad for which Father and his forefathers laid the first stone in construction was now to carry him to his death. All was left for the new masters who claimed credit for everything and who even changed the names of our once proud cities, universities, hospitals, palaces, museums, industrial and other enterprises, regarding which they had nothing in common except the desire to blow them up at the first opportunity. They renamed them after the worst thieves and murderers in all history.

Petrograd, built by Peter the Great, they changed to Leningrad after that murderer, Lenin, whose body upon his death became black and so badly decomposed that the poor chemist was shot because he was not able to complete the process of embalming.

The leaders went into the prisons where among thousands of innocent officers, clergymen and others, they found a man resembling Lenin. At four o'clock in the morning they shot the innocent victim and his body was embalmed. Later that same morning Lenin's body was disposed of. *(Editor's note: boldened for emphasis as new information for editor)* Today millions of tourists see this mausoleum on Red Square close to the wall of the Kremlin. Within a short distance of the red brick wall lie the Holy Sanctuaries. *Here are the remains of the murdered man under glass. If you should see this man, do not condemn him, for he is an innocent victim, but pray for him that his suffering was not long. I have heard this from a friend who met a sister of the nurse who was present at this event.*

The curtain had fallen on the travellers-Father, Mother and Marie. They had left. The new day could not draw the curtain aside to permit one look into their uncertain future. Only our anxiety could keep them from continuing the trip and force them to return. Perhaps the river would prove im passable and they would have to wait for the thaw, when we could all go together. If Alexei's illness had not delayed our trip, perhaps we would all have been taken to Moscow.

Probably Mother would have given her consent that the children go abroad, and she and Father would have stayed in Russia. This matter was laid before her, but she would not listen. She emhasized that the trial was only the preparation of the spirit; she was willing to die for her country. She prepared us to believe her belief. Olga, Marie, Alexei and I were not willing, Tatiana accepted the inevitable.

We received no news to break our apprehension; no sunshine dispelled our dread. Dread loomed everywhere, but we knew we must not give in but hope this trip would bring betterment to our lives. There was Alexei to cheer and there were new guards to win over.

At night we heard heavy footsteps and the clicking of arms. Every sound suggested fear. We heard that Count Benckendorff was negotiating with Mirbach for our rescue. Olga kept warning us to be particularly careful. "Now that we are alone, we must be cautious with those cruel men," she said. When Dr. Botkin left us, we lost one of our staunchest protectors. Now our good friend and tutor, M. Gilliard, played the role of a brother to us. Other friends who had moved into our house were now fellow prisoners. They were helpless but at least we had them as consultants. Colonel Kobylinsky, that blessed little man, was still with us. If gave us comfort. Others too were protecting us, including General Tatishchev, Mlle. Bittner, Shura Tegleva, and Alexei's faithful Ukrainian servant, Nagorny.

The guards continued to flow into Alexei's room to check on his health. They still did not believe he was ill. We sisters were anxious for Alexei to be well, so that when the river thawed we should be able to follow our parents. Meantime one of the men who drove the family half way to Tiumen brought a letter from Marie describing the incredible condition of the river. It was a miracle that Mother had survived that trip. We were sick at heart that they were suffering there, while here we suffered just as much. The new guards were rough and frightening. We submitted to their tyranny, making no challenge to their disagreeableness. But we were eager for any news which might come to us through Colonel Kobylinsky. Now the poor man had grown nervous and troubled, his hands shook and a strain was noticeable on his face.

The following day Colonel Kobylinsky brought word that the family was safely on the train. The destination was not mentioned. Then came a short note from Mother addressed to us all. It said the journey had been very difficult but they were on the train. We tried hard to read between the lines but found nothing more there.

Day after day followed monotonously; anxiety made us too tired to think; and we lost interest in our studies. In spite of M. Gilliard's and Mlle. Bittner's gentle approach, we could not concentrate on our lessons.

We grieved for those we loved most. Every turn we made, the emptiness reminded us of the former times and we were unable to escape from that feeling. Our hearts beat painfully without refreshing news.

The Holy Week was unbearably sad. Almost four days passed without news. At last on Good Friday, Colonel Kobylinsky received a telegram. It read, "We are safe."

The only comfort we had was when we noticed an improvement in Alexei's health. We tried to amuse him, but he too had no thought beyond what was happening to Mother and Father. Now I realized why Mother had taken Marie with her. In case of separation from her husband, she would not be left alone. Marie had the patience of a saint, her presence would be comforting to both.

Olga was frail in nature. Mother had wished to spare her this trip if possible. Tatiana would take the responsibility for Alexei's care. To alleviate the boredom, I had been given the responsibility of keeping the family accounts and soon assumed the role of family banker and bookkeeper. A special permit was required each day for our food purchases. Every evening, I entered in the ledger all our expenditures; General Tatishchev made me believe I was indispensible in that capacity.

Nagorny was a godsend to Alexei. He slept in Alexei's room and kept the boy busy, amusing him with tales of his province in the Ukraine; of the great poet Taras Shevchenko, and he recited some pastoral and other poems, including "Naimichka" (The Maid), a beautiful poem. This great poet asked to be buried in the expanse of the golden wheat fields on the broad Dneiper River. Here Alexei used to wade and play in the sand at General Headquarters in Mogilev.

Our days were long, but the nights were even longer. On Easter Eve we were permitted to attend the midnight service in the big drawing room. It was a sad performance. We heard that the guards had completely disrobed the priest and searched him thoroughly. They searched the nuns, too, who came to sing in the service. They insulted them. During the service the guards were disturbing and hurled improper remarks. Had we known what would happen, we would not have requested the service at all.

Outside there was the constant sound of footsteps on the wooden sidewalk. Now that the snow had begun to melt, the garden was full of slush. Soon we were not allowed to go out at all.

We waited anxiously for Alexei to get well and for the ice to melt on the river. Then we received a letter, ominously brief. It said the family had halted at Ekaterinburg. They were safe, but there was no detailed explanation. All three of them were accommodated in one room. Marie slept on the floor. We were grateful that Father, in particular, had not been taken to Moscow where he would have met a disastrous end, because he would never have agreed to sign a treaty harmful to his country.

We knew of Ekaterinburg from Father and General Tatishchev. We had passed around the city on the train en route to Tiumen the summer before.

Coincidentally the founder of Ekaterinburg was an ancestor of General Tatishchev who had dedicated the name Ekaterinburg to the Empress Catherine the Great. General Tatishchev was destined to be shot in his ancestor's city of Ekaterinburg years afterwards.

My Father had many friends and relatives interested in different business enterprises. The Imperial family owned the stone cutting works and had other commercial operations. Close friends of ours had extensive businesses in this region. Knowing this vicinity General Tatishchev spent several evenings telling us about the city, where two months later my family, and he as well, were destined to be murdered. (*Boldened to bring awareness to the extensive ties the Imperial Family had to the Ekaterinburg area which may have helped in Anastasia's escape and possibly Alexei's*)

The condition of the river had improved to the point that we might be able to depart any day soon, although Alexei was still recuperating. We were ordered to let the commandant know via Dr. Derevenko the very moment that Alexei was well enough to travel. During yet another search of our house many of Father's belongings were confiscated.

We had never had such vicious guards as we now faced. They laughed at our embarrassment as they verbally harangued and bullied us. Rodionov who was the new commissar was a Latvian with a thirst for blood. He stole some of most valuable belongings as personal souvenirs.

Now the majority of our guards were new and fully unknown to us. The friendly ones who were able to stay due to the intervention of Colonel Kobylinsky stood post at each door. Only the colonel's men were allowed into our private rooms. However, we had just received orders to not lock our doors at night so that the last vestige of our privacy had suddenly been stolen from us.Without asking for permission and for any reason at all, perhaps even on the flimsy excuse to see if we were asleep a guard could enter our bedrooms and private quarters. Without Marie, we three remaining sisters slept in the same room and took turns at night guarding our door at night. One would stay awake wrapped in a blanket while the others slept. We could sense a guard was pproaching as the floorboards creaked. The sister on guard would quickly feign to be asleep as well.

We became inured to the annoying conduct of our captors. Our greatest anxiety came from waiting for news from Colonel Kobylinsky who failed to appear for an inordinate amount of time.The meaning of this unexpected absence filles us with dread. We learned, however, that our beloved Kobylinsky had taken ill and would not able to bid us good-bye. He had been sent away shortly before our departure, and we children hoped that our parents would not find out, leading to their ever-growing anxiety.

The guards were ubiquitous posted even at the entrance to our bathroom. Shura or Mlle. Schneider never left our side. Tatiana crossed the hall to her dressing room oblivious to the fact that she was being closely followed by a guard. Suddenly, she heard his footsteps close by causing her to turn back swiftly only to bump into Rodionov causing her to fall against the wall. She was in pain and frightened, as she had been hit in the breast by whatever hard object he had held in his hand. She let out a cry and became terribly palid. It took her some time to overcome the shock. Subsequently, none of us dared to go unaccompanied to the bathroom.

Volkov, Mother's old reliable groom of the chamber, or Nagorny made their constant rounds pacing up and down the hall.We began to feign an air of respectfulness in an attempt to appeal to the men's conscience. Only an awakening of their sense of honor would repel them we hoped. hoping to shame these men and to arouse their conscience. They continued to humiliate us with their lecherous and untoward base humor. They were capable of all kinds of malice and would have carried it out if we had not had Father, Dr. Botkin and Colonel Kobylinsky with us.

Julian Calendar May 6th, dubbed Old Style, was my Father's birthday, the second we marked during our captivity. For the first time in our lives we were not able to congratulate him, which distressed us greatly. Our parents wished to commemorate the day with a Divine Liturgy that day in Ekaterinburg, yet no priest was allowed to fulfill this plan.

We had no greater wish than to depart on our way. However, we wanted to take no action which would be detrimental to our brother. We wanted nothing more than to be reunited with our parents. Much distress was caused by our lack of communications from our family. Dr Botkin did send a few for his son Gleb and daughter Tatiana. The letter contained the word "well" so that we knew that all were alive but could not communicate freely with us because they were censored and thwarted from writing with liberty.

Alexei was finally able to sit up in a wheel chair, and the river was clear enough for navigation. Perhaps this trip would afford our brother an opportunity to regain his strength. The idea that he was on his way to Mother might be just the right elixir. Firmly believing this we convinced Dr. Derevenko to inform the commandant that Alexei was now sufficiently recovered to travel. Even he was happy to be on our way as the current conditions in which we found ourselves was in all ways pathetic.

We had packed our suitcases quite some time before in anxious anticipation of our trip. We had few frocks with us, although Anna Demidova had written cryptically on Mother's behalf that we were to carefully pack the *medicine*. (*She was referring to jewels that we had secreted in the seams and folds of our clothing*) Inventory was taken by General Tatishchev and although the pieces were not numerous they were invaluable. The General put the value of the gemstones and other items at between three and four million rubles. He and Gillek (M. Gilliard) and Shura Tegleva placed them carefully clothes, suitcases, and pillows. These were possessions that we could carry with us. At Tsarskoe Selo we had removed them from their settings, while had secreted away some small pieces of lace of incomparable worth.

We had now been separated from our parents for three weeks when we received the news that we would be departing at 11:00 am the next morning. We were quickly taken through the streets fo the dock. "Rossia," the same boat that brought us to Tobolsk almost ten months before, now was ready to launch. We were not followed by any other vessels. Although we were onboard by noon, we did not begin to move until late in the afternoon.

Even though no one was permitted to be on the dock, crowds gathered, nonetheless, on the river banks trying to catch a glimpse of us. We saw them wiping tears from their eyes with their handkerchiefs, while some blessed us by crossing themselves or making the sign of the Holy Cross in our direction in the air. The crowds became larger in size so that the guards told us to go back to our cold, damp rooms.

Permission was given about an hour later for us to ascend to the upper deck. Some familiar faces were visible on the banks of the river but not those of the Botkin children. We were not able to explain their absence later to their father, Dr. Botkin. When we informed him that we had not seen his children the doctor wrote to Voykov about their coming to Ekaterinburg.

Nagorny later informed us that one man had loudly exclaimed, "Lunatics, what are you doing to this innocent family? God will punish you for your brutality." In reply Rodionov retorted, "Your friends called us lunatics." Had the boat not already been underway, not one of them would have been left alive.

※

# PART V

## *Ekaterinburg*

# XXII   REUNION

Those accompanying us on the "Rossia" included General Tatishchev, Mlle. Hendrikova, Iza Buxhoeveden, M. Gilliard, Sidney Gibbes and Mlle. Schneider, who had once taught Russian to Mother and Aunt Ella; also Alexei Dmitriev, the hairdresser; Alexandra Tegleva, governess; Elizabeth Ersberg and Miss Tutelberg ("Tootles") and Alexei (Diatka) Volkov, Mother's groom of the chamber; valet Trup; Leonid Sidniev, Klementy Nagorny, Ivan Kharitonov, and a few others.

Alexei's condition worried us as well as Dr. Derevenko, who was, however, not permitted permitted to see my brother. Such cruelty was protested by the physician and Nagorny. With a menacing voice, Rodionov shouted back, saying, "You will see who is running this boat." He uttered curses in Russian and expressions in some foreign language threatening us: "I have orders to shoot anyone who resists." We had no recourse with this monster, but we were thankful that Nagorny was with Alexei. Our doors again were not allowed to be closed.

We realized that the trip to Ekaterinburg would not be long! Our only worry was that Alexei's condition might suddenly worsen before our arrival. The scant air which reached us though our windows from the River Tobol carried with it the sweetness of spring. On the other hand the air was damp and cold. We were allowed to sit on deck the next day. The early buds on the trees created a beautiful spectacle of color on the shoreline. The rivers were swollen with the spring thaw which created little spontaneous lakes along the way. In contrast to our personal condition, the world of the river seemed tender and lovely. Was this a portent of our beginning or our end?

Armed guards with bayonets were everywhere which depressed us to the point that we had little desire to allow ourselves any kind of conversation. When someone wished to address us they had the obligation of speaking in a louder than normal voice and use exclusively the Russian language. Not only that, they could not sit close to us, rather at some distance. It did fill our hearts with gladness that Alexei was allowed to come on deck in his wheelchair. He sat quietly in the sunlight following M. Gilliard whenever he momentarily left him. Gilliard was his faithful protector and ally. Alexei sat quietly yet preoccupied. He realized how serious the trip was which filled our hearts with great sadness. Even if we tried to play some innocent game or other, none of us could concentrate. We were in a constant state of fear.

On the second morning, May 22nd, we arrived in Tiumen. The level to which the guards were armed was greatly increased and even included machine guns. Our captors were afraid of riots so we were not allowed to leave the boat. Either the crowds on the banks were interested in the first boat of the season or they had heard that we were onboard. It was several hours before we were finally allowed to go on shore where we undertook the opposite routine of the year before walking from the platform across tracks to the waiting train.

When petals and flowers were thrown at our feet from a group of women gathered nearby, we were deathly afraid to acknowledge them, but did perceive that they were crying and wiping away tears with their handkerchiefs. As had been done by the group before, many cross themselves or blessed us by making the sign of the Holy Cross in the air in our direction. Some stood without moving, their lips trembling. An elderly man knelt but a guard cursed at him pushing him over. How reprehensible that old people could be so abused without respect for their elderly years. I was ashamed to witness such behavior. By the cut of his clothes and posture it was obvious that this Russian gentleman belonged to the older generation. Somehow he looked familiar as though we had once seen him somewhere else. When Tatiana asked Rodionov if Baroness Buxhoeveden could be at our side, he grinned with malevolence and sputtered *Panie, nyet* (Lady, No!)

We were listless and famished as we had had nothing to eat since noon the day before. A long trip was still ahead of us. Brave Nagorny finally managed somehow to get us a bottle of milk. Presumably someone had given it to him and he then rushed to pass it along to us. Each of us sisters took only half a glass and left the rest for Alexei. We were then transferred to a train where one car was reserved for Alexei and us sisters. One side was for us girls, Hendrikova, Buxhoeveden, Schneider and Ersberg, while the opposite side was set aside for General Tatishchev, Alexei and Nagorny. The travelers from one side were not allowed to speak to the travelers on the other side. M. Gilliard, Alexei's beloved and devoted teacher, was now separated from our brother. The rest of the retinue, we had heard, were in a car behind ours. We were not allowed to speak with those on the other side.

With the guards pacing up and down the corridor, we did not dare to undress that night. We could sense that we were approaching Ekaterinburg as the guards spoke of Bazhenovo, the village near Ekaterinburg. We were treated as common criminals by the guards. The shades were pulled down at night with our car lit only by dim lights which were not turned off. The train screeched to a halt around midnight. We remembered our father having told before that this area was near the famous emerald mines.

At 9:00 am we were told by men who had entered our car, "Please carry your own personal luggage." No one made any attempt to assist us in any way. They guarded Nagorny more heavily that anyone and ordered him to pick up Alexei. Silently Nagorny carried our brother off the train. It was such a gloomy day, gray and dark with clouds. There were a few people standing under the trees slightly green with the new spring buds. Evidently the news of our arrival had made its way around the town. The people were ordered to turn away showing us their backs. We carried our own heavy suicases and other belongings. Olga had been ill during the night hardly able to walk in her dizziness. She could not carry very much of her load. Dr. Derevenko who had traveled in the other car was not allowed to see her, and we had truly worried that she might suffer a heart attack. Four or five carriages awaited our arrival near the tracks, which I presumed were on the outside of the city. We had passed through Ekaterinburg the year before on our way to Tiumen. Of the two stations in the municipality we were surely stopped at the one less likely to be the gathering place for a demonstration of the people in protest.

Alexei was placed in the first carriage by Nagorny who immediately came to lend us a hand. He was viciously pushed aside when he tried to help Tatiana with her heavy luggage in one hand, the dog and a blanket in the other. The ground was mixture of mud and cinders on which we each struggled with our personal baggage with no helping hand to assist us. Alexei and Nagorny preceded in the first carriage while we followed in ours in which a commissar rode in each. As it had begun to rain, the hood of the carriages were raised. I recognized Zaslovsky in my carriage.

We soon entered a broad avenue on the left of which I immediately spotted a church, then a chimney behind a wooden fence at the end of which the carriage came to a stop. I remembered this church the day I entered the Ipatiev House.

We descended from our carriages trembling in trepidation. It was must have been about 9:40 A.M. or perhaps a little later when we entered the Ipatiev gate. Goloshchekin, the commissar, stood at the gate. Olga was the first to enter after whom we followed. A rough looking man stood in the entrance from which we were escorted through a wide stairway passing into another room which was the commissar's office.

Individually we each had to present an identity card with a serial number and photo of the bearer which had been taken in Tobolsk. On the card was printed the place and date of birth, first name, patronymic and family name as well as our Tobolsk address.

Father embraced us with full hugs when he saw us at the threshold. Nagorny placed Alexei in Father's arms, while our mother and Marie met us there too. We all collapsed in deep sobs, but when Alexei was brought to our mother, it was she who placed her head on his chest and bitterly wept, "My baby, my precious one!" We rejoiced at hearing these tender expressions which had been so sorely missed in Tobolsk. Our reunion was a mixture of joy and overwhelming sorrow.

Mother looked pale, haggard, and prematurely aged. Even Marie had lost her glow. Father's once clear blue eyes were circled with dark shadows and his hair was sprinkled with gray. His hands were thin and I noticed dark spots on them. "It is his liver," Dr. Botkin said. Marie gave her bed to Alexei. In Father's and Mother's room were the three folding beds which had been brought from Tobolsk. We four sisters moved into one room.

Late in the afternoon, our cook Kharitonov, his helper Leonid Sidniev and the valet Trup arrived. They reportedly had been interrogated for hours. Their extra clothing had been stripped of them while other belongings of theirs had been confiscated. The interrogators were not willing to forget Nagorny's angry exchange on the boat during his protest of Alexei's mistreatment.

We could not fathom the news when they told us that General Tatishchev, Countess Hendrikova and Mlle. Schneider had been arrested and taken away to prison. Sadly, they were unable to find out what had become of Dr. Derevenko, M. Gilliard, Buxhoeveden, Tegleva, Ersberg, Father's valet Kirpichnikov and the others. All of our money which had been guarded by General Tatishchev had been confiscated from him. We now had nothing. Father asked Voykov in a letter why these people had been taken to prison demanding to know of what they were guilty.

In spite of all the unpleasantries Mother was thankful that some of these men were still with us, especially as Father's valet of many years, Chemodurov, had been sent to a hospital during our time in Tobolsk. Now we were searched upon our arrival. Our luggage was rummaged through, although, fortunately, we had brought precious little with us. Iza Buxhoevden, who wore a size 4 ½ as did I, had promised me a pair of her shoes but she was forbidden to give them to me.

The trunks brought from Tobolsk reached the house and were immediately dispatched to the attic. We could hear them being opened above us, having taken the keys from General Tatishchev for this purpose. They removed our belongings from these pieces of luggage. Commissar Yurovsky's room sported a piano on which Olga was bid to play. We immediately recognized our table linens and even one with the Imperial Double Eagle embroidered on it. Despicable Yurovksy even appropriated Father's clothing which were ridiculously too tight and short for him.

Olga suffered excruciating pain and a nervous stomach again. Most of Mother's, Father's and Marie's clothing were in a closet when they first arrived at Ekaterinburg, but most of their belongings had been in their trunks. One misfortune quickly happened after another even to the point that Alexei had knocked his knee against the bed when trying to get up. The pain was unbearable and he fainted. This affliction was due to an internal hemorrhage causing him untold suffering. There was no medical help or any means to alleviate his pain. Yurovsky, after Dr. Botkin's pleadings, allowed Dr. Derevenko to administer some medical treatment to our brother. The physician did not reply to Mother as she attempted to talk to him during the treatment. He trembled and looked pale as she continued to attempt to elicit a response, until Mother realized that he had been threatened and was not allowed to speak to her. In her state of distress, Mother broke down into tears which caused the doctor's face to become beet red, while he regarded her with pleading eyes. The physician left her lotion, salve, clean gauze and epinephrine so that Tatiana could take over the responsibilities of ministering to Alexei's needs. After giving a salute, Dr. Derenvko disappeared as quickly as he had arrived, creating a phantasmogorical impression. Employing the gauze, Tatiana was charged with applying compresses of epinephrine to Alexei's knee, but when the gauze was used up, Tatiana had to wash it inorder to reuse it. When that finally disintegrated, Tatiana used bits and pieces of Father's old shirt and our worn out blouses. Alexei's suffering was continuous so that he became weak and thin. His stiff knee led to a partial paralysis of both feet with one leg becoming shorter than the other. The physical torture of our Bolshevik captors continued in that the physician Derevenko was not allowed to attend to Alexei's needs. (*Editor's note: one is left with the impression that Yurovsky would have welcomed a natural death for Alexei eliminating the need to murder the youngest of the children*) We were not able to use the foam treatment apparatus.

A trunk in the hallway held the instruments, but it would have been futile anyway, because there was no electricity and scarce hot water. As there was nothing in this particular trunk which our captors desired, it was the only one turned over to us.

We were being mocked and denigrated continually. Our morale was under attack by the use of restrictions and distrust. One bedroom served for all four of us girls. We had to sleep on the floor covered by blankets for the first days of our incarceration. We created "beds" with odd groupings of blankets, coats and cushions as the rugs and carpets had been removed before our arrival. The floor was chilly and damp. Olga and Tatiana experienced pain on the floor as they had become so terribly thin that their bones hurt when they were on the floor. Because I seemed to have more natural padding I felt a little less discomfort than they. Eventually bedding made of sacks filled with straw was delivered to us. We turned them every day, but the ensuing dust terribly aggravated Mother's sinuses. As we had done before, one sister kept watch while the other slept in order to keep us safe at night.

Marie described the trip from Tobolsk to Tiumen which was filled with distress and danger. For example the ice on the Irtysh River had begun to break with a noise like thunder. Even the armed guards under Rodionov's supervision had become unnerved. The horses had struggled in the thick slush which reached their bellies. They could not raise their legs so they pushed the slush instead. The spokes of the wheels had broken when pieces of ice became wedged in the wheels. Right in front of Rasputin's house, a huge block of ice slid towards them so that one of the horses fell. He could not be raised up until a plank of wood was employed. Had not Rasputin prophecied, Marie recalled, that we would one day visit his village and that our deaths would follow his own? Fear entered Marie at this thought, yet Mother tried to lift her spirits.

Before they ever reached Tiumen Father, Dr. Botkin, and Prince Dolgorukov walked in the marsh to lighten the burden of the horses which were wet, steaming and foaming at the mouth. In the evening the group was given hospitality in a peasant's cottage where some tea and food were served. Mother's clothes were soaking wet. She became so chilled that her lips turned blue and trembled, her teeth chattering and her body in shock.

Father experienced an odd moment when he recognized one of his former generals passing by dressed as a peasant. They caught each other's eye and knew the one another's identity. However, neither revealed what they knew in order that the general would not be executed. In this trip Dr. Botkin got violently ill, but they continued on due to weather conditions.

They arrived at a spot near to Tiumen early in the morning. Portions of the ice had melted near the banks of the river requiring a temporary bridge to be put up. It was just after dawn but all kinds of gaurds were there of which only a few spoke Russian. The others were comprised of foreigners. The soldiers were armed with grenades and guns. They were escorted thus from the boat to the train. The entire party was seated in one car with Father, Mother and Marie on one side and the others on the other side. Those accompanying Marie and our parents included Prince Dolgorukov, Dr. Botkin, Chemodurov, who was Father's old valet, Anna Demidova and Sidniev who had once been footman to us girls. The family was not allowed to speak to any one of them.

Yakovlev continually changed the path of the train; he was secretly a supporter of Father's. Moscow had once been the destination for the train but Yakolev felt that Father and the family would be executed there if Father refused the order to leave Russia. Yakovlev was clandestinely an opponent of the traitors in Moscow. Father was convinced that all orders in Moscow originated with Count Mirbach. Hence, Yakolev wanted to stall any arrival in Moscow. Soon after Yakovlev received orders to take us to Ekaterinburg. Soon thereafter Yakovlev received orders to proceed to Ekaterinburg. They spent Palm Sunday on the train. As the train slowly approached Ekaterinburg a commissar arrived demanding to see everyone's identity documents.

Father had only one identification card he always carried in his leather walled on which was embossed with a crown in gold. It bore his name, the date and the place of his birth, his religion and marital status. It also indicated the issuing office: the Imperial desk. Additionally, he had the identification card that had been issued to him at Tobolsk. This showed his photo and the statement: words: *Nicholas Alexandrovich Romanov, ex-Emperor, Citizen, Tsarskoe Selo.*

Commissars Sverdlov and Goloshchekin, both Jews, took photos of the five in Ekaterinburg. People on the street near the train station fell down on their knees and kissed the ground on which my family passed. The same guards on the train were now here. Each gave a name was admitted upon arrival at the Ipatiev House. However, when Prince Dolgorukov identified himself, he was immediately placed under arrest. Father's friend of many years was now separated from him.

Prince Dolgorukov pulled out of his pocket one of his general's epaulettes which had been removed from his uniform in Tobolsk. He handed it to Father and said: "It came from my Emperor and I give it back to my Emperor." There was no chance to shake hands. He saluted Father and said, "God be with You, Your Majesties."

He was whisked away, but Father was so shaken by this incident that he wrote a note to Goloshchekin, in charge of all prisoners, but it was for naught.

A great gathering of people assembled in front of the house at 2:00 am but several shots were discharged. The sound of screams informed us that several must have been killed. An ensuring search through the house resulted in Father's money being taken as well as Mother's jewels. Even Anna Demidova, the maid, was also robbed. A foreigner spoke to Mother in German and to Father in French even though he spoke Russian. His words were unmitigated insults. We heard that it was a cohort of Yurovsky, Trotsky and Mirbach. Purportedly he was was sent from Moscow to the Ipatiev House in his capacity of a antiques expert for a Swiss firm. His name began with a "K."

Father bristled at this treatment saying he did not need a foreigner to remind him that he was a prisoner not of his own people but rather of traitors, convicts and foreign agents. foreign agents.

Even though the guards were Russians, their orders originated with foreigners in Moscow. Most of the guards were ex-convicts whose orders were issued by foreigners in Moscow. Even though most of the guards were exconvicts, they could see the injustice that was being done. Gradually, they became more lenient in their treatment of us. Soon, however, they were replaced by more compliant recruits. Such was Marie's account of their trip and stay in Ekaterinburg.

The arrival of Kharitonov, our chief cook; Trup, the valet; and Leonid Sidniev, the 14-year-old kitchen helper, brought a needed moment of happiness to our depressing residence. Dr. Botkin was overjoyed to see us and embraced us with a kiss, his tears welling with tears. In less than a month we had all begun to undergo changes in our bodies and health.

Arthritis affected Father's knuckles which now swelled, while his kidney problems caused him to suffer terrific back pain. Mother's hands swelled as well, so much that she could no longer hold a needle and thread.

Dr. Botkin made a special effort to affect some kind of a happy look even though he had noticeable bags under his eyes. Although he anxiously awaited news of his children, he did not receive any. He had only heard unconfirmed rumors on the boat. He was a tender and caring man whose only pastime now was reading. We affectionally called him "Papula." Commissar Yurovsky was particularly abusive to him. Why should he be punished so? Dr. Botkin had only wished his children be brought to Ekaterinburg for which he begged Commissars Avdiev and Yurovsky to allow it, but it was denied. In retrospect, it was a blessing that they did not arrive, because it saved their lives, for they would have perished with their father. We found it hard to believe that Yurovsky could be so cruel as his his father had been a rabbi who would have taught him to be kind, especially to children.

Food for our parents had been prepared and brought in from outside, but with the arrival of Kharitonov meal preparations became normal again. We were initially allowed only fifteen minutes of outdoor activity each day, and only in the small and muddy garden. The spring, however, caused the grass to begin to sprout and the deliciously fragrant lilacs began to blossom. We brought Mother violets and lilacs.

Before taking them to Mother, however, they were also inspected in the office. The horses had chewed off bark severely affecting the trees in the garden. Especially impacted where the white birch trees and the poplars. ther, but they had to be examined at the office before they were taken into our apartments. A few trees showed considerable abuse, as the horses had chewed off much of the bark on the white birch and poplar trees. We harvested the blossoms of the linden tree, dried them and used them to make tea. Even in this house of denigration God had provided fragrant flora in the garden. The acacia was exceedly pleasant and pungent. On occasion Mother went out with us in the yard especially when Alexei was feeling better. After Nagorny had been taken away and Father was ill, Dr. Botkin or Marie carried Alexei down into the garden. Dr. Botkin carried Alexei downstairs one day when our brother threw his arms around his neck and kissed this good friend on both cheeks in gratitude.

Guards watched our every move when were exercised in the garden. They were bedecked with hand grenades in their belts. Surely, some of these men were good people, but few stayed over a few days. At one point we overheard them say, "Where there are devils, there is Hell, and that is what we have now." Our window panes had been whitewashed outside to impair our view except for a tiny space at the top through which we could glimpse the blue sky. Father wrote Yurovsky asking him to remove enough paint so that we could see the thermometer which was on the left side of the window frame outside. We saw nothing but walls, prison walls.

Alexei made a request to Father that M. Guilliard return to continue his lessons. Yurovsky would not hear of it. Our brother also asked Father how long we would be in the Ipatiev House, and Father could only tell him honestly, "It might be long." Alexei never raised that question again.

There were nights when we would hear a shot, a scream, and then silence. Our living area was searched yet again. We girls still had no proper beds. An odd request was received that we were to set our clocks two hours ahead. Our breakfast, therefore, arrived at 12:30 pm. Kharitonov had to prepare our food and that of the staff, but also for the thugs who had us under lock and key.

When the delicious smells of tasty dishes and fish reached our rooms, we had to realize that this food was not for us, but for the commandant and the guards. All we were given was a thin fish soup or a half cooked veal cutlet at for lunch and a cold one for supper. Father found it impossible to eat such things, so he often went without. Mother's fare was somewhat different consisting usually of noodles and tea which Leonid made for her using a small kerosene burner. She refused to sit at table with her repugnant captors. We had to take our meals at the same table as those who abused us. On the other hand we either ate it or would starve, while the guards ate off the fat of the land at our expense.

*(Editor's note: It is evident from Anastasia's account that Yurovksy and his crew were involved in a systematic program of denigration and deprivation. Whether the Romanovs were aware of it*

at the time or not, the reader who knows today what eventually happened at the Ipatiev House can clearly deduce that Yurovsky probably knew all along that the family would be assassinated in the end. There is also a tinge of psychological torment in that Yurovsky would have known that his prisoners were hungry, ill and despondent. His case is deserving of a psychological analysis as he was raised Jewish and converted to Lutheranism which implies he should have otherwise had empathy and compassion, especially for children. Instead it seems he indulged in public Schadenfreude.)

# XXIII   DEPRIVATION AND COURAGE

Guards stood by the entry to the doorway to the Commissar's room once a week when Father was interrogated. After having been questioned for two hours one day, Father returned totally out of sorts. He had been shown a war document which was called "The Orange Book" from which certain pages were missing, which was the impetus for our captors to accuse Father of having removed them to substitute a letter from Emperor Franz Josef (Francis Joseph) of Austria in which he insisted to our father that he wished only to live in peace in his old age and assuring him that he had no territorial ambitions.

They were willfully ignorant of the fact, that these communications had been read by Father and the General Staff, then archived at the Ministry of War. It was their lack of understanding that Emperor Franz Josef could have written such a missive that fueled their ill informed suspicions.

Had we been in a real prison we would have been afforded more privacy than we had here. Since our arrival in the Ipatiev House, all the doors had been removed. Our rooms were open invitations for instant, spontaneous inspections and intrusions at any hour of the day or night. Every three hours they would disturb us. We could smell the alcohol on the breath even before they appeared at the door. They used our glasses to drink their swill. Anything they saw which caught their fancy they took with impunity. They approached in groups of twos and threes. As we had only our most essential and treasured items with us by now, their loss even more painful. We were willing to part with them without a murmur in order to that we would be left alone with an end to their constant interloping.

Their incursion into our private world became more frequent; they made us the butt of their jokes and tested our patience hoping for us to lose composure. They stood in great contrast to the rather well behaved guards at Tobolsk. These ogres did not appear to be real soldiers with their course manners. Nightly we were rocked by their drunken carrying on which reached us from their quarters below which inspired Dr. Botkin to try interceding on our behalf. The kind doctor had begged the commandant to demand order of his troops, but they continued as unruly as ever. Father himself rarely exchanged words with the commissars. When he wanted to communicate, he wrote it down asking his valet Trup to deliver it in writing to Yurovsky.

Whenever any of us came down with any illness or were not feeling well, Dr. Botkin voluntarily cared for us. We girls had been trained to be prim and proper with those people with whom we were not familiar. Mother's example taught us to be rather reserved. Mother rarely engaged in conversations with her personal help beyond giving orders, yet she was, at the same time, very kind to those who needed assistance. In fact, Mother was spontaneously generous with financial help in those instances when it was necessary. With Anna Demidova's loss of her personal possessions, came a promise from Mother to all of her help that she would personally replace their own losses.

Kharitonov once became ill, so we sisters prepared the food for him. A burlap sack of potatoes arrived in the kitchen with the order that we should peel them. How we delighted in these simple products of the earth and actually enjoyed our task. A small pile of peelings was left over after our praiseworthy service. Not one potatoe was put aside for our consumption. On another day we helped to bake bread in the kitchen. Kharitonov was appreciative of our attempts to assist him as he had been feeling poorly of late and was exhausted from cooking for so many commissars, staff, guards, our help and us.

Two maids cleaned our quarters, washing the floors and changing our bedding twice a week. We enjoyed seeing new faces in our space, but we were not allowed to converse with these ladies. The guards oversaw their every move from the positions in the doorway. Once the rooms were cleaned, they were searched again each time. In some savvy way, these maids related to us that some of our friends had been taken prisoner our friends had been imprisoned and some even executed by gunshots.

The Bible became our clandestine means of communication using a code based on verses of the Holy Scripture. While the maids scurried about with their chores, Mother or one of us sisters would read aloud certain verses from the Book of St. John. Our hope was that the maids would understand the meaning and relay it as a message to someone on the outside. When the maids came the next time one or the other would raise one or two fingers. We took it to mean that we should read Chapter One or Chapter Two. At other times we realized we were being told to read other chapters of the Word of God. We sincerely believed that there was some kind of communication with someone on the outside. We began this tradition when conditions inside the house had detiorated, as it was the only method left to us to signal that we hoped someone would rescue us at some point in the future. We were never sure if any of these messages reached any one at all.

The closest monastery in the area had been sending food to the Ipatiev House for our consumption, but hardly any of it ever reached us. Most of it was confiscated by the commissars for their own consumption. Avdiev sat at our table when as did the guards when we took meals. We noticed that when he was present that our fare was greatly improved. The few servants who remained with us did not feel comfortable sitting to take meals with us at the same table. They approached Dr. Botkin asking him to broach the subject with Father who made it easier for them by saying:

"We are all in the same boat, and if we are to sink we might as well sink together." They were exceedingly sympathetic and showed us more kindness. We could read the grief in their faces, but they were as brave as the rest of us."

Voykov wanted Trup and Kharitonov at the Commissar's Club located in a house away from the Ipatiev House. Both would have nothing to do with that suggestions. They preferred to work without compensation for their old employers. Mother's incessant prayers seemed to help Alexei who began to actually feel better. Sensing this, Yurovsky entered our quarters to declare without preparation on our part that Alexei no longer needed Nagorny. He was immediately taken away. Soon after our young footman, Sidniev, was also removed.

Our silver cutlery also disappeared suddenly except for the few pieces which kept with us in our rooms. The majority of pieces had been confiscated from us in Tsarskoe Selo during the Era of Kerensky. My sisters had repurchased some pieces with their own money, while Count Benckendorff also purchased some of these pieces.

When we took our meals, the guards did not let us get a word in edgewise and also told jokes on end. They had no table manners at all and ate like animals. One of them even lit his cigarette from a candle near Dr. Botkin, dragging his sleeve through the latter's food. Spontaneously, I handed him a napkin upon which he suddenly seemed sheepish.Gradually we noticed a slight amelioration in the guards' attitudes. Some became tolerant and a few were even friendly (Editor's note: insight into night of tragedy).

One guard used the occasion of our walk around the garden to utter in a voice loud enough for Father to hear, "How cruel and senseless to hold and abuse an innocent man." He and others suddenly were no longer among us. New replacements arrived daily to relieve the ones who were being shipped out, as they were showing sympathy and empathy for us, which surely was the cause of worry to Yurovksy.

Candles were items we used at night to help create some atmosphere of homey coziness. Even though our bodies were hungry due to lack of food, our souls were filled in these candle-lit hours spent together as a family. We were only allowed to burn one candle at a time or use one kerosene lamp. We complied with this rule for some time or we would go to bed early or sit in the dark. There was almost never electricity though we heard promised reiterated day after day that it would be restored. For the time we were there no electric lights were ever on.

Kharitonov had a box of gold candles among our personal kitchenware. Even they inspired suspicion so that guards melted them to see if we had hidden anything of value in them. Yurovsky made his office in the house. It sported a massive and impressive desk and an army cot with a military blanket on which various members of his staff would take turns napping. The room was a pigsty, filthy and smelly. Many glasses of tea were consumed from a samovar which was placed on the table, and nearby rested a German newspaper. A black horn handled knife with a pointed tip was on the table, and Yurovsky used it to spear his cutlet at suppertime. A samovar graced a table, many glasses of tea were consumed. A

German newspaper rested majestically by the samovar. He sported a curly black bushy beard and moustache, but saliva was always at the corner of his mouth. He ate with animal like voraciousness polishing off a mound of butter at one sitting. We had not had butter for ages, while the doctor had prescribed it for our main captor due to his weak heart. Ironic that this brute sought sympathy as reprehensible as he was.

The table was covered with an elegant damask table cloth with a woven double eagle and a crown in the center. We also recognized Prince Dolgorukov's handkerchiefs, presumably taken away from him during his arrest. His coat of arms displayed a hand holding an arrow. Dolgorukov means "long arm."

The guards often asked to be amused by Olga with her playing the balalaika or the piano. She even performed her pieces of her own composition. As long as the songs were not misconstrued to have double entendres Father consented to her playing. We tried to comply to the guards requests especially if it were something positive and constructive such as music, for these moments were moments of respite for us too. The guards, however, encountered blazing resistance when they insisted that Olga sing "We Abandon the Old Regime" at which moment she arose and assured them firmly, "I will not do it, even if you kill me." Her courage startled them.

Once when she played *Andante Contabile* by Tchaikovsky, they screamed "No" at the top of their voices, "It is sad, play something else, please." Then she played a war song, "He Died in the War Hospital." "No, no, please stop it; it is sad too, play something else." They were somehow seeking cheer and happiness through her playing for they had long forgotten what joy was. Father always stood at the doorway when we played or sang for them. Mother was, however, never ever left alone. This custom of never leaving her was something we had instituted in Tsarskoe Selo.

As the majority of our jewels and valuables had already been taken, the regular searches focused on escape routes and possible ways out. They always came with a fresh excuse to invade our privacy. They invented ways to incriminate us insisting we had hidden guns. They were impervious to reason. We knew when they stole things from us even if we did not see it, we sensed it intuitively. We observed them taking our silver spoons, soap and even pencils. They would slip the stolen booty up the sleeves of their jackets. They even had the audacity to dismantle a photo in a heavy enamel frame with the excuse that we may have secreted something underneath the frame or might have something hidden in it. Underneath they did find a photograph of Mother's beloved brother Ernest. She had been afraid for a long time at the ramifications of displaying her German brother's photo, hence she covered it with one of our photos. Surprisingly they did not mention it at all. Over Alexei's bed there was a gold chain with an icon hanging from it. They even made off with that. We never resisted or tried to stop them as Father said not to give them the pleasure of letting them know how much they annoyed us.

Dr. Botkin was able to persuade Yurovsky to have a window opened in one of the rooms for ventilation. They unlatched two other windows and illogically accused US of opening them. In the night we girls would move our mattresses closer to the window in order to be able to catch a breath of cooler air. Our parents' beds were moved closer to ours and to the open window yet also closer to the guards' booth. Dr. Botkin, Sidniev, Trup and Nagorny had no privacy at all which we lamented. It was close to the end of the staircase which the guards used to go downstairs. Two doors stood opposite each other in the room. One led to a hallway and the other into an apartment.

Before the sweltering heat had started Nagorny and Sidniev had been taken away. Poor Kharitonov and little Leonid had slept in the hot kitchen. Each day was different from the previous one due to the disorganization by our captors, although we did arise at eight o'clock every morning. After waking up we would have a morning service at which we sang prayers. All the staff including Father, Mother, and Dr. Botkin joined in this half hour of meditation and prayer. These were the best moments of the day, because our friends were beside us.

Mother was preoccupied more with Alexei than anything else, because he was malnourished leading to his increasing weakness. He no longer had the vitamins and minerals as well as other nutrients he needed to build up his body. Dr. Botking pleaded with the commandant to somehow provide gelatine, vegetables and fruit for the ill boy. Dr. Botking, our "Papula," implored Yurovsky to assist in this endeavor but was ignored. Father addressed Yurovsky in a letter but this too was rebuffed. Such anxiety weakened Mother's heart, and her trembling blue lips indicated she would soon suffer a heart attack.

Helpless to assist his children, Father looked stricken. We were aware that he was able and willing to undertake any necessary actions in oder to promote the cause of Russia and his family. He did his very best to disguise his anxiety from us. Her perceived our individual heavy hearts and often told us sisters what we were thinking.

# XXIV   THE NIGHTS ARE LONG

When we heard that Nagomy and Sidniev had been taken away we were absolutely heartbroken. They had had no previous notification to get ready and were ordered to leave within moments (*Editor's note: this modus operandi would be repeated when the Imperial Family were ordered to make their way in minutes to the basement of the Ipatiev House*). We learned from Dr. Botkin that both had wanted to see us one last time before they left. Nagorny had confided to him, "I am employed by my Emperor and I am going to see him." Quite to the contrary he was roughly pushed along to the stairway. Our poor little Leonid had lost his only living relative, his uncle Sidniev, who had devoted his life to this little orphaned boy. Leonid now took care of the dogs. Alexei and all of us were encouraged and uplifted to see someone who had been with us in Tobolsk. Leonid's quick smiles were a gift to all of us, yet he too was a prisoner with us sharing our restricted fate. Alexei and he played at naval games with toy boats and ships. Alexei realized that Leonid was an orphan and so dedicated himself to educating his little friend and helping him in any way he could. Nagorny's absence made it necessary for Father to carry Alexei downstairs so that he could enjoy his thirty minutes of out door activity. Father's back was beginning to give out as it was in a compromised condition. We choked up each time that we witnessed Father's tenderness. With the lovely garden tainted with surly guards we now wanted to go out less and less. The mere thirty minutes of outdoor time was not worth the detrimental effects that taking Alexei out was causing him. Father persisted, however, as the fresh air was like a tonic to Alexei which is all we had until the time that God would answer our fervent prayers.

Mother insisted that Alexei go to the garden and walk a little bit each day, although we did not bring down the wheelchair (Editor's note: in The Art of the Authoress of Anastasia *the reader will see a painting signed OTMA in which the wheelchair appears*).We did not take the wheel chair down into the garden. We had the custom of taking turns to support him under his arms, as his legs would crumple under him had he not had some assistance. Dr. Botkin was sure that leg braces would assist in this endeavor, but the rubber on his existing braces had totally disintegrated. With great ingenuity and creativity, Olga and Tatiana fashioned leg braces using pieces of our corsets, such as the stays, hooks and other support materials. To replace rubber we used cotton to act as padding. With these homemade braces under his trousers, Alexei was able to now go outdoors.

One day a group of birds in the garden began to sing and chirp wildly. One was so insistent and incessant in this warbling that our spirits were lifted as though we were in Divine Liturgy. I wondered if he might have come from the Crimea. From that point on we all listened intently to our little friends as they represented the outer world from which we were being held against our will.

Our thirty minutes outside were now curtailed to fifteen. No sooner had we left the house, then we were back inside. Olga had a saying that we were going back "into the vault." It was a very occasion when Mother would go outside with us, but she so eagerly breathed in the fresh air that surrounded us when we reentered our quarters. Our monotony was growing steadily, nonetheless. Finally the books which had been confiscated from us upon arrival were returned. on our arrival, were now restored so that we could resume our reading but our thoughts wandered far from Ekaterinburg.

Father had a lovely custom of reading aloud from the Bible and would begin serendipitiously wherever the Holy Scripture was opened. The lack of yarn and good light made our girl's tapestry and embroidery work so challenging that we gave up. Mother could no longer sew as her eyes had worsened in the dim light. The strain was just too unbearable.

Alexei no longer had his toy soldiers, the guards having seized them some time earlier. Now he passed many hours cutting out paper soldiers with his little friend Leonid-lining them up in formation on the squares of a chessboard. We sisters helped to design different uniforms and color them. Anything to help the boys forget the dreary hours. The guards leaned over the boys' shoulders commenting on the play. Father wrote Yurovsky requesting a priest to come and hold a service. After a long debate with Dr. Botkin, one of the Commissars came at last to inform us that, on the next day, a priest would come to hold a service in the house, the first one in Ekaterinburg. Mother was ecstatic. We selected our choice icons and, with the help of our friends, we put up in the sitting room a small altar, a table covered with a hand embroidered cloth. With the coming of the priest and the service a little light crept into the Ipatiev House. Just before the service began, Alexei's bed was brought into the room. He had been suffering from the cold as well as from swollen hands and legs partially paralyzed from his knees down. Yurovsky leered at us from one corner of the room but we ignored him. The priest's voice trembled. He was upset for fear of making a mistake, probably knowing the fate of Father Vassiliev in Tobolsk.

It was an inspirational day; the simple ritual, the chanting, the Communion and its consummation, our lips kissed the cross, and our souls feasted on the Blessed Bread. Exaltation swept through us and we soared to an enveloping oneness with God. Father read the Holy Scripture and we all sang. What a day it was! After the service Mother said: "The priest and the deacon seemed so sad. Priests are in great danger these days. I pray they get into no trouble for coming to the house." Did the guards feel as we felt that day? They did not interfere with our taking Holy Communion. God's hand was upon us and we felt safer. The world of prison and persecution was not real. We had glimpsed the real world, that world where our souls were filled and a new life flowed into our withering flesh. Mother kept repeating: The Communion has been such a healer." Perhaps it was the influence of this Communion service which gave us inspiration.

> *(Editor's note: In The Art of the Authoress the reader will see a painting created by the woman known simultaneously as "Evgenia Smetisko" and HIH The Grand Duchess Anastasia Nicholaevna of Russia which depicts this scene described above. The family face away from the viewer and stare out of a window to a spiritual reality in which doves fly in golden light, while the interior of the room in the Ipatiev house is in darker tones. Empress Alexandra is in a wheel chair while Alexei watches from his bed. They seem to view eternity as their liberator and destiny, a welcomeone full of peace and love.)*

We girls put our heads together and wrote a prayer of seven verses, one for each member of the family. We memorized each verse completely so that we could destroy the written copy in order to keep the prayer to ourselves. We agreed that if we were ever separated, we could communicate with each other by using one or more of the verses as a sort of unwritten code. We were delighted with the idea and worked on its composition, each member contributing. Olga put the prayer together in its final form. Then we memorized it verse by verse. When everyone had· mastered the prayer we tore into the tiniest bits the paper on which the prayer was written and disposed of them, a little at a time, every day. Six verses of the prayer follow:

> Our Father of all men, Giver of our lives, In our
> saddest, stormy hour of this day, We stand at the
> Gate of our Lord,
> Give Thy courage and nourishment to our innocent bodies.
> Watch over us in the hour of our fate, bathed by our tears.
> Almighty Father, though men may stain their hands in martyr blood,
> Fill our hearts with forgiveness,
> Grant Thy salvation to us—defenseless-
> As we pray for the sickness of the souls who have gone astray.
>
> O, Father in Heaven, light up the land of Russia.
> Enlighten her way from darkness to understanding, Stretch Thy
> Blessed hand over those in need of Thy help. Lighten their
> sorrows and heal their wounds.
>
> Almighty Father, breathe into us Thy power, Thy strength;
> And when the storm breaks, grant us patience.
> With prayers on our lips, numb the pain in our bodies;
> With compassion, close our eyes with Thy blessed hand forever.
>
> > When we are no more, open Thy doors to the hungry
> > spirits of our souls.
> > Guide them in a prayer to be worthy of Thy Kingdom,
> > And grant that we may receive Thy mercy on the day of
> > judgment.

Blessed Father, Thou hast bestowed life upon us with the great power of Thy hand.
Grant that, when Thou takest our lives' spirits to be born free again,
We may rest in peace in Thy heaven, O blessed Father of all men.

# XXV   ACCUSATION

Yurovksy became more and more surly, even more so when his men were nearby. He ignored how nasty the men became when they caught us washing our drinking glasses after they had used them for their own use. Dr. Botkin again interceded and Yurovsky feigned concern, yet did nothing. Imagine our horror when the maid approached quietly and whispered that Nagorny and Sidniev had been shot to death a few days after being taken away.

Commandants alleged that Father was in still in contact with the outer world and that he had sent a letter instructing the recipient how to get into the house. Ironically, Father had no knowledge whatever of the layout of the house. We had all been confined to our quarters, most of all Father, from the very moment we had entered the house. Our view of the street was occluded due to the whitewashing of the outer side of the windows in our rooms. We were able, nonetheless, to hear, the guard on duty outside our window who sang obnoxious and bothersome "songs" for us to hear. Two tall wooden fences (*Editor's note: also visible in a painting in The Art of the Authoress of Anastasia*) surrounded the house, but we had no idea how far the fences were from each other.

Yurovsky and Goloshchekin informed Dr. Botkin that both Father and Mother knew of a future escape plot. Dr. Botkin firmly denied this allegation. Although a suggestion had been made in Tobolsk dealing with this subject, Father had flatly rejected it. Yurovsky accused us of communicating with our friends. There was nothing that they had written in Tobolks which was incriminating in any way, and our parenst were well aware that all their communications had been read with the contents thereof known full well to the authorities in Moscow. However, Mother had indeed complained in those letters about the leaders selling out Russia to the enemy. She had openly complained of the foreign policy coming out of Moscow and that Father would always remain steadfast and committed to Russia.

Yurovsky and Voykov appeared one morning with some papers which were photostatic copies of letters written by Mother to Anna Vyrubova and others in Tsarskoe Selo and Petrograd. Others were directed to Mother and the family by Mlle. Fredericks and Mme. Sukhomlinova, the wife of the previous Minister of War. Soloviev, Rasputin's eldest daughter's (Matriona) husband, had carried them fromTobolsk in a scheme hatched by Anna Vyrubova.

Some letters were in handwriting which was purportedly Mother's but was really someone elses. Voykov remarked, "You thought Anna, Yaroshinsky, Markov and Soloviev were your friends. We have photostatic records of all the letters and activities in Tobolsk." When Father recognized Anna's handwriting and what he thought was Mother's his face turned white and the "Otsu mark" on his forehead reddened.

There is an interesting story behind the "Otsu mark": before his marriage, Father had stopped in Japan invited by the Emperor to make a visit in temple in which no Christian had ever set foot. Father's riksha was followed by that carrying Prince George of Greece. Police lined both sides of the road. At the end of the line a policeman fiercely struck Father drawing blood with his sabre on the head close to the hair line. Father's hat saved him, but he was struck yet again on the arm. Father fled to a nearby shop blood pouring into his eyes so that he could no longer see. The fanatic followed Father, but again Father fled into the street where Prince George stopped the would be assassin. Chaos broke out so that police started to use their sabres on one another. The physician examined Father's wound and happily informed him that it was not life threatening, yet from that day the permanent scar would sometimes redden causing Father immense headaches. From that day on, the family dubbed the vestige of this wound, the "Otsu scar" or "Otsu mark."

Yaroshinsky, a rich banker, was known to Marie and me for he had financed our hospital during the war. He had once explained to us that he had arrived from Poland penniless with his to work in the mines. Marie pressed him about his financed, "But where did he get all the money?" The conversation came to an abrupt end.

Mother had expressly warned Anna to be careful about whom she was sending to Tobolsk. She admonished Anna to destroy all our letters and to please not involve people not known to us. Anna did not heed Mother's directives, and it is sad reality that Mother died with a feeling of bitterness toward her old friend who may have been well-meaning, but was obviously careless and naïve. Surely, Anna did not do anything intentionally but out of ignorance. Yurovksy was right this time for we, indeed, had been betrayed. Our beloved Father had had no part in this matter whatsoever. The leaders in Moscow knew of Father's resolute nature, but Yakovlev (in charge of Father on the train) believed that if Father were in Moscow that he would compromise with Mirbach, Ludendorff, Lenin, Kamenev and Trotsky. Father would never had done any such thing as Yakovlev had understood unequivocably from Father that he should never expect any appeasement from him while there was breath in his body. He would rather sacrifice his right hand than to do anything to bring harm to Russia. Indeed, Father had gone so far to declare that he was prepared to sacrifice his life for his country. Father knew that Yakovlev had telephoned Moscow with the news that Father was being stubborn. Father's existence was dangerous, because the people wanted him back on the throne. For this reason Father was kept far away in Ekaterinburg. Yakovlev had disobeyed the directives issued from Moscow and kept Father on the train which went back and forth without destination. This continued for four days until we were finally detained in the Ipatiev House. Yakovlev had given informed Father that he too was opposed foreign invaders and the traitors.

The Emperor and his family belonged to Russia and were there to serve it not to be masters over the people. Our father was Father of All Russia and we children were the Children of Russia as well. He wanted us to be simple and humble as well as kind toward all people and serve them in good faith. It was decay and disunity that had poisoned and divided the people from the Emperor splitting various elements of the Imperial family into opposing factions.

No cyclone had decimated the Russian nation, but rather a disaster had been planned years before from outside Russia by insidious men who exploited the first opportunity to strike a blow at this Slavic Empire. Innumerable ancient empires had all suffered the same fate-Egypt, Babylon, Persia, Rome, and others. The people did not recognize what Mother and Father knew full well, that it was an era of short-sightedness on the part of the people who were not able to see or comprehend what the Emperor and Empress saw. Instead the people now poisoned by propaganda looked blindly to the very murderers of the Russian nation.

It was not easy for Father, the Tsar of Russia, to die, yet it even more excruciating to leave this world knowing this his death was the death of Russia. He had opportunities to save himself by signing the disastrous Brest-Litovsk Treaty, but he could not bring himself to have his country treated like that. Even at the moment of greatest personal peril, he refused. Unto death he remained loyal to his coronation oath for which he never complained and to which he dedicated himself full-heartedly. He served to his utmost for twenty-two years. Many do not want to understand the full extent of what happened during those days of demoniacal events; neither do they care to look truthfully at the noble and admirable deeds accomplished by this great man, my father, Tsar Nicholas II.

There were those who suggested that Father was too weak, too frail, too indecisive to wear the crown of Russia. Little did they understand the great fortitude required for Father to represent the myriad ethnicities and cultures within its borders. Any normal man would have crumbled under such a burden. The Tsar was made the unending victim of intrigue, lie and innuendo, but the endurance of his character and loyalty were well beyond that of any of his contemporaries.

Anyone who had intimate knowledge of Father would agree that his chief characteristics were fearlessness, kindness, honesty, loyalty and firmness. In every occasion that he knew he was correct in his assessment of situations and of his judgment, he would not falter. Hence he was dubbed "Stubborn Tsar." He firmly rejected murmuring, court gossip, and coddled idleness, but he also refused to listen to those who tried to inform him of his enemies and spies within his ranks.

I once heard from a former officer who assisted me in my escape from Bolshevik Russia that he knew the names of several officers who had been disloyal to Father. Some were of respected social reputation including the son of a high Finnish diplomat who had been appointed to his position by Father. Although he was the son of an officer, he was a coward, afraid of being wounded. The Germans paid him money to act against Father.

Father and I knew one another for seventeen years of my life, especially during our incarceration during which we were together without separation. His strength and character were shown in his refusal to save himself and us while betraying Russia. Under extreme pressure from Moscow, Father maintained his stance and with deep emotion said,

"My family and I will never agree to what they ask me to do, no matter what happens. Anything they have to say, they should say to me and leave my family out of it. They have taken everything away from them, their youth and freedom, but none of them will yield to German spies and convicts who do not represent Russia, and will never forsake the Russian people."

Father was keenly aware of what the final outcome of our imprisonment would be. He understood how Moscow was involved in a campaign of a big lie to discredit him before the Russian people, yet he remained implacable. As the hour of greatest danger loomed, Father's stance in all ensuing official conversations would not be mollified. Dr. Botkin was usually the man via whom both sides communicated as Father wanted nothing to do with anyone associated with the man known as "Lenin." Good Dr. Botkin confided in Father, "When I needed your help you were very kind to me, and I have made my mind up never to leave you as long as I am needed."

The moment of all truth had now arrived and any hope of future freedom seemed impossible. In utter desperation I often pressed by body against the dame wall that imprisoned us wondering if the sunshine would ever make its way into our room again.

# XXVI  FEAR AND DREAD

With the discovery of the intercepted letters associated with Mother, her hair seemed to turn white overnight. She weakened daily after that event and needed to rest on someone's arm to move at all. Prayer was her consolation and strength but even in those moments her hands shook incontrolably and her voice faded into a mere whisper. She resolutely refused to believe that anyone could betray us which caused her unending agony for over a month. She did repeat frequently, nonetheless, "It is God's Will!" She craved the peace that surpasses all understanding as the Scripture says in her intense desire to partake Holy Communion in which she found her ultimate consolation. Father had the custom of regarding Mother but turning his head ever so slightly so that no one could perceive his tears; in this way he helped us all to carry our burden as we knew that he was doing the same inwardly for us all. This quiet and brave suffering was strengthening for our souls. If he did allow himself a rare moment of dejection, he quickly stood upright again believing that Russia would one day repent and believe in him (*Editor's note: In 1981 the Russian Orthodox Church Outside of Russia canonized the Tsar and his family as martyrs of the faith, a fact which adds another dimension to this story of survival and how the narrative would have to be addended after new information emerges a century after this crime against humanity. The Tsar's prescient pronouncement that he and his family would be believed in again leads to the fact that on October 1st, 2008, the Supreme Court of the Russian Federation ruled that Nicholas II and his family had been victims of political repression and rehabilitated them, thereby proving the Tsar correct in his prophecy. It should be noted that in 1981, when ROCOR canonized the Imperial Family, the woman known as "Evgenia Smetisko/Anastasia Romanov," visited the Holy Trinity ROCOR Monastery to make plans for her collection of Romanov artifacts and yearly annuity in perpetuity to be given to the future museum there. When her companion, the executor of her will, was asked who the "little old lady" was, he exclaimed, "Why, THAT is HIH Anastasia Nicholaevna Romanov! The juxtaposition of iconography and reality is poignant. It must be reiterated that when this "Anastasia" died, the monastery buried her with the date of birth of the grand duchess on her grave cross, not that of "Evgenia Smetisko" most likely the name created for a false and protective alternative identity in the United States.*)

Our freedom of religion and faith were greatly infringed upon here as we were not allowed to go to Church. Our captors only allowed the priest to come to us twice. We had to rely on ourselves to conduct personal services. Mother would read aloud from the Bible, while the rest of sang the chanted prayers. We held these house services daily. The comfort they gave us was immeasurable.Throughout the day, in the morning, at midday and at night our faith in God was quickened and strengthened with our family devotions.

The Bible became the most important book in our family, and no there is no other book which will ever take its place or be as precious. It is the Word of God and will never die. Even the hovering guards listened in quiet, their heads bowed. We were astonished. (*Editor's note: in light of their sense of impending death and daily depravations, the family of Nicholas II would have been very aware of the Bible verse: Matthew 16:18: And I say also unto thee, That thou art Peter, a small stone, and upon the large rock I will build my Church {Gr. ekklesia – called out ones}, and the gates of Hell shall not prevail against her. RUSSIAN: От Матфея 16:18 и Я говорю тебе: ты– Петр, и на сем камне Я создам Церковь Мою, и врата ада не одолеют ее*)

The hard façade of the guards began to crack, while an inkling of shame began to emerge. In their rough way they tried to atone for their treatment of us. They extended pity when all we wanted was to be left alone. They even gave us some of that by lessening their intrusion into our privacy. (*Boldened to give insight to various factors the night of the execution*) Mother declared that there had been an answer to our prayers. The very moment, though, that the highers-up perceived that there was a new leniency towards us, the guards were immediately discharged and replaced. By late June, early July they were replaced with the toughest lot of guards we had ever experienced. They were the lowest of the low, beasts even. Courtesy on part was to no avail. Upon noticing our comfort in the Holy Scripture, our Bible was taken from us. They were unable to take our faith away from us.

Mother said, "This is another test. Is there not enough of Christ in us to do without the Bible?" But Mother was more shaken than I had ever seen· her as she said this. Father looked at the guards and accepted the humiliation.

The guards had now become nothing but cruel and abusive, harsh and persecuting. We had grown inured so that we almost did not see them or hear them. We had built a psychological wall around ourselves: in the outer world we were surrounded by a hell like wall of fear, hardness, darkness yet this was contrasted by our inner world which was soft, mystical and full of love. We became detached from the mundane world, living in the world but not of the world, the Body of Christ impervious to Satan's demons in our midst. Curiously, each day of suffering we became calmer and focused on the Lord. We were helping Christ to carry His burden. We had been pre-ordained to suffer for Christ.

In the last days of our life uncertainty reigned so supreme that we never truly undressed, especially as the men surrounded us with lascivious glances and an undue repulsive curiosity on their part. We began to pull our skirts aside when they were near just as one draws away from rats and snakes. The new guards were not Russian at all. We heard every kind of language: Polish, Latvian, Hungarian, German and Yiddish. (*Editor's note: more insight into the chaotic reality of the dreadful evening to come*)

Although we did not even touch them we did see German newspapers scattered on the dining table. The guards seemed ready to make trouble any way they could. Their facial expressions telegraphed accusation and hatred. Yurovsky seemed to delight in a noxious way our being dragged into conversation by him. We wished to remain aloof but did not want to anger him either. We were on pins and needles. His mouth was continually full of spit ready to spray out at any moment without notice. The house was searched yet again by Yurovsky, Sverdlov, Goloshchekin and Medvediev along with four Letts and Hungarians. They yanked out our suitcases, books, photos and clothes so that all was left disheveled when they were finished.

Father read copiously in order to divert his attention from the odious goings on around us. He gave us the task of memorizing this or the other passage in a way to alleviate our anxiety. He never gave up believing that our family's fate as well as that of Russia's was in God's hands. This notion brought us great consolation. As if by miracle, our Bible was finally returned to our possession.

Yurovsky entered our area one day with an unlit cigarette dangling from his mouth. Out of his pocket he pulled a match which he ignited on the heel of his show. He wanted us to see that he was smoking one of Father's own cigarettes which were gold tipped with an embossed Russian double eagle on the paper. These had been especially created for Father by Benson and Hedges with Father's name on them. Interestingly, since the war Father had smoked many of them. Of course, Yurovsky wanted to show his "superiority" over Father by smoking these elegant aristocratic cigarettes in front of their original owner. We girls also recognized that he was wearing some of Father's own clothes taken from our trunks in the attic. He wanted to offend Father's sensibilities, even to the point of leaving the gold-tipped butt for us all to see in the ashtray. No matter whose clothes he wore, Yurovsky was always untidy with his shirt open at the neck, his bushy black eyebrows fanning out over his eyes which NEVER looked at us directly, but always to one side.

To our horror we could no longer lock our bathroom door, so that we always went in pairs. One day Marie and I crossed the hall when I espied something shining from the floor. When I picked it up it was a key with the inscription, "Made in U.S.A." We wondered if there were an American in the house, perhaps for the purpose of saving us. Mother thought she had heard some one talking in English, but she was not sure. (*Boldened as could be a hint rarely if ever read about in any other accounts*)

Yurovsky used this name with the goal of sounding more Russified (*Editor's note: Anastasia, aka Evgenia, may have been thinking of Yurovsky's mother's maiden name which was Moiseevna*). Many of those in the revolution had changed their names to sound more Russian thereby attributed the overthrow of the Tsar directly to the Russian people. On the other hand, there were many Russians who were initially involved who then found themselves too compromised to change the course of events. They now had no opportunity to repent for the horrors which were to play out. As Bolshevism albeit Communism are inherently atheistic, the revolutionaries attacked the churches, smearing human blood from those they had murdered on the altars which had stood since the Byzantine time. Russia had adopted Eastern Orthodoxy, the Christianity of the "Eastern Church," when the faith was still being persecuted. German propaganda had poisoned many of the leaders of the revolution.

Germany, I have heard, spent many tens of millions of dollars of Russian money to promote the Revolution; this money was made available to them for the care of the Russian prisoners of war. Instead they used the money to overthrow Imperial Russia, while our warriors were starving in dirty barracks.

Father was falsely accused of being instrumental in a Jewish pogrom in the Ukraine. Father had no idea of this even until one of the Grand Dukes heard of it while traveling to the Crimea and then immediately telephoned Father. The Preobrazhensky Regiment was dispatched immediately to quell the violence. Jews were not the only casualties at that time as other nationalities, such as Bulgarians, were confused with the Jewish population and also attacked. The catalyst for the pogrom was a falsehood passed from mouth to mouth that a small Jewish sect had purportedly seized a young Gentile to sacrifice him for his blood, as they believed him to be without sin. His blood had been let and in the process had died.

The fantastic story continued in that someone had heard a scream and witnessed a shopkeeper carting a barrel to a field in which the boy had been nailed. The boy was found dead and the barrel traced to the shop. This supposedly sparked the pogrom. Dr. Vatrik who had taken care of Alexei and was a famous surgeon had explained this to us children. A variant on the story said that the the Jews had had nothing to do with this incident at all, but rather could be traced to the boy's own relatives.

The Imperial family never hated the Jews. Jews were received in all military hospitals with the same care as any other men during the war. Many Jews fought heroically for Russia and died on the battlefield.

Others, however, did not want to fight for Russia and crossed the border to the Austrian and German side, where they supervised Russian prisoners of war and caused them untold suffering.

Father did more for the Jews than any Emperor before him. My parents always advocated the principle of freedom of religion.

There were also many Roman Catholics connected to our family, including Count Benkendorff. Father was now questioned several times in the next few days, because a new commissar had arrived from Moscow. He intimated that Father and we could be released into freedom if Father would just sign some certain documents which he had brought with him. Refusing to have anything to do with Moscow, Father told the emissary from the new government that there was no longer anything to say.

After Father had returned from one of these negotiating sessions he posed the question to us if we would allow ourselves to go to freedom in Germany or remain in Russia to suffer. We were unanimous that we would prefer to stay in our country.

Father was pleased that we all shared this same point of view. We could not believe that the situation with the guards could become any worse, but it did with the arrival of yet a new group of guards. Their clear goal was to increase our humiliation and suffering.

Voykov came one day and demanded to see whatever jewels we had left with us. He took Mother's engagement ring created with a rare red diamond, which we called a ruby as it such a lovely red, perhaps the only one of its kind in the world. At age eighteen Father had asked jewelers in St. Petersburg to search for rare gemstones. The famous jeweler, Bolin, found the gem and sold it to Father who had it created into an engagement ring for his future bride. Voykov had the audacity to take Mother's ring as a "souvenir." He wore it disdainfully on his little finger. Father was helpless to say anything and tried to not let it vex him further. However, a few days later just before the impending tragedy, he was still wearing it. Another moment of denigration occurred when a true believer in the Bolshevik cause entered our area without notification and began a soliloquy about Ulianov (Lenin) and Pilsudski, claiming that the two would soon be considered two of the world's most important men. Voykov was still wearing the ring when we saw him again a few days before the tragedy. On another day, this man again came into our living room without warning and began a long discourse about Ulianov (Lenin) and Pilsudski. He claimed that these two would soon be regarded as the world's greatest men. Father ignored the prattle by picking up a book and reading. Later Voykov continued on the diatribe to which Father replied that he must be right, that no doubt that all he said was indeed true. (*Editor's note: perhaps a kind of reverse psychology*)

# XXVII OUR FINAL DECISION

Our final decision occurred on Saturday July 13th, 1918 (*New Style, id est Gregorian*) after Father's last interrogation. Yurovsky and Voykov pretended to take a special interest in Alexei. Our trepidation revolved around the belief that they might take him to Moscow to use as leverage to force Father to yield to their demands. He told them that they would have to kill him first before they would be allowed to touch any of his children. They surely had no doubt that Father meant every word that he said. These perversely cruel men sat on Alexei's bed watching him cut out paper soldiers and annoyed him with constant chatter and attempts to engage him in conversation. Perhaps, we thought, they were trying to gain his confidence in order to poison him. We admonished Alexei to not eat anything that they might offer him.

In contrast to the other commissars, Yurovsky constantly followed us. We could not ignore his omnipresence. His guards were foreign and the smell of alcohol emanated from the clothes and breath, yet Yurovsky did not appear to imbibe. He confided to Dr. Botkin that he had suffered pneumonia the year before, and that his doctor had forbidden him to drink any more. We were sure that these current guards were very dangerous.

One of the guards was named Mebus or perhaps Nebus who informed us that Trotsky himself had sent him to search our house yet again. He must see everything of value. For the umpteenth time he rifled through every drawer, suitcase, bed, mattress and cushion. In one medice bottle he found Persian grey powder (*Editor's note: perhaps referring to Persian Powder, a natural substance used as an insecticide but here purportedly a sinus cure*) It was errantly deemed to be dynamite, even though Dr. Botkin assured them it was a treatment for Mother's sinus problems. The chemists assured our captors that it really was a harmless powder. The next idiocy was when Mebus purportedly found bullets in women's garments in the bathroom along with hidden guns. The blouse shown to us was one taken from our trunks, trunks we had not seen or touched since leaving Tobolsk. (*Editor's note: one such blouse which belonged to one of the sisters is on display at the museum located at Holy Trinity Orthodox Monastery in Jordanville, New York*). The commissars had apparently taken the keys from their guardian, General Tatishchevk, who was separated from us when we arrived in Ekaterinburg. Besides, we did not even know where the entrance to the attic was. This blouse was originally sent to us by Anna Vyrubova when we were in Tobolsk. Mebus or Nebus, whichever his name was, came in with the blouse accompanied by Commissar Horvath, an Hungarian, along with others who spoke German. We did hear one use the word "Kishason" (lady) so that we detected their origin was in Hungary. One of these men wore a cross hanging from a black cord and a small square bag of dirty white cloth which contained something.

Thousands of prisoners of war had joined the terrifying Cheka for a variety of reasons. Horvath's companions included two Jews by the name of Beloborodov and Goloshchekin (Russified names they had adopted). These two made a remark to which we did not reply when they espied our icons. Yurovsky, Beloborodov, Goloshchekin and Horwath appeared walking through our rooms, demanding that we place all our jewels on the table. We only wore our gold baptismal crosses and silver rings with an inscription "Save and Protect us". (*Editor's note: the author has one such ring*) They looked at us with focused suspicion so that we were afraid to not show them everything. They made no effort to examine our travelling clothes and for that we were thankful. They took everything they saw. A detailed list was drawn up with a scrap of paper given to Father as a kind of receipt, which all four thugs signed. Father was asked to give an evaluation of each item. Father said, "They have great sentimental value to us, since many of them are gifts from my wife's family and her grandmother-Queen Victoria-and from myself." Yurovsky asked: "But how much would such a piece cost if purchased today?" Father answered, "I am not a jeweler by trade, I cannot put a value on them." Their grasping hands trembled when they took our treasures and placed them between layers in a cushioned bag.

The dining room was now searched in which they found some goldcoated candles which aroused their suspicion to the point that they melted some and naturally found nothing at all. We could hear them drinking and clinking glasses all night keeping us awake well past midnight. Surely they had sold off our jewelry before we were even asleep. These treasures, stolen booty and tainted with innocent blood, were sold abroad to foreigners. Surely they adorn many high society ladies all over the world at this time.

(*Editor's note: an article from NPR titled The Mysterious Disappearance Of The Russian Crown Jewels by Corey Flintoff, December 20, 2012, URL: (http://www.npr.org/2012/12/30/168219426/the-mysterious-disappearance-of-the-russian-crown-jewels), proves the point made in the authoress' quote. Flintoff reports that a sapphire brooch was auctioned in London in 1927. Other pieces once included in the official list of jewels are no longer anywhere to be found.*)

Early in the evening of this Saturday, Yurovsky stood, noticeably excited, stood at the door of our parents' bedroom and said, "Nicholai Alexandrovich, your request is granted. The priest will be here tomorrow to conduct Sunday services." (*Editor's note: one suspects that Yurovsky was giving them a "last meal," that is one last wish before death; he was "excited" because he was going to inflate his own ego by orchestrating and carrying out their execution. Truly demonic.*) We gathered some icons that evening while Father's valet helped us to prepare a table in the center of the rear wall which we covered with a white cloth. We prayed that the service would continue without disturbance and without the untoward incursion of those noxious men watching over us and the visiting priest.

The morning arrived, Sunday July 14th, 1918, and we began to assemble in our room; Yurovsky entered asking if we were ready. "Right, we are," said Father. We wheeled Alexei's chair into the room. We exetended a greeting to the few friends waiting for us to enter the large room. To our surprise an error had been made in communicating to the priest what we were expecting. In his written note to Yurovsky, Father had clearly asked for a service called *"Obiednya"* at which the Holy Communion, the Eucharist, could be celebrated. We were astonished to learn that the *"Obiednitsa"* was being conducted at which no Communion is offered. It is a liturgy to commemorate the dead. (*Editor's note: Clearly this was a change ordered by Yurovsky who would have been sufficiently versed in Orthodoxy to know what the implications of the Obiednitsa were. It seems to have been another page in the scheme of psychological torment which had gradually and relentlessly been employed in the Ipatiev House to denigrate, humiliate and debase the Imperial Family.*)

Father asked Dr. Botkin to check with Yurovsky, because he had requested a Communion. Yurovsky motioned to the priest, saying, "A Communion is requested." Evidently Yurovsky knew that the service for the dead was meant for our own funeral service. No doubt Father must have known that the tragedy was near because he specifically requested Communion.

While the priest prepared the homemade altar and arranged the Communionware covering the chalice with a fine embroidered cloth, Yurovsky started to remove the chalice from him to see what was in it. Father Storozhev grabbed it back and in a voice trembling with justified anger informed, "I will not let you touch this Holy Sacrament with your hands." We were not allowed to make our Confession in a normal way as the priest was at some distance from us. At the raising of the cross he intoned, "God shall forgive your sins." Instantly we fell to our knees in humility in tears while Yurovsky lorded over us. We four girls wept throughout the entire Liturgy. We were so distraught that we could not even chant as we normally would have. We rose to our feet to receive the Precious Body and Blood of the Lord Jesus Christ from the priest while the deacon sang the creed. (*Editor's note: The Nicene-Constantinopolitan Creed in its form from 381 AD with its clarification of the reality of the Holy Spirit, still in use today:*

*We believe in one God, the Father Almighty, Maker of heaven and earth, and of all things visible and invisible. And in one Lord Jesus Christ, the Son of God, the only-begotten, begotten of the Father before all ages. Light of Light; true God of true God; begotten, not made; of one essence with the Father, by whom all things were made; who for us men and for our salvation came down from heaven, and was incarnate of the Holy Spirit and the Virgin Mary, and became man. And He was crucified for us under Pontius Pilate, and suffered, and was buried. And the third day He rose again, according to the Scriptures; and ascended into heaven, and sits at the right hand of the Father; and He shall come again with glory to judge the living and the dead; whose Kingdom shall have no end.*

*And [we believe] in the Holy Spirit, the Lord, the Giver of Life, who proceeds from the Father; who with the Father and the Son together is worshipped and glorified; who spoke by the prophets. In one Holy, Catholic, and Apostolic Church. I acknowledge one baptism for the remission of sins. I look for the resurrection of the dead, and the life of the world to come. Amen.)*

Father Storozhev provided the prosphora- a small biscuit like piece of bread which is given to each communicant-but Yurovsky insisted on opening each one by breaking it to see if there was anything hidden in it. A group among us, including Dr. Botkin, who had until now retained their composure, collapsed in tears. Now the priest used a white napkin and broke the prophora into pieces for distribution thereby concluding the Liturgy. This service brought the light of hope to our souls even though the room was dimly lit. Father greeted each with the customary Russian kiss on both cheeks including Dr. Botkin, Trup, Kharitonov and little Leonid. Mother and we girls kissed Anna Demidova, our loyal maid.

Mother extended her hand to Dr. Botkin who bowed and kissed her fingertips. We all perceived his odd countenance. After hearing "Peace to the Soul" he had become oddly nervous. While he cried he kissed us children on both cheeks.

Dear Papula, his suffering was beyond measure on our behalf. He had paid dearly for his loyalty to us. Whenever he saw me, his face brightened, and we frequently engaged in conversation. He was somehow closer to Alexei and me than to the other sisters. At the end the end of our travails, this kind man became brave even though he too was becoming frail. He was a bit older than Father who was then fifty years old, while Mother was forty-six. There was an odd peace surrounding us after receiving Holy Communion.

Father said, without bitterness, "A great crime is being committed, but I feel we have been true to ourselves and to Russia. The Russian people have been betrayed." Olga, who could say things so beautifully, added from her tender heart, "The Russian people have been hypnotized and one must not judge them by the present. They are good people." Dr. Botkin added, "Be true, do not fear, in a minute all will pass."

*(Editor's note: a premonition or perhaps Dr. Botkin, who was the one who actually verbally communicated with Yurovsky had actually been informed of what was to happen and protected the sensibilities of the family by not divulging what he knew.)*

Such words from him were rather startling and later I wondered whether he had realized what the deeper meaning of his pronouncement was. He must have known of our destiny.

While Yurovsky and his minions were meddlesome during Father Storozhev's service, we continued to have the sensation that we were felt we enveloped by God's sweet grace and filled with power to ignore the brutality of the guards. Invariably, one of us would stand up whenever a guard would come into the room while Father was reading in order to occlude their view as much as we could. On Monday, July 15th two maids arrived to commence cleaning the rooms as usual. Ostensibly they feared something and wanted to divulge information to us, but the presence of the guards made any such communication among us impossible. *(Editor's note: obviously the maids had heard the men boasting or even bragging to them directly, that they were about to participate in the heinous event at the Ipatiev House. The air was heavy with the impending malice.)*

That very day Yurovsky and his cadre arrived including Voykov, Goloshchekin and Jacob Sverdlov all Lenin's comarades as well as of Trotsky and other international conspirators. All day long we saw them in and out of the house, two steps behind us always even during our precious fifteen daily minutes in the garden. Sverdlov mentioned to Father that in 1913 during the Three Hundred Year Anniversary of the Romanov Dynasty he was ready to "blow upt the whole Imperial family with a bomb." Father did not miss a beat and retorted quickly, "What kept you from doing it? I probably would not be here today nor would my family be."

The young kitchen boy, Leonid, who used to come to play with Alexei for an hour every day, came on July 16th and had no sooner arrived than a guard announced that Leonid's uncle, Ivan Sidniev (our former footman) had come to see the boy. Leonid excitedly got up asking us to forgive his leaving us. We knew that this was untrue and that something was wrong. The captors assured Father that Alexei's playmate would come the next day.

Also on July 16th, despite his hands and feet being swollen and being still somewhat paralyxed, got out of bed. We took him to the garden in which he was able to walk just a bit. Marie remained inside with Mother who had not gone outside now for some days.

While in the garden we saw a pidgeon fly toward the porch frantically flapping its wings then suddenly to the other side of the house where we were not allowed to go. Mother had perceived it too and seen it fluttering against her window through the white wash which covered the outside glass. She reminded us, "At the coronation we were presented with two birds; and, as you remember, during the Three Hundredth Anniversary a pigeon flew inside the Cathedral when the service was held; and today a bird came into the picture again."

Dr. Botkin was sent by Yurovsky well before the tragedy to ask Mother if she wished her sister Ella to come to see her with the promise that Yurovsky would arrange transportation. Immediately Mother wrote to Aunt Ella informing her that she would welcome her visit. Very late that afternoon, Father and the rest of us were asked by Goloshchekin and Yurovsky to write letters to our friends and relatives here and abroad to the effect that we were in the far North, in Sweden, and that we were quite happy In our new surroundings.

With anger Olga interjected, "If we get there, we will write to our friends from there and not from here". Due to fear for his children's fate Dr. Botkin had already written such a letter or letters. His letters had been sent to Madame Elizabeth Narishkina and one or more to his children hoping they were still in Tobolsk.

Yurovsky's compatriots had the intention to lead the world to believe that we escaped at night and were hiding somewhere in the wilderness. Our friends after receiving such letters would be satisfied that we were safe. (*Editor's note: a kind of early 20th century fake news by which a narrative is promoted to attain a desired effect, even if the content of the messages is fallacious)*

In this way they wanted to obfuscate their criminal act. Suddenly, while reading, Father directed his attention to us and explained, "It is exactly twenty-seven years this month (July 1918) since I returned from Japan and that is the icon which was presented to me in the Government of Ufa upon my arrival there."

Someone commented that it seemed more than coincidental that Father would suddenly now at this particular time remember that unpleasant event which took place in Japan, where he almost lost his life. Jemmy, my little dog, went after Yurovsky that night when he came into the room. My docile pet snarled at our captor which was a very unusual behavior. I called her back, but it was too late. Yurovsky grabbed her gruffly by the scruff of her neck carrying her away demanding, "Who brought this dog up here?" Callous Yurovsky continued oblivious to our reaction to his abusive to our dog. We could only ponder what had happened to our beloved dog. (*Editor's note: Many may not have heard about the remarkable escape and survival of Alexei's pet spaniel, Joy, which was taken care of by a guard at the Ipatiev House after the murders, then taken to Great Britain after the White Army had entered the city and the Bolsheviks had fled. Colonel Pavel (Paul) Rodzianko with the British Epeditionary Force in Siberia cared for him until the dog was brought to Windsor Castle for the rest of his natural life. An interesting article titled Royal dog fled from Siberia into British exile, living in shadow of Windsor Castle by Kate Baklitskaya can be found at URL: http://siberiantimes.com/other/others/ features/royal-dog-fled-from-siberia-into-british-exile-living-in-shadow-of-windsor-castle/*)

This duplicitous man sat on Alexei's bed as though they were on the friendliest of terms. Perversely he pulled out a pistol which he handed to Alexei telling him it was American and did he want to see it. Alexei promptly rejected the strange offer. (*Editor's note: worth remembering that Empress Alexandra had thought she had heard English being spoken one evening in the Ipatiev House, after which Anastasia finds a key stamped "Made in America," followed by an American revolver being shown to Alexei*). Against his will Yurovsky shoved into Alexei's hand who asked if it was loaded. With malicious intent our jailor gloated, "It is not loaded now, but IT WILL BE!" Father was incensed and told Yurovsky to leave his son alone, especially as he was unwell. This mass murder seemed amused at Alexei's fear.

Now alone, Mother opened a book from which she wished Father to read aloud, and it happened to begin with this verse: "Let us take courage and be strong, look straight with our spiritual eyes up to Christ." Followed by: "Do not fear those who kill the body, but those who wish to kill the soul." Father was difficult to hear as his voice was just a tad above a whisper. Below us the drunkards were at it making all kinds of noise with their obscene humor and inebriation. Mother suddenly seemed to be in a moment of heavenly connection, as though privy to a private apparition from Paradise. She went to the window and assured us that she heard the AVE MARIA being sung, and so clearly as though it were being played right in our midst. None of us, however, could hear it, but we were sure that she indeed was being given a private moment of consolation.

Although I had the best intentions of meditating on Father's quote I could not stop thinking about my beloved pet. I was fearful they might have already killed her. Father assured me, "Most of the Russian people are kind to animals," but was Yurovsky a Russian? (*Editor's note: his behavior was culturally much different that what young Anastasia had ever witnessed. It is logical that she would have considered him "foreign" in all senses, but the truth is that Yakov Mikhailovich Yurovsky,1848-1919, was the son of Mikhail Yurovsky and Ester Moiseevna of Tomsk, Siberia. There are historians who report that the family was Russian Orthodox but that Yakov had acknowledged his maternal Jewish roots and studied the Talmud as a youth. Later, before adhering to Bolshevism, he is reported to have converted to Lutheranism, oddly the state religion of Kaiser Wilhelm so detested by the Imperial Family, and perhaps why there were German newspapers on the table in the Ipatiev House.*)

One fact was undeniable and that was the condition of the guards downstairs who were more intoxicated than we had ever witnessed. (*Editor's note: another hint as to the conditions which might have made an excape of any one of the family more possible, especially if there was extreme drunkenness on top of chaos and reduced visibility due to gun discharge and horse hair plaster dust in the air*)

Father laid the book down and said: "The best thing we can do is to go to bed and forget about it."

That evening as Father crossed the hall he saw several extra guards examining some rifles in the middle of the hall near the doors between the office and the stairway. When they saw Father, they lowered the butts of their rifles to the floor. Father knew every make of gun. He said, "These are the highpowered, German army rifles holding usually five cartridges; they can be fired singly or in rapid succession." Olga replied, "I remember at the hospital, soldiers used to come with their bones shattered and their flesh mutilated. We always knew the type of gun which inflicted such wounds. Russian guns caused clean wounds." Then Father added, "If Wilhelm had enough poison, he would have poisoned all the bullets." This was the last time he mentioned the Kaiser's name. It was four or five hours before the tragedy.

Father was well aware that the Kaiser desired victory at all cost, even it required the sacrifice of his own godson, Alexei, to whom he was bound to protect according to the mandates of the Orthodox religion. It meant that he would also sacrifice his cousins, my parents, and their daughters along with them. He had professed great love for us on his visit in 1912. This must have weighed upon his conscience. Nevertheless, the Netherlands gave refuge to this man who had enslaved not only Russian but Germany. The powerful and deadly German arms in the Ipatiev House were capable of unheard of wounds and death, but it did not occur to us deep down that he would allow us to be assassinated; on the contrary we knew that the

German High Command had demanded that we be delivered to Moscow unharmed, probably when the news reached them about how horribly we were being treated.

I came to learn only later that the plan for our assassination was not known to Wilhelm until afterwards, and that the German High Command itself was responsible with the collaboration of certain of our former Allies. They had allowed or sent these hooligans into Russia in order to bring out a revolution. It was obvious that if the former government regained power that those responsible for such misery would pay a painful price.

Only after my successful escape did it come to my knowledge that the Kaiser had collapsed emotionally when he heard of our family's demise, of the Grand Duchess Elizabeth and other Romanov family members. According to first hand accounts he cried incessantly for hours repeating, "I have lost my best friend. Nicky was my best friend. I loved them all. My hands are clean. Why have the other cousins permitted such crimes to take place? My conscience is clean. I did not know what they were doing. I had nothing to do with it. It was Mirbach and Ludendorff, supported by those Nicky believed were his friends."

During our last hours together in the Ipatiev House in Ekaterinburg Father spoke to us, so that his words are still fresh and vivid in my mind to this very day.

He said: "It is the end of Russia, but of the Allies, too. They have dug their own graves and soon they too will lie in them, and Germany will pay retribution for her deeds of treachery. No one can escape consequences, no matter what they do to avoid them; sooner or later they will have to pay. The taste of blood is an epidemic and it will soon flow all over the world."

Cousin Wilhelm could not disgrace Father before the world, but did manage to disgrace himself in before the world. The orders to kill us emanated directly from Voykov, Beloborodov, Goloshchekin as well as from the top Bolshevik leaders: Trotsky, Lenin, Sverdlov, Apfelbaum and the other men I have mentioned previously. They were in constant contact via telegram. Yurovsky had spoken with the Moscow contingent for hours on July 16, 1918. It was on that afternoon that he came into our sitting room. Mother could not abide his sight, stood up and exited to her bedroom. Feeding his own ego he chortled that Sverdlov, Beloborodov and other comrades in Ekaterinburg had been in contact by telephone the entire morning talking with comrades in Moscow. Dr. Botkin told us later there had been a great deal of activity in the office that morning and that Lenin and Trotsky had both been on the line. He went on to recount that Goloshchekin or Sverdlov or both had just returned from Moscow. In fact the Kremlin leaders were responsible for the guards we had had for the last two weeks consisting of Austro-Hungarians and Letts. Father explained, "They use the same tac tics as the Chinese did in the Boxer rebellion. But the danger here has come to the native people in their own land but not to foreigners."

These two weeks our lives had hung by a thread and on the 16th of July between 9:00 A.M. and 12:30 P.M. our destiny was sealed.

I gathered much information from the man who rescued me, during our escape. He confided in me that the outside guards were Russians and had been plied with vodka that evening, encouraged even to drink as much as they wanted. They had no idea what would happen that night. He assured me that the crime never would have occurred if the that inside guards had been Russians and if they had not become inebriated that night on free vodka. The outside guards, he went on, would have surely taken up arms against the foreign inside guards as they would have understood that it would be ultimate humiliation for Russia.

# XXVIII    DAWN TURNS TO DUSK

Early in the evening of July 16 we were disturbed by loud noises coming from below our rooms. It seemed that large and heavy objects were being moved. We could not fall asleep at 10:30 pm due to the repeated drunken rabble rousing penetrating in to all our rooms. From Yurovsky's room we heard lewd and lascivious talk even though it was somewhat removed from our area so loud were they speaking. Without warning heavy footsteps approached our area. The light was turned on and exceedingly deep voice, that of Yurovsky, was heard. He directly made his way to Father's room.

Father rapidly appeared in the doorway to tell us in a quivering voice that we must be ready to leave within forty minutes. We cried quietly and prayed as we washed and dressed. Before we were ready another message with a guard was given to us to NOT pack anything as there was no time. We took only a few essential things, while Tatiana scurried into our parents' bedroom to help Alexei with his leg braces. Olga busied herself packing Alexei's medicine as he was till rather ill and in need of assistance. At this moment he began to weep just as we did.

White blouses, grey skirts and jackets were the clothes we wore that evening though we also had top coats into which had been sewn some of the treasures which were still in our possession. Father and Alexei had on their military coats and Mother in her black suit. Dr. Botkin entered with a small satchel and coat over his arm. For the last minutes before our descent from our floor, we knelt in humility to pray fervently before an ancient icon of Christ.

We now shared the holy *prosphora* given us by the priest on the previous Sunday. The icon before which we now prayed was a family heirloom over many generations. There was a catalogue of all of our valuables and treasures in which this icon was also listed. This icon had gone with us from Tobolsk to Ekaterinburg, because it was one of the oldest and most venerated of its kind. It was even more precious than other icons encrusted with diamonds and other gems.

This framed cloth icon was said to have been made from the piece of toweling that had been used to dry the Lord's face of blood and perspiration while being taken to Calvary and his crucifixion. One could see faintly the imprint of his faith on the cloth. Subsequent tests proved that the material was the same used in those days in Jerusalem, and that the stains creating the outline of a face were really remnants of human blood and sweat. No mortal hand could have created such an image so it is called the Icon Not Made by Hands (in Russian

*Nerukotvorenny Spas*) as it was created by the Saviour himself not by the intervention of human hands.

As we left our rooms prayers poured from all of our lips. Again as we descended I was struck with the violent premonition which had been plaguing me all day long. My heart palpitated and I grew cold; I had even had a premonitory dream the night before which had caused me to tremble. In that dream I was in the doorway of a small wooden house akin to a fishing shack or cabin. The platform was of wood. The water began to rise from below the surface so that the platform began to float in the water. Suddenly, through the encompassing mist, I could only see water. There was no land, no mountain, no forest which could give shelter. All was absolutely silent, so much so that I felt enveloped by this sadness and began to sink.

In the midst of reliving this nightmare a man suddenly appeared to us, now assembled at the dining table where the family, Dr. Botkin, Ivan Kharitonov and Anna Demidova were also gathered and asked if we were ready. Father answered affirmatively and we were ordered to follow him. Anna, who had our two big pillows, suddenly handed one to Tatiana. They concealed still more of our jewels. The dim light of the lantern lit our way as we made our way out into the courtyard, Alexei being in Father's strong and protective arms for he could not walk himself. All of a sudden I remembered Jemmy, the dog, and I asked that she be returned to me. "Downstairs you will get your dogs," came the answer.

We supported Mother so that she could follow behind Father. The man moved the light side to side to better illuminate the stairway. Upon reaching the ground floor, Mother almost collapsed. Shadows moved around the courtyard. I can remember, however, that the night was cool with a bright moon. (*Editor's note: a painting of this scene is included in The Art of the Authoress of Anastasia*).

Now we entered into a secondary entrance to the house, through a hallway and went into the second room to the right. It seemed to have the same layout as our space upstairs, and it was from here where we surely had heard the bothersome noises earlier. At that time we were sure they were moving heavy furniture and other large objects. There was not a single piece of furniture in this space.

Dr. Botkin and Anna put their bags on the far side of the room as they were told to do. We too had to put our jackets and top coats there as well. This room was actually one step up or down from the ground floor. Yurovsky went before Father and said something to him pointing to the first door we had just passed.

Father held Alexei while three chairs were brought in. Alexei was then placed on one of the chairs, and Yurovsky left the room. Mother sat to Alexei's left. Eight men already awaited us when we entered; I assume these were the men whose shadows we had seen in the courtyard. Dressed in military uniforms they had revolvers in their holsters and hand grenades attached to their belts.

Although ill Trup had followed us, although he had been absent for some days in his sickness. Either the guards had forgotten to wake him up or they had decided at the last moment to seal his fate to ours, he appeared in his night garment holding his clothes in his hands. We had not been able to see him for a few days and though he was only about thirty-five years of age he was thinner now and blue in the face.

Tatiana arranged the pillow Anna had given her to help make Alexei more comfortable while we waited for Father to return. The group of men formed two separate units. Father passed between them ashen faced with the Otsu mark irritated and red as fire. His left shoulder and eye were twitching. He pulled out a handkerchief to wipe his face and sat next to Alexei at his right. No one will ever know what Yurovsky said to Father in that private moment.

I stood to my Mother's left side and Dr. Botkin to her right and behind her. Behind just a bit were my sisters while the men were about eight feet in front of us. I felt trapped and claustrophic as I am sure the others did as well. We could say or do nothing.

As Father entered Mother had attempted to raise herself from the chair but she began to shake and fell into her chair as her head slumped toward Alexei to the right. (*Editor's note: perhaps she mercifully suffered a heart attack or stroke before the bullets rang out*) I screamed while grabbing Dr. Botkin's arm not hearing exactly that Yurovsky was saying. I then heard the others screaming. I could feel no pain nor did I see anyone fall, but my lips were frozen cold and a feeling of clamminess claimed me. I was paralyzed and I heard a violent ringing in my ears before I entirely lost consciousness.

I have no idea how long I hovered between life and death yet all too soon I woke up to horror and dread. I do not have any recollection of my coming back to life. However, I realized I was indeed alive and in terrible pain. I was surprisingly clear minded and perceived I was in the midst of a catastrophe of great magnitude. I shrieked, but was afraid really to breathe or open my eyes. It dawned upon me that I had been unconscious and was now coming back from it. Fear suddenly overwhelmed me. Perhaps I had fallen on the floor and being taken for dead had been buried alive without a coffin. I controlled by screams understanding what had just happened. I had no desire to open my eyes as I did not wish to witness what I already knew in my heart. My pain was intense, my neck swollen, and my left eye was swollen.

Was I next to the others? Were they too alive but afraid to stir? I heard no sounds, I felt no body warmth and I could hear no sounds of anyone's breathing. I then remembered the screams of the others. The contrast between the absolute quiet and the memory of the shrieking of the others was all encompassing. It was the quiet that a tomb brings with it. I could smell wet earth but my eye was so swollen I could not open it. I suspected that someone must be near me so I moved my hands cautiously to test my belief. My right eye was able to open, but when I did I closed it suddenly. On my right was a crumbly earthen wall. Had I been entombed alive? When I dared to open the right eye again I could see a tiny opening just above me.

The slightest movement created great pain. I was nauseated and my head was wracked by a headache of intensity. The convulsion passed and I lay totally bathed in sweat only to await the death I felt I could not escape. I did not want to escape now. I truly wanted to die and quickly. I wondered why we had not been buried together, as we had always wanted to be together in life and in death. There was still silence even after the noises I have must have made in my convulsions. If only someone would hear me and end my agony. My ears were ringing loudly and I felt disoriented and dizzy. Again I was convulsing.

✳

# PART VI

## *After The Tragedy*

---

# XXIX  DUGOUT

A hand suddenly touched my forehead, but I reacted by stiffening in terror unable to cry or even to feel nausea. Perhaps it was the hand of death come to take me. I was chilled to the bone, yet the hand imparted warmth to my forehead. The hand was removed, and intuitively I waited for a weapon to descend. I was not able to look out of fear, hence I kept my working eye shut. The suspense grew.

My eye opened just a sliver but I could see the faint light of a candle. I opened the eye just a bit more. A woman approached, and my reaction was to scream in fear shutting my eye. The warm hand again comforted me though I was hardly breathing. Another eternity. The hand was lifted yet again. Was this woman real or an apparition? I had never seen her before. She approached and offered a cup of water lifting it to my lips, yet I could not life my head to drink it.

"Where is your pain?" she said in Russian which was colored with an accent I did not recognize, but knew was foreign. It was my intention to answer, yet no words formed. I indicated my stomach, gagging just a bit. The nausea returned. In a flash, a piece of preserved lemon was put between my lips. There was pain as the acidity irritated my lips so that I clutched them with my hand. Something was not right with my lips, my left arm, my head, my ankle and my nose. The unknown lady had bandaged my stomach area. Gradually, the lemon soothed my nausea. The lemon was so soaked in tears that I could hardly taste it although I sucked on it eagerly. I was if in a stupor, gazing at the candle. My thoughts raced and attempted to make sense of it all-the tomb, the candle and the lady. As she moved, the candle flickered and almost extinguished itself.

I continued to be startled with suddent movements; in a moment the mysterious lady was again at my side. She placed the candle a bit closer to me on a table next to my bed. Now she drew back my covers and undid the bandage around my stomach. She never looked at my face but focused on washing my wound and then expertly rebandaged it. She went from my abdomen to my leg, bathing it and then rebandaging it too. Next my head wounds were dressed washing then my hands and face. With efficiency she picked up the basin of water and disappeared through the space in the ceiling.

I tried to focus on the spot through which I had seen my caretaker disappear when suddenly two feet appeared, then a skirt as the lady came down once again. Again she approached and put yet another slice of preserved lemon into my mouth. She regarded me for only an instant and departed yet again.

Still I had no idea where I was, yet I could make out a trap door with a rung ladder of not many rungs leading up to it. I can still remember the lady's face which was pleasant with fine features and black eyes. Her now partially gray hair, probably brown when she was younger, was pulled back tight into a knot at the back of her head. In age she struck me as being similar to my mother. Long slender hands attached to a tall thin body. She did not appear to be a peasand, nonetheless she appeared to have had her share of hardships in life. Apparently she was not a professional nurse, however, she was efficient and confident in her care of me.

Curiosity helped me forget my aches and pains for just a a moment. Who was this unknown woman? How could I be with an utter stranger? How long had I been here? How long had passed since the end of my family? I guessed several days as I sensed crusted blood at the side of my eyebrow, nose and cheek. My hair was also encrusted with blood making it stiff and matted. The soreness in my left leg made it painful to move. My fingernails were full of some kind of a stained substance. I still needed to know where my family was. Truly I was afraid to imagine. My head still ached terribly, my jaws too and that ringing in my ears! Every movement, every emotion was agonizing for me.

I woke up sobbing so frightfully that I imagined that I had also gone to sleep crying. Could it be a nightmare? How it could it be that I, the little one, could have been spared and be now alone? The lady was now at my side anew. I allowed myself to wonder if the rest of my family too were being taken care of by strangers. I could not calculate any measure of time so I slept when I could cry no longer, and then awoke only to cry myself to sleep again.

Such crying iniatied yet another attack of nausea so that the woman hurried up the rung ladder again to fetch me some water. She used a sponge with which she dabbed at my lips and then fed me with a spoon. Now I understood why my lips were sore, for my two upper front teeth were broken and driven almost all the way through my upper lip. Dr.Kostritsky had filled one of those teeth in Tobolsk who also was in charge of Mother's false tooth and Father's teeth as well. Several lower teeth were also loose.

In my right cheek a piece of flesh was missing creating a bit of a hole. Only sleep could offer me any respite for when I was awake I experienced only horror and haunting memories. When I had sharp pain I though of it as a welcome diversion from my constant thinking. I do not know how long this bacchanal of crying, weeping, sleeping and waking continued. As I began to feel better, I did experience moments of composure. The moment I began to weep again, the feeling that I wanted to die returned.

The kind woman in the cellar working without pause to make sure I was well taken care of and comfortable. I felt bad that she had to climb up and down that rudimentary ladder especially as I felt her many tireless efforts were not making me better very quickly. She was gentle but also thorough. I was thankful that she continually changed my dressings. When she was working on me, I remained quiet, because if I had looked at her I would have felt even more lonely. She did not try to make my friendship and could even be described as cruelly impersonal, although her care was full of determination and dedication. Were she able to talk with me and give me some sympathy I would know that she was indeed friendly. With discipline she avoided meeting my eyes though now I could now see even if only through small slits sore from crying.

Though her care of my body was impeccable, she seemed oblivious to the hunger I felt for human warmth in my soul. She did wash my scalp but did not even try to brush and comb my matted hair. I noticed, however, that there was less and less dried blood on my pillow. There were two spots on my scalp where she finally cut my hair in order keep the wounds clean. There was still a hole, deep and round, in my ankle, and my back wounds still caused me substantial pain.

Now that I was able to control some of my mental torment I became more and more curious wanting to ask her questions, but I refrained. As long as I did not know things, I could hold out hope, so in a way I was somehow glad for her lack of sympathy. The greatest kindness I felt was when she placed her warm hand on my forehead, though the touch of that kind hand was also a catalyst to sense loneliness. The kind but distant woman did everything she could to alleviate my nausea except to offer a word of kindness. (*Editor's note: It is possible that the woman did not want to initiate a friendly relationship during which information about her identity might be divulged which could put her in danger at a later date.*)

My heart was torn to bits by uncertainty, because I sometimes wanted desperately for her to talk and then immediately hoped she would not. It could be that she did want me to suffer a relapse and hoped for me to grow stronger before confiding the truth to me which is the last thing I truly wanted to hear. Perhaps if I knew that my family was also being cared for, I would endure more bravely this pain and could tolerate the separation much better.

The proverbial moment of truth did arrive at the instant of its own choosing. As my wounds were being rebandaged I managed to whisper and ask her where I was. She did not want to answer immediately, but did divulge in the lowest and quietest of voices, "You are in a tiny room underneath a house. It is very dangerous so never talk out loud lest we be heard."

I was beginning to feel just a bit better, especially because the nausea was almost gone. More and more I slept soundly, while my youth was also in my favor. I allowed the lady to continue to tend my wounds, but as they were not sufficient to kill me, I had little desire to examine them. I had not taken much nourishment in these days, perhaps due to the danger of nausea and vomiting.

Eventually I was brought some very delicious soup containing barley which had a very strong flavor. It seemed to have healing properties as I felt stronger at the very moment of eating it. Ironically, I did not want to get better, perhaps as I already knew the worst. Now that I knew she seemed even more distant. I suspect she feared for her own life. When she had completed her perfunctory duties, she quickly left me. Why on earth was she nursing me. I had no idea. I understood only that I was alone and would not die. The prayers I had helped my sisters to compose kept coming to mind. The words seemed to have lost their meaning even as I tried to recite the memorized words.

I was tormented with haunting thoughts. How had I escaped death when it was intended for the entire family? For what reason did the leaders in Moscow want us dead? We could have gone to a foreign country never to return to our beloved Russia. I quickly remembered Mother's frequent assertion that the throne had brought nothing but unhappiness to the family. We all loved Mother Russia and would have been content to live as common citizens in some remote corner of this enormous country.

I pondered whether Father had ever imagined this ending to our suffering? Was he hoping for an amelioration of our condition or was he facing death head on to show how bravely a Tsar could die when he held his head up high and erect? Althought it would have seemed disloyal to Russia, he could have saved himself and us. Not one of us, however, would be saved at Russia's expense. The only time I saw my father bitter was when his epaulettes were removed, otherwise it was sadness that I most witnessed that he could not spare his country from the tragedy of revolution. It was noxious propaganda and contrived, fallacious news reports which kept the nation from knowing the truth about Father's goodness, and that he was the one who wanted to do what was right for Russia. The people did not hear how the Kaiser had made Father a victim of intrigue. Mother was also continuously misrepresented and misunderstood. She too had done only that which she thought was best for Russia, a country she loved too. From this vantage point I could now see it all; they had had no chance from the very beginning.

We were continually moved inland so that we would be less likely to escape, so we were moved to Tobolsk and Siberia, far from the the mecca of refugees-Finland. Kerensky had made Father believe that being farther away would increase our safety when it was really a way to make us easier targets. I could only hope and pray that Mother had suffered a heart attack before the assassin's bullets reached her. I missed her, but I also hoped that she had cheated Yurovsky and his henchmen. I should have felt great satisfaction it this were the case. At no moment did Yurokovsky fool Mother in the least. She understood and discerned all, just as Olga who also had the same gift.

We never doubted that God would take care of us. Little spontaneous prayers would come forth naturally when we were suddenly faced with challenges and persecution. We prayed as new humiliations were piled upon us. All these underscored the words of the psalm, "Though I walk through the valley of the shadow of death, I will fear no evil, for Thou art with me." In retrospect perhaps we should have been more active in helping God to save us with his help.

These thoughts of despair swam in my mind when suddenly I heard voices, quietly speaking, allowing me enough information to understand that there were organized parties searching in the woods, going house to house. They had found nothing. The voices continued that no one suspected them yet, but they all believed they were in danger. He said much more than that, but this is all I could understand.

"Which one of your sisters was very tall?" the woman asked. "Tatiana," I replied excitedly. Turning to the man she said, "It is too bad. Just think, she too, could be alive if ..," her voice faded away, as if she was trying to keep me from hearing.

I wanted to know the rest of the sentence and I tried to get out of bed while asking but fell back in great pain. I stretched out my hand to her pleading for some information

She begged me to not ask her any more questions and then rushed up the rung ladder without divulging any more information. My torture did not seem to end. I almost had a bit of truth to hold on to, but now would never possess it, except to know that Tatiana was no more.

I did struggle to understand what it was that made her not survive as I. Had she lived we could have mutually found a reason to live. I noticed that man's voice I had heard had the same accent as the woman who was caring for me. I gleaned from bits and pieces of whispers that I heard that he had not been the actual rescuer, and spoke as though he were in close contact with the actual rescuer who had confided information to him. He felt some level of fear because of me too. Had the rescuer or rescuers saved me for humanitarian reasons or had they found me still with life after having tried to rob me thinking it wiser to nurse me back to life than to dispose of me?

I became aware of my surroundings: the low ceiling which one could touch with one's hand while the space seemed to measure nine by ten feet. All the walls were earthen and even some roots protruded through them. The floor was dirt also but was covered by a woven and oval straw mat. It was now easy to understand how I had first thought I was in an unsealed grave. There was a tiny window, dirt-stained, measuring about five by eight inches. Hardly any light at all could shine through. An army cot was my bed. There was also a wooden ladder leading up to a trap door, and to the right of the ladder a wooden bench piled high with blankets. Next to where I slept was a tiny wooden table with a marble top and a drawer. On it a small candle did give me some light. The only other piece of furniture in my dugout was a chair.

What had become of my clothes-my white blouse, gray plaid skirt? Now A white cotton nightdress was now my standard wardrobe, and I felt dwarfed in its large size. Certainly it belonged to the lady taking care of me. Had anyone found the gemstones which had been embedded into my heels? What of the jewels sewn into my clothes including my buttons? In the belts of our skirts we girls had also sewn money. I would have given then anything and all if they would only divulge to me Tatiana's fate. Both the man and women knew why my sister did not survive, yet no one would inform me of anything.

The man opined that I could be moved until realizing that I could not stand on my feet. The woman approached to place a heated, tightly wrapped rock in the bed with me. The warmth was welcome, so much that I embraced it which sent warmth through my entire body.

My body made daily progress, while my head throbbed less and less. Sensing this, the kind lady removed my bandages noting that my wounds were less painful. She wisely placed a pillow behind me thus sitting me up in bed. Soon thereafter, while sitting up in bed, I noticed something brown and bunched up on the table next to me. I almost swore it was a piece of dried apple. When I examined it, however, I could not believe my horrific realization that it was a handkerchief which Grandmama Marie had given to me and each of my sisters. From where had it come? I had no recollection of ever having picked it up as we never used this fine lace bordered handkerchiefs as they were too beautiful. They were heirlooms which we cherished and stored away with us. I do remember having retrieved it from the floor the last time our rooms were searched after which I had placed it on the small table in Mother's room. I must have had it with me quite by chance, perhaps absent-mindedly. The lady in the dugout had recounted that on that fateful morning when I had arrived at her abode I was clutching it tightly in my hand. It had accompanied me from Tsarskoe Selo to Tobolsk and then to the Ipatiev House in Ekaterinburg. When the day comes when my museum is opened I will exhibit it there.

The efficient lady who cared for me did so at regular intervals although I had lost all notion of time. I wore one of her white cotton jackets with starched pleating around the neck and down the front. Although I literally swam it in, it was her very best. The sheets were of course cotton as was the pillow case. The pillow case was edged with pretty lace and buttoned together. She had placed a warm army blanket over the sheet.

Hardly any light whatsoever ever shone into the dark confines of the room. Day and night were hardly distinguishable. Above me hay covered the little window at the top of the wall I later discovered. At night a dark colored cloth was hung over the little pane of glass. The continuous dim light of the candle made my eyes sore so that I extinguished it except when the lady came to assist me. News of the outside world did not reach me either, while the day, the time of year, the month-I was in a space devoid of light or time or context. My room I could tell was always cool and damp.

I had, however, an unique opportunity to mentall review all the experiences that I had had with my family over the last seventeen years. Perhaps I was confused, I allowed myself to ponder, as there had been so many brusque changes in the quickly unfolding chaos and hysteria which had marked the last few years. I had the opportunity one day to ask my guardian if all the turmoil was a reality of some kind of a bad nightmare. She was swift to respond that I was not dreaming, but that all was indeed true. Because I was now propped up in bed I could hear the man better than before. I really did not know for sure if he was to be trusted or feared. The only thing that was clear to me was that the woman had not helped to rescue me and that her only duty was to make me better. me well.

A certain phrase did remain in my memory: "You see how careful we must be." I assumed from that the man and the woman were working together. Were others involved and were others saved? I would ask the man when he arrived back, as I wanted to piece together my last recollection to my current condition with information from the interval that he could give me. I still guarded some hope that Tatiana had somehow survived.

The man had descended the rung ladder during this time of deep thought totally unperceived by me. There he was suddenly at my side. The lady stood behind him with the dimly flickering light. He had just been outside as I could sense the fresh air which still surrounded him. He asked me how I felt. My lips said, "Better, thank you," but all the time I was thinking, he sounds friendly. I will ask him. There was no time to ask him anything as he quickly interjected that I must never ever speak out loud, admonishing me to speak only in a whisper, as it was very dangerous. As quickly as he came, he left without a word, followed by my kind nurse.

I was able to regard this man with great scrutiny to the point which I realized he had not been a guard at Ekaterinburg nor was he anyone I had ever seen before. He seemed to be wearing shabby English clothes, so that I had no clear idea of his origins. His posture was that of a soldier, while his hair was neat and combed, while his manner seemed kind. He looked at me straight in the eye and did not hesitate to issue me his orders.

My food on a rough wooden tray and gradually contained more solid food such as potatoes and fresh fish. I was always careful to not swallow one of my very loose teeth. Various wounds and disfigurements made themselves known as I suddenly realized that I could only chew on the right side of my mouth. I could feel various welts up and down and around my face, one more painful than the other. Feeling around my head, I realized I was covered with welts, one more painful than the other. There were also two long grooves with one of them behind my ear on the right side of my head. Had I gotten this from an accident or was it something I had inherited as Mother also had a sensitive spot on her head which the hairdresser was aware of when doing her hair. Perhaps mine had been caused by a bullet grazing my head. From the intense pain I sensed my nose was also broken.

Here I was, a partially toothless, homeless girl alone in a world which did not care. No matter what, the Lord was still my shepherd as the psalm insisted and He was my sole consolation. My abdomen was whole; nothing had been shot off that I could see underneath the bandaging. However, my skin was grazed as though it had been cut by shards and pieces of glass flying through the air.

The idea that I was well enough to be interested in my wounds seemed to please my caretaker. She confided that she had pulled out small pieces of blue glass from my flesh. She had used honey as a kind of drawing salve to extract these pieces of glass from my skin. Due to the many pieces of glass she asked me candidly if I had been carrying any kind of glass container with me. Mother, however, often carried a bottle, small and blue, of smelling salts, at that time. Then I was shown a gash in my left leg, deep and oval shaped. There was another round one in the back with a corresponding hole in the front. That was the end of any information she gave me, almost as if she did not want me to have the opportunity to ask anything else.

More and more the man visited me in the cellar. His friendliness exceeded that of the lady. He always began with a pleasantry about the weather or an appropriate salutation. After a period of time another man appeared, dressed differently in peasant type clothing as he evidently was one. They seemed anxious for me to be get well as they asked how soon it would be for me to be better. Ostensibly they were afraid of being caught. The man dressed in English clothes had a newspaper folded in his pocket one day. It was not written in Cyrillic script but another language which used Latin script, however, I could not detect in which language it was printed.

They were patient for me to get well. They were inquiring about my progress, asking the woman how soon I might be up and around. From their nervousness I could see they were in constant terror of discovery.

I experienced a mixture of fright and excitement when the men arrived, as I always held out hope that one or the other might tell me something definitive about Tatiana. How difficult it was for me to believe that they were all gone, no longer in this world. I was terrified by the thoughts which raced through my mind and also by my overwhelming uncertainties. Tsarskoe Selo was the only world I really knew. Perhaps, I pondered, that this was the retribution of Fate, as I had once envied girls who could come and go as they wished. What a shielded life I had led as a young girl. It was not until the war that I realized how serious that life really was.

Here I had no shield between these walls of dirt and the real world What I could sense, however, was that beyond these earthen barriers a lurking power was menacing me. Days and days, weeks, perhaps months seemed to pass. It was already a milestone that I could sit up in bed. Now I could stand on my feet so that the straw rug made of braids was under me so that I could feel its roughness. Suddenly I reeled in dizziness and hurried back to bed. The lady put me on my feet again the next morning; this time I felt stronger and I did not get dizzy. After a short time I returned again to my bed. We repeated this therapy, even though I protested somewhat. These exercises shook me out of the thoughtfulness in which I found myself engrossed.

Before I knew it I was walking the entire length of the rug several times. In defiance I shed tears as she urged me along. Though I staggered, I forced myself to walk as well as I could endure. My caretaker was satisfied when I could finally master this exercise.

A new chapter had begun when the lady brought things from above down into the dugout. Clothes arrived including heavy long underwear, followed by old stockings of black cotton, a slip, and a faded dress of gingham, so that I could only see with difficulty that it has originally been bluish grey. My small feet were stuffed into old fashioned peasant shoes which were two or three sizes too large. A babushka was tied around my head, and a coat thrown around my shoulders with the order that we were now going outside.

How my heart began to palpitate. Would I be killed? I noticed that I was not afraid of death now. Even though my body lagged, my mind was ready for death. I grabbed the rung of the ladder but could not raise my leg without help, because my lower back was injured. The assistance of my physical therapist, this kind lady who had nurtured me with few words, lifted them up one at a time. Her hands were next to mine on the rungs. Up we went slowly but with determination until we went through the trap door.

On my hands and knees I climbed out as I had been instructed. We continued through a dark corridor, about two yards wide, and into a room on the other side. The two men who had visited me in the dugout were waiting here. The only light was a candle on the table. The windows were tightly covered with cloth so that no light could stream out of them and no one could look in. I was led to the table seating me to face the men, at which time my body began to shake uncontrollably.

The first man who had visited me encouraged me not be afraid as they were trying to thelp me. I calmed down a bit when I realized his sincerity.

"We are in great danger," he continued. "Spies have been everywhere, searching for missing bodies. If anyone comes near you, and tries to speak to you, pretend to be deaf and dumb. Make signs with your hands but never speak to anyone, not even to us, unless we first speak to you. We cannot be careful enough."

He then broke the sad news to me which I had not wanted to hear. His voice was gratefully gentle and consoling, but it brought the news I had feared, "I grieve to inform youthe others are no more. I can tell you nothing more." There was no need to go any further, as I understood exactly what he meant. Nother more was said.

In a moment he continued, "It is becoming too dangerous to remain here. We must go away, but first you must accustom yourself to the outdoors. Ahead of us is a long, strenuous journey. We dare not risk the daylight, so the trip must be made after dark. Tonight will be a starter. Tomorrow we will see you again."

I was gripped by the guilt felt at times by other survivors when their loved ones have died, but they are still alive. Everything about me was a reminder of all that had to do with my family. While I grieved inwardly, I could no longer cry outwardly. Under the watchful eyes of the man and woman I lost my balance and collapsed on the ground. Quickly I was helped up, rushed into the house and back down the ladder.

The darkness and damp earthiness of my surroundings were welcome. I felt close to my family in this enclosed space in contrast to the sparkling stars and fresh air to be found outside. The world which did not share or know of our tragedy was of no interest to me, and I had no interest in interacting with it.

In the night I realized that I was walking around in this cellar area, totally confused, disoriented, not knowing where I was. I was barefoot but could feel the soft dirt and then the braided rug which thankfully led me back to the bed and the hot stone which gave me warmth.

I had got a slight cold from walking around barefoot in the damp coolness. This upset the woman, though she thought it had been provoked by my first foray outside and the cool night air. Early in the morning the men were there as planned. They were not happy that I had a cold and agreed to defer the trip a bit longer so that I would feel more well, though they urged the lady whose name I did not know, to speed up my recovery.

I became lost in thought. The men had told me that there were no survivors, yet I could not believe it completely. I would never cease to keep hoping, especially as I saw how incredibly difficult it was to die. Surely God could not fail them in their nobility of character, their faith in Him, their character, all more grand than the events of that night.

Nonetheless were certainly separated. I was to be taken to a new place in the world, a place that was indifferent, a world that would not bend its knee to me as in the old world I had known. I must suppress my identity and make a new life, all alone. God knows how I missed them. (*Editor's note: it seems she did indeed surpress it brilliantly with the pseudonyms Evgenia Smetisko and sometimes Eugenia Smith*)

I still felt intimately close to my family while the woman continued her care of me so that I was oddly suspended between two worlds belonging neither one or the other. (*Editor's note: A similar thought was expressed by Johann Wolfgang von Goethe in his masterpiece, Faust, with which Anastasia would well have been aware, perhaps even having read it in German. It follows here in German with English translation:*

*Zwei Seelen wohnen, ach! in meiner Brust, Die eine will sich von der andern trennen; Die eine hält, in derber Liebeslust, Sich an die Welt mit klammernden Organen; Die andere hebt gewaltsam sich vom Dust (= Staub) Zu den Gefilden hoher Ahnen. (Faust I, Vers 1112 1117)*

*Two souls reside, alas, within my breast,*

*One wants to release itself from the other; one remains with organs clutching in the earthly desire for love*

*The other raises mightily from the dust*

*To the upper realms of renowned ancestors translated JF-P)*

If I had not had the strong faith in God nurtured in my upbringing, I would have seriously considered suicide, but the years of prayer which emboldened my belief in the Lord would not permit me to entertain this thought.

My cold had soon passed when I was again climbing the rung ladder and exiting through the trap door. The two men were again there. The only light remained the dim candle on the table, while the windows were covered as before. I wanted to wish them a good evening, but refrained as I remembered not to speak. They began the communication without flourish. They were interested in a clarification of some facts. In Tobolsk and Ekaterinburg interrogations had evoked frightful memories, while Mother's admonishment to be courteous but to offer no information came suddenly to mind.

The men wanted to know if we had been ill treated during during our time in the Ipatiev House. I had to admit that our captors had been very unkind. When they continued plying me for information they seemed to desire details, but I was unwilling to relive many of the unpleasantries we had undergone with Yurovsky. There were certainly myriad cases of denigration and depravation but all seemed trivial now in contrast to the great tragedy which had just befallen us. I could only answer, "Everything to contribute to our unhappiness and humiliation." When asked about who we were with in Tobolsk I did answer that our friends and household help had been there. Again another question whether these people had gone with us to Ekaterinburg was asked.

Pondering the answer to this question I could see another room to the right through which I saw light and what seemed to be a the shadow of a person going back and forth. I was temporarily distracted from my train of thought. I knew that I must answer these questions, and as I had growing confidence in these men, I did not worry that there might be other people in the house with the two men and the lady.

I began, "Some went first with Father, Mother, and Marie, Dr. Botkin, Prince Dolgorukov, a maid and Father's valet. When our parents left Tobolsk the others stayed to take care of us children who were left behind to go later when Alexei should be better." What kind of quarters did we have in Ekaterinburg? Did we have enough to eat? Did we ever go outdoors? Did we see our friends? How did we pass the time? These questions were meant to pave the way for more questions that were to come later and to encourage me to answer them. In a way I was glad to confide my sorrow.

When this period of questions and answers had ended one of the men made a signal to the lady who then accompanied me outdoors. This was the second time I had been out in the fresh air. I did not want to look up into the sky. Holding on the woman's arm, I took short breaths and walked around the house. I could feel that one of the men was walking behind us. Not long after we were back at the entrance of the house. Into the dark house we went where I descended into the dark subterranean room with earthen walls. A cloth was nailed over the trap door, perhaps so that no sound would emanate from it. I was self satisfied that I had been able to walk around in the fresh air. I fell into a deep sleep.

When I woke up I was cognizant that my recuperation had reached a new level. I would no longer struggle so tenaciously to not enter the outer world. I felt as though I were an autumn leaf on the surface of a rushing stream in which I would sink if I did not agree to float. The outer world got closer day by day. It would have been daunting enough to live this life in good health, but to live it with ill health and loneliness was more than I could bear.

The lady was now folding all the bedding, tucking the pillow under her chin to carry the entire burden up and out of the trap door. I sensed this was an end to this part of the odyssey. These were her things, for she had been sleeping downstairs with me since I arrived. Sensing that I was now well enough, she was going to sleep upstairs. I had hardly been aware of her constant presence due to the misery which deadened me to much in my environment. Now, seeing her leave, I was a bit unsettled and missing her watchfulness.

My only way of telling time was by her appearance for I had no clock. It was morning when she appeared. She never said anything more than "good morning" which was the extent of her verbal communication with me. I never heard her name. If I needed anything, I could only whisper, "Lady, please." However, I believe she was named Iliana or Irina as I seemed to hear the man call her that. While she was not verbally intimate me she was gentle, for example, when she combed my hair. She was tender in all she did for me. There seemed to be a resemblance between the first man and her. I wanted to know more about them.

That day we ate an early supper, after which I was dressed in the clothes from before which seemed grotesque to me. We went to the upper room where the two men were. Another shadow appeared again in the next room. Where the questions before had been rather general, these new inquiries were more specific.

Point blank they wanted to know about Madame Vyrubova. Had she influenced my mother? Had she had intimate relations with Rasputin? Was she a resident at the Palace? I wanted to answer none of these questions, yet how could I refuse? Who was the man whose shadow I could see nearby and was he taking notes on everything I was saying? I became exhausted all of a sudden and almost fell out of my chair. The men noticed my condition and excused me. The lady took me outside for fresh air and then took me back to my dark hole. She returned upstairs deftly, lowered the trap door quietly but ever so firmly. A few days later she brought me a piece of meat and vegetables. I could not bring myself to eat the meat. My wounds were sufficiently healed so that the woman no longer had to rebandage them. The wounds began to itch which the woman felt was progress and this pleased her. She assured me that my hair would grow back over the shaved placed on my scalp. I could even braid it now. The nightly interrogation continued, but each time I went outside I felt better and more independent. My kind interrogators now focused on my mother.

"Did your uncle come from Germany to see the Tsarina?" The shadow in the next room seemed poised for my answer. Suddenly I was glad of the recording. Here was the opportunity to show Mother as the eager helpmate that she really was, trying to report to Father the facts as she saw them in·his absence. "Did the Tsarina listen to Rasputin, because she believed in his honesty, foreseeing, and experience?" I answered, "Whatever Mother did, she did it only for the good of Russia. When Father did not agree with Mother, she accepted his decision as final, knowing she could have no further influence."

242

I wanted all my answers to be accurate especially as I realized they were being recorded. Two weeks long these nightly interrogations continued. I seemed to have a fever each time the period of questioning ended. This was perhaps as the questions were personal and unending. The range of inquiries led from the Imperial Family to the household staff, and well as employees. I lost my patience one night, "Why are you asking me all this?" They replied, "We only want to know."

With time I became aware of the setting of my location. There were forests and low hills, and I could see that the house was square low house like many othe peasant homes. Shingles covered the roof. I could see that the little window to my underground chamber was occluded by mounds of hay which was another reason why it was so dark all the time down there. There was a long dirt driveway from the main road to the back of the house, and on the side of the home there was an old abandoned barn in which there were no longer any animals. I did hear cows somewhere in the distance. Perhaps my daily milk came from them. There were no chickens nor were there horses, although somewhere in the distance there was the sound of a train whistle though I did not see trains on tracks. Did these men come from the neighboring houses and walk across the fields? What went on in this house was a complete mystery to me. Did these two men and the woman live in this house? There was another young woman. Was she behind the ill-fitting door? I had only seen the hall and the question room, but I felt sure there must be another room in the house.

There was not much such furniture so that I came to the assessment that this was an abandoned farmhouse of perhaps a vacant servants quarters which had one been part of someone's estate. All my observations were based on what I could perceive after the sun had gone down and it was dark outside. I had the distinct sensation that these people were in someone else's service and were hiding out here. While the woman continued her care, the men actually joked about my recupation. Suddenly, I could no longer repress the question which plagued me, and I asked directly why they had rescued me.

Both men reddened in the face. The first man I had met seemed shocked, while the second man's eyes were blazing in a kind of fury. My feelings were hurt, and I suspected the worse must lie ahead. One thing was clear, however, that I must soon leave this place. These people would pay the penalty for helping me. I wanted to stay in my dugout forever now. I had become part of the earthen walls, the darkness and the dampness. I wanted to inscribe my name here but I had nothing with which to write. A hairpin met my glance; it would serve to engrave my name in the drawer in the table near my bed. I withdrew the drawer, set it upside down on the bed and with the hairpin I scratched my name into the wood: "A.N.R. 1918."

Though it was hardly legible, it would serve as an historical marker and witness to my habitation there. Some days later the lady took even greater care with my grooming, taking pains to braid my hair and dressed me up in one of her jackets. She arranged the bed very neatly and gave me a new pillow case with lace at the edges against which to rest when the men suddenly came down the rung ladder.

They returned with several photographs one of which I had with my manuscript until it disappeared. One could see the lace on the pillow, but I was, to my mind, deformed with swollen nose, jaw caved in and light dots in my eyes. The first man insisted it was a wonderful likeness.

They did not forget to remind me of the danger outside, with the news that people were being lined up and shot for no reason. They were in growing danger with my presence, but they persisted in their interrogation. My parents would have been so proud of my skill in diplomacy.

This pattern continued for some time until the day when I sensed that I would soon be departing. They reminded me that I was deaf and dumb and only to use hand gestures to communicate. They were going to take me to a different place, but reminded me it was risky. They told me we would start in the morning and that I should sleep until they awakened me. (*Editor's note: this play acting with life and death implications fits perfectly with Anastasia's personality and skill at make believe for which she was known growing up with her older sisters. In this case, it was a gift that would help preserve her life.*)

I was put to bed earliy and I began to cry as I was reminded of our night at Ekaterinburg. The lady's face with white and exhausted with the many preparations she had undertaken to assure that my departure would be seamless. She brought me a cup of milk, but her hand shook as did mine, so that the milk spilled on my dress. She tried to dry it and turned away, but our souls were now knit together. She rushed to dress me in the same peasant clothes as before. Only now this dress had a hem which reached my ankles hiding my black stockings, high laced shoes, topped off with a babushka on my head. Silently she handed me a label which had apparently been removed from someone's coat or dress. Stamped on brown taffeta in gold were a double-headed eagle and the words, "Mikhailov Moskva." Mikhailov was the name of a well-known Moscow firm. I could not recall having ever seen such a label and could only guess at her motive in giving it to me. Possibly she thought I would recognize it and surmise something as to what had happened to its owner. I still have it.

I asked once more what had become of my old clothes that I had had on that fatal night. Puzzlingly she replied, "They were so badly bloodsoaked that I had them burned." I wished to ask her again what became of the items I had had hidden in my clothes. I was afraid. I was at their mercy. I had no choice. There were some fifty large diamonds and pearls and about twenty-five rubies, emeralds and sapphires.

I took a final glance at the room and thought of the un certain future ahead. Now that I was leaving this tiny spot, I knew that I owed it a great deal. The only thing I had to give I had already given-my initials. In front of the ladder I knelt down to pray for a moment for my dear ones. I dreaded to leave the dugout for fear that I might never again visit this part of the world where 1he remains of my beloved ones no doubt were buried-somewhere nearby.

My mind went back to a question I was once asked: Why did I always stand at some distance from my sisters? I now realized that I must have unconsciously had the premonition that we would some day be separated.

I blew out the candle and groped my way through the room to climb the ladder, and out through the trap door. A clam was being torn from its shell.

In the hall I was greeted with a rush of fresh air. Our departure was to be immediate, with no light of any kind. In a few seconds the woman led me outdoors.

# XXX   WESTWARD TREK

**I** sensed that there were people scurrying mysteriously back and forth to and from the house. As my eyes began to focus I could make out a man who led me to the back of the hay wagon where he was to instruct me in the plan to spirit me away. He guided my hand so that I could feel a little door unlatch, further pushing my arm into an empty space within. There was a bedding of hay and a blanket, over which arched hoops covered with a tarp so that the hay would not fall through. He wanted me to touch the sides of the wagon and the arched top over which lay the hay. I would escape within this kind of human chicken coop which was made to look like a pile of hay for farm animals. I understood immediately to what lengths these people were going to save me and in what danger they were placing themselves. At once I was being hoisted through the little door. I was given a bottle of water after which I was locked in. I could hear many footsteps outside, and after a strong lurch we were on our way. In some way I felt like a little calf or piglet being hauled off to market. However, I had good reason to place my trust in these people of which I had become convinced witnessing their careful preparation, discreet silence, and meticulous attention to detail. I could not understand their motivation but their kindness was clear. I wondered if I would be met at our destination. The serious and elaborate measures being taken were indicative of the immense peril were were in. As the sun came up I could perceive a sliver of light coming in from the back of the wagon.

It must have been hours that we had been underway. The horse trotted at a brisk clip, and when we went up a hill or knoll or down I could feel it. The road as a rough on so that I ended up being shaken to and fro. Such country paths were noted for their ruts and bumpiness. The dust from the road entered into my space and clogged my nose, so that breathing became difficult. I needed water so badly for my dry thoat using the bottle I had brought as a temporary solution. I wiped my face with a bit of it.

At least my hidden space was long enough for me to lie totally extended full length with enough space to turn over if I needed to. Trying to catch a breath of fresh air, I pressed my face to the little door trying to gain a whiff of it. I did not dare to call out to the drivers for fear that I would implicate us all and give away my cover. From the maneuvering it seemed the the driver of the carriage was well acquainted with the rough little country highway. It had no springs and it jolted brutally and ceaselessly. The cart had no springs to absorb the shock making my head ache terribly. I feared for my wounds hoping that they would not now break open. Dust and sweat created an odd mask on my face. The miserable ride continued for quite some time more. Eventually more light entered through the little door at which moment the carriage took an unexpected and sudden turn. We descended quickly and then back up when the cart stopped. Were we being searched at a checkpoint? Had someone jumped from the driver's seat? Someone approached the little door to brush away the hay. In an instant the door flew open.

A gush of fresh air entered which was welcome, but I was suddenly dizzy, so much so that I fell into the arms of the woman who had taken care of me for so long. I was pleased that she had come along on this journey. She smiled and seemed equally pleased to be with me. She supported me for a moment until I could move my tense body and loosen it up.

How pleasurable this momentary freedom in the middle of the forest in the daylight. It was said that there were no problems in this particular area. The rest also served to take care of the horse. My eyes were red, swollen and unfocused. I bathed them with water, after which the lady wrapped a cloth around them and sat me on a log to rest. I lifted the cloth just a tad to see first a bit of green, then a forest, a bubbling brook, with bushes and thickets which kept us hidden from view. It was a perfect spot to go undetected and take a break. In the evening we commenced our trek anew, stopping now every once in a while to rest. Dawn returned with its penetrating light into my coop, and I could sense again that the horse had turned. Again this rest stop had been chosen with great care ahead of time.

The air was unforgettable, filled with the freshness of the morning dew. Wild asters and deep orange flowers were natural ornaments to our surroundings. Quietly I gathered some seeds to scatter to the wind in a childish hope that they would fly through the woods toward the direction where my family must lay. If I were permitted to kneel at their graves for just a moment; alas, it was not to be. I was perturbed because I knew so little of the fate which had befallen them. Here there were no prison walls; the water gurgled in the brook above which humming insects flittered.

My kind nurse, friend, caretaker spread out the army blanket on the ground motioning for me to sit. Thereupon she opened up a lunch basket in which she had packed hard boiled eggs, one a piece, fried fish, and bread. How sumptuous this feast seemed to me. What a glorious feeling for a change to be surrounded by birch and pines over which the deep Siberian blue sky, so typical, presided. The horse grazed contentedly while the leaves did not stir creating a divine silence, perhaps in sympathy as we hungrily enjoyed our lunch. I felt a deep sense of gratitude for these daring people. Soon all three were asleep in their naps, giving me an opportunity to ponder if I might make their lives easier if I just ran away, but conscience would not allow me such a thankless gesture.

We later stopped at a small house where we spent the night. My own sleep seemed to have been but a twinkle of an eye in length. The lady was awakening me while it was still dark outside. She had a candle in her hand and brought me to a table on which milk and bread awaited me. We then went outside to the wagon which was waiting. The stars were remarkably brilliant so much so that I could see in their light. Oddly, she did not take me to the back of the wagon but to the front where one of the men was already in the driver's seat.

The second man made a gesture as were he to help me up, at which moment I glanced at the woman seeking some explanation. Sensing this she pressed her lips to my forehead and motioned me to the man who assisted me to take my seat next to the driver. Off we went, but this time there were two horses, while the woman had been left behind. I would never see her again. With a man on either side of me, we left the front yard and made our way onto the country road. Did my rescuers have misgivings? Rigidly my companions sat upright alert to every sight and sound on the way. They had planned all along to leave the woman behind at that juncture. It was a milestone we had reached together. She had done her expected duty; now it was up to these two men to carry on with their appointed task.

With her departure was gone the last vestige of the feminine world. Judging by the level of the men's alertness we were still in danger. Why had they not returned me to the coop? How brave they were to even attempt this journey. I became confident as I saw how vigilant they were remaining. Even though one of the men had annoyed me greatly several days before, I was now sitting at his side.

Further and further we traveled adding distance between my lady caretaker and me. I had taken her care of me and her protection for granted. I had guarded a mixed feeling for her, one of wonderment and resentment also. How I had wished that she would talk to me one day and inform me of all I had wanted to know. resentment. That day was now gone forever. She had been faithful and I must now be grateful.

When we had looked into each other's eyes that last night in the cellar dugout, she had understood what I most earnestly desired to know. I should have liked to have been able to verbalize it. I had felt a certain bond with her at that moment. There was now greater and greater distance between us. Had she returned to her normal way of life or had we, perhaps, deposited her at her home? Had the dugout been near or far from Ekaterinburg?

Between themselves the men spoke of Uktus and Mramorskaya. Had that been the location of my dugout? The mystery irritated me. As of yet there had been no resolution, now less with the departure of the woman who had not divulged any thing at all to me.

The light of the countless stars this night made our journey a bit easier, so that the men continued on. Now the dawn raised her head to drive away any other darkness. The sun appeared in all its radiance. Even though I was cold and numb, I welcomed our stop to stretch and rest the horses. They handed me the basket and army blanket unharnessing the horses horses. We were now beginning of our fourth day on the road. My task was to attend to the food while the men cared for the horses. In the basket we found our provisions which included black bread, eggs and a bottle of water. While we were asleep the woman had baked the bread for us. We ate in a sunny spot which I had found for us.

No sooner had we finished eating, they jumped to their feet expecting me to do the same in order to continue our journey. We sat three abreast in the driver's seat. We were but a peasant family moving between work fields. My faded clothes were perfect for this image we wanted to create. Now the horses seemed to know this path as well as the drivers. Obviously, both had been on these byways many times before. A village was visible in the distance from our vantage place on a hill. Never once did I ask the men their names, nor did they ever offer them to me. Other wagons passed us by. The men were obviously less stressed here, so I assumed we were past the zone of most danger. Again we stopped for a bit of nourishment, although very little was left. The men were so exhausted they could hardly eat. After our sparse meal they harnessed the horses and made a bed for me in the hay in the cart. I was touched by their immense kindness which greatly reassured me. Now I was out of their sight so that I allowed myself some private tears. I slept soundly until the wagon suddenly came to a stop. I sat up in absolute fear. IT was a dark night. The horses were being helped out of their gear, so I knew that we were to spend the night here. After some time sleeping I was sure I heard a scream from somewhere. It repeated. It had turned into a shriek and the horses even neighed. Immediately the men sprang to their feet pulling hay off the wagon. With the hay they made a fire saying that two wolves were nearby.

I now was able to stay awake much easier after this scare. These poor tired men were awaked various times that night, until I finally heard them sturrying in preparation for our continued journey. Using my fingers for a comb and my palm for a brush I tried to look as presentable as possible. I knew I did not really look well groomed, but I did not really much care either. One helped me down from the hay, while the other poured some water over my hands so that I could freshen my face. After this scare it was easy to keep awake. I felt sorry for the men who were up and down several times during the night. At last dawn appeared and I heard them stirring in preparation for a new departure. The night had been spent not far from a farmhouse known to my companions.

Our path took us from the forest to an open field and then into another forest. The position of the sun informed me that we were headed in a southwesterly direction. After awhile we made yet another stop for food and rest. This time we had only bread which we washed down with water. After lunch not another word was spoken, while our odyssey over this rutted country lanes and roads continued without major incident. Along the way we encountered men and women of frail health accompanied by barefoot children in tattered clothes. As soon as we emerged from one rut we got into another the vibrations of which were beginning to make me feel nauseous.

The farms here were great distances apart. They had very little grain which indicated that they must be struggling to raise enough food to feed their children and keep them warm. It was the vision of an society living at the level of bare existence. They had no interest in what was happening in the large cities, nor had they probably even heard of the the mass shootings of innocent people or the assassination of their Tsar and his family. Only later did I hear that the grain had been taken away from the peasantry causing many to die in the winter of 1917-1918. At this point my companions were talking freely about their journey and even joking about how frightened they had been. They did manage to exchange a few pleasantries with me, yet they did not address me or use my real name or title. (*Editor's note: following this precedent it is no wonder that the name on the tomb cross in Jordanville, New York is Evgenia*

*Smetisko, but the date of birth is that of Anastasia, June 18, 1901)* Now the men talked freely about their journey. They even joked about their fright. But they exchanged only a few words with me. They did not address me nor use my real name or title.

Later in the evening the wagon halted once again. A veritable eternity, it seemed, had passed since the lady had left our retinue. The men released the horses from their harnesses and tied to them to tree. Our food had now run out. An eagerness between them to reach our destination was tangible. In the mid afternoon the horses suddenly we entered an open field upon a hill. We could see the village in the distance. The horses were allowed to graze at will as they were now hitched to long ropes which allowed them to walk around. The men stretched out by the wagon and soon enjoying a well deserved nap. On the other hand, I had no idea where we might be. In the early evening, the men jumped up saying that we were going to get going. We were to leave the horses and wagon taking off on foot. Making sure the horses were safe they looked back several times. I felt a tinge of sadness as I had become quite fond of these animals. We began to walk three abreast. We went down a hill and then up another, and down other a few times until the village came into closer view. One of the men gave the other one directions only to return to the horses we had just left. I could see our companion to this point going back up the hill losing himself in the widening distance.

My boots of course were too big for my tiny feet and were terribly uncomfortable. I wondered how my wounded leg would endure and if it would open up again. My feet sloshed around inside the oversized footwear. By the time we reached the village it was dark. Here and there dogs barked and ran around in the streets returning then to their houses. One could see the occasional flickering of a candle or kerosene lamp in the window. All seemed to be sleeping already in the silent village. Eventually we came up to a dimly lit house. My traveling partner gave two short knocks on the window upon which a tall lean man with a cane came to the door.

He held the door open for us and said, "I have been expecting you for the last two nights." I extended my hand to him. He held it in both of his hands, kissed it, and looked into my eyes, without a word. A tear rolled down his cheek. He stood in silence ... overcome with emotion, then said; "My dear, you must be tired and hungry after such a trying trip." His voice and words were touching and more friendly and warm than I had heard in several months. He drew me to a chair at a table and when I was seated the two men sat on either side of me.

*(Editor's note: After reading Anastasia's account of events as she remembered them over and over, there are hints that even while in captivity there may have been plans underway to save the family or those they could. One wonders if the hasty way they were executed could have happened because of such a fear or tip off of such an attempt. The initial lady who tends to Anastasia's wounds seems to have been in a "safe house" en par with the Underground Railroad. Had Anastasia's rescuer truly just "popped in" on this peasant woman or had the route been preplanned? Indeed, as we will read shortly, part of her new identity may have already been schemed ahead of time, perhaps even in the USA as the closeness to the Kohlsaat sisters with their ties to the executive branch of the federal government via their father could indicate.)*

# XXXI  ALEXANDER

The man who received us asked us if we had any trouble on our way to get to his house. My companion responded that we had had very little. Although he did recount how we had used a few matches to make a fire to scare away some wolves, a special event as matches were scarce. Our host asked us if we wanted some and handed him some loose ones. The man who had brought me here assured our host that the surroundings were very pleasant, but that we must not tarry.

The host called a woman by the name of Marushka to bring us some tea. Instantly, thinly sliced ham with bread and cheese appeared on the table with a small samovar. The kind gentleman was a bit surprised when I refused the meat, as it was such a luxury at that point. However, ever since Ektarinburg, I had not been able to stomach the sight of meat. I did feel somewhat guilty taking sugar in my tea, but the host insisted. I did not stir it as I anticipated a second cup. It was so refreshing, especially given our arduous journey.

When we had finished my companion informed me in front of the host, that it was the host to whom I was indebted for my rescue, and that my life was saved due to the intervention of this kindly gentleman. Immediately, the man who had just received us stood up and handed my companion a very old and thick envelope, so that I was sure it contained paper money and jewelry. As we looked on my companion opened the flap, glancing inside. The host said "Take some bread and cheese to your friend. He must be hungry." "Are you really leaving?" I asked. "Yes," he said, "my part is done."

At that moment I did not know what the my companion meant, although I had instant confidence in my host. I assured him that, although I had nothing to offer him as a token of thanks, that I did feel immense gratitude for saving me in the name of my family and myself, for he had risked so very much in helping me.

With bow he was suddenly gone. Each farewell indicated a loss of a little bit more of Russia. The chapter of my recuperation in the earthen cellar dugout was now over. Yet the man had said that I owed my life to this host. What part exactly had he played. I did have a sense of security however. Honestly, he seemed like one of my own people so that I could freely talk to him and find out who he really was. I began by asking him if the house was his to which he answered with a riddle, "Yes and No."

He explained that the cottage had been part of a former estate on which Marushka's husband had worked. However, he had gone missing in the war and had not been heard of since. He went on to explain that the woods and fields had also been part of the estate which had belonged to relatives of the Gier Family of Ukraine. I remembered that there had been a governor by that name as I had met him and his daughter once before. He affirmed that my recollection was correct. An instant bond joined us at that moment.

At that moment Marushka came in to announce that everything was ready for me. Thanking my host I followed her. Besides the kitchen the house contained two rooms . The host slept where we had just enjoyed tea while Marushka and I were in the other room. I fell into a deep sleep on an army cot while my hostess slept on a small wooden bed next to the wall. There was a basin, a water pitcher with water, soup and a towel, with a kerosene lantern nearby. This house, like the majority in the countryside and small villages, did not have inside conveniences. (*Editor's note: inside plumbing and toilet*). In the morning I enjoyed the sight of a vegetable garden outside the window. The cosiness was only more complete with the presence of a joyful little dog who came to sniff my leg each time I bathed the wound on my leg. When I allowed myself a tear or two in my continuing misery the dog regarded me with compassion showing me his sympathy. He even licked my hands! I felt an immediate affinity for this canine to which I was drawn from the first instant. In fact I could not fathom having to leave him soon. day. He followed me everywhere in the day time and slept by my cot at night, as if to protect me from danger. It was as if he had always been my pet.

After breakfast my host informed me, "We will not hurry. You need the rest and time for your wound to heal better. We will remain here a week or so." This was music to my ears, as I was finally comfortable in body, mind and spirit. My host was desireous to converse with me, for which I was also thankful especially after weeks of silence.

Alexander was his name, and he had been an officer during the war. A recipient of St. George's Cross for his distinguished service in the Russian Army he had also been decorated with the medal of St. Vladimir, 3rd class, usually given to commandants of large units. He had met my father's mother; on one occasion had even met us children at G.H.Q during a visit with Father.

During the war he had been nursed for an abdominal wound at the hospital in Kiev or Rovno where he had also become acquainted with my Aunt Olga. (*Editor's note: Alexander knew the Tsar, had met the children, knew Dowager Empress Marie and Grand Duchess Olga, the Tsar's sister. One assumes that this familiarity and access to funding to help with an escape plan may have been seminal to Anastasia's rescue.*)

Our conversation one evening turned to the topic of Father; Alexander shared his view of him insisting that His Majesty was kind, really too kind. To his mind, Father had been patient and understanding throughout the time of his banishment. We were of the same belief that only Christ could understand Father's suffering. He believed that Their Majesties had suffered a long time. He bent his head and tears rolled down his cheeks. "It is all finished for all of us and for Russia."

My father had also shed tears on that final night of July 16th-17th after his talk with Yurovsky. (*Editor's note: one senses that Nicholas had been been told what fate awaited the family. Perhaps to keep them calm he had held it all in, so they would not perceive it and become anxiety-ridden, giving them in a sense the gift of temporary peace before eternal rest for the Christian soul as a result of human torment and murder.*) Our weeping was mutual and simultaneous. How I thanked the good Lord that He had led me to such a good and sympathetic individual. Our talks were numerous, yet we never broached the topic which was so delicate to both us but ever on my mind. Alexander avoided speaking in much detail about the fate of my family and the particulars of my rescue. I did relay much information and commentary to him about my excellent care in the cellar and how well the kind lady had taken care of me, also I had been frightened by the questions the men asked me.

"They questioned you?", he said. "What about?"

"About my family, the imprisonment," I answered. He was surprised at this news.

"Do you think they knew who you were?"

"Yes." I said, "They never came out with it, but, judging from their questions, I suspected they had guessed."

"Then we must leave immediately," he said. "There will be trouble." (*Editor's note: evidently the men, though efficient and helpful, had overstepped their boundaries and were never authorized to interrogate Anastasia. Understandably they were caught up in the momentous events of the time in which they were all involved, but Alexander's reaction shows that it was not part of the plan and could mean danger to Anastasia's and his well-being.*)

Alexander had suddenly become agitated calling to Marushka to prepare for our departure. This happened on the third evening of my stay at the cottage of my host. We had both looked forward to a week of respite, but this was now cut short.

Well before dawn on the fourth day, Alexander and I departed on our journey. By the Russian (*Julian*) calendar it was September. I realized this when I glanced at a calendar on the wall in Marushka's room. Wittily, she had reused last years calendar and changed the dates to correspond with the current year. Marushka wept, as she so commonly did for her deceased husband, as we left. After a quick good-bye, we took our leave while the dog also seemed puzzled. I felt the pain of separation from this furry little creature.

Off we went. I carried absolutely nothing with me, although Alexander did carry a small canvas bag with some food and a medicinal salve for his wound. Our journey by foot was unremarkable reaching a small town by late morning. He was extremely quiet, at times not quite sure which road or path we should take. After an hour's rest he assured me he now knew where we were as he recognized a church steeple and was familiar with this part of the country. After walking several more hours, we neared the ruin of a factory. Sitting on the rocks and fallen bricks we ate our lunch. Our provisions were bread, hard boiled eggs and a bottle of sour milk with some apples we had purchased.

Now for the first time in this arduous trek I knew approximately where we were. We had a magnificent view passing the ancient city of Ufa, high up on the banks at the junction of the Ufa and Belaya Rivers. Vast stone quarries and stone-cutting mills spread before our eyes. The numerous smoke stacks were a witness to the size of Russian industries. Now they lay idle with not smoke rising from them.

Bashkirs inhabited part of Ufa (*Editor's note: a Turkic people indigenous to Bashkortostan*), but now many people including foreigners, were buying grain from the new government using prescious stones and platinum to avoid starvation. This was sold by the Bolsheviks to foreigners, while Russians were going hungry not able to buy their own products. Alexander informed me that were going to leave by train that very afternoon catching it in Ufa.

There was no train at the depot on the other side of town when we arrived. It was farther down the track we now heard. Walking down the track some distance we did find it. It was filled with Russian peasants but also many foreigners with their purchases, and the latter were boarding first. Some of the country folk actually got up on the roof of the cars. Alexander and I managed to squeeze into the doorway standing up all night. Although there were restrooms on the train, even these were filled with people. We decided to not get off the train for fear that we would never be able to get back on again. But we did disembark at Bulgulma where we caught another train to Simbirsk which was later changed to Ulianov to commemorate that heinous man known as Lenin. The Volga was marvelous here with the city of Simbirsk on its banks dotted with numerous church steeples. A genealogical note of interest occurred to me that Miss Rita Khitrovo, former lady in waiting, had once spoken of her ancestors who had founded Simbirsk, and how we had hoped to make a trip to this historic city when the war was over. Boyar Khitrovo had constructed palisades here in the seventeenth century to defend the city from the Tartars.

Many legends about the the famous robber of the Volga River had originated here, while all Russians know the song "Stenka Razin" which talks of him. Here was also a statue of the Russian historian Karamzin, while Alexander pointed out the Club of the Noblesse at the Nicholas Garden.

A great pain ached in my chest as I regarded all of this. I had wanted to enter the Convent of the Redeemer as we walked past, but Alexander would not hear of it informing me that nuns, priests and monks had been driven out and some even executed. This was no time to remain in Russia. Entering the church might tip someone off to our whereabouts, so I contented myself with a silent prayer very time we passed a house of God, the sight of which lifted my spirit and calmed my nerves.

Alexander was evidently well acquainted with this city as we walked intently to a house in front of which was a wooden gate some distance from the station. Upon knocking an attractive woman in her forties opened the door. Her name was Alexandra. They were happy to see on another, and he told her that his side was giving him pain. "You need a rest, I will have tea ready in a minute." She invited us to sit down. "Nikolai will be back any minute; he will bring some bread," she said. "Usually the bread line is quite long and one must start very early in the morning."

That a lady as lovely as this lived here in this house came as a surprise to me. Indeed, she looked aristocratic, so that I wondered what her relationship was to Alexander. Nikolai soon arrived, dressed as shabbily as Alexander in civilian clothes, with a loaf of bread tucked under this arm. It was evident that Alexander and he were close friends. They chatted busily while we enjoyed our tea.

As we finished, he turned suddenly to Alexander and asked, "How did you ever happen to go to E.K. (that is, Ekaterinburg)?" Alexander answered at length: "I wanted to join Admiral Kolchak's army but was arrested and put in prison for a time. While there, I had a fresh attack and they let me out of prison. Instead of going to a hospital, I went to Ekaterinburg. There I met a priest by the name of Father Storozhev whom I visited several times. He informed me of the desperate condition at the Ipatiev House. It seemed he had been summoned to conduct a service there and was alarmed about the consequences. He suggested I contact a man by the name of Voykov who was in charge of hiring the guards and other workers. I applied as a worker, but did not get the job.

"One day I went to the guard house next to the Ipatiev House where I became friendly with the guards through a guard whom I had met previously and with whom I later played chess. I returned to the guard house several times. Some of the guards were jolly but rough; most of the outside guards were Russians, former convicts. They did not object to my presence. They remained guarding the house to the last. The inside guards, I was told, were replaced by foreigners two weeks before the tragedy."

Of course, Alexander was indeed correct that they were foreigners, mostly exprisoners of war. It seemed to me that Alexander was allowing me to hear the entire story by listening to his narration of it to Nikolai. Ostensibly, he must have felt that I had the right, indeed the need, to know.

"I saw Father Storozhev a few days before the night of July 16-17th," he continued. "I went to the guard house again, after dark, because the priest had given me a feeling of danger. I did not tell him where I was going nor did I see him again. When I came upon the guards with whom I played chess, I saw most of them had been drinking heavily.

"They asked me to drink a toast to Comrade Yurovsky; he sent the liquor in appreciation for their services. I refused to take anything pointing to my wound. 'Never mind, tovarishch,' one of the guards said. 'More will be left for us. You are sick and only good for the dogs.' They seemed to be drowning something in drink. I am sure they were not aware of the forthcoming murder. I began to feel uneasy and feared there was real danger. I was afraid to leave the place. I wished I had four or five armed men with me. After dinner it was announced that no one would be allowed to leave or enter the place. They looked at me and said jokingly, 'We have a new prisoner.' "Some of the guards left drunk for their various posts. With several other guards I entered the courtyard. I heard a truck drive up to the house about eleven P.M. I offered the truck driver to help him back up the truck. He accepted my offer. It flashed through my mind that this truck might be for the purpose of secretly taking the family away. After a while the driver fell asleep, giving me the opportunity to get into the back of the truck. I lay down flat in the back of the truck. Imagine the shock when I felt warm, twitching objects thrown next to me. I knew then what had actually happened."

Tears spontaneously poured forth from Alexander's eyes at this moment. I could not stand to hear more and ran out of the room. With hope beyond hope I had so desired to hear that some one or other of my family was still alive, but his tears told me otherwise.

This topic was only brought up twice-initially by Alexander followed by Nikolai who told me the rest of Alexander's heroic rescue. Out of pure fear Alexander had remained in the truck, stricken with horror, motionless as he realized the dangerous situation he was in. He had no option other than to stay hidden next to bodies which still had the remnants of life in them, even still warm and moving. He would have been immediately shot too, had he ever been discovered. The guards that night were for the most part totally inebriated. Out of the courtyard and into the streets, the truck speeded away with haste. As it reached the country roads, however, it slowed down because of the many bumps and ruts.

Alexander had heard a moan among the bodies. The truck turned slowly at the bend of the road and threw out two bodies, tossing them into the bushes. There were guards on horseback quite a ways farther back, so that my rescuer lay in the ditch among the bushes until they were well past. He quickly returned to the bodies and examined them. One appeared to be lifeless, so he wrapped the other one in in his coat and carried it a long way to the first house he could find. This was the house with the cellar dugout, in the vicinity of Uktus and Mrammorskaya. The strain of carrying such a burden for this long distance caused his wound to rupture allowing infection to set in. Ill and blood soaked, he did the only thing that he could do and that was to ask total strangers to care for me, offering them a generous reward. If, at the beginning, the strangers had known my true identity, the might have rejected the offer out of fear for their lives.

One of these men kept Alexander up to date on my condition. It was understandable now why the journey from the dugout to Alexander's cottage had been so difficult. I informed both Alexander and Nikolaie about valuables I had sewn into my clothes. Both agreed that that was probably the reason that they had burned by clothes and cared for me as they did, for they had been well paid. On top of that Alexander had paid them too with the contents of the brown envelope. I did not ask nor did they tell me how much had been in it. He did tell me, however, that I had been fully clothed when he had delivered me to the house, but that the garments were soaked in blood-my own and surely that of my family. The only thing I carried with me when I left the dugout was the blood stained handkerchief, the piece of blue glass and my soul. If at this writing anyone is still living who was with in Tobolsk, he would recognize the handkerchief from there.

There had been no mention up to now of leaving Simbirsk, although I was sure it was understood that we eventually must. However, our respite here was welcome and did me good. Honestly, I was quite unnerved by all I had gathered from these latest conversations. Alexander surely also needed a rest before continuing and more of this trip. On the third day in the evening a truck appeared. Alexander and I bade Mlle. Alexandra farewell and were again moving.

Alexander was in the front seat with Nikolai, while I rode sitting on the straw strewn on the floor of the truck. All night long we drove, making rest stops along the way in wooded areas and to change drivers. Alexander seemed to me to be exceedingly thoughtful and kind, trying to make things easier for Nikolai and me as best he could. He made light conversation about the weather, for example, saying that we had been lucky this year in this season.

How ironic that the truck transporting me belonged to a factory in Kursk where Nikolai worked and who was delivering it to them. (*Editor's note: The unintended justice of the fact that a vehicle belonging to the Bolshevik government was saving the life of the Tsar's youngest daughter cannot be overlooked.*)

It was now late in the afternoon when we stopped in a wooded spot with tall poplars, birches, walnut and elm trees which grew profusely in this area near Penza. For a short while we rested and then proceeded toward the city, an old historical site. Although the prices were exorbitantly expensive we did buy some food there. A woman was selling shawls nearby, but her asking price was also ridiculously expensive. Alexander knew I was cold with no coat, but a shawl here would be impossible to buy. All of a sudden, the woman came close to me and stared into my eyes. I was naturally qutie frightened. Changing her mind for some inexplicable reason she told me she would take a fourth of her original price she had first asked. She picked out the very best one she had and put it gently on my shoulders. As I glanced back she made the sign of the cross in the air in our direction. (*Editor's note: this is reminiscent of Biblical stories in which the elderly, by inspiration of the Holy Spirit, recognize holiness in their midst unbeknownst to all others in the area. Notably, one remembers the Presentation of Christ in the Temple when Anna, a prophetess, and Simeon, of great age, both acknowledge that the baby of the Blessed Virgin and Joseph the Guardian is the Messiah.*)

By this time the fact that the Imperial Family had been murdered was known all over Russia. At this point of our journey out of Russia we met people of many ethnicities and cultures including Tartars, Buriats, Kirghiz and others. We The impressive Lermontov statue was here in a lovely park. We came to Sadovaya Avenue which was reminiscent of the Sadoavya in Tsarskoe Selo. Descending, we passed Sadovaya Avenue. It reminded me of the Sadovaya in Tsarskoe Selo. I suddenly remember the canal, the pond, the orangeries, the Chinese Village, the Siberian blue bridge and the palace.

On we continued when Nikolai suddenly glanced at me, allowing me to perceive that he truly felt sorry for me. Both of these kind men tried in whatever way they could to somehow make up for the loss I had suffered such a short time ago. When we passed Tambov, Alexander spoke to us of some friends in Voronezhat whose place we could perhaps get some sleep. In the afternoon we arrived at Voronezh where we stopped in front of the Convent of St. Mitrophanes. Nikolai and Alexander gave me their consent to walk to the convent to ask if I might rest a bit there, while they went to seek a doctor to tend to Alexander's wounds and find the friends about which he had spoken.

These wonderfully sweet and kindly nuns washed my clothes, prepared me a hot bath, washed my hair and bandaged the sores on my legs. When I left some hours later, they had prepared food for me to take, all that they could spare. I prayed with the nuns, at which times something remarkable happened. A spontaneous feeling of peace and well being came over me and I felt a breeze fly over my shoulders three times. I turned to see, but could see nothing. In my mind's eye I could see my family at church in Tsarskoe Selo coming in through the side door where we prayed in the Feodorovsky Sobor. The choir there sang so beautifully with such a perfection that we never wanted them to stop. I could see my loved ones in the winter church at Tobolsk.

At once I was back in my present surroundings encompassed by a few humble women. The voices were few and diminutive. For all the kindess I had received here I gave glory to God. I left the church to find Alexander coming towards me, his face ashen and excited. He informed me that there was no need to go to the Crimea, as he had heard from reliable sources that my grandmother, my aunts, their husbands, and all their children have been killed. Others including Vostorgov (a high ranked clergyman in Moscow), together with a great many others, had been assassinated last month. The young Ministers Maklakov and Khvostov, who had replaced the old Minister Goremykin, Minister of the Interior, had also perished. Khvostov's wife, Anastasia, had also been shot in Moscow. No tears would form, but I shook as if I were wracked with a high fever. Obviously, we too were in great danger and had to put out of my mind that I would be with my family withing a week in the Crimea. That was no longer a possibility.

The tragedy in Sevastopol came to our attention in which the revolutionaries had killed and tied stones to the feet of the young cadets and thrown them into the Black Sea. No one could explain their disappearance until a young woman on her way to market saw some bodies and reported them. Officials turned her away at the scene where the bodies had been spotted. A diver rose to the surface screaming that the bodies below were alive and walking on the bottom of the water. He lost his mind. Another diver came up to report that the bodies were upright, being held down by heavy stones tied to their feet, while the action of the waves moved their bodies making them seem to walk.

It was only faith which helped me to listen to this odious news about my relatives. Only later did I learn that it had not been true at all. Another account relayed by Alexander was that late one night in June, 1918, Uncle Misha and his English secretary, Nicholas Johnson (who thought his presence might help the Grand Duke), were taken away into the woods near Perm where they mysteriously disappeared. Unfortunately this time it was true that they had been executed, as I was to learn much later. Father was right in his insistence that the taste of blood begets an epidemic. Having heard all this about the Crimea, we knew that going there was an impossibility so we did not go through Tula as we had previously envisaged. Instead we headed to Kursk where Nikolai delivered the truck. We purchased food while he was doing his business task. Bread was not too out of the ordinary as far as cost, but the other products were outrageously expensive. We now headed toward the border with Romania.

The terrain had been mountainous with craggy ravines lined with fir trees when we first started this trip. Now the countryside was flatter dotted with many graneries. We had to traverse forests and muddy wheat fields. We would rest and proceed, rest and proceed in a pattern which kept repeating itself. We slept in sheds on heaps of hay, happy to be anyplace dry. We crossed railroad lines where we spotted cars full of sacks of moldy wheat which had sprouted and was growing through the holes in the burlap. Even though the people were starving to death, they were not allowed to take this grain. Later on when we had run out of food, Nikolai and Alexander had bought some fresh wheat from a farmer which they chewed on, but the grain swelled inside of them causing them great pain and causing them to drink water whenever they could find it. I would have too but for the problem with my teeth. We even heard that some peasants had died when they had eaten raw wheat.

Supposedly Lili Dehn was living close to Kremenchug on the east bank of the Dnieper River. Fighting was going on in the area so we did not try to find her, and we continued on westward. In abandoned railway cars, some people lived trying to hide their identities. They patched walls with canvas to keep out rain and cold, and many children were born here but died due to starvation and exposure. No one claimed the bodies which were buried in shallow graves near the railroad tracks. There were more than a few grain elevators which were filled with charred corpses. Foreigners, well fed and well dressed, received the best attention. This was the "liberty" which Kerensky, later the Bolsheviks, had orchestrated to pollute the minds of the people. Alexander was lagging behind we noticed. Nikolai found pus on his shirt. We applied the salve Alexander had brought with us hoping it would serve well enough until we could find a doctor. We gathered leaves to make him a bed, while Nikolai and I sat next to him hoping he would be well enough to reach the next village. What I would have given to be able to help this dear friend.

There were surprisingly other people in these woods which we detected by the sound of crunching leaves and crackling branches. We heard footsteps approaching when two men appeared. They were somewhat afraid of us, and darted back in the forest when they saw us. Nikolai, however, called out to them to join us. He asked what was wrong and they answered in a language we knew was Serbian.

"Our friend's wound has opened and is infected," said Nikolai, "and we do not know what to do."

In broken Russian the Serbian suggested that we take our patient to the nearest house under the cover of night. He would volunteer to look for and secure a house. The other man, we learned by talking to him while the other was away, was Croatian. They had not been able to board the train in Kursk and decided to walk to the border. Both had been officers in the last war, one for Russia and one for Austria-Hungary. Now they were together going to their respective homes.

In about an hour the Serbian returned having found a house not too far away. As the sun set, Nikolai and the Serbian helped Alexander to his feet supporting him all the way to the house which was a thatched-roof, white-washed house in which a young woman about thirty-five years old lived with her four children. I was reminded of Alexei at the same age by her little boy, five years old, with his blond curly hair and big gray eyes. I was immediately drawn to him when he looked at our invalid and asked, "Is the father ill?" Indeed, they had been waiting for their father to come home who had also been wounded in the war. He probably imagined that his father had been wounded in the same way.

Even though the house was tiny, we all spent the night there with the two women in one room with all the children, the men in the other room. By morning Alexander felt much better. We waited most of the day to make sure he would be strong enough to make the rest of the journey. How generous this woman was sharing the scant food she had for herself and her childen. In order to beat the heat of the day, the Serbian and Croation decided that they would leave early in the evening. Alexander heard about their leaving insisting that Nikolai and I go with them. In spite of our protestations, Alexander insisted that all would be easier if we did what he suggested. We were convinced enough to leave him, I reluctantly, with the promise that Nikolai would return for him as soon as we crossed the border. (*Editor's note: This is where we first hear of "the Croatian, and it is the identity of a Croatian man whom Anastasia later uses to create a new identity for herself as Mrs. "Evgenia Smetisko." In the Ocober 18, 1963 Life Magazine, Mr. Marijan Smetisko, a Croatian with an Ukrainian sounding name, insisted he had never met her let alone married her. We will soon read that this early 20th century version of a "coyote" or a paid guide who crosses people without documentation across frontiers, tells a border official that "Evgenia" has no papers, is his wife, and is just taking her across the border to seek medical attention. Surely it is HIS identity she uses to put on documentation to gain entry to America. However, it could not have been done so efficiently without much outside help and, seemingly, organization albeit planning before the escape. Smetisko, if he is the Croatian in her narrative, would have had to insist he had never met her, as it would have placed her in jeopardy as the real Anastasia if he were questioned by authorities during the Cold War. One thing is sure: the escape of "Evgenia," here described almost as serendipity, may have seemed as such to her, but must have been previously and intricately devised. One assumes that the version she writes was enough to her mind to explain fully her escape without implicating or endangering those who had helped her and were still living at the time she penned her intriguing tale. The Kohlsaat sisters she credits with being of such assistance seem to be a link to the planning of her story. Edith Kohlsaat leaves 1918 to go to Great Britain for "relief work" and "Evgenia" may have been the person she would assist.*)

# XXXII ESCAPE

pportunity only knocks once, so when it does it must be seized upon and not rejected. We four started out on foot at ten o'clock at night. I was beside myself that we had seemed to leave our dear friend behind to die when he needed us most. All night long we made our progress towards the western border. Perhaps we would find a peasant home in which we could take a meal, as our last one had been with the young mother and her children. Indeed, we had had no breakfast or lunch. Neither did we have enough money for train fare or even documents to cross the border.

A benevolent farmer provided us with food and shelter for the night. We slept till the following morning and took up our journey anew. We learned from the farmer that the war had not really stopped, and that socialism was making its way to Germany and Austria. Daily the crime rate was increasing with criminals from aboard crossing into Russia to kill and rob. A third prisoner formerly in the Austrian army now joined us. Luckily and gratefully he shared his supply of food with us. As we came closer to the border, the number of refugees increased which caused our apprehension to grow. Nikolai wondered if we might be turned away from the border even put into prison. No matter what would befall me, I would not let anyone know who I was. At once we emerged from that unpleasant forest and crossed a small stream where we drank some water and filled our bottle. The Serbian began to question me as we continued onwards. Both Nikolai and I became worried about so many questions. Nikolai went ahead and walked with the Serbian to find out what was in his mind while I walked with the Croatian and the former Austrian soldier.

Finally Nikolai returned, satisfied and said, "He knows the facts, but will not betray us, I am sure." The Serbian was a loyal friend, offering considerable protection to me all the way. When we were near the border, he scouted ahead to see what could be done to make the crossing successfully. (*Editor's note: How the Serbian knew "all the facts" is a mystery as Nikolai would not have offered them voluntarily. Perhaps the rumor and belief that Anastasia had survived and escaped was already whispered about among the people.*)

In case of our separation, the Austrian and Nikolai devised a plan of where we would meet. As far as the eye could see there were refugees in rags-thin, undernourished, ill. We heard that there were still German troops in Kiev and we saw troops going by in trains. On their way to the border countless people, dressed partially in civilian clothes, partially in military, continued their trek. Those who had no passports were being arrested on the spot. With the help of our latest companion we found our way to the border. He had been a soldier fighting on the Austrian front on his way to Bukovina. Our group had grown to five as we approached dangerous territory. Two prisoners of war had the necessary documents for crossing the line. The Serbian's papers were in order. Someone suggested I pose as the wife of one of them in order to enter Romania. The Serbian was not appropriate, while the Croatian was a better choice. He had fought on the German side, and Nikolai would become my brother.

At this time we were exhausted and famished as we had not eaten properly for the last twenty-four hours. Another peasant could feed us but not give us lodging so we used the haystack as our sleeping place. While I slept at the top, the men slept at the base of the stack. Suddenly a clap of thunder shook me out of my sleep and the rain began to pour. I was totally soaked by the time I had made my way to the bottom again. All five of us dug ourselves into the hay and remained there huddled, warm and steamy until we fell asleep. The rain lasted for hours coming down cats and dogs. When the time came to again set out, the fields were a muddy mess. My ankle was bothering me a great deal; on top of it all I was itching all over adding great discomfort to my already lingering fatigue. Perhaps there was some poison ivy or something similar in the hay which caused my skin to itch so. It was decided that if we were somehow separated that the Nikolai would come later in four weeks with Alexander and find us via the Austrian soldier.

Nikolai had endless messages from me to deliver to Alexander, as I wanted Alexander to know how grateful I was and how close I felt toward him for saving my life. Nikolai was my last link to my beloved Russia, so to say goodbye to him was extremely difficult. I wanted to throw my arms around him to thank him from the bottom of my heart for all that Alexander and he had done for me. I intuitively felt that our separation would come soon. He warned me not to cry but to walk steadfastly as though I were accompanying my husband and not look back. We grabbed some tiny potatoes which were still in the ground using rain water to clean them eating them raw. My face was swollen covered with small red pimples.

The Serbian had just returned from a scouting search when suddenly we heard the command,

"Halt. Where are you going?"

"We are going to a doctor," answered Nikolai.

"All of you? And for what?" said the guard.

"Look at the lady for our answer," said Nikolai.

"It looks like cholera. Who are you?" asked the guard.

"Her brother," said Nikolai, and the Croatian assured the guard that he was my husband. Three of them, the Serbian, the Croatian, and the Austrian soldier produced their papers.

*(Editor's note: Perhaps this is the Croatian Smetisko who claimed later he had never met Anastasia, but whose last name she appropriated from this incident)*

Facing Nikolai, the guard persisted, "Where are you from?"

"The village over there," answered Nikolai, pointing back. "There whole families are ill, all needing medical care. When we obtain some drugs we will return to the village. We must locate a doctor soon."

"What doctor?" asked the guard.

"There used to be a doctor over the bridge," said the Serbian, pointing straight ahead.

"But you cannot go that way. It is under German occupation. Do you really know a doctor?"

"We'll surely find one." Nikolai retorted.

"But you absolutely cannot cross here," said the guard pointing to Nikolai.

"How far are you going?" the guard turned to the Croatian. "How soon will you be back?" he inquired. "You are all right, but where are your wife's papers?"

*(Editor's emphasis as seems to relate to the man known as Marijan Smetisko)*

"Does she need papers to see a doctor?"

The questions were answered, but no one heard or cared what they were; we were all but drowned in the terrific rain.

"All right, go on." said the guard at last with a gesture of hopelessness, "but be back in one hour."

He turned to Nikolai saying, "Not you!"

Four of the five of us crossed the flimsy, temporary structure which shook as we did. We could see only darkness in the waters below. All of nature raged with anger. I had made a cross in the air toward Nikolai as we parted in the dark. I offered a prayer to God that He might spare him and that Alexander, Nikolai, and I would meet again.

A new hazard arose. Several soldiers approached us as we reached the line of demarcation. They demanded to know our destination. The two former prisoners of war could speak German and presented their documentation. The Serbian brought forth his papers, while the guards asked the Croatian about our situation. He told them that I was his wife. Hours of conversation and interrogation ensued, but finally we were allowed to enter Bukovina.

I now had my last look toward my troubled coun try only to leave it under the darkness of night. At the beginning of this odyssey I had had no real desire to leave my country. I was not well and wished for nothing more than peace and rest and quiet. I was too weak to resist, so I went with my early rescuer, then Alexander and Nikolai to finally finish with these new acquaintances.

My lips quivered as I left the country of my birth where, hidden in the wilderness, the remains of my parents and siblings lay hidden. Also Alexander and Nikolai were left behind. God had designed it that they would lay down their swords and lives at the altar of their country. May He grant them eternal peace in heaven.

Father departed with his very young family, but in true Christian faith and fidelity to Russia. Now free from the cruel human lies, injustices and misunderstandings, he left the world not in pomp and glory, but in greater glory. He died for his country and his people whom he loved best.

With these thoughts in my mind I left behind the land of my heritage forever.

# XXXIII    REFUGE

The rain was torrential yet it washed the tears from my face. These strangers and I were drenched, tired and terribly hungry. We had no hope of finding a place to sleep. In the distance we espied a light and made our way in that direction. No Russian money was accepted at his house, but the Austrian soldier had some of his own money which he had been saving and he offered that as they bargained with the proprietor to allow us to briefly stay. I consulted with the woman of the house about the terrible itching, and she recommended pouring sour milk on a sheet within which I would be wrapped. I felt like a mummy as she had done it so well that only my eyes and mouth were left uncovered. This treatment did indeed bring comfort, and even my leg seemed to have improved.

I was well enough to travel again, and the kind woman had packed enough food for us to last several days. She gave me rags with which to wrap my feet so they would not slide around in the oversized boots. By wheat fields and tall oak trees we contined to trudge. There were trenches which were uncovered, deserted and barren out of which the rain had made rivers. War had turned this into a true battleground. and deserted and the rain made rivers of them. The war had turned this area into a battleground. We could make out pieces of clothing, brass artillery shell cases, chains, pieces of iron and other odds and ends of metal buried in the trunks of trees-mute testimony to the destructive military power of artillery. Tragedy was ubiquitous.

All the blood which had been shed here over the last four years had been washed away by the rains. In the midst of this devastation a geranium appeared. Around it were pieces of blankets and rusty canteens. I screamed suddenly when I stepped on some leaves out of which poked the remnants of a pair of feet, devoid of flesh now. They were the remains of an unknown Russian soldier. The uniform was so decayed that we could no longer tell if he was an officer or not, but a rusty watch was still wrapped around his wrist bone. Such were the tragedies exposed in this forest.

I remembered that Father knew this battlefield and had even come under shell attack while inspecting the troops. Alexei and he had both received their St. George medals for their devotion and bravery. In the end they too sacrificed their lives so that Lenin and Trotsky could fill the void. The day before the way began in 1914 I had dreamed of woods like these engulfed in flames. I had heard the crackling of trees as flames made their way skyward. Even then I had sensed that war was unavoidable, especially when Father arrived late for dinner for the very first time. As I regarded this place of great suffering I could not help but recall my dream. I left this scene in great distress.

Like true gentlemen the man carried me over the puddles, taking turns, but I was afraid I was too heavy for them. I really only weighed forty kilos, not even ninety pounds. The Austrian soldier knew these villages well, especially as this was the region from which he hailed. He volunteered to be our guide. About two days later we arrived to a part of the forest where women were gathing wild mushrooms, yellow ones. One of the young women already had her basket full. She was on her way home which was half way to the village. We joined her, and the men carried her baskets for her. When we reached the village we learned that our Austrian companion actually had relatives here. Through his intercession we were able to find shelter for the night here.

An elderly woman came out and in a Slavic language I understood, said, "Come in, my child, I hear you have an injured foot. I know you are hungry. I will have supper ready for you in a minute." She seemed so clean and kind and motherly, I was drawn to her immediately. We followed her into the house and there we met her daughters who also welcomed us. (*Editor's note: probably Slovak or Czech*)

As I sat shivering on a low stool the daughters of this kind lady removed my muddy stockings and poured warm water over them to removed the majority of the caked on mud. As a disinfectant, the mother scraped off some salt with a knife from a block of it, in order to create a kind of disinfectant. After this foot care, supper was ready which consisted of warm mamaliga, a yellow mush made out of corn, called maize by some. Over this was poured warm milk. I had never had it before, but it was delicious, and nothing had ever tasted better.

The mother examined my wound. While she washed it a tear dropped on my ankle. Our eyes met. "I think it will be all right, I do not see any infection."

The warm milk soon stopped the chattering of my teeth. The good girls had already made up a bed for me: a small wooden bed with linen sheets spread over a narrow mattress. They had hardly left the room when I was fast asleep. The girls shared the same room with me, but I was not aware of them. When I woke up the next day, the girls told me that the men had been waiting for me since eleven in the morning.

"What time is it now?" I asked.

"Four in the afternoon," they laughed. "Several times the men came in and looked to see if you were asleep or dead, and were reassured."

Evidently I felt safe at last. The girls told me excitedly that the men had slept in the barn and later had helped their mother clean the stable. The Germans had left her one horse and one cow, confiscating all the rest of the livestock before the Russian invasion, fearing that the Russians would take it. When I started to dress, to my surprise I could not find my wet travelling clothes. Instead of my clothes I found a new outfit: everything from a cotton dress to a pair of shoes.

This humble family had presented me with Sunday clothes belonging to their youngest daughter, six months my junior.

I located the men in the garden eating half-dried plums still on the trees. They were relaxed, free and happy after getting me safely across the border.

I, too, was relaxed and free.

At long last I had found a peaceful refuge with this unknown but friendly family which had taken me into its midst and made me a welcome member.

It was October 24th, 1918 . for me a new day .. and the beginning of a new life.

# PHOTOS

*Black and white image of formal portrait of HIH Anastasia Nicholaevna Romanov by Barbara Green, nee Korr/Kur based on Anastasia Again: The Hidden Secret of the Romanovs and the 2D/3D visual face recognition analyses of Robert "Bob" Schmitt. Froebel-Parker Collection*

*Plaque on grave cross of aka "Evgenia Smetisko" clearly showing the date of birth of Anastasia Romanov-18 June 1901*

*3D side by side analysis of Anastasia Romanov and the woman known as "Evgenia Smetisko" using technology of Robert "Bob" Schmitt*

*Portrait of adult HIH Anastasia Nicholaevna Romanov, commissioned by author of Barbara Green, nee Korr/Kur*

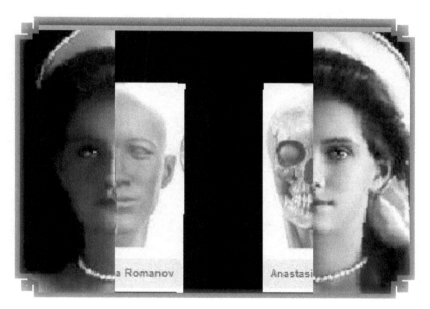

*2D analysis of alleged skull in Russia of Anastasia which really matches her sister, Maria.*

*Anastasia's MISMATCH to her purported skull reconstruction in Russia*

*2D side by side analysis of Empress Alexandra Feodorovna and the woman known simultaneously as "Evgenia Smetisko" and Anastasia Romanov, showing a haunting similarity.*

*2D overlay of Empress Alexandra Feodorovna and "Evgenia Smetisko/Anastasia Romanov" showing a congruence one could expect of a mother and child.*

*Formal portrait by Richard Banks titled "HIH Anastasia Nicholaevna Romanov, Grand Duchess of Russia" by Richard Banks (1963). Froebel-Parker Collection.*

The Enigma of Evgenia
from the Russian version in English
By Dr. Larisa Head-Semenova

*Moscow State University*
*Universidade do Minho, Braga, Portugal*

On July 17 2018, it will be the 100th anniversary of the Czar Nicholas II, his family and others of his household who also had the fate of the czar. At the time, the details of these murders of the imperial family were kept secret in the USSR, concealed by false information about their deaths. Some Soviet historians and political scientists wanted to prove that such an action, taking the life not only of the czar but also of his young daughter, was necessary!!!

During the time of *Perestroika*, the truth concerning the barbaric murders became public knowledge. The remains of those murdered had been thrown into pits and bathed with acid. The bodies were exhumed and submitted to examination, but the results were inconclusive. The remains were buried again in the Cathedral of the Fortress of Saint Peter and Saint Paul in Saint Petersburg. The doubt concerning the identification of the bodies gave rise to some sensational material regarding the possible miraculous escape of the youngest daughter, the Grand Duchess Anastasia Romanova, who was seventeen years of age at the time. There were news stories about various women declared that they were the daughter of the czar. Films were made, and novels were written concerning this intriguing topic.

On May 25, 2014, at the largest Russian Orthodox monastery outside of Russia, in Jordanville NY, an exhibit was inaugurated at the Museum of Russian History. Two months earlier, the New York Times had published an article about Eugenia Smith, holder of a passport from the United States, who had donated a vast and valuable collection of belongings of the family of Czar Nicolai Romanov. Some of the objects (paintings and embroideries) were not included in the exhibit, and they were acquired by Professor John Froebel-Parker, who began to cultivate an interest in Eugenia Smith, who could perhaps be the Grand Duchess Anastasia Romanova, as she had stated in her autobiography. In order to determine whether Eugenia Smith and Grand Duchess Anastasia Romanova were the same person, John Froebel-Parker had biometric tests conducted. He compared photos of Eugenia Smith at age sixty with photos of Anastasia Romanova as a young woman. The comparison of the photographs, while not conclusive, provided almost 100% support for sustaining the hypothesis of identity. Other materials provide indirect support for that hypothesis. How could Eugenia Smith, who lived on a small pension, establish a foundation with articles valuing millions of dollars? How could she have in her possession items from the imperial family? Is it a mere coincidence that the date of birth indicated of the tombstone of the grave of Eugenia Smith (*Editor's note: aka "Evgenia Smetisko*) in Jordanville is the same as the date of birth of Anastasia Romanova? The paintings of Eugenia Smith represent scenes from Russia from the life of Anastasia Romanova. It is known that Anastasia Romanova had lessons in painting. The embroideries of Eugenia Smith are signed with the letters "OTMA", which correspond with first letters of the daughters of the czar: Olga, Tatyana, Maria, Anastasia.

Some time ago, a lie detector indicated "false" when Eugenia Smith responded negatively to the question as to whether she is the Grand Duchess Anastasia. J (Johannes) Froebel-Parker believes that the DNA tests which can be conducted in Russia can resolve the question of possible identity of Eugenia Smith and Anastasia Romanova, finally providing the truth concerning this enigma.

Visual Face Recognition
*Guest essay by Robert (Bob) Schmitt*
www.visualfacerecognition.com

Face recognition started out as a technology to try to identify people using only their faces for comparison. The early days of the technology were fraught with all kinds of problems, but the biggest one was what happens when you get a false accept? In other words, how do you know for sure that you identified the correct person?

The simple fact that face recognition proved was the people do look alike. Sometimes they look alike because of a facial feature that is prominent, but does not mean it's the same person. Sometimes it's the shape of the face, the style of the hair, or even the complexion of the person.

It's also a fact of life that when you grow up in one society, you are able to distinguish faces from the races that are prominent in that environment.

A simple example is that people in the US have a hard time telling a Chinese person from a Japanese or Korean, because they simply have not had the experience to understand facial features.

It became evident very early in the face recognition arena that there had to be a way to quickly tell if two people were the same or not. The answers will never be 100% positive, because the face recognition biometric is unlike a fingerprint or an iris image. In the case of a fingerprint or an iris, the result of a comparison is binary: it's either the same person or it's not. A face is much more complicated because of the number of features that have to be compared and the fact that pose can have a big impact on how easily a comparison can be done.

Let's consider Brad Pitt and Benicio Del Toro. They certainly look alike in the pictures, but then they both have facial hair that is similar, hair styles that are similar, and even clothes that are worn the same way (open collar). So when we compare them, what do we learn?

The first thing we learn is that they look very much alike. The proportions of the face are pretty much identical. The hairline seems to match pretty well. The mouth is in exactly the same position. The eyebrows seem to be in the same position also.

Is this the same person? If we said it was and took some kind of action based on these pictures we might have a strong case that it's the same person, but we would be wrong. Let's look more closely.

The first place it starts to fall apart is the nose. They are close, but they are not exact.

Del Toro's nose flairs much more than Pitt's, and the nostrils are completely different. The eyebrows are also different. One is much higher than the other one. Eyebrows are often the distinguishing mark that people don't pay enough attention to.

And finally we have the chin line, which looks the same until we compare them closely and then we can see that Brad Pitt has a longer face than Benicio Del Toro

The two men look alike, but they are not the same person.

*The Elements of Face Comparison* The first concept that is critical for understanding face comparisons is the 'normalization' of faces. No two pictures of the same person are going to be exactly the same size. In fact, they are often of very different sizes so we have to figure out how to make them exactly the same size so we can compare features.

This is done simply by making the distance between the center of both eyes the same for each image. By having the eyes the same distance apart, if it's the same person then the features will line up exactly the same.

This normalization process is easy to do when the images are facing the same way. So, for example, if we were comparing mug shots of criminals, 99% of the time they would be facing in the same direction on each photo. But what if they are not facing in the same direction? How do we do face comparisons then?

The answer is with 3D face technology. The process is very sophisticated and very computer intensive, but what it does is allow us to set faces at exactly the same angle so we can compare them accurately.

Rather than taking two points on each face (the center of the eyes), 3D technology takes over 40 points from different parts of the face for comparison. Using those 40 points, the 2D image of the face is electronically placed over a mask of a face for that type of person, and a 3D image is created.

Now if we look at a comparison of Brad Pitt in 3D and Benicio Del Toro we can see how different the two noses are.

That is what 3D allows us to do better than just a 2D image. hat you can't see in these examples are the movement of the image comparisons and how obviously different they are when done in real-time. This is the key to both 2D and 3D comparisons.

When done in real-time, the differences between two faces is striking. On the flip side, when it's the same person the similarities are also striking. Even with the passage of time, the features stay the same and the facial structure stays the same.

What can change a face? Great weight gain and loss will change a face. The proportion of the features will stay the same, but the features themselves may look very different when there has been significant weight differences. Face lifts won't change much of the facial structure.

Accurate face comparisons are important for a number of reasons, but most importantly, so that the use of a technology like face recognition does not identify the wrong person.

(*Editor's note: A great debt of gratitude and heartfelt thanks is due to Mr. Schmitt. He departed this world in 2019 leaving behind his 2D/3D analyses of aka "Evgenia Smetisko" and Anastasia Romanov which have opened new insights into history, a history not yet fully understood or codified.*)

> *The comparison of the faces is one of the most accurate I have seen especially considering the difference in ages. There is little doubt it's the same person.*

> Robert "Bob" Schmitt

# ABOUT THE AUTHOR

(Johannes) Froebel-Parker graduated from a small town Central School in Marathon, New York. He taught English as a New Language for almost 3 decades in an upstate New York Central School District, having previously taught English as a Foreign Language for one year at the Marie Curie Oberschule in then West Berlin in an academic exchange program sponsored by Akademischer Austauschdienst. He completed his undergraduate B.A, M.A. (German Language and Literature) and M.S. (Education) at the University at Albany in Albany, New York-USA. From the earliest age he was captivated by the stories of his maternal and paternal grandparents who shared with him their oral histories from both sides of the Atlantic. Via his maternal grandmother there are a number of ancient genealogical connections to Queen Victoria via the family "von Juelich-Kleve-Berg" hence to Tsar Nicholas II, Taritsa Alexandra and their children. He is fascinated by the interconnected nature of genetics and family lore leading to the very Froebelian concept of "Einheit" (unity). Indeed, the Kindergarten founder is quoted as insisting "Jedes Dinges Wesen ist Einheit" (Unity is the Essence of All Things). With his research about Anastasia Romanov and the woman aka "Evgenia Smetisko" he hopes to contribute to such a notion. He is the author of various other books based on characters from his "Ahnentafel" (family tree), many with Authorhouse.

# ABOUT THE ARTIST

Barbara Green, nee Korr/Kur was born in Brooklyn, New York and graduated in the same class from Erasmus High School as another well-known personage in the arts - Barbra Streisand. Her undergraduate training was at New York University, followed by two years at the Instituto Allende in San Juan de Allende, Mexico. There she studied printmaking, stone lithography, and etchings. She completed her MFA at Allende. Known for expertise in figure work, she gained invaluable experience with Harvey Dinnerstein at the National Academy of Design (New York) and the Arts Student League (New York). Perhaps her most unique live figure experiences were in the boxing gym run by Cus Damato in Catskill, New York, where the young Mike Tyson honed his skills. Her portraits of Romanov personages include HIH Anastasia Nicholaevna Romanov, HRH Maria Pavlovna Romanov Grand Duchess von Sachsen-Weimar-Eisenach, HSH Ekaterina Ivanovna Konstantinova Romanov, and an double portrait of HIH Alexandra Feodorovna with Catherine the Great (anno 2020). Froebel Gallery has enjoyed a relationship with Barbara and her artist husband, Francis Eugene Green, since the 1990s.

Lightning Source UK Ltd.
Milton Keynes UK
UKHW051012070223
416609UK00009B/2408